STARK

The Life and Wars of John Stark
French & Indian War Ranger,
Revolutionary War General

STARK

The Life and Wars of John Stark
French & Indian War Ranger, Revolutionary War General

Richard V. Polhemus
and John F. Polhemus

BLACK·DOME

www.blackdomepress.com

Published by Black Dome Press Corp.
649 Delaware Ave., Delmar, N.Y. 12054
blackdomepress.com
(518) 439-6512

First Edition Paperback 2014

ISBN-13: 978-1-883789-74-9

Library of Congress Control Number: 2014944098

Front cover painting: *The Battle of Bennington, August 16, 1777*. Oil on canvas by Alonzo Chappel. Collection of the Bennington Museum, Bennington, Vermont.

Design: Ron Toelke Associates, www.toelkeassociates.com

Printed in the USA

10 9 8 7 6 5 4 3 2 1

For our children,
with love and pride:
Jenn, Julie, Michelle, Amy,
Jeff, Martha, John and Luke

CONTENTS

ACKNOWLEDGMENTS

Many people helped us during the long course of researching and writing the life of John Stark, and if we fail to mention any by name, please rest assured that the omission is not intentional.

To begin, all history is written on the shoulders of those historians and researchers who came before. Many authors of previous books have shed light on John Stark and the events that crowded his life. First among them was Howard Parker Moore, who published the general's biography in 1947. In an era without the Internet, when all inquiries were typed or handwritten and posted through the mail, Moore pursued the facts of Stark's life with stubborn persistence. And when he could find no publisher for his work, he produced 500 copies at his own expense. His work has been a foundation and inspiration for all who followed.

Special thanks go to the people at the libraries and museums that we consulted: to Jeannie Sherman at the Connecticut State Library; Christopher Fox at the Thompson-Pell Research Center at Fort Ticonderoga; Tyler Resch and Callie Stewart at the Bennington Museum; Jeffrey Barraclough and Ben Baker at the Manchester Historic Association; David Smolen and William Copely at the New Hampshire Historical Society; Nancy Finlay and Sierra Dixon at the Connecticut Historical Society; and Ellen McCallister Clark at the Society of the Cincinnati in Washington, D.C.

Special thanks to John Colburn and the members of the Weare, New Hampshire Historical Society for trying to solve a mystery about Robert Rogers.

We benefitted from guidance from Dr. Edythe Quinn of Hartwick College, and from Edward Knoblauch at nyhistory.com.

We were fortunate to have friends who helped us, especially Pat and Tom Freiler, who gave us a tour of the Saratoga battlefields and provided gracious hospitality to boot. And thanks to Bud Macey, who showed us some of Lake Champlain from the deck of a sailing vessel.

We had a great tour of the Hubbardton Battlefield with Carl Fuller, who knew the history and geography of the site thoroughly and very kindly shared some of his knowledge with us. Thanks also to Elsa Gilbertson of Vermont State Historic Sites for her kind assistance.

We extend our appreciation to Rich Strum and all the staff at Fort Ticonderoga for the excellent "war colleges" given there.

We owe warm thanks to Jenn Calabro and Maria Polhemus for their help with the manuscript, and further thanks for Jenn's photography.

Special thanks to Julie Polhemus for finding antique maps for us, and especially for the maps she drew for us. And thanks to Chris Jones whose computer expertise made this job so much easier.

We were very fortunate to have Dr. Michael Gabriel of Kutztown University read the manuscript. His careful commentary opened new lines of inquiry we had not foreseen, and we are grateful for the close attention he gave the work. Thanks, also, to Ray Andrews for his thoughtful comments on the manuscript.

We are grateful to Ron Toelke and Barbara Kempler-Toelke of Toelke Associates for their design of this book.

We extend appreciation to our editor and publisher, Steve Hoare of Black Dome Press, who was always ready with aid and counsel when we needed it.

All of the above gave us assistance, but if there are errors in this work, either of fact or interpretation, they are ours and ours alone.

Prologue

August 15, 1777

All day long a summer rain soaked the two armies facing each other across the valley of the Walloomsac River in northeastern New York. The Americans, most of them farmers from New Hampshire and Massachusetts or Green Mountain men from the newly proclaimed Republic of Vermont, camped in makeshift huts on a long hill west of Bennington. They wore homespun clothing and cowhide shoes with buckles, and they carried an array of primitive weapons. Their hill faced into New York where their adversaries crouched behind log and earthen breastworks.[1]

The King's troops, a mixed force of German auxiliaries, British regulars, Canadians, Indians and Loyalists, held a strong position on a height across the shallow river. They had marched over the hills from the Hudson River. The German dragoons usually rode horses; this time they had walked, and the August heat wore them down. The roads had turned to deep mud from the rain. Maneuvering was difficult and gunpowder was wet; both commanders decided to wait out the weather.

The Walloomsac River valley lay between the enemy forces, a scene of gentle hills carved up into homesteads so new that stumps still littered the landscape. Most settlers lived in cabins, with log outbuildings for oxen, hogs and chickens. Corn and flax ripened in the fields. Like farm people everywhere, these folk expected their livestock and crops to improve their lives; they had not expected a war to come to them.

British General John Burgoyne had ordered an expedition as far as the Connecticut River to capture horses and provisions for his army that slowly advanced south along the Hudson River toward Albany. His supply lines stretched all the way from the St. Lawrence River, across wilderness and lakes, through a hostile country. His army needed to live off the land, but American farmers drove their livestock into the woods and either destroyed their crops or let them go to ruin. When Burgoyne learned that the rebels maintained a supply depot at Bennington, he changed the mission of the raiding expedition into New England and ordered Lieutenant Colonel Friedrich Baum to attack Bennington.

In late June, angered by rebellious Americans, Burgoyne had published an ultimatum to the citizens of northern New York and New England. He addressed them as a "froward and stubborn Generation" and exhorted them to cease hostilities. Otherwise, he warned, if the "Phrenzy of Hostility should remain … The Messengers of Justice and of Wrath await them in the Field, and Devastation, Famine and every concomitant Horror that a reluctant but indispensable Prosecution of Military Duty must occasion, will bar the Way to their Return."[2]

Americans knew that he meant every word. During the past year British warships shelled and burned seacoast towns; British and German troops torched, looted and raped their way across New Jersey; American prisoners of war starved in chains on prison ships. Now, the King's force threatened a different region—northern colonies that had long endured Indian raids and invading French armies. These Americans had a history of reacting fiercely to such attacks. Thomas Paine wrote: "Beneath the shade of our own vines are we attacked; in our own houses, and on our own lands is the violence committed against us." The perceived injustice of Burgoyne's invading army provoked a rage that sought retribution.[3]

A plain New Hampshire lumberman commanded the Americans. Militia Brigadier General John Stark, age forty-nine, was a lean, tough, seasoned soldier. Historians have variously described Stark as "unpredictable," "cantankerous," and "independent as a hog on ice." The novelist Kenneth Roberts called him simply, "that sour-faced feller."[4]

By most accounts Stark was thin, blue-eyed and weathered. His soldiers, the men who knew him best, believed in him. They demonstrated time and again that when John Stark led, they would follow. He and his army of militia had marched under orders from the New Hampshire General Court and Committee of Safety, orders that made clear that Stark owed no allegiance to the Continental Army's chain of command. His only mission was to protect New Hampshire and the Hampshire Grants (Vermont). The Committee of Safety had given Stark broad discretion in how he carried out his task. He would not have undertaken the command otherwise.[5]

Stark had earlier served as a colonel in the Continental Army, but he resigned his commission in March 1777 when Congress promoted officers above him who had less seniority and inferior qualifications.

On August 7, when John Stark rode down the mountain into Manchester, Vermont, at the head of a column of troops, he found that a Continental general, Benjamin Lincoln, had already ordered the advance party of Stark's troops to march to the Hudson River to reinforce Schuyler. Stark defied Lincoln to his face, countermanded the order, and headed for Bennington.[6]

His decision placed his men directly across the line of march of Baum's raiders. When they met, John Stark took action. On this day of driving rain, he reported, "I sent out parties to harass them."[7]

Baum's men soon began to doubt their own commander. Roving Americans attacked them from the woods, shooting from behind trees and killing several soldiers. One British captain complained, "Now they will become bold—we leave them too much time, for they will gather by the thousands during the night."[8] Baum sent an officer riding off toward Burgoyne along the Hudson, asking for reinforcements.

The Americans fought like woodsmen, always on the move, slipping from tree to tree. The German commander's soldiers were intimidated. One of them wrote, "every 40 paces a man is standing behind a tree." The Germans had never experienced such warfare. They had been trained to fight masses of uniformed men, locked in tight formation with drums beating and flags waving. The constant splatter of raindrops muffled all sound, silencing the footfalls of frontiersmen gliding through the trees. Baum's men could not see their foes in the mist and rain. These silent unseen killers scared them.[9]

John Stark excelled at such tactics. He had fought as a ranger officer under Robert Rogers during the French and Indian War. "Ranging" tactics, with constant patrols and raids, kept the enemy off balance and provided intelligence. Like George Washington, Stark learned the soldier's profession in that brutal wilderness war where combatants on both sides used the cruelest methods to defeat their enemies.

For the past twenty-six months, Stark had been in the thick of combat—at Bunker Hill, Trenton and Princeton. He knew firsthand the brutality the King's troops brought to these battlefields, where they often refused to grant quarter, clubbing or bayoneting defenseless men to death. He knew the fate of prisoners of war in British hands. Despite all this, word had come down from the highest councils of the rebellion that Americans would pursue a "policy of humanity." Immediately after the victory at Princeton, where redcoat bayonets had mortally wounded General Hugh Mercer as he lay helpless, Washington wrote an order concerning prisoners held by the Americans: "Treat them with humanity, and let them have no reason to complain of our Copying the brutal example of the British army in their Treatment of our unfortunate brethren."[10]

Civilian leaders approved of the policy. John Adams wrote to his wife Abigail: "I know of no policy, God is my witness, but this—Piety, Humanity and Honesty are the best Policy. Blasphemy, Cruelty and Villainy have prevailed and may again. But they won't prevail against America, in this Contest, because I find that the more of them are employed, the less they succeed."[11]

Noble sentiments. But how would they work in the face of not just one, but four distinct foes? A mixture of British, Germans, Indians and Loyalists made up Baum's force. Stark and his men brought different perspectives to bear on each of them. Thomas Paine had expressed American attitudes thus: "a line of distinction should be drawn, between English soldiers taken in battle, and inhabitants of America taken in arms. The first are prisoners, but the latter are traitors. The one forfeits his liberty, the latter his head."[12] Almost to a man, Stark's soldiers were native to the territory threatened by Burgoyne's advance. Most of them came from Vermont, New Hampshire and Massachusetts, and they believed the enemy posed an immediate threat to their homes and families. Washington and Adams were hundreds of miles away. John Stark had already demonstrated his independence from the Revolution's leaders. It was one thing to voice high-minded ideals, another to put them to the test in the ferocity and chaos of battle.

For a few hours the summer storm maintained an uneasy peace; neither army could fight with wet gunpowder. When the skies cleared on August 16, a human tempest burst. Events of that day would shock General John Burgoyne and cause him to write: "The Hampshire Grants in particular, a country unpeopled and almost unknown in the last war now abounds in the most active and most rebellious race of the continent, and hangs like a gathering storm upon my left."[13]

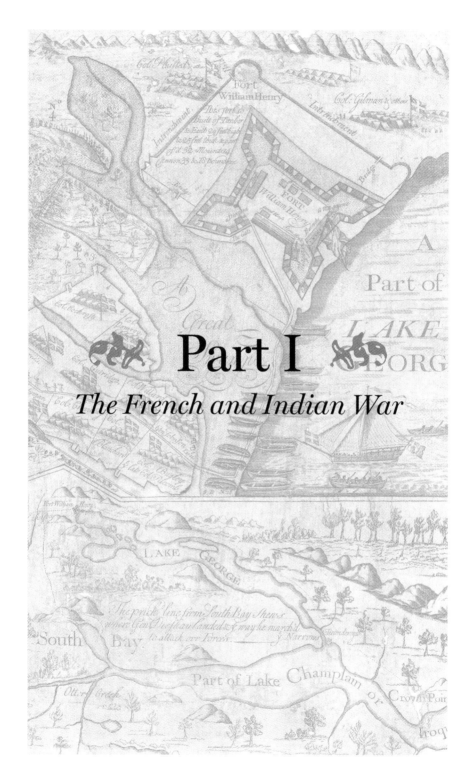

Part I

The French and Indian War

 **1**

ORIGINS

A Hiding Place from the Wind

John Stark was born on August 28, 1728, at Nutfield, a settlement on the frontier of the northern wilderness in what would become New Hampshire.[1] John's parents, Archibald and Eleanor Stark, both born in Scotland, had emigrated twice—first to Northern Ireland, and then to America. They were Scotch-Irish, part of waves of migration of their countrymen to the New World that began in 1717.[2]

Eleanor's father, James Nichols, and her mother left Ireland before them and arrived in Boston in 1718. Their pastor, Reverend James MacGregor, led an entire Presbyterian congregation to America, where the Massachusetts Bay Puritans gave them a cold welcome. Puritans strove to perfect their insular version of Christianity and practiced open intolerance toward other faiths. They had even been known to hang Quakers. The Presbyterians sought to distance themselves from these stern folk.[3]

MacGregor's flock wandered for a time. Then, an ally of English descent, Squire John Goffe, helped them acquire the Nutfield land grant in the Merrimack Valley. In April 1719 the congregation gathered on Horse Hill in Nutfield, overlooking their new land, to hear their pastor preach from Isaiah: "And a man shall be as a hiding place from the wind and a covert from the tempest; as a river of water in a dry place, as the shadow of a great rock in a weary land."[4]

Reverend MacGregor's people carried a collective memory of oppression. Cromwell's armies had driven their lowland Scot ancestors from their homes after fierce struggles.[5] In Ulster, Northern Ireland, English armies again harried the Scots. The people of Londonderry endured a siege through which they fought and starved for one hundred and five days until relief arrived. In honor of the memory of this trial, their descendants renamed Nutfield as "Londonderry."[6]

The Scotch-Irish in Ulster continued to chafe under British rule. When farmers established woolen and linen industries to complement their husbandry, the Irish Woolens Act ruined their endeavors. When the terms of their land leases ended, English landlords doubled or tripled the rents—a practice known as "rack-renting." When the Anglican Church required funds, Presbyterian Scots tithed for its support.[7]

Scotch-Irish clergymen like MacGregor thus led a series of migrations to the American colonies as entire congregations boarded ships bound for a new life across the Atlantic. Life in the new land would be hard, but at least the people could endure the hardships as a group. And, as a group, they would remember and pass down to their descendants stories of oppression by the English.

Archibald and Eleanor Stark followed her parents in 1720, sailing from Port Rush at the mouth of the Bann River where, from 1718 to 1720, smallpox struck. They had their three small children with them.[8] At first the tossing ship spread only the usual misery of seasickness among the passengers. Then, one by one, each Stark child fell ill and died of smallpox. Sailors cast their bodies into the sea. Not even their names survived. The distraught parents, childless now, sailed on toward a strange land.[9]

When the disease-ridden ship entered Boston harbor, local authorities refused to let the passengers disembark. The vessel's master sailed down the coast of Maine and into the channel of Sheepscot Bay. Scotch-Irish settlers at a community later known as Wiscasset welcomed the voyagers and sheltered them through a harsh winter.[10]

In the spring of 1721, the Starks joined the James Nichols family in Londonderry (Nutfield), where Archibald found work as a joiner, or carpenter. They lived with the Nichols until the fall of 1722, when Archibald paid £24 for thirty acres of land next to his father-in-law. There he built a small dwelling fronting the "direct road to Kilrea."[11] That year Eleanor gave birth to a daughter, Anna. More babies followed in regular succession: William in 1724; Isabel in1726; and John in 1728. Three generations of the family lived side-by-side.[12]

James Nichols was a leader in the community and served as Moderator of the Town Meeting in 1723, a job usually reserved for the most respected citizens. Then his health failed. Archibald Stark and two neighbors signed as witnesses when the old man made his mark on his will shortly before he died in 1726.[13]

The Scotch-Irish of Londonderry shared the community with a handful of colonists of English ancestry including Squire John Goffe and his son, John, Jr., both of whom signed the list as original proprietors. The elder Goffe served as town clerk.[14] John, Jr., was a bold man who inspired imitation. His neighbors called him "Hunter John" because he made daring excursions into the forests north and west of Londonderry. That wilderness stretched all the way to the Hudson River and the St. Lawrence River and was inhabited only by wild beasts and Indians. Relations between the native population and the colonists varied between tension and violence. Only the rare English settler dared venture far into the woods.[15]

The Pennacook Indians made the Merrimack Valley their home. Their principal village lay a few miles north of Londonderry. Each spring they gathered to fish at Amoskeag Falls on the Merrimack. After King Philip's War in 1675, white hostility had driven many of them to withdraw to Quebec, Canada. There they joined the Abenaki at the village of St. Francis, along with other refugees from white encroachment. French traders and Catholic priests encouraged their resentment against the Protestant New Englanders who had displaced them.[16]

A few Indians remained near Londonderry, however. John Goffe, Jr., befriended a Pennacook named Christo who lived in a hut at Amoskeag Falls. The Indian taught young Goffe to hunt and trap and find his way in the forests. Hunter John developed a passionate love for the wilderness, a trait that neighboring Scotch-Irish boys readily adopted.[17]

Archibald and Eleanor Stark had arrived at the New Hampshire frontier at the very time hostilities between whites and Indians worsened. From 1722 to 1724, warriors from St. Francis raided settlements in New England, and the attackers struck closer and closer to Londonderry.[18] John Lovewell, a militia officer from Dunstable, petitioned the Massachusetts General Assembly for funds to support a proposed expedition against the Indians. Lovewell wrote that he and his company "are inclinable to range and keep out in the woods for several months together in order to kill and destroy their enemy Indians." His militia would be a party of "rangers."[19]

The General Assembly voted to award a bounty of £100 for each Indian scalp the rangers brought in. "Lovewell's War" began in 1725 when his men attacked a small party of sleeping native hunters.[20] John Goffe, Jr., joined Lovewell's force, and they ventured north toward Ossipee Lake. Goffe remained at a makeshift fort near the lake while Lovewell and his company combed the woods looking for the enemy. Indians found Lovewell first; they ambushed his party and killed several men, including Lovewell himself. The survivors, with John Goffe, barely escaped back to the settlements.[21]

Lovewell's War served only to worsen matters, promoting distrust and hatred between the races. Christo left his hut one day and, while he was gone, white men torched his home. They failed to drive him away, however, for he lived at Amoskeag several more years.[22]

As his family grew, Archibald Stark worked at farming and carpentry to provide for them. With the help of two nephews, Robert and James Walker, he drew gum from pine trees to distill into turpentine; it was a forest occupation similar to tapping maple trees for their sugar. The boys remembered spending part of three years helping their "Uncle Stark" labor in the woods.[23]

Together with the entire community, the Stark family attended religious services at the Presbyterian Meeting House in Londonderry, where Archibald purchased a pew "on the north side of the west dore next to said dore." Later events would show that the hours young John spent on the hard bench of the meetinghouse failed to make him a committed Christian. When the time came for Archibald to sell the Londonderry farm, he conveyed his pew along with the land.[24]

In the spring of 1736, the Stark's house burned to the ground. Homeless, with seven small children, and Eleanor pregnant again, the family moved in with relatives until Archibald could build new quarters. He turned this disaster into an opportunity to improve their lives. On June 15, 1736, Archibald purchased six hundred acres in Derryfield, the settlement just to the north of Londonderry. The land was on the high ground east of the Merrimack River at Amoskeag Falls. In September, Archibald sold the land in Londonderry, and they moved north. Christo became their neighbor.[25]

Archibald built a cape-style home on his new land and constructed a sawmill on the small stream nearby. He designed the house around a central chimney, where a great hearth became the source of heat, light, food and education.[26] The conversation of adults informed the minds and spirits of eighteenth-century children; on long winter evenings, talk was the sole entertainment for the family. The fireplace was the heart of the house.

It would take the Starks years of labor to make their place a proper farm, but the move had added one vital new asset to their balance sheet—fishing at Amoskeag Falls.

New Hampshire settlers quickly learned the value of the Amoskeag fishery. It was seasonal work, a pleasant break from plowing and seeding, but the catch provided real economic value. Fish could be packed in tubs, salted down and kept through the year. For several decades salt fish constituted a kind of currency of a known value that could be traded for other goods and services. Men of all ages, from childhood to dotage, returned to Amoskeag for every spring run of fish.[27]

Long before white men appeared, Indians knew that the falls on the Merrimack interrupted the upstream migration of fish on their way to the spawning beds. Salmon, shad, alewives, sturgeon and eels milled around below the white water. Indians spread a net partway across the river below the falls, trapping the fish. Then warriors speared or netted the catch from canoes.[28]

When the tribes moved away, white men took over the fishery. They netted salmon and shad from weirs stretched across the river or its tributaries. They speared fish from rocks or angled from the shores. Fishermen gave colorful names to their favorite spots: Eel Falls, Todd Gut, Little Pulpit, Point Rock and Black Rock. Children participated at the smaller streams, throwing alewives ashore with shovels and scoops. The fish were so plentiful and so easy to catch that farmers fertilized their corn with the carcasses.[29]

Eels became a staple food. Men armed with eel pots and spears handled the slippery creatures with wool mittens. A local poet called the eels "Derryfield Beef." He concluded a verse on the subject with a light-hearted refrain: "And before they walked—it is well confirmed that the children never walked but squirmed."[30]

Men fought over fishing sites. One day a group tried to evict John Dickey from Todd Gut, but he refused to budge. His competitors built a platform of slabs and planks over him and began fishing right on top of him. Another time, bystanders stepped in to break up a fistfight over Little Pulpit, but one combatant kept swinging. "His blood be upon his own head," he hollered.[31]

More often, the fishing offered an opportunity for men and boys to meet and socialize with their counterparts from neighboring settlements. John Stark made a lifelong friend of Matthew Patten from Bedford, across the river from Derryfield. Matthew fished at the "Patten Seine," downstream from the falls.[32] Young Robert Rogers and his brothers came to the falls, and they probably first met the Stark brothers along the river.[33]

The Merrimack grew into a wild, dangerous torrent in the spring when it carried off the mountain snowmelt. Men had close calls with the raging water; others drowned after slipping off a wet rock or overturning a canoe. Youths earned reputations for hardiness and courage at the falls. Their companions came to identify certain fishing sites with the strong characters who claimed them. Local lore acknowledged young John Stark's right to three sites: Near Gut, Snapping Place, and Crack in the Rock.[34]

The Stark brothers learned three trades early in life: farming, lumbering and fishing. Otherwise, they received only rudimentary educations. All of them could read and write, but their spelling amounted to phonetic guesswork; most of John's extensive military correspondence was written for him by aides.[35]

In 1734, John Goffe, Jr., moved to Derryfield. He built a home and sawmill on Cohas Brook, south of the falls on the Merrimack. He and Christo were now available to teach their young Scotch-Irish neighbors two additional vital occupations—hunting and trapping.[36]

James Rogers, Robert's father, had moved his family to the New Hampshire frontier in 1739. He had acquired a parcel of land a few miles northwest of Amoskeag Falls in November 1738. It was an area of low hills that reminded James of his home in Ulster, and he named it for his native place, "Mountalona."[37]

John Stark and Robert Rogers grew up in similar ways, both members of large families with several scrappy brothers. Neither received much schooling. Rogers's letters revealed the same careless phonetic spelling characteristic of Stark's writing. Both boys sought a wilderness education.[38] "Hunting," Rogers wrote later, "was at that period the most agreeable and profitable business in which the hardy youth of New England employed themselves."[39]

This passion for the wilderness became a notable trait of Scotch-Irish youth. Jeremy Belknap, the eighteenth-century New Hampshire historian, found such boys remarkable. "They frequently lie out in the woods several days or weeks together," he wrote, where "they pass the coldest nights and awake vigorous for labor the succeeding days." Belknap distinguished the Scotch-Irish young people from others: "By these methods of living, the people are familiarized to hardships; their children are early used to coarse fare and hard lodgings."[40]

Rogers and Stark became friends as boys. They hunted and trapped together and explored the New Hampshire forests. Rogers could have been speaking for both of them when he wrote of himself: "His manner of life from early youth, having been brought up as it were, in the hunter's camp, and inured to hardship, rendered him peculiarly qualified for the service in which he afterward engaged."[41] This life was no hardship to such boys; it was a celebration of their freedom, and they gloried in it.

France declared war on England in 1744, and another round of frontier violence spread across the American colonies—King George's War. Attacks by French-Canadian partisans and their Indian allies terrorized New England. They struck suddenly at remote farms and outlying settlements, then the raiders melted back into the woods. Their home was the village of St. Francis in Quebec, but their advanced base stood on the shore of Lake Champlain, the high stone fortress of the French at Crown Point—Fort St. Frédéric.

They attacked first in the Connecticut Valley. Twelve Indians captured a man cutting wood outside the fort at Great Meadow. Then they killed a man at Pembroke. New Hampshire Governor Benning Wentworth called out the militia, whose commander, Colonel Joseph Blanchard, ordered John Goffe, Jr., and his company to "range the woods and to intercept Indian bands which might possibly be on their way to frontier settlements."[42]

Goffe and his men took to the woods on snowshoes in January 1746. They travelled north along the Merrimack to the mountain valleys where they hoped to find the enemy. But the raiders had vanished. The Americans patrolled the frozen woods, but they found no sign of Indians. Goffe vented his frustration in a letter to Governor Wentworth: "It is enough to make ones blood boyl in ones veins to see our fellow creatures killed and taken upon every quarter and if we cannot catch them hear [here] I hoop the general Cort will give Incorigment to go and give them the same play at home—."[43]

Goffe rejected the strategy of trying to waylay the small bands of raiders in the forests, where encountering them was pure chance. The French and Indians, he believed, must be attacked "at home."

An uneasy peace settled over the land in the spring and summer of 1746. New Englanders planted their crops and tended their stock, all the while keeping a careful eye on the nearby woods. Sentinels watched over the workers in the fields. Young children of both sexes learned to load and fire muskets.

Captain Daniel Ladd's militia company walked into an ambush between Rumford (now Concord, New Hampshire) and Hopkinton. Indians killed five men, scalped and disemboweled them, and fled with two captives. Only one man escaped.[44]

Robert Rogers, age fourteen, enlisted to replace one of the dead militiamen. He patrolled the woods through the remainder of 1746 in Captain Ebenezer Eastman's company. But the enemy had disappeared.[45]

Some people couldn't adjust to this pattern of frontier life—months of uneasy peace, followed by sudden vicious attacks where no quarter was given and torture and dismemberment were real possibilities. While such tactics terrorized some, it inspired a thirst for revenge in others. Christo read the temper of his white neighbors; he abandoned his hut and left Amoskeag.

Communities constructed stockades or garrisons where people could find shelter if attacks threatened. These were log fortifications surrounding a house or farm, where the defenders could shoot back from relative safety. Early in 1746, Archibald Stark helped build a garrison on his own land at the outlet of Swager's Brook from Fort Pond. It enclosed about a half acre, and the pond and brook supplied both water and fish. Hunter John Goffe commanded the militia unit based at "Stark's Fort."[46]

A year passed with no attacks. Then, in August 1747, alarm bells rang near Rumford. The McCoy family of Epsom hurried out on the road to the garrison and safety. Husband and wife became separated. Indians sprang from the woods, grabbed Mrs. McCoy and dragged her away. Mr. McCoy escaped; he insisted that he had recognized one of her captors as Christo.[47]

The people at Rumford imagined the worst for Mrs. McCoy—torture, rape or murder. Instead, the Indians took her to Canada. They treated her kindly and never abused her. In Quebec they sold her to a French family, and she worked as a servant until the end of the war. When peace was declared in 1748, Mrs. McCoy returned to her family in New Hampshire.[48]

In April of 1748, the French and Indians made Robert Rogers a lifelong foe. One night at the hill farm at Mountalona, the Rogers family heard the alarm bell tolling. They escaped to the garrison at Rumford. When they returned to their farm, they found the house and barn burned to the ground, their animals slaughtered and their orchard cut down.[49]

Robert Rogers did not stay to rebuild the farm. He became a wanderer. He lived in the wilderness north of the settlements, hunting, trapping and, perhaps, smuggling. He visited Quebec after the end of the war, passing through miles of forest that he called "the uncultivated desart."[50]

John Stark experienced a very different war. His family lost nothing, neither lives nor property. They did not have to start over like the Rogers family. In fact, the building of Stark's Fort had raised their status with their neighbors. In addition their sawmill gave them a commercial relationship with people that farming could never provide. The wilderness attracted John Stark, just as it drew Robert Rogers. But while Rogers wandered, Stark kept a foothold in Derryfield.

2

Captivity

There'll Be War

In 1740 New Hampshire became a province, independent of Massachusetts. Much of the province lay within an old grant to a Captain John Mason dating from the early 1600s. In 1746 investors or speculators (called "Masonian proprietors") purchased the claims of Captain Mason's heirs to that portion of his grant lying within a radius of sixty miles from the sea at Portsmouth and, by 1748, they were selling "townships." Where these townships already contained settlers, the Masonian proprietors quit-claimed the land to its occupants. Their business strategy was to populate the townships quickly, thus increasing the value of the lands they retained.[1]

In 1748 several men petitioned the proprietors for a parcel located west of the Merrimack, a tract that included the farm of James Rogers at Mountalona. The first signers of the petition were Archibald Stark and his three eldest sons.[2]

James Rogers and his neighbor, Joseph Pudney, hired a lawyer in Londonderry to press their claims to their farms in opposition to the Starks. The proprietors settled the matter by granting two hundred acres each to the petitioners and also to Rogers and Pudney. James had claimed significantly more land than that, but he accepted the outcome. Because Archibald's signature appeared first, the township was named Starkstown.[3]

The Stark family continued to reside at Derryfield. When Archibald, Jr., reached majority, he moved to Starkstown and, later, William Stark also moved there. The Stark family's connection to the new settlement grew stronger as the years passed. A wealthy English colonist, Caleb Page, built a large house at Page's Corner, near the road to Rumford. He had a son, Caleb, and a daughter, Elizabeth. As a girl, Elizabeth had carried a musket to the fields to keep watch against attacks while the men worked. John Stark, who was nine years older, liked to tease her by calling her "Molly."[4]

Land grants at Starkstown didn't come free. To "prove up" their claims, settlers had to clear three acres, build a dwelling and have a family living in it by the spring of 1752. The proprietors wanted to see signs of progress. Farmers had to provide for their families and livestock, defend against Indians, and race against the clock to settle their land claims.[5] The drought of 1749 made their lives harder. These pioneers were gamblers. They came from poverty, so poverty in a new place didn't frighten them. They dared much because they had little to lose. Such daring occasionally meant disrespect for law and order. Some men turned to counterfeiting and smuggling, and some quickly became violent.[6]

John McNeil and Daniel McNeil in Derryfield attacked sixty-year-old Archibald Stark with "clubs and stones." Archibald sued them, claiming that he was unable to work from April to August in 1751 and that his "life was for a long time despaired of." The justice of the peace awarded him £34 damages and fined the McNeils twenty shillings, but he made no record of the cause for the assault.[7]

Accidents took their toll. One day in 1753, James Rogers followed a forest trail on his way to visit a friend's hunting camp. He may have been wearing a hide coat with the fur side turned out, because his friend mistook him for a bear and shot him dead.[8]

Back at Amoskeag, John Goffe, Jr., and Archibald Stark joined forces to improve the neighborhood. They petitioned for a township charter for Derryfield, which was granted in 1751, incorporating the sections known as Cohas, Amoskeag and Harrytown, along with a large tract inland from the river.[9]

The next year, Goffe and Stark, in their capacities as Selectmen, petitioned the Court at Portsmouth for a road to be laid out along the east bank of the Merrimack, "… not only for the Great Benefit of Travelors up and Down said River, but as our River has become a Maritime Place for Transporting Timber, Plank and Board." The court authorized the construction of the road but, because both Stark and Goffe dealt in timber, plank and board, their constituents may have resented the two lumbermen; neither was reelected the following year.[10]

⁂

John Stark was a grown man by 1750. Later descriptions of him focused on his grim appearance in portraits made when he was an elderly man. These paintings failed to capture the spirit and passion of the young Stark. Most observers reported that he was tall, lean and narrow of face, with blue eyes and a weathered complexion. One man noted the "peculiar" intensity of Stark's gaze when he looked a man in the eye.[11]

If his speech resembled his writing, it was not the language of the gentry. He did not "go" somewhere; he was "agoing" somewhere, and his destination was a place he called "them parts."[12]

His manner amounted to what might be expected from a young man who grew up in the cornfield, the sawmill and the hunting camp. He appeared, one observer said, to be frank, undignified and ordinary. He spoke his mind plainly, and he never seemed to care what impression his words made on others. He would have made a poor showing in the drawing rooms of Boston, Philadelphia or Fairfax County, Virginia. He was a common man except that, when circumstances required action, he became a most uncommon man.[13]

⁂

In late March 1752, John, his brother William, and two friends, David Stinson and Amos Eastman, set out on an extended hunting and fishing expedition. The ice on the Merrimack had melted, so they travelled by canoe, headed for the remote Baker River, which flowed into the Merrimack from the western hills. The river was named for Thomas Baker, a militia lieutenant who led a mission there in 1712 and slaughtered several Pemigewasset Indians for their scalps.

Baker River was a gentle stream, winding eastward through a forested valley with high mountains looming on the north. The four young men pitched their camp on the south bank of the river, opposite the mouth of a small stream that flowed down from the north (Stinson Brook). They set traps along the river and the tributary streams, and they settled in for weeks of hard work in the wet and cold.[14]

The trappers built a fire in front of their lean-to for cooking and for warmth. The smoke probably betrayed their presence, because they soon found moccasin tracks nearby. On April 28 they decided to pull their traps and retreat downriver with their furs.[15]

The group selected John Stark to collect the traps while the others broke camp and packed the canoes. John went out alone in the afternoon, walking beside the dark river searching for their trap sets. When he found one, he bent over to pull the trap. Indians suddenly sprang out of hiding around him; Stark told his grandson that, "A sharp hissing sound as of a snake accompanied the movement." Within seconds they made Stark a prisoner.[16]

His captors were ten warriors from St. Francis, led by their chief, Francis Titigaw. They may have been a hunting party that happened on the four young men by chance. The capture took place only a few miles from a favored Indian site at a bend of the Connecticut River known as the Cowass Intervales. Indians revered the site and sought to keep white men away.[17]

The Indians asked Stark the whereabouts of his companions. He pointed upriver, away from where he knew the three men would be. With muskets aimed at his back, he led the warriors in the wrong direction. But his brother and Eastman and Stinson had become alarmed when it began to grow dark and he didn't return. They fired their muskets to guide him back. Now the Indians knew Stark had deceived them. They quickly reversed direction, but it was too dark, so they bivouacked for the night.[18]

The two parties spent the night near each other, both in cold, fireless camps. The Indians moved out before dawn and caught the white men just starting downriver. William Stark and David Stinson paddled the canoe, and Amos Eastman walked along the riverbank. John Stark yelled to them, trying to warn them to escape. Indians raised their muskets and aimed at the fleeing men, but Stark forced some of their gun barrels into the air, causing shots to go astray. One ball struck and killed David Stinson; his body slid into the river.

Amos Eastman surrendered. Now, Stark paid for interfering with the warriors' aim. They beat him, but stopped short of hurting him seriously. Thereafter the Indians abused neither white man. They pulled Stinson's body from the river and carved his scalp from his skull. Then they bundled up the furs and headed toward the Connecticut River with their prisoners.[19]

William Stark escaped in the canoe and made his way, alone, to Rumford to report the ambush. Days later he led a party back to Baker River, where they found Stinson's body and buried it. The rescue party returned to Rumford with the sad news. People feared the worst for Amos and John.[20]

Titigaw's band rested one night at the Intervales, then proceeded north to a place known as Upper Cowass. Three warriors split off from the band and headed farther west with Eastman. The others moved north along the Connecticut River to the mouth of John's River.

The Indians spent several days hunting and trapping along John's River. Each day they released Stark and urged him to trap. He brought two beaver pelts back to camp. The warriors knew he would not try to escape; they knew the country—he was lost. It was a bewildering country of rivers and lakes. Alone and unarmed in this huge forest, he would surely die. He stayed with the Indians, and they reached St. Francis on June 9.[21]

The village stood high on the east bank of the St. Francis River, less than ten miles south of the St. Lawrence. It was more than one hundred fifty miles, through total wilderness, from Baker River. People from many tribes lived there, and they were collectively known as St. Francis Indians. Many of them were refugees or descendants of refugees displaced by the expansion of white settlement in New England and elsewhere. The village was not a primitive encampment; French priests had built a mission and church there many years before. The homes resembled French houses more than traditional Indian dwellings.[22]

The French encouraged the raiding parties from St. Francis. The Indians' motivations for the attacks were complex; they wanted to stop white encroachment and they wanted revenge for old grievances. But one motive stood out—raiding was good business. They kidnapped white settlers so they could extort ransom from the colonists. The practice had been going on for decades.[23]

Fifty years earlier, in 1703, Indians raided Deerfield, Massachusetts, and carried off Reverend John Williams and his wife. When Mrs. Williams proved to be a poor traveler, her captors killed her.[24] At St. Francis, Reverend Williams found English children who had been kidnapped as he had been. They had adapted to life as Indians and were treated as members of the extended family of the village. A Jesuit priest tried to convince Williams to worship at the Catholic Church, which was already a fixture in the Indians' lives, but the Reverend declined.[25]

Eventually Williams was freed and returned to Massachusetts, where he wrote an account of his captivity, *The Redeemed Captive Returning to Zion,* first published in 1707. It was widely read. John Stark probably knew the Williams's story before his own encounter with St. Francis.[26]

ᏨᎪ ᎾᏦᎧ

The Indians welcomed Stark and Eastman to the village by making them run a gauntlet in which parallel lines of Indian youths, all armed with sticks or cudgels, stood ready to beat the new prisoners as they passed between them. Eastman went first. The warriors thrashed him so severely that he collapsed on the ground.[27]

Stark followed, but he had broken the rules of the game by picking up a long stick of his own. He told the story to his grandson, Caleb Stark, who reported it: "After receiving a blow or two, he turned his pole right and left, dealing a blow at each turn, and made his way without much injury, his enemies making way for him to avoid the sweeping blow dealt by his pole."

The Indians tried to make their captives work. They handed John Stark a hoe and ordered him to clean the weeds out of a patch of corn beside the river. While the Indians watched, Stark grubbed out the young corn and spared the weeds. Then he threw the hoe into the river, saying it was "the business of squaws and not warriors to hoe corn."[28]

His bravery and defiance earned him the respect of the elders and warriors of St. Francis, and thereafter they treated him as one of their own. His grandson reported that they called him "young chief." Caleb wrote, "In the latter days of his life he often related, with much humor, the incidents of his captivity, observing that he had experienced more kindness from the savages of St. Francis, than he had ever known prisoners of war to receive from more civilized nations."[29]

⚔ ⚔

In mid-July, two Massachusetts officials arrived at the village seeking to ransom or redeem prisoners from their colony. When they found none, they paid to free Stark and Eastman instead. After six weeks of captivity, the young men were free to leave. They accompanied their redeemers to Albany, along with the very Indians who had captured them and who hoped to sell the young men's furs. At Albany Stark watched merchants buy his furs from his captors, an experience that fueled his lifelong contempt for the people of Albany.[30]

When they reached home, Stark and Eastman found that they were indebted to Massachusetts for buying their freedom. Stark owed an amount equal to $103. For some reason Eastman owed less. To raise the money, in 1753 Stark ventured into far northern New Hampshire to trap along the Androscoggin River. The furs he took on that trip paid the redemption debt and more. Further, his expedition demonstrated that he had not been intimidated by the St. Francis experience. He still sought the freedom of the wilderness life.[31]

The two young men resented having to pay back the ransom money, however. They reasoned that, if Massachusetts paid to redeem its citizens, New Hampshire should do likewise and, in 1754, Stark and Eastman petitioned for reimbursement for their lost furs and ransom. They calculated that the furs amounted to "five hundred sixty pounds, at least, old tenor." Caleb Stark never reported whether the province reimbursed his grandfather, but John Stark's petition revealed one important fact—he identified himself as "John Stark of Starkstown." He now lived closer to Molly Page.[32]

⚔ ⚔

The New Hampshire Provincial Assembly, alarmed by Indian activity along the Connecticut River, resolved to build a road from the Merrimack Valley to the Connecticut River at the Intervales. They selected Molly's brother, Caleb Page, to serve as surveyor for the expedition. John Stark was appointed "pilot" for the group, because he was one of the few colonists who had ever traveled the route. Robert Rogers also joined the mission.[33]

The Indians sent a message to the New Hampshire authorities, protesting the building of the road into territory they considered sacred. Nevertheless, on March 10, the men set out, blazing a trail to the Connecticut, following the same route Stark traveled in 1752. They had finished their work and returned to Rumford by March 31, but threats of war convinced the Assembly to abandon the project. The road was not built.[34]

That year, Robert Rogers is said to have correctly predicted that, "There'll be war before another year."[35]

In the late fall of 1754, Robert Rogers went hunting in the woods in Goffstown, south of his family home at Mountalona. A stranger appeared in the forest. He introduced himself as John McDaniel and told Rogers that he wanted to buy cattle. He gave the young frontiersman bills of exchange to make the purchases, and then he disappeared.[36]

In fact, "John McDaniel" was the notorious Owen Sullivan, leader of an extended counterfeiting ring in New England and New York. Sullivan had plied his trade in Boston and Providence. Over the years he had been caught and punished several times. Lawmen had jailed, flogged and branded him, and then cropped his ears for good measure. He always escaped, and he always returned to counterfeiting.[37]

Rogers began passing Sullivan's fake notes in the winter of 1754–55.[38] Other local men joined the ring—Benjamin Winn, James McNeil, and a pathetic fellow named Carty Gilman. Sullivan soon developed contempt for his henchmen. "Damn you for a pack of fools," he told them. "I never was concerned with such a pack of damn fools before." He left New Hampshire early in the winter, probably worried that some of the fools would be his undoing.[39]

The law swooped down on the remaining members of the gang. Matthew Patten, Justice of the Peace in Bedford, issued summonses for the suspects and the witnesses. On February 3, 1755, Patten set out from his home after midnight, bound for Amoskeag. He found John Stark on the Sabbath and gave him a summons as a witness.

Patten could not locate some of the suspects; they had "obsconded," he wrote. His diary recorded that he "… setout with Capt. Chamberlin and went to Goffes and Starkstown to apprehend Counterfeit Money makers. Travelled all night and got to Mounterloney [Mountalona] by morning."[40]

Lawmen sought the other members of the band as well. Undersheriff John Light caught Carty Gilman, who was carrying two fake bills and a message from Robert Rogers. Gilman popped the message in his mouth and tried to swallow it. But Undersheriff Light wrenched the paper from his mouth and read it:

Mr Cartee Gilman at Exeeter, Gilman Sr. for gods sake do the work that you promised you would do   by no means fail or you will destroy me for ever for my Life Lays at your proodence   now ons mor I adgure you by your maker to do it for why should such an onest Man be Killed. Sr, I am asoured freend   Robert Rogers[41]

Warrants had been sent out from Portsmouth for nineteen suspects, including Robert Rogers and his brother Richard. Magistrates examined witnesses. Since Rogers had approached Stark about buying cattle for Sullivan, John's testimony was taken and transcribed:

THE EXAMINATION OF JOHN STARK who says Robert Rogers some time last fall asked him if he had any oxen to sell. He answered yes, six oxen. Where are they. And he [Stark] said they were at McCurdy's. And he asked Rogers what he was going to do with them. Who said a Gentleman from Boston [Sullivan] wanted 3 yoke of oxen—Some time after he saw Rogers and asked him what he had done with his oxen and he said he sold em but not to the man he purposed them for, and said he was cheated for he intended the oxen for Sullivan and thought to have a large quantity of Counterfeit money. But said he would not be concerned anymore in such things.[42]

It is unclear whether Stark ever received money for the six oxen or if he knew from the beginning that his friend was passing counterfeit money, but he certainly knew by the time he testified. Stark's words directly contradicted Rogers, who swore he didn't know the money was fake. But, John's final words demonstrated his loyalty to his friend by repeating Robert's promise that he would reform.[43]

The case against Rogers was put over to a later term of the court, and it languished. In 1755 the colonies faced more serious problems than a handful of petty criminals. The prediction made by Robert Rogers had come true. Another war with the French and Indians broke out, and New Hampshire needed troops. Rogers had already enlisted twenty-four volunteers to serve for Massachusetts, men that New Hampshire Governor Wentworth wanted for his own forces. Rogers now had a way out of his legal difficulties; he transferred his company to the New Hampshire Regiment, to be led by Robert Rogers, captain, and John Stark, lieutenant.[44]

The counterfeiting episode ended without consequences for Robert Rogers. Owen Sullivan wasn't so lucky. He made his way back to his hideout in the mountains of the "Oblong" in Dover, New York. There, a militia officer named Eliphalet Beecher found him hiding under a woman's bed and dragged him off for trial in Manhattan. Upon a verdict of guilty, the court sentenced Sullivan to hang.

The authorities had to postpone the hanging twice—once because Sullivan's admirers sawed down the gibbet, and a second time because no volunteer could be found to do the actual hanging. When his time finally came in May of 1756, Sullivan faced his end bravely: "… just before he was hanged he took a large cud of tobacco and turning to the people said: 'I cannot help smiling as 'tis the nature of the beast.'" Sullivan was just the kind of man Rogers and Stark would need in the forests around Lake George and Lake Champlain. It so happened that there were many like him.[45]

3

STARK AND ROGERS GO TO WAR
May God Be with Us

While Robert Rogers and John Stark sorted out their personal lives, powerful men across the ocean made decisions that would affect them for years to come. The long series of wars between the French and the English had settled nothing. Both nations competed for a variety of economic prizes, several of which were in the New World.

The islands of the Caribbean and the Maritimes of Canada were two sources of friction, the first for sugar and rum, and the second for control of the fisheries. For England's American colonists, the important struggle was for the expanse of wilderness that stretched from Maine across northern New England and New York, past the Great Lakes to the Mississippi River and, ultimately, to the Gulf of Mexico. This vast region, inhabited by scores of Indian tribes, tempted adventurers from both countries and provided the spark that set off the next war.

In 1753 the French built a series of strongholds in western Pennsylvania along the Alleghany and Ohio Rivers and their tributaries. A small French military unit had passed through the area in 1749. Its leader, Captain de Bienville, buried lead plates beneath marked trees. The plates were inscribed with a notice: "We ... have buried this plate ... as a token of renewal of possession heretofore taken of the aforesaid Ohio River, of all streams that fall into it, and all lands on both sides to the source of the aforesaid streams."[1]

By such slender means the French attempted to control a wilderness of unknown breadth and some 3,000 miles in length. It seemed like an impossible task. French Canada was a sparsely populated ribbon of land, inhabited by about 60,000 Roman Catholic Frenchmen settled most densely near the St. Lawrence River and its tributaries.[2]

The English colonies to the south, by contrast, contained over a million and a half people, most of them Protestant. The huge disparity in numbers, however, did not translate into military advantage; overall the French maintained an army nearly ten times the size of Britain's army. Canadian militia units were well trained, experienced and unified under a single command. In British America each colony maintained its own militia, with independent training and standards, and with no tradition of serving with other colonies. The weakness of the provinces provoked the British Board of Trade to call a conference at Albany, New York, intending to discuss relations with the Indians and to provide for mutual defense.[3]

Benjamin Franklin attended the conference in June as a commissioner for Pennsylvania. On the journey north from Philadelphia, he drew up a proposal for, "the union of all the colonies under one government, so far as might be necessary for defense." At Albany the delegates met with the chiefs of the Six Nations—the Iroquois—who were essential to the colonies' mutual defense because of their location between the antagonists. Franklin's plan, with amendments, was adopted and sent for approval to the Board of Trade and the colonial assemblies, where the plan foundered. Franklin wrote that the assemblies thought that there was "too much prerogative in it," and in England it was judged to have "too much of the democratic."[4]

In Franklin's view the royal governors played a heavy role in the defeat of the plan. They refused to recommend raising taxes to pay for defense, "unless their vast estates were in the same act expressly excused." He thought that both England and America suffered from these decisions. "The colonies, so united, would have been sufficiently strong to have defended themselves; there would have been no need of troops from England; of course, the subsequent pretence for taxing America, and the bloody contest it occasioned, would have been avoided."[5]

Even had the Albany Conference succeeded in organizing a united defense, events were moving faster than men could adapt to them. The month before the conference, a bloody incident in Pennsylvania caused the antagonists to stumble into war.

French incursions along the Ohio River system elicited a strong reaction from Governor Robert Dinwiddie of Virginia. In October 1753 he dispatched young Major George Washington of the Virginia militia to the French outposts to deliver a letter that warned the French to move away from lands that Virginia claimed. Washington and his companion, frontiersman Christopher Gist, handed the letter to a French officer at a post near Lake Erie, but they received no reply. They hurried east to report, and almost died in the effort. Along the way an Indian shot at them, and they nearly drowned in the icy Alleghany River.[6]

In May of 1754, Washington, recently brevetted to colonel at age twenty-two, led a detachment of about 160 men westward to deliver a more forceful message to the French. On May 27 they learned that a large French force was nearby. Washington met an Iroquois ally, Tanaghrisson (known as "Half-King"), that night. Before dawn the Americans and the Iroquois moved out to track the French. They soon located a camp hidden in a ravine in the woods. Silently, the Virginians and the Indians surrounded the camp.[7]

The encirclement was complete by eight o'clock. French soldiers were rousing and cooking their breakfast. Smoke and flame spewed from the Virginians' muskets. The French would later claim that Washington ambushed them without provocation. Washington insisted that the French had run for their guns when they sighted his men, and only then did he order his men to fire. Either way the skirmish only lasted a few minutes. Twenty-one Frenchmen surrendered amidst the bloody bodies of their dead and wounded.[8]

The French commander, Joseph Coulon Sieur de Jumonville, was among the wounded who gave themselves up. Suddenly, Half-King sprang forward, tomahawked Jumonville to death and scalped him. The Indians then killed and scalped the rest of the French wounded.[9]

George Washington must have been dazed, it happened so fast. If he was aware of the gravity of what had happened, he never acknowledged it. In fact, his first combat seemed to exhilarate him. "I heard the bullets whistle," he wrote, "and believe me, there is something charming in the sound."[10]

The French prisoners told Washington that Jumonville was a diplomat carrying a letter to the English, warning them off the French domain. This was the version of the event that reached Quebec and Paris. It infuriated the French, who viewed Jumonville's death as an assassination.[11] Washington never accepted that idea. He regarded Jumonville's men as a group of spies. "In strict justice," he said, "they ought to be hanged as spies of the worst sort." If the slaughter of the wounded troubled him, he did not dwell on it. The next day he wrote a letter to Governor Dinwiddie in which his main message was that he was not being paid as much as a regular British officer of the same rank; only after finishing that complaint did he tell the Governor about the attack.[12]

That his rank and pay scale should loom so large in the young officer's mind at that moment seems strange, given the nature of the firefight and its aftermath. By year's end he would resign his commission because the British failed to promote him to full colonel.[13] He plainly did not comprehend the gravity of his actions that fateful day in the wilderness. Historian Francis Parkman saw the matter in a more serious light: "Judge it as we may," he wrote, "this obscure skirmish began the war that set the world on fire."[14]

The Seven Years' War, also known as the French and Indian War or "the Old French War" in the colonies, took place in myriad locations, on land and sea, around the world. John Stark fought his war in the valleys of the upper Hudson River, Lake George and Lake Champlain. From 1755 to 1759, the combatants sought each other throughout this wild expanse, and they found each other often. Virtually every encounter took place within the sound of a musket shot from one of the three bodies of water.

In 1749, Swedish naturalist Peter Kalm recorded his journey up the Hudson and then north the length of Lake Champlain to Canada, and back again over Lake George. His journal described the stage for the battlefields of the wilderness war that threatened.

Kalm's travels came about at the behest of the Swedish Academy, which had instructed him to "obtain plants and seeds from the northern latitudes, whose climate was comparable to that of Sweden." He landed at Philadelphia in the fall of 1748, where he met and befriended Benjamin Franklin. Then he moved north to New York where he spent the winter. The following spring he sailed up the broad Hudson where he watched porpoises and sturgeons.[15]

He formed a low opinion of Albany. The merchants, he said, "traded with the very Indians who murdered the inhabitants of New England … by purchasing articles such as silver spoons, bowls, cups, Etc. of which the Indians robbed the houses in New England."[16]

Kalm and his associates rowed and paddled up the Hudson past the burned ruins of Saratoga (now Schuylerville), which had been destroyed by the Canadian partisan Joseph Marin in the last war. Rather than travel on to Lake George (then known as Lac du St. Sacrement), the naturalists entered the south end of Lake Champlain at South Bay. Kalm called this part of the lake a "river." Passage was blocked by downed trees deliberately felled across the narrow channel to block French and Indian invaders. Kalm reported:

> The country which we passed was the poorest and most disagreeable imaginable. We saw nothing but a row of amazingly high mountains covered with woods, steep and rough on their sides so that we found it difficult to get to an open place in order to land and boil our dinner. In many places the ground, which was very smooth, was under water …; for this reason the Dutch in Albany call these parts the "Drowned Lands."[17]

They rowed north on the serpentine lake past a wide place at Benson Bay to a promontory on the west where they spent the night. That high, rocky peninsula lay between a river and the lake. The La Chute River was the outlet stream from Lake George that emptied into Lake Champlain. The place was uninhabited in 1749, but soon the French would construct a fort there, which they would call Carillon and which was known to the Americans as Ticonderoga. Kalm noted a profusion of snakes; rattlesnakes infested the hills around the two lakes.[18]

The next morning they floated north along the west shore of Lake Champlain to the stone Fort St. Frédéric at Crown Point. In Kalm's mind he had been travelling on a river up to this point, and the French fort was situated at the southern end of Lake Champlain. "The breadth of the river is here about a good musket shot," he wrote. Chimney Point protruded into the east side of the lake only a couple of hundred yards away. Kalm penned a complete description of the scene:

> The fort is built on a rock, consisting of black lime or slate, as mentioned before. It is nearly square, has high, thick walls made of the same limestone, of which there is a quarry about half a mile from the fort. On the eastern part of the fort is a high tower, which is proof against bombshells, provided with very thick and substantial walls, and well stored with cannon from the bottom almost to the very top; and the governor lives in the tower. On one side of the fort is a pretty little church, and on the other side, houses of stone for the officers and soldiers.[19]

One visitor counted eighteen houses, some on either side of the lake, and Kalm noted a windmill nearby. Retired French soldiers farmed in the neighborhood. Beyond the little settlement lay virgin forest.[20]

On July 5, 1749, Kalm witnessed the aftermath of an Indian raid. Several days before, Indians had attacked and killed a New Hampshire farmer and kidnapped his son. Now they paddled past the French fort on Lake Champlain, displaying the dead man's scalp hanging from a pole in the bow of a canoe. "Their faces were painted with vermillion," Kalm wrote, and "most of them had great rings in their ears." The commander at the fort issued provisions to the Indians for their trip back to Canada, because "he did not wish to exasperate them."[21]

North of Crown Point the lake widened into a kind of inland sea almost six miles across. It was studded with islands, most of them forested. On the western shore the high mountains came right down to the water. On the east a rolling plain bordered the lake, and farther east rose the high rampart of the Green Mountains.

They reached Split Rock, about twenty miles north of Crown Point on the western shore. Farther north, near what is now Rouse's Point, New York, they saw a stone windmill on a point across the water. From there it was only about eight miles to the fort at St. Jean in Canada.[22]

Kalm spent several months in Canada. On his return journey south on Lake Champlain, he observed Indians at close range and noted that they wore tattoos on their bodies. He didn't reach Lake George until late October, and he passed up the lake from north to south (the water flow proceeds from south to north, and the outlet stream is on the north end of the lake). Kalm's descriptions of this phase of his journey are reversed here to accord with the direction of travel of John Stark's and Robert Rogers's expeditions a few years later.[23]

On the south shore, where Fort William Henry would later stand, Kalm found a sandy, sloping shore, ideal for launching boats and canoes. The lake was wide with low mountains on either side. To the north he could see the "First Narrows," clogged with tiny islands sprouting pine and spruce trees. He found few deciduous trees, "small, miserable specimens, surrounded and crowded by the firs." He heard wolves howling nearby.[24]

The mountains on the east side became higher north of the First Narrows. They dropped to the water's edge, creating steep shores where it was difficult to find a landing place for canoes and bateaux. The mountains channeled and accelerated the wind. In a squall, Kalm found that the lake was "almost like a boiling kettle." On the west a steep mountain particularly impressed him. "It was awe-inspiring when we rowed at the foot of the mountain and looked up, for it seemed as if the mountain hung right over our heads as we proceeded."[25]

Peter Kalm never mentioned a large promontory north of the mountain— Sabbath Day Point. But he did observe an Indian camp nearby:

> The canoe lay upside down on the shore, as was the custom, and a short distance above in the woods, the Indian had made his hut. … He had placed pieces of birch bark on top of slender rods as a roof over himself where he lay and had hung an old [blanket] … to protect himself on the side from the winds and the storms. … The native men had pulled out the hair from the front part of their heads as far up as the part above their ears, so that the whole of this part of the head was bare.[26]

High hills flanked the lake north of Sabbath Day Point, "quite steep and covered with forests." They rowed past a mountain with a lofty cliff face that seemed to fall right into the lake; this was later named Rogers Rock. Kalm found the lake water so pure that he could see the bottom even at a great depth.[27]

Large flocks of ducks and cranes rose from the water at the lake's northern outlet. On the La Chute River, midway between the two lakes, the travelers found a waterfall where the French would later build a sawmill. Downstream from the waterfall, the narrow river was navigable in small boats all the way to Lake Champlain. A high, forested mountain with bare ledges and cliffs bordered the river on the south; it would become known as Mount Defiance. Across the lake from the river's mouth lay a long, low hill, the future Mount Independence.[28]

The Swedish naturalist's American guides regaled him at night around the campfire with tales of Indian atrocities. He had already witnessed red men with a scalp they had taken, and these stories frightened him. "The long autumn nights are rather terrifying in these vast wildernesses," he wrote. "May God be with us."[29]

Peter Kalm survived his tour of the northern wilderness, despite his fears; the scenes he described became one of the stages of America's first great war.

In 1755 the combined British and American forces planned a four-pronged campaign against the French. General Braddock led an expedition against Fort Duquesne (Pittsburgh). Governor Shirley of Massachusetts, a newly minted major general, proposed an attack at Fort Niagara. General Monckton sailed against Fort Beausejour in Nova Scotia. William Johnson, the wealthy Irish-American baron of the Mohawk Valley, had orders to take the fort at Crown Point. The company led by Robert Rogers and John Stark was slated for the Crown Point attack.[30]

New Hampshire mustered a regiment composed of three companies for Johnson's expedition, all under the command of Colonel Joseph Blanchard. Their troops were mostly farmers who had signed up for one season's campaign. They carried their own muskets, which were weapons used for hunting, not for war. Some of them slung hatchets from their belts for close combat.

Most of them had never soldiered before. Young boys marched side-by-side with older, more experienced men. One lad proudly wrote his family: "I am agoing to war." Clergymen accompanied the regiment and conducted daily prayer services, with frequent lengthy sermons. There was a religious element to this war—they were about to fight heathen and "papists."[31]

To make a show of force for any lurking Indians, New Hampshire authorities decided to march Blanchard's regiment to the Connecticut River following the trail blazed by John Stark and others in 1753. From there they were to strike off across the Green Mountains, aiming to join Johnson's forces near Crown Point. The plan overlooked the reality that there was no road, not even a blazed trail, across the Green Mountains.[32]

Someone wisely countermanded the marching order, but not before Rogers and Stark and their men had reached the Connecticut River. The company then marched south down the east bank of the river to the stockade fort at Number Four, crossed the river to Fort Dummer and, by August 25, started west for Albany. It was already late in the year for beginning a military campaign along the northern frontier, but the inexperienced soldiers were full of enthusiasm.[33]

⚔ ⚔

News of Major General Braddock's defeat and death on July 9 must have reached Johnson's army by the time it mustered at Albany. Braddock had marched west across the mountains of Virginia into Pennsylvania, hauling heavy wagons filled with provisions. The British general ignored advice about fighting in the wilderness and scorned his Indian allies, causing one chief to say, "He looked upon us as dogs, and would never hear anything that we said to him."[34]

On July 9, Braddock moved his forces down a narrow road in thick forest near the Monongahela River when the French and Indians attacked from cover. Redcoats were massed in the open, and they died by the scores. Braddock had four horses shot from under him before a ball struck him. George Washington did what he could to restore order to the panicked soldiers as they retreated. Braddock died of his wounds four days later, and his men buried him in the rutted wagon road so the Indians would not find and desecrate his body.[35]

The defeat happened despite American officers warning Braddock that massed formations would be vulnerable in forest warfare. The event caused a stir in the colonies. Benjamin Franklin wrote, "This whole transaction gave us Americans the first suspicion that our exalted idea of the prowess of British regulars had not been well-founded." Franklin stated the germ of an idea that would grow as the war proceeded. Few colonials ever questioned the courage of British regulars. But it would grow painfully obvious that some British generals failed to learn the lessons of Braddock's defeat.[36]

Johnson gathered his army along the banks of the Hudson River north of Albany at a place known as the "Flats." He began the march north on August 8, before the New Hampshire troops arrived. Blanchard's half-starved regiment had marched many more miles than necessary and had eaten all their provisions. When they arrived at the Hudson River, special arrangements had to be made to feed them.[37]

The first mission for Rogers and his men was to escort a train of wagons north along the river to the "Great Carrying Place"—the northern terminus of navigation on the river, from where all travel northward was by road. The Hudson made a great bend to the west nearby, and then large waterfalls choked off all boat travel. It was sixteen miles overland from the carrying place to the south end of Lac du St. Sacrement, where Johnson planned to stage his attack on Crown Point.[38]

At the carrying place, Colonel Blanchard's troops engaged in their first combat—a brawl with New York soldiers. It was not an auspicious beginning for the New Hampshire men. They arrived late, required charity to feed them, and then fought with their hosts.[39]

4

Battle of Lake George
The Bullets Flew Like Hailstones

Johnson renamed beautiful Lac du St. Sacrement "Lake George" for his king, and he set about building a fortified camp at its southern end. He faced hard decisions. He had orders to push north through the forests to attack Crown Point, but his army was all that stood between the French and Albany. A new stronghold, Fort Edward, was under construction at the carrying place, but it was incomplete. If Johnson moved his forces farther away from the Hudson River, enemy forces might simply slip around behind him and threaten populated areas. Johnson also feared that September was too late to begin a campaign this far north. He elected to stay at Lake George.[1]

Meanwhile, a new French commander arrived at Crown Point, the Baron de Dieskau. He was a more aggressive leader than Johnson. Dieskau explained his plan:

> At length on the 27th of August, a Canadian named Boileau, returned from a scout and informed me that about 3,000 English were encamped at Lidius' House [Fort Edward], and they were constructing a fort that was pretty well advanced. I immediately resolved to go forward and to put myself in an advantageous place either to wait for the enemy should he advance, or to anticipate him myself, by going in quest of him.[2]

Dieskau knew that part of Johnson's army was at Lake George; he meant to flank them in order to attack Fort Edward. He would use Canadians and Indians, leaving most of his French regulars to defend Crown Point. The raiding party, about 1,500 men, paddled canoes south on Lake Champlain toward South Bay. They reached Fort Edward on September 7.[3]

Dieskau's Indians had never laid siege to a fortress before, and they refused to attack the palisade at Fort Edward. However, they told Dieskau that they would attack Johnson's encampment at Lake George. The Baron changed course and marched north toward the less fortified camp.

At the same time a detachment of Johnson's army proceeded south from Lake George, straight toward the advancing enemy, who laid an ambush. The Americans moved along a narrow trail, in column, and without any scouts in front or on the flanks. Volleys of musket fire from attackers in the woods cut down the Americans. Survivors ran pell-mell back to Lake George, pursued by the Indians. It seemed a repeat of Braddock's disaster.[4]

The provincials at Johnson's camp crouched behind flimsy barricades. When Dieskau's men came in range, the Americans picked them off. Dieskau himself was wounded and captured, and his Canadians and Indians withdrew.

A provincial surgeon, Thomas Williams, described the day in a letter to his wife: "The wounded were brought in very fast, & it was with the utmost difficulty that their wounds could be dressed fast enough, even in the most superficial manner, having in about three hours near forty men to be dressed. … The bullets flew like hailstones about our ears all the time of the dressing."[5]

Some of Dieskau's force blundered into a surprise reinforcement by New Hampshire militia commanded by Captain McGinnis; his counterattack "made great slaughter amongst them."[6] After the shooting stopped, dead soldiers from both sides were dumped in a nearby pool, known thereafter as "Bloody Pond." The initial ambush earned the bitter sobriquet "the Bloody Morning Scout." William Johnson took a stray shot in the buttocks; he and Dieskau were both out of action.[7]

Stark and Rogers missed this first action of the war in New York because they were on a scouting mission along the Hudson that day. Dieskau's decision to change the objective from Fort Edward to Lake George may have saved Rogers's company. Had they been near Fort Edward, an attack there might have wiped them out.[8]

Dieskau blamed his situation on his Indian allies. "I owe this misfortune to the treachery of the Iroquois," he wrote. He believed that, prior to the ambush, they had warned Mohawk scouts working for Johnson. The baron's low opinion of the Indians worsened; while he lay wounded in the American camp, "one of them entered my tent, sword in hand, on the morning following, to dispatch me; but an English officer threw himself before me." The Indian was one of Johnson's Mohawks.[9]

Perplexed by the rage of the Mohawks toward himself, Dieskau asked Johnson what they wanted. The American commander replied: "To burn you, by God, eat you, and smoke you in their pipes, in revenge for three or four of their chiefs that were killed. But never fear; you shall be safe with me, or else they shall kill us both."[10]

Afterward, Baron Dieskau had only praise for his treatment by Johnson and the Americans. The war would not always be so civilized.[11]

The surprise attack taught Johnson that he could not function without accurate intelligence. He could no longer rely on the Mohawks, who left for home within days after the battle. Colonel Blanchard suggested that some of his New Hampshire troops could fill the vacuum left by the Mohawks. Rogers and Stark accepted a new mission. Rogers wrote, "The 24th of September I received orders from the General to proceed with four men to Crown Point, and, if practicable to bring a prisoner from there." From that day forward, his company ceased to be just another militia unit; thereafter, they were rangers.[12]

Robert Rogers published his *Journals* in 1765, after the end of the French and Indian War. He apparently reworked his book from a diary or journal he kept during the war itself. Some excerpts from the original journal appeared in colonial newspapers within a matter of days of the events described. The newspaper accounts often named members of his company and narrated their exploits. Years later, when the book appeared, it omitted much of this detail, focusing instead on Robert's own story. It is thus often difficult to ascertain whether John Stark or other individual rangers took part in the early "scouts" or missions in the fall of 1755.[13] Given his wilderness skills and his courage, plus the fact that Rogers was a friend from his youth, it is probably safe to assume that Stark took part in at least some of these scouts, but there is no way of knowing for certain.

On September 24, 1755, Rogers and four men rowed north on Lake George. They landed somewhere on the west shore. Two men stayed with the boat while Rogers and the two others moved off through the woods. Five days later they emerged within sight of the fort at Crown Point. They spent two nights watching the fort and the village, counting soldiers and gathering the information they could, then they made their way south long the west shore of Lake Champlain. At the peninsula the French called Carillon, they saw smoke and heard shooting. The French had arrived at Ticonderoga. When Rogers returned to the boat, he found the men, the boat and all the food gone. It took two long and hungry days before he and his scouts reached Johnson's camp.[14]

Once Johnson learned of the activity at Ticonderoga, he ordered an immediate reconnaissance of the area. Rogers and five men travelled north again to the "point at Ticonderoga." They saw two hundred French soldiers there, sawing wood, hewing timbers and laying out the foundation of a fort overlooking Lake Champlain. Returning to Lake George, the scouts discovered "a bark canoe, with nine Indians and a Frenchman in it, going up the lake." They fired at the canoe, killing six men, but they had to flee when two other canoes appeared.[15]

Rogers and his men went out on several more missions in the fall of 1755. If possible, they were to bring back prisoners who, fearing for their lives, usually talked freely. The Indians called prisoners "live letters"; the Indians were more likely than the Europeans to kill and scalp their prisoners, so surviving as a "live letter" depended on the captor.

The ranger missions became larger. Rogers went out with thirty or forty men on occasion. Increasingly, they dared to confront the enemy. On October 26 they approached the fort at Crown Point. Toward dark they crept closer until they were only a few hundred yards away, where they remained all night. Rogers reported in his *Journals*:

My men lay concealed in a thicket of willows, while I crept something nearer, to a large pine-log, where I concealed myself, by holding branches in my hands. Soon after sun-rise the soldiers issued out in such numbers, that my men and I could not possibly join each other without a discovery. About 10 o'clock a single man marched out directly towards our ambush. When I perceived him within ten yards of me, I sprung over the log, and met him, and offered him quarters, which he refused, and made a pass at me with a dirk, which I avoided, and presented my fusee to his breast; but notwithstanding he still pushed on with resolution, and obliged me to dispatch him. This gave an alarm to the enemy and made it necessary for us to hasten to the mountain.[16]

The account in the *Journals* differed somewhat from the report Rogers wrote for General Johnson, in which he claimed to have scalped the man in full view of the fort. The contemporary report also acknowledged that another man had been with him behind the pine log. Both narratives reflected the boldness Rogers brought to the missions.[17]

On December 21 he and his men spent a bitterly cold night in a French hut at Ticonderoga under the very noses of five hundred French troops. They acted with an aggressive spirit that Johnson found in no other unit.[18]

General Johnson ordered other militia companies to scout the enemy. The reports of the officers of these units reflected the terror most soldiers felt in this dangerous wilderness. In early October a Captain Syms sent a message to General Johnson from a bivouac on Lake George:

Sir, We are now incamped about three miles from you. Immediately on our coming here we sent out two scouts, both came in and did not discover anything towards Evening I posted Century [sentry] out one of wh was shot and scalpd & a hatchet was left in his head, Shall be glad to receive your further orders   some of my men seem frightened and fear that some will run off to night as they seem much frightened. P.S. I believe some fresh hands will be necessary.[19]

A day or so later, Lieutenant Jelles Fonda came across Captain Syms and his men. He ordered them to proceed with their mission. Almost all of them refused to go. Fonda then told them, "all of you that are Cowards Come and Ile take yr names Down and they came so thick that I could see but 10 or 12 Left of the whole party."[20]

A Captain Doolittle echoed Syms's anxiety. On October 24 he noted, "God knows weather ever we get home if we do I would Humbly Present these few lives to Gen'l Johnson." Doolittle had just viewed the growing French force at Ticonderoga.[21]

Captain Angell took a company by boat to the north end of Lake George on November 3, but he judged it "not safe to land there that night as it was so near the Enemy's Camp Knowing Capt. Rogers had been there a Day or two before and that likely he Might have alarmed them." Captain Angell considered his options and decided it was "Better to Return unsuccessful than to run so big a risk of being Discovered."[22]

James Connor's unit discovered an enemy camp on the lakeshore in early November. They kept a tight watch through the long night. In the morning the "whooping of Indians" alarmed them and they retreated to Johnson's camp.[23]

Lieutenant Waterbury could not even induce a third of his twenty-man scout to begin a mission; he set out short-handed. By the time his two boats reached the islands at the First Narrows, Waterbury discovered that one boat crew had conveniently forgotten their provisions. He sent that boat and its crew back to camp, and he and the remaining seven men stayed the night on an island, terrified that the enemy knew they were there. The next morning Waterbury seems to have allowed his men to vote on what they would do next: "… and it was the General Note of the popel [people] to Retorn By Being discovered and for Want of provisions for We had Not any at all So we returned with sped [speed]."[24]

The accomplishments of Robert Rogers and his company contrasted sharply with these stories. His reports of the growth of French strength, particularly at Ticonderoga, disheartened Johnson. Johnson believed that the French were too strong for him to attack, and instead he used his time and manpower to build a fort at the south end of Lake George—Fort William Henry.

Johnson sent an aide, Peter Wraxall, to Manhattan to report on the French troop strength. British officers refused to believe the reports brought back by Rogers, and they ordered Wraxall to tell Johnson to send out more reliable scouts. Wraxall told them he did not believe "there was another Man in the Army [who] would go." The British hooted at him. "Try if there is not," they told him.[25]

General Johnson did try, again and again. Only Rogers and his men would go.

※ ※

The term of enlistment for Blanchard's New Hampshire regiment ended in October. Johnson's army was going nowhere. So, one by one, units began the long march home. Rogers, Syms and a skeleton force remained at Fort William Henry for the winter. Lieutenant John Stark joined the column on the walk back to New Hampshire.[26]

In later years the only documentation of Stark's participation in the 1755 campaign was a certificate he signed seeking a pension for a disabled fellow veteran.

> This may certify whom it may concern that Peter Bowers of Salisbury was in the Provincial service in the year 1755 under the command of Major Rogers, who was then a Captain, and that the gun of Charles McAuley was discharged accidentally being loaded with a ball which entered the head of said Peter near his right eye and blew same out, I being personally present and see same. Dec. 24th, 1770 John Stark, Lieut. To said Company.[27]

※ ※

Back home in the Merrimack Valley, the war seemed remote from people's lives. John Stark's friend, Matthew Patten, made no mention in his diary of the return of the New Hampshire regiment. He did note that Archibald Stark kept the sawmill running in John's absence; on October 3 he wrote that he "spent the afternoon in going to Stark's mill."[28]

Patten was a carpenter, farmer, logger, surveyor and justice of the peace. He also kept his diary (with some omissions) every day from July 1754 until his death in 1795. He recorded his accounts and his daily work, along with observations on the weather, religion, friends, enemies and how much rum he drank.

In October, while Stark was marching home, Patten leveled the sills of the new meetinghouse and then worked two days raising the structure itself. On October 16 his entry read, "my wife was Delivered about 8 in the morning of a Son and sold a Cow to Willm Macneal of New Boston."[29]

John Stark had probably reached home by November 17 when, in Matthew Patten's words, "about Four of the Clock in the Morning There was an exceeding great Earth Quake … seven Different shocks they were all in about an houre or less the first was exceeding hard and of some minits." An aftershock struck five days later. This was the great "Cape Ann" earthquake of 1755.[30]

Patten never mentioned John Stark, the war, or any of the local soldiers through the winter and spring of 1756. If the war caused him any hardship or prompted any sacrifice, he bore it in silence. Yet his neighborhood, the Merrimack Valley, always readily provided new recruits for the conflict.

Robert Rogers spent his first winter as a ranger at Fort William Henry. With a thick layer of ice on the lake and a deep blanket of snow in the woods, he and his men had to change tactics. By turns they travelled on ice skates and on snowshoes. They could not move without leaving obvious tracks. Their dark figures, outlined against the snow, stood out at great distances to Indian observers.

In January, Rogers succeeded in capturing French soldiers and some provisions. He and his men "proceeded down the lake, on the ice upon skaits."[31] They crossed Lake Champlain and laid an ambush on the east shore. Two teamsters driving sledges loaded with beef fell into their trap. Rogers brought his prisoners back to Lake George. Captain Jeduthan Baldwin was at Fort

William Henry when the rangers arrived. He noted in his journal, "… in the morn about ½ after 6 o'clock We was all allarmed by Capt. Rogerses fiering as he came in on the Lake from ye Lake Champlain Where he took 2 Prisoners & Brought them in with him."[32]

Baldwin was a military engineer. He kept a diary that gave a daily account of Fort William Henry through the winter of 1755–56. He commanded the construction that was being done at the new fort, but other needs soon pulled him from his task. On December 4, Baldwin and his men commenced killing all the livestock at the fort because there was no forage to feed the animals. They butchered the carcasses and salted down the meat in barrels. On December 6 the diarist noted that Ensign Stone died and was immediately buried. Smallpox struck and made the rounds at the fort.[33]

On December 13, Baldwin wrote: "I was took Sick. In the afternoon I had 2 Blisters Drawd & Polticed, in the Evning Exceeding Bad." He grew worse and suffered "Extream Pain" in his head. He was ill twenty-eight days, "almost to the Gates of the Grave," he said.[34]

Baldwin was bedridden until January 12 when he wrote, "blessed be God for his Great Goodness … I have bin [able] this Day to Walk out of Doers [doors]." Several more soldiers died in January, but military discipline prevailed. The troops watched as one of their own, "John Doughty tried & rcd 10 Lashes." On February 19, Baldwin noted that he dined with Captain Rogers.[35]

※※　※※

Later in February, Jeduthan Baldwin accompanied Robert Rogers and his men on a scout to Lake Champlain. The British thought an engineer should examine the works at the two French forts. Rogers's account of this mission amounted to one paragraph. Baldwin, probably unused to such an adventure, created a full narrative of their journey. Captain Israel Putnam, later to be a general, accompanied them.[36]

On March 1, Baldwin wrote, "We sent back 5 of our men Not well. … Saw a wolf chase a deer into the Water." That night they made a comfortable camp, probably with a fire for warmth (Baldwin made note of fireless nights), and "loged not in a fither-bed but on hemlock boughs."[37]

It snowed on March 3 and March 5. Their patrol came near Crown Point and they no longer dared to build campfires, so they made cold camps, "without fier." Thin ice on Lake Champlain prevented them from crossing to the east side. While scouting the route, Rogers fell from a rock ledge twenty-six feet into the lake. "With much difficulty he gott out."[38]

They scoured the countryside trying to capture a prisoner. On March 8 they set fire to several homes and barns, and then were shocked to discover that one of their own men, an Indian, had been asleep in one of the barns. He was burned so badly that they had to carry him.[39]

Rogers and Putnam and a few others stayed with the burned man while Baldwin led the rest back to Fort William Henry. They planned to send boats back to Rogers so he could transport the invalid to the fort. Baldwin's men learned that the enemy lurked in the woods around them; they found messages on the trees. "[T]hey wrote on the trees that if they could catch us they would Burn us."[40]

Baldwin and the main body of men arrived at the fort on March 11, "… the men very Weak and faint having Nothing to Eat for some time." Rogers and Putnam returned on March 14. Neither Rogers nor Baldwin said anything further about the fate of the burned man. After two weeks in the cold wilderness without proper food or rest, at sunset the very next day Rogers set out for a meeting with Governor Shirley in Boston.[41]

In early spring, troops hauled provisions from Albany and Fort Edward, preparing for the campaign of 1756. In April the garrison at Fort William Henry expected to be attacked any day. Baldwin's men "filled Sand bags, layd 2 platforms & made all the preparation for an attack that is possible. The Enemy apear very Bold and Dareing."[42]

The enlistments of the winter soldiers at Fort William Henry ended on May 1, just as Rogers and his men returned from a mission to Crown Point. Baldwin's journal for the winter ended on May 4 with this entry: "James Fowles died in the morning 4 o'clock."[43] It had been a grim winter.

At some time during the war, Jeduthan Baldwin received a bad leg wound. The surgeons advised amputation. They prepared to tie him down and proceed with the operation despite his protests when Baldwin seized a bayonet and threatened them, "saying if he went we would go together." He kept his leg and lived.[44]

5

ROGERS RANGERS

An Independent Company of Rangers

The British made changes to their army in America before the campaign of 1756 began. With the death of General Braddock, overall command fell to Governor Shirley of Massachusetts. As one of his first acts, he had summoned Robert Rogers to Boston.[1]

It took a week for Rogers to reach Shirley, but he found the governor receptive. "On the 23rd, I waited on the General, and met with a very friendly reception; he soon intimated his design of giving me the command of an independent company of rangers, and the very next morning I received the commission, with a set of instructions."[2]

Shirley's orders gave Rogers the freedom to make war on civilians as well as on soldiers: "… from time to time, to use my best endeavours to distress the French and their allies, by sacking, burning and destroying their houses, barns, barracks, canoes, battoes, etc. and by killing their cattle of every kind; and at all times to endeavour to way-lay, attack and destroy their convoys of provisions by land and water, in any part of the country where I could find them." Shirley's orders sounded like they had been written by a lawyer, but they made clear that he understood one thing—the French in the Champlain Valley operated far from their base; the way to defeat them was to deny them food and fodder.[3]

Shirley displayed originality in creating an independent company of rangers by a stroke of his pen; the company could be disbanded just as easily. They would not be part of any colonial or British regiment, but they would be subject to regular army orders and discipline. Their independence and their pay scale provoked resentment from other units.[4]

His commission authorized Rogers to enlist 60 privates at 3 shillings per day, three sergeants at 4 shillings, an ensign at 5 shillings and a lieutenant at 7 shillings. Rogers's pay was fixed at 10 shillings per day. Shirley specified that Rogers was to "inlist none but such as were used to Travelling and hunting, and in whose courage and fidelity, I could confide."[5]

To find such men, Rogers returned to his home ground in New Hampshire, where his brother Richard signed on as his first lieutenant. Although Shirley's order authorized only one lieutenant, Rogers prevailed upon John Stark to serve as second lieutenant, third in command of the company. It took almost a month to fill the rolls; then Rogers marched his men to the fort called Number Four, along the Connecticut River—"then a frontier town greatly exposed to the enemy."[6]

Richard Rogers took some of the men to Albany, intending to march north from there to Fort Edward. Pursuant to orders, Robert Rogers and Stark headed west, through the "deserts and mountains," directly to Crown Point.[7] For the second time in two years, the high command had ordered a military force to traverse territory no such force had ever crossed before. It was an era of travel by water. No roads existed across the Hampshire Grants, and none would exist until John Stark built one in 1759. This time, however, Rogers succeeded in getting his force across the Green Mountains to Lake Champlain.

John Stark did not finish the journey with Rogers. Two days out from Number Four, he became so ill he required evacuation back to the fort. Rogers sent six men with him. Stark evidently made a rapid recovery, for a week later he reached Fort Edward. Along the way he had a close call. He eluded a large party of Indians near the Hudson River, three or four hundred strong according to Rogers.[8]

That could have ended his military career in brutal fashion. Three weeks earlier a small American scouting party camped on an island on Lake George about twelve miles north of Fort William Henry. At four o'clock in the morning of April 12, sentries at the fort heard musket shots down the lake. Ten soldiers set out to investigate the shooting. They returned that afternoon with the bodies of three soldiers which, in the words of Jeduthan Baldwin, were "all Stript Shot Scalpt and cut in the most awful manner. … We suppose that the other three are Either killed or taken as they are not found."[9] Both sides now used terror as a tactic.

※ ※

By early in 1756, after only a few months as leader of the rangers, Robert Rogers had gained a considerable reputation. Reports published in newspapers in New York and Boston referred to him as "the famous Rogers" or "the famous scouter" or "the brave Captain Rogers." In February, officers in Albany raised funds to buy him "a handsome Suit of Cloathes," and the New York General Assembly "voted 125 Spanish Dollars to be sent to Capt. Rogers, for the Service done to his Country."[10]

Regular reports passed through Albany to various journals with details on the numbers of French soldiers killed or captured and the number of scalps taken. The papers rarely identified the authors of the letters; either some loyal "Boswell," or Rogers himself, kept the columns filled with his exploits.

※ ※

Rogers reached Lake Champlain a few miles south of Chimney Point on May 5. Unable to snare a French prisoner, they "… Killed twenty-three head of cattle, the tongues of which were a great refreshment to us on our journey." The rangers made their way south, crossed the lake on a raft, and met Stark at Fort Edward on May 11.[11]

During the next six weeks the rangers made two sorties for intelligence and prisoners. They estimated that a thousand soldiers manned the new fort at Ticonderoga that the French called "Carillon." Soon, Rogers raised that estimate to three thousand soldiers. This news shocked the high command. General Shirley, in one of his last acts as commander in chief, ordered the rangers "to Lake Champlain, to cut off, if possible, the provisions and flying parties of the enemy." His order led to a remarkable mission for the entire ranger force.[12]

Shirley sent six "light whale boats" up the Hudson from Albany to Fort Edward, where they were landed, carried across the portage to Lake George and made ready for action. The boats were long and slim, "light but sturdy, with a bold sheer, sharp and raking at both ends," according to Rogers.[13]

Fifty men in five whaleboats pushed off from the beach at Fort William Henry on June 28. Each boat had been armed with a swivel gun mounted in the bow. In addition to its complement of rangers, each boat carried provisions for a long expedition. Although the boats were built of cedar and thus very lightweight, the food and armaments added several hundred pounds to each craft.[14]

The company rowed north on Lake George and camped on an island that Rogers did not identify. The next day they proceeded north about five miles and beached the boats on the eastern shore. Then the rangers began an epic portage that Rogers recounted in one sentence: "… we landed our boats and carried them about six miles over a mountain to South Bay, where we arrived the 3d of July." In the full heat of summer, the fifty men hauled five whaleboats laden with food, firearms and gunpowder over the high mountain ridge east of Lake George. Five days of labor, averaging about a mile a day, brought the rangers to the south end of Lake Champlain. They had chopped down trees to make a passage. The rangers accomplished this feat despite the danger that their slow progress and noisy presence might make them obvious and vulnerable to the large French force nearby.[15]

After dark the whaleboats moved north on the lake, passing Ticonderoga with muffled oars, "so near the enemy as to hear the centry's watch-word." Rogers calculated that only four hundred yards separated the peninsula of Ticonderoga and the hilly promontory on the eastern shore.[16]

They hauled the boats ashore before daybreak and spent the day hidden in thick undergrowth. The sky the following night was too bright, and they laid up another day. They counted almost a hundred enemy boats passing their hiding spot, seven of which landed nearby while French soldiers disembarked for a meal break.[17]

After dark on July 6, the rangers rowed past the high fortress at Crown Point within easy range of French guns on both sides of the narrow passage. Once north of the fort, the whaleboats moved freely for two nights on the wider lake until they reached the vicinity of Jones Point, about twenty-five miles north of Crown Point where Lake Champlain is nearly five miles wide. Ranger scouts brought word that a French schooner lay at anchor nearby. Rogers prepared to board her.[18]

His plans changed quickly when two enemy lighters, or barges, turned toward the rangers' hiding place. "[T]hese we fired upon, and then hailed them, if they would come ashore; but they hastily pushed towards the opposite shore, where we pursued and intercepted them."[19]

The rangers killed three men, wounded two others, and captured the rest of the crews. Rogers reported that one of the prisoners was wounded so badly that he "could not March therefore put an end to him to Prevent Discovery." But the French on the nearby schooner probably already knew of their presence.[20]

The rangers sank the lighters with their cargoes, salvaging a few kegs of brandy, which they buried for future consumption. They hauled the whaleboats into the woods and covered them with saplings and leaves. Then the whole company slipped into the forest and began the long walk back to Lake George. They reached the lake four days later, far north of Fort William Henry. Most of the men were too weak to finish the journey. Richard Rogers walked to the fort to obtain boats to carry the rangers home. Their prisoners survived to warn the Americans and British of a "great" enhancement of the French forces.[21]

⊱ ⊰

The whaleboat foray mystified the French. They could not figure out how their enemies could have launched a "navy" on Lake Champlain. Their Abenaki allies discovered the whaleboats in October and reported their find to French officers.[22]

The Marquis de Montcalm, who had recently arrived at Quebec as the new commander in chief of French forces, had sent his brilliant aide, Louis Antoine de Bougainville, to the Champlain Valley. Bougainville struggled to solve the mystery of the whaleboats. In his journal he devoted almost two full pages to theories on the question. "It is still to be learned," he wrote, "by what route these barges got to Lake Champlain." A mathematician by education, Bougainville proposed five possible solutions to the problem, but he rejected the correct answer: "It does not appear probable that they portaged these barges ... from Lake George."[23]

That the small ranger fleet was able to strike the French troubled Bougainville and his fellow officers. He sent out two reconnaissance missions to learn how the Americans had managed the feat, but they could not answer the question. The whaleboat adventure accomplished little of substance, but it earned the rangers respect from their enemies.[24]

Like the French, the British also changed commanders in 1756. Lord Loudon replaced Shirley with Major General James Abercromby. Shirley had planned an aggressive war, with attacks at both Ticonderoga and Crown Point. Abercromby changed everything. There would be no strikes against French forts in 1756.[25]

When Loudon replaced Shirley, Robert Rogers sensed a threat to his new independent status. "I therefore, upon my return [from the whaleboat expedition], wrote his Excellency, desiring to lay before him the minutes of my last scout, and to recommend to his consideration an augmentation of the rangers." In addition to his capabilities as an Indian fighter, Rogers also possessed considerable political skills. In July, Abercromby summoned him to Albany. Rogers narrated the scene: "The General permitted me to wait upon him at Albany. In this interview we discoursed on the subject of my letter, in consequence of which he immediately ordered a new company of rangers to be raised."[26]

Richard Rogers was to command the new company, Noah Johnson to be first lieutenant, Nathaniel Abbott second lieutenant and Caleb Page ensign. Robert Rogers would continue to command his company with John Stark as first lieutenant, John McCurdy second lieutenant and Jonathan Burbank ensign.[27]

Of these eight ranger officers, six would call Starkstown, New Hampshire, their home at some time in their lives—Robert Rogers, Richard Rogers, John McCurdy, Caleb Page, Jonathan Burbank and John Stark. Thus, each man knew his fellow officers, knew their character and courage. It was an arrangement that inspired confidence and loyalty. The brotherhood from Amoskeag formed the nucleus of the rangers.[28]

Twice in 1756, British and American commanders strengthened Rogers's hand, augmented his forces and raised their pay. The mere fact that this backwoods fighter sought and obtained personal meetings with the top commanders demonstrated that his prestige had increased since the days of guarding wagon trains in 1755. Shirley and Abercromby knew of the contrast between the boldness of Rogers and the timidity of other field commanders, and they knew that the army needed him.

Where Robert Rogers succeeded with his British superiors, George Washington failed. Washington went to Boston in February of 1756 to persuade General Shirley to accept his Virginia militia unit as a regular British regiment. The British army insisted that junior regular officers outranked senior provincial officers. A British major, under this system, was superior to Colonel Washington.[29]

Shirley seemed sympathetic. He wrote an order giving Washington seniority in one specific instance. However, unknown to the Virginian, Shirley also posted an order elevating an inferior ranking officer over Washington, who learned of it only after his return to Williamsburg. He immediately informed Governor Dinwiddie that he would resign his commission. Once his anger subsided, however, Washington remained a colonel in the provincial service.[30]

The British command structure came directly from King George, whose royal order of May 12, 1754, decreed: "… all general and field officers with provincial commissions were to take rank only as eldest captains when serving in conjunction with regular troops." Major General John Winslow, the new colonial commander at Lake George, pointed out that the order meant that any British major might command the entire provincial army.[31]

The egos of American officers were further wounded by a 1754 ruling of the British Solicitor-General; he ordered that all provisional troops would serve under British military law and discipline. Americans with any military experience knew that meant floggings and hangings; British officers ruled their lower-class conscripts with an iron hand.[32]

Shirley and Winslow feared that no American army would serve under those conditions. Men from Massachusetts and Connecticut enlisted "for the campaign"; their obligation ended at the close of the annual campaign season.

In theory their enlistments also ended if the stated goal of the campaign were changed. They viewed their enlistments as "contractual" arrangements. To avoid problems Shirley planned to send the regulars west to Lake Ontario, and hold the Americans for service at Lake George and Lake Champlain. He intended to separate the Americans from their British cousins.[33]

When Lord Loudon learned of the conflict, he summoned General Winslow to Albany and asked him point-blank if provincial officers would serve with regulars. Winslow's answer appalled Loudon; provincial soldiers viewed their service in a different light than the British soldier, Winslow told him. Loudon knew he could not defend the northern frontier without the Americans. At his insistence, provincial officers signed a pledge of loyalty, in return for which he accepted an understanding that colonial officers would lead colonial troops.[34]

General Shirley recruited a company of fifty "Stockbridge Indians" to serve with the rangers. These men were Mohicans who had settled near the Housatonic River at Stockbridge, Massachusetts, site of the Stockbridge Mission. Founded in 1734, the mission's goal was to convert and "civilize" the Indians. John Sargeant, a Yale graduate, served as the first pastor in the remote valley, where he built a church and a school. With the enthusiastic cooperation of their chief, Konkopot, the Indians rapidly adapted to Sargeant's teaching. The community thrived for a time. In theory, the native people owned the land at Stockbridge.[35]

Eventually, white settlers appeared in the neighborhood. By 1750 they had divested the Stockbridge tribe of more than sixteen thousand acres of land. When the war began, trust between the races evaporated. In the spring of 1753, white men beat a Schaghticoke Indian to death. The killers got off with punishment for manslaughter instead of murder, on the subterfuge that it was difficult to distinguish a "good Indian" from an ally of the French.[36]

Hysteria over imagined Indian attacks infected the Housatonic Valley. Perhaps to prove their loyalty, many Stockbridge Indians volunteered to serve with the colonial army. When they arrived at Fort Edward in August of 1756, John Stark gave orders for their first action, according to Robert Rogers: "… thirty privates and a Lieutenant, would scout and scour the woods under my direction, which party had arrived while I was out upon my last scout, and Lieutenant Stark strengthened their party with some of our people, and sent them out with particular directions what route to take, the day before I arrived."[37]

The Indians returned from their first mission "with two French scalps, agreeable to their barbarous custom," according to Rogers, a scalper himself. News of the Indians' success so enthused Loudon that he ordered the rangers, with the Stockbridge Indians, "to penetrate into Canada, and distress the inhabitants, by burning their harvests (now nearly ripe) and destroying their cattle."[38]

Early on August 16, rangers rowed two whaleboats north on Lake George, one commanded by Rogers, the other commanded by Stark. They beached the boats and marched overland to the point on Lake Champlain where they had hidden the whaleboats in July. Rogers reported that they sailed north toward Canada, but whether they got there remains unclear. They found no Frenchmen to attack. An enemy schooner sailed past them, moving too fast to be caught and boarded. They returned to the eastern shore of the lake near Chimney Point, where they captured a French farmer and his teenage daughter, the only fruits of this long mission. The Stockbridge Indians performed well, however, and under their own commander, Captain Jacob, they served on many later missions.[39]

A relative handful of Indians allied themselves with the British and American side. The French, however, attracted warriors from many tribes. Some came to the Lake Champlain region from as far away as the western Great Lakes. They had heard that scalps, plunder, captives and martial glory awaited with the French and Canadian forces.[40]

Montcalm attacked Fort Oswego on Lake Ontario in August. His force of three thousand men far outnumbered the fort's defenders. When a French cannonball beheaded the fort's commander, his successor quickly asked for terms of surrender. The French set the terms. Montcalm promised that he would protect his prisoners from the Indians, but he could not keep his promise. The Indians murdered and scalped the invalids in the fort hospital, plundered their possessions and made off with captives. French officers took hours to restore order. Montcalm paid ransom to rescue some of the prisoners, setting a precedent that made it likely there would be further such rampages.[41]

Lord Loudon knew that the chances of a similar attack at Fort William Henry or Fort Edward had increased with the loss of Oswego. A concentrated French movement might even threaten Albany. He abandoned any plans to take Crown Point.[42]

* * *

The English desperately needed accurate intelligence, and the rangers provided the only dependable information. Other units continued to fail. They would not brave the dangers or the hardships. Colonel Jonathan Bagley at Fort William Henry reported, "I have sent out skulking parties some distance from the sentries in the night, to lie still in the bushes to intercept them [Indians]; but the flies are so plenty, our people can't bear them."[43]

British officers entertained the idea of creating their own ranger force. They asked Rogers and his officers to train regulars in frontier warfare. By September, redcoat officers and enlisted volunteers accompanied the rangers on occasional scouting expeditions. One such combined unit discovered that the French were building a sawmill on the La Chute River at the falls west of Carillon.[44] On September 19, Rogers reported that "Captain Abercrombie, Aid-de-camp and nephew to General Abercrombie, did me the honor to accompany me."[45]

But Loudon placed little faith in the American rangers. He wanted to develop his own regular force, "fit for that service." He wrote to the Duke of Cumberland, "I am convinced that till we have everything necessary for carrying on the War here, within ourselves, Independent of Aid from this Country, we shall go on very slowly." But, for the time being, he recognized that his troops could not manage without the Americans. He lamented, "some Rangers I shall be obliged to keep all Winter."[46]

That fall the rangers began to build a permanent camp for themselves. They constructed huts and a log hospital on a large, flat island in the Hudson River across a narrow channel from Fort Edward. Eventually it would be known as Rogers Island.[47]

The opposing armies retired to winter quarters by December 1756, but they did not leave the theater of operations. According to Robert Rogers:

> Both armies now being retired to winter-quarters nothing material happened to the end of this year. The rangers were stationed at the Forts William-Henry and Edward, to which also two new companies of rangers were sent this fall, commanded by Captain Spikeman and Captain Hobbs, in one of which my brother James Rogers was appointed Ensign.
>
> These two companies were stationed at Fort William-Henry, mine and my brother Richard's at Fort Edward.[48]

Three Rogers brothers and three Stark brothers now served with the rangers. All were officers, making a strong corps of leaders from Starkstown and Derryfield.

6

FIRST BATTLE ON SNOWSHOES
To Play at Bowls

Back home in New Hampshire, with many of the young men gone, families carried on as best they could. John Stark's oldest sister, Anna, married William Gamble, a forty-seven-year-old widower with three daughters.[1] On November 16, 1756, Matthew Patten, over in Bedford, reported: "… about 3 or 4 of Clock in the morning there was a shock of an Earth Quake so hard that it wakened my wife and I out of sleep."[2]

Robert Rogers and John Stark were at Rogers Island when the New Year came in. A barracks had been constructed for the rangers, but they preferred smaller huts to communal living. They constructed an isolated "hospital" at the south end of the island for smallpox victims. An infamous whipping post stood on the parade ground. Soldiers reached Fort Edward by a pontoon bridge part of the year, and across the ice or by wading the rest of the time. The camp was known in 1757 simply as "the Island."[3]

On January 15, 1757, the commanding officer at Fort Edward ordered the rangers to march to Fort William Henry and prepare for a mission to Lake Champlain. Rogers took fifty privates picked from the two ranger companies, led by Lieutenant John Stark and Ensign Caleb Page. The rangers spent two days at the south end of Lake George packing food and powder, making snowshoes, and choosing more men from the rangers stationed there.[4]

They marched out on the lake ice on January 17, 1757, and camped the first night in the forest east of the First Narrows. Rogers sent back several men who were unwell, and proceeded north with "seventy four men, officers included." They moved on snowshoes.[5]

Four days later, with their weapons rain-soaked, they emerged from the woods on the west shore of Lake Champlain, "about mid-way between Crown Point and Ticonderoga, and immediately discovered a sled going from the latter to the former."[6] In the initial published report, Rogers wrote, "on which I dispatched Lieut. Stark with a Party of 20 Men towards Crown Point to head the Slay."[7] Rogers did not wait, nor did he reconnoiter further to determine if more enemies were nearby.

Rogers himself led a party south toward Ticonderoga, leaving a third unit under Captain Spikeman where they had first spied the sled. Rogers planned for Stark to cut off the French teamsters on the ice so that Spikeman's men could attack but, Rogers reported, "I soon discovered about 10 slays more coming down the Lake, and immediately sent two Men to tell Lieut. Stark not to discover himself, and let the first Slay pass." Stark led his men out on the ice before the messengers could reach him, however. French soldiers on the advancing sleighs spotted the rangers, and their teamsters turned about and fled back to Ticonderoga.[8]

The commandant at the fort, M. de Lusignan, had dispatched the teams to Crown Point to haul brandy and forage back to Ticonderoga. Eight horses drew each sleigh, which were heavy and cumbersome when loaded. When the sleds were empty, as they were that morning, they were relatively light and fast. A guard detachment, led by a sergeant, hurried their charges back to the fort.[9]

The rangers chased and caught some of the Frenchmen, but most of the teamsters made it back to the fort, where they roused the garrison. The prisoners informed Rogers that six hundred regulars, two hundred Canadians, and forty-five Indians manned the fort. Rogers knew his force was in trouble. The larger enemy force might cut off his retreat back to Lake George; the French knew his location, and the rain had rendered ranger muskets useless. Rogers decided to return to their campsite of the previous night, hoping to rekindle the fires and dry their weapons. To get there, they followed their old trail through knee-deep snow.[10]

They reached the old camp and managed to dry their weapons, "and then marched keeping a good rear Guard:—Myself and Lieut. Kennedy took the front: Capt. Spikeman the Center; and Lieut. Stark brought up the Rear."[11] Very soon, when they had walked barely half a mile from their camp, the

French attacked them. The enemy soldiers were arrayed in a semicircle at the brow of a hill, waiting for the rangers.

When the teamsters had raced into the fort at Ticonderoga and reported the attack, de Lusignan sent out a force of about a hundred soldiers with some Ottawa Indians to pursue the rangers. Montcalm's aide, Bougainville (who learned of the events afterward), gave the French version of what happened: "The detachment went to lay out an ambush on the road of the English whose advance guard appeared three hours after midday."[12] His use of the expression, "on the road of the English," suggested a well-used route or trail—one the French were quite sure the rangers would follow.

A ranger veteran of the event remembered how the encounter came about:

> In regard to the battle of January 21, 1757, the late venerable Mr. Shute [John Shute] of Concord, N.H. remarked that Rogers did not act with his usual prudence. He states that after taking the sleds, a council of war advised to return by a different rout, from a that by which the party came, which was the usual practice of the Rangers, and on this occasion would have enabled them to escape the hazards of battle. Rogers, however, said in regard to the enemy, that they would not DARE to pursue him, and took the same rout back. The first notice the Rangers had of the enemy was the noise of cocking their guns … .[13]

The official French report of the action continued the story: "About three o'clock in the afternoon this party [the French] halted and waited for the English, within three leagues of Fort Carillon, and seeing them come singing, allowed them to approach within musket-shot, then saluted them with one-half of our musketry, the other having missed because of the rain."[14]

The French fired the first volley at point-blank range, killing several rangers outright. Robert Rogers was wounded in this salvo, but he was still on his feet and in command. He wrote, "… then I ordered the whole to Retreat to the opposite side, where Lieut. Stark and Ensign Brewer, with about 40 Men had made a Stand." The rangers regrouped on a wooded hillside on the opposite side of the valley. The French and Indians pursued them, wounding Captain

Spikeman and taking several prisoners but, Rogers reported, they "were beaten back again from the Bush Fire of Lieut. Stark's party that covered and secured our retreat." Ensign Caleb Page was killed in this part of the battle.[15]

The French sent out flankers, "which Lieut. Stark discovered and called out to acquaint me of." Rogers deployed Sergeant Phillips with several men to head off the flankers. The rangers had been badly mauled by the initial attack, they were outnumbered, far from their base, and it was nearing dark. But they held a strong position on the hillside, with large trees for cover. At about sunset a French musket ball struck Robert Rogers "a slanting Wound in my hand, through my wrist, which disabled me from loading my Gun."[16]

Ranger John Shute remembered being wounded in the first volley, "by a shot which ploughed the top of my head." Shute lay unconscious for a time, but he recovered; "… on coming to himself, the first sight which met his eye, was one of the Rangers cutting off Roger's cue [queue] to stop the hole in his wrist through which a shot had passed."[17]

As darkness fell in the snowy, dripping woods, Rogers wrote, the French began to call out to the rangers:

> … desiring us to accept Quarters, promising that we should be used with humanity, and treated kindly, and at the same time called me by Name, and threatened me that if we did not embrace their Offer, as soon as the Party joined them from the Fort, which they expected every moment, they would cut us to Pieces; but we absolutely refused to receive their proffered Mercy; and I told them, that we had men sufficient to repel any Force that could come against us; and that we should have it in our Power to cut them to Pieces and scalp them.[18]

When darkness fell, the shooting stopped. Rogers conferred with the remaining ranger officers, "who unanimously were of opinion, that it was most prudent to carry off the wounded of our party, and take Advantage of the Night to return homeward, lest the Enemy should send out a fresh Party against us in the Morning."[19]

The rangers filed off silently through the dark woods. They kept on the move all night and arrived at the frozen shore of Lake George the next morning. Many men could not walk without help. They were all exhausted. John Stark and Thomas Burnside volunteered to hurry down the lake ice to seek help.

⨯ ⨯

The rangers didn't carry off all the wounded. In the darkness and confusion they left some injured men behind. Captain Spikeman and Private Thomas Brown of the rangers, and Robert Baker, a British volunteer, were all badly wounded. After Rogers and the main force left, they huddled around a small fire in the enemy-infested woods. Brown lived to tell the story; "… the Major [Rogers] took the advantage of the Night and escaped with the well Men, without informing the wounded of his Design, lest they should inform the Enemy and they should pursue him before he got out of their Reach."[20]

After talking it over, the three wounded men decided to surrender. Suddenly, Brown spied an Indian creeping toward them. Brown crawled away from the fire and hid. The Indian reached Spikeman first and "stripp'd and scalp'd him alive." The Indian then seized Baker and hauled him away. Brown went back to try to help the captain, who begged to be put to death. Brown refused to kill him. He listened to Spikeman gasp his last words: "He desir'd me to let his Wife know (if I lived to get home) the dreadful Death he died."[21]

Brown kept moving through the night despite the bitter cold and the pain of his wounds (he had been shot in the knee and the shoulder). The next morning a band of Indians caught him and, to his astonishment, they "took me buy the Neck and Kiss'd me." They dressed his wounds with dry leaves. Then they took him to the French, who made him identify some of the dead rangers, including Ensign Caleb Page. Brown saw Captain Spikeman's head fixed on a pole. But the British soldier, Mr. Baker, still lived, and he and Brown supported each other on the walk to the fort at Ticonderoga.[22]

⨯ ⨯

John Stark never told the story of his long rescue mission on the ice of Lake George. The lake was thirty-two miles long, and his relief effort the night of the 21st began several miles from the lake itself. He made it to Fort William Henry quickly enough that Hobbs's company of rangers sallied forth with a sled and met Roger's main party at the First Narrows on the morning of January 23. The remnants of the whole battle-scarred company reached the fort on the evening of that day.[23]

Rogers figured that he had lost fourteen men killed, six wounded and six missing. He later learned that the six missing men had been taken prisoner.[24] The French reported losing eleven men.[25]

One of the wounded rangers, Sergeant Joshua Martin, suffered a shattered hip and a ball through the stomach. The rangers thought Martin was dead and left him behind. They watched behind them as they moved along the lake, and one of them "descried a small dark object on the ice." Sergeant Martin had followed their tracks. He survived to fight again.[26]

The firefight, known afterwards as the "first battle on snowshoes," represented a stunning defeat for the rangers. Although they gathered intelligence about the enemy, the cost was high—the loss of over a third of their force with three officers dead. Even so, the toll could have been much worse; wet gunpowder caused many French muskets to misfire, and deep snow robbed the French of mobility. Bougainville reported, "Our soldiers, who had no snowshoes fought at a disadvantage, floundering in the snow up to their knees."[27]

Rogers had decided to return by the same route his force had followed earlier, a violation of his usual procedure, and clearly the French had expected him to do just that. His decision that January day to return by the same route led to disaster. Nevertheless, it was probably the prudent choice.[28]

Had the rangers been unable to dry their weapons, they would have been massacred in any encounter with a French force. Their trail would have been obvious in the deep snow, and they would have been breaking trail for their enemies. The French guessed correctly that Rogers would travel a certain route, but ranger discipline and dry gunpowder made the battle competitive.

The real cause of the defeat was Rogers's earlier decision to attack the sleighs on Lake Champlain without first assessing the enemy's strength. Once he saw the additional sleds approaching on the ice, it was too late to stop the unfolding events. On January 21, 1757, Robert Rogers had less than two years experience commanding a military unit. He had demonstrated that he was outstandingly bold and aggressive, but he had insufficient experience to develop judgment. It remained to be seen if he could learn.

Once back at Fort William Henry, Rogers wrote to General Abercromby's aide, Captain James Abercrombie, recommending replacements for the slain ranger officers. He favored promoting John Stark to captain to lead Spikeman's company. The badly wounded Joshua Martin earned a promotion to ensign.[29] On February 6, Captain Abercrombie wrote back, congratulating the rangers for their conduct and expressing his thoughts on war itself:

> I am heartily sorry for Spikeman and Kennedy, who I imagined would have turned out well, as likewise for the men you have lost; but it is impossible to play at bowls without meeting the rubs. We must try to revenge the loss of them. There is few people that would believe it; but, upon honour, I could be glad to have been with you, that I might have learned the manner of fighting in this country. The chance of being shot is all stuff, and King William's opinion and principle is much the best for a soldier, viz: "that every bullet has its billet" and that it is allotted how every man shall die; so that I am certain that everyone will agree, that it is better to die with the reputation of a brave man fighting for his country in a good cause, than either shamefully running away to reserve one's life or lingering out an old age, and dying in one's bed, without having done his country or his King any service.[30]

Given subsequent events, John Stark probably read this letter, or knew of its contents. The captain's letter portended future events. His enthusiasm for

"King and Country," his bravado, his belief in the expendability of soldiers' lives, all revealed a prevalent British idea of leadership for which John Stark had only contempt. In 1758 such leadership would bring tragic results.

Rogers's report of this battle revealed for the first time John Stark's leadership ability. The French attack might have destroyed the entire ranger force had Stark not made his stand on the hillside, covered the withdrawal and thwarted the enemy flankers. Years later, one old ranger remembered Lieutenant Stark's contribution. Stilson Eastman, of Concord, told this story:

> … on receipt of his second wound, Rogers thought of ordering a retreat, as the only safety of the party. Lieut. Stark who was almost the only officer fit for duty, declared that he would shoot the first man who fled, said he had a good position, and would fight the enemy until dark and then retreat; and that in such a course consisted their only safety. While he was speaking a ball broke the lock of his gun; at the same time, observing a Frenchman fall, he sprang forward, seized his gun, returned to his place and continued the action.[31]

7

Fort William Henry

Each Man for Himself

Robert Rogers's wrist wound became worse at Fort William Henry, and he had to be evacuated to Albany for medical attention.[1] Meanwhile, General Abercromby wrote to Rogers to convey Loudon's order that the terms of service of the rangers be altered. The size of ranger companies would be expanded to one hundred men, but they would serve for the duration of the war (as opposed to one season's campaign, which had been the standard term of colonial enlistment). They would also serve at reduced pay. Loudon's order was an open insult to the rangers. Many in the British high command regarded the rangers as undisciplined and unreliable.[2]

Abercromby instructed Rogers that, if any men resisted the pay reduction, "you are at liberty to discharge them, in case they refuse to serve at said establishment." The general closed his letter with the admonition, "You are to inlist no vagrants, but such as you and your officers are acquainted with."[3]

The British adamantly refused to pay Rogers's men for their service in 1755. Under the custom of the day, a commander assumed personal responsibility for paying his troops. Some of his old soldiers sued Rogers and obtained money judgments against him amounting to several hundred pounds. "But for all of which," Rogers wrote, "I have not at any time received one shilling consideration." Still, the British refused to underwrite his debt.[4]

Loudon hoped to eliminate the concept of "contractual" service on the part of all provincial troops; he planned to use them alongside regular British soldiers and make them subject to regular army discipline. He planned to form his own British-led and British-manned ranger units, but first he had to find regulars who could fight like rangers. Lord Loudon suffered the presence of Rogers's force until his redcoats were ready for the mission.[5]

The strain in the relationship between the British regulars and their colonial allies grew throughout 1757. There seemed to be no officer willing to work out the problems, and the English officers took an increasingly hard line. Rangers resented the change.

Smallpox appeared again as spring approached. Robert Rogers remembered, "On March 5, I was taken ill with the small-pox and was not able to leave my room till the 15th of April following, during which time my officers were recruiting."[6] Rogers was still in the hospital at Albany. A skeletal force manned Fort William Henry—346 men, of whom 128 were invalids. John Stark commanded the ranger company at the fort.[7]

On the night of March 18, sentries heard the sound of axes chopping from across frozen Lake George. Then came the sound of many footsteps on the ice. Sixteen hundred French Canadians and Indians approached the fort carrying three hundred scaling ladders. The attackers first sought to parley, but British Commandant Eyre declined. The defenders opened fire.[8]

The French attempted to burn the outbuildings and the boats locked in lake ice along the shore. A heavy snowstorm halted hostilities for a time. When the weather cleared, British and American soldiers watched the attackers set fire to a sloop, and then both sides waited to see if the flames would spread to the fort.[9] When the French tried to burn the rangers' huts outside the fort's walls, Stark and seventeen men sortied out to drive them off. In the firefight a spent musket ball struck Stark but caused no serious wound.[10]

Though many boats were lost in the raid, the invaders failed to take the fort—but they came close. The French battle report explained the failure: "The fort remains isolated; 'twas saved from the flames only because no wind was blowing during the conflagration."[11]

Finally the attackers gave up and began the long trek back to Ticonderoga through deep snow. They had lost eleven men, while the English suffered only seven men wounded.[12]

Loudon, with the encouragement of William Pitt back in England, concocted a plan for a daring attack on Canada. Loudon wanted to strike the fortress at Quebec on the St. Lawrence River. Instead, Pitt wanted him to take Louisbourg at the northeastern tip of Cape Breton Island first, and then lay siege to Quebec. Pitt's plan would require a well-timed convergence of forces from the colonies with an armada from England. If Montcalm took the bait and moved his army to defend Quebec, the plan had merit. If, instead, Montcalm attacked the undefended northern frontier of the colonies, Pitt's plan might lead to disaster.[13]

Loudon ordered the provincial troops and most of the rangers to move to Manhattan to await embarkation. The ranger companies of Robert Rogers, Stark and Buckley started south in early May. Richard Rogers's company manned Fort William Henry, together with provincial troops and an inexperienced unit from New Jersey.[14]

The American force for the Louisbourg expedition waited for weeks at the ports until Loudon received news on June 20 that the fleet from England had sailed. Only then did the American contingent set sail.[15]

The delay was long enough to prevent John Stark from going on the expedition. He came down with smallpox and had to be hospitalized. Several rangers died of the disease that year, but Stark seemed to make a rapid recovery. Then, strangely, a junior officer arrested John Stark and had him jailed. Lieutenant Jonathan Brewer may have been concerned that his superior had not completely recovered, and confined him to protect soldiers who had not yet been infected. Whatever the reason, John Stark was furious that he missed the voyage to Nova Scotia. Brewer was subsequently court-martialed and convicted for "confining his Captain illegally." Loudon approved the sentence, that Brewer be cashiered from the service, but then pardoned the lieutenant. Brewer continued to serve with the rangers. It was an awkward event that seemed to result in no lasting harm, and now John Stark knew that he need not fear smallpox ever again.[16]

Two days after the expedition sailed for Louisbourg, Richard Rogers died of smallpox and was buried outside the walls at Fort William Henry. Two regiments of regulars and one provincial unit were divided between the two northern forts, William Henry and Edward. Overall command fell to a timid officer, General Daniel Webb, at Fort Edward. Lieutenant Colonel George Monro commanded at Fort William Henry.[17]

The French knew that Loudon's Louisbourg foray weakened the British-American defenses at the two forts. The knowledge spurred them to recruit heavily among their Indian allies.[18] Among the tribes, the conquest of Fort Oswego and the resulting opportunity for scalps, booty and ransom made another campaign against the English attractive. They rallied to Montcalm in large numbers, almost 2,000 strong, some of them making the journey almost halfway across the continent to gather at Crown Point and Ticonderoga. In addition to the ever-present Abenaki, warriors from the Iowa, Chippewa, Pottowattomie, Micmac, Delaware, Nipissing, Algonquin, Iroquois, Huron, Ottawa, Menominee, Miami, Winnebago and Sauk tribes gathered by Lake Champlain, eager for war and its spoils.[19]

Montcalm planned to take Fort William Henry using siege tactics. He intended to ship cannons by bateaux over Lake George to a point just north of the fort on the west shore, entrench there, and then batter and starve the defenders until they gave up.

In the face of this threat, Webb and Monro commanded troops with relatively little experience of war. With only a small contingent of rangers, they could gain no intelligence about French activity north of them. On July 23, Monro sent five companies of "Jersey Blues," an unblooded provincial unit, to reconnoiter the north end of Lake George. Bougainville, Montcalm's aide, related what became of the Jersey Blues near Sabbath Day Point:

At daybreak three of the [English] barges fell into our ambush without out a shot fired. Three others that followed at a little distance met the same fate. The [remaining] sixteen advanced in order. The Indians who were on shore fired at them and made them fall back. When they saw them do this they jumped into their canoes, pursued the enemy, hit them, and sank or captured all but two which escaped. They brought back nearly two hundred prisoners. The rest were drowned. The Indians jumped into the water and speared them like fish. … The rum which was in the barges and which the Indians immediately drank caused them to commit great cruelties. They put in the pot and ate three prisoners."[20]

The surviving Jersey Blues, less than a third of the original force, made it back to the fort and told the tale.[21] Hunter John Goffe recognized the danger. All their boats were lost. The British and Americans at the two forts were, effectively, blind. Webb and Monro had no idea of the size of Montcalm's army nor its location.[22] In the midst of this fog of ignorance, the Canadian partisan Joseph Marin struck at Fort Edward. He killed and scalped thirty-two men and took one prisoner. Marin's raid thoroughly unnerved General Webb.[23]

Montcalm's Indian allies wanted action. Waiting for the French commander to muster his complex force with all its weaponry and provisions seemed strange to them. They made a camp at the north end of Lake George and managed to set fire to it, earning the place the name "Burned Camp." Another band of warriors stayed near Sabbath Day Point, where they amused themselves on the rocky hillsides by killing rattlesnakes.[24]

Finally, on August 1, Montcalm's army, more than 7,000 men, set out on Lake George. An armada of canoes, bateaux, and cannon-bearing platforms cruised south to their staging point, where the soldiers encamped. They could look to the southeast and see Fort William Henry near the south shoreline of the lake. It was a log and gravel structure, with corner bastions overlooking the lake and a swamp on the north and east sides. Deep ditches flanked the south and west ramparts, and cannons faced out from the fort's walls.[25]

Lieutenant Colonel Monro commanded 2,200 men at the fort. Fourteen miles south at Fort Edward, General Webb led a complement of 1,600, which he promised he would lead to Lake George if the French attacked there. Once Monro saw the size of the French force before him, he wrote to Webb requesting reinforcements. Webb did not respond.[26]

Montcalm sent a messenger under a white flag to the fort with a letter demanding that the British surrender. Monro immediately declined. The cannonade began, and the barrage continued for several days. An anonymous British artillery officer kept a journal during the battle. He wrote that on August 5 in the afternoon, the French artillerists "got their distance very well, several of their Small Shells falling into the Parade. One of their Shott carried away the Pully of our flag Much rejoiced the Enemy; but it was soon hoisted tho' one of the men that was doing this had his head Shot off with a Ball, and another wounded."[27]

The entire garrison believed that General Webb would send reinforcements from Fort Edward. They remained in "high spirits," expecting to see Webb's regulars appear at any time. Every event was a hopeful sign. "A party of Indians were seen advancing with great Speed towards the road that leads to Fort Edward which Confirmed us in our Belief of Relief," one soldier wrote.[28]

Daniel Webb could hear the cannons from his quarters at Fort Edward. Unknown to the men at Lake George, Webb had sent a messenger to Monro carrying a letter that informed the unfortunate lieutenant colonel that the general "does not think it prudent to attempt a junction or to assist you till reinforced by the militia of the colonies." There was no such militia available that could relieve the two forts in time to save them.[29]

Indians waylaid and killed the messenger, however. They took Webb's letter to Montcalm. He now knew that no reinforcements would interfere with his attack. He sent a special courier to Monro. Bougainville, blindfolded, carried Webb's letter to the fort and presented it to Monro, who thanked him "for the courtesy of our nation, and protested his joy at having to do with so generous an enemy. This was his answer to the Marquis de Montcalm." Monro must have been astonished, not only at Webb's refusal to come to the fort's aid, but at his stupidity in putting the refusal in writing. Still, Monro soldiered on.[30]

Bougainville returned to the French lines, and the cannons commenced firing again. The artillery duel took an increasing toll on the defenders. More than half the fort's cannons overheated and burst, driving hot iron into human flesh. Meanwhile, French guns pounded the log walls and bastions to splinters. The morale of the exhausted defenders sank. The fort hospital was full of soldiers suffering from wounds and smallpox.[31] Monro tried to put some spirit in his troops by threatening to hang over the walls any cowards or shirkers. But his officers knew the battle was lost. One man wrote, "We now began to believe we were much slighted having received no reinforcements from Fort Edward as was long expected."[32]

Early in the morning of August 9, Monro held a council of war. His officers handed him a letter advising surrender signed by all of them, regulars and provincials, including John Goffe. Monro concurred and sent a flag of truce to the French camp.[33]

At Fort Oswego the defenders had demonstrated little resistance before giving up, and Montcalm, following the military usage of the era, had demanded unconditional surrender. At Fort William Henry, Monro and his soldiers held out for seven days under brutal attack and only agreed to capitulate when they knew the situation had become hopeless. In Montcalm's mind they were thus entitled to honorable terms, and he agreed that they could leave the field with the honors of war. The British and Americans would march to Fort Edward under the protection of French troops. In return the vanquished soldiers would agree not to take up arms again for eighteen months, and all French prisoners in British hands would be freed. The arms and provisions in the fort would become French property. It was an understanding between gentlemen in the European manner.[34]

Down at Fort Edward, General Webb must have noticed the silence of the guns, and he must have known what it meant.

Montcalm consulted with the Indians before he accepted Monro's surrender, and he believed the warriors had consented to the generous terms he proposed. Accordingly, the surrender proceeded. The troops who could walk marched out of the fort and gathered in the adjacent entrenched camp. The sick and wounded remained in the fort, defenseless.[35]

Indians immediately scrambled into the fort bent on plunder. When they found helpless men in their bunks, one witness remembered, "the Indian Doctors began with their Tomahawks to cure the sick and wounded."[36] They killed and scalped all who came into their grasp. A French priest, Father Raubaud, wrote later: "I was witness to this spectacle. … I saw one of these barbarians come out of the casements with a human head in his hand, from which the blood ran in streams, and which he paraded as if he had got the finest prize in the world."[37] Montcalm personally tried to stop the slaughter, but only time and exhaustion halted the killing. By evening the fort was quiet.

The next morning the defeated troops and their camp followers lined up to march through the forest to Fort Edward. The New Hampshire soldiers were in the rear. As the ragged group began to walk, small bands of Indians ran into their lines, grabbing clothes, hats and equipment. Then a brave tomahawked a man and scalped another. The pace of attacks quickened. Warriors dragged women and blacks into the woods. Ultimately the sporadic violence erupted into total mayhem. Colonel Samuel Angell of the Rhode Island troops reported: "All this did not satisfy them; but they fell to stripping and scalping without distinction; which put our men to flight, each man for himself."[38]

The New Hampshire men fared badly. Some of them escaped into the forest. John Dinsmore, one of Goffe's soldiers, ran out of his shirt when it was snatched by an Indian. He prowled the woods for two days, hiding from every noise and shadow, until he reached Fort Edward.[39] John Stark's neighbor, the sutler Samuel Blodgett, hid under an overturned bateau on the lakeshore. The Indians found him, but then let him go.[40] Ezekiel Stevens of Derryfield fell into the Indians' hands. They scalped him and left him for dead, but French soldiers rescued him and took him to Fort Edward.[41]

French officers counted forty or fifty bodies once the rampage ended, not counting the invalids murdered the day before. They tried to ransom men, with some success, but the Indians left with about two hundred prisoners the next day, defying all efforts to free them.[42]

Montcalm ordered the fort to be demolished and burned. While the flames crackled, the Indians dug up and scalped the corpses in the fort burying ground, including the body of Richard Rogers. Now the dead took belated revenge; the scalps and the clothing that the warriors carried back to the Great Lakes triggered an outbreak of smallpox that decimated the tribes.[43]

General Webb feared that the French would march south to attack Fort Edward. But the victors were running short of food and fodder. Their Indian allies, with plunder, scalps and prisoners, abandoned them. Montcalm ordered his army to withdraw toward Ticonderoga, leaving the smoking ruins of Fort William Henry behind.[44]

Scores of terrified British and American soldiers struggled through the forest, trying to find Fort Edward. Cannons were fired periodically along the Hudson to guide the lost men, who straggled in for days afterward.[45]

≈∂к ж∮ъ

After the slaughter at Fort Oswego in 1756, the Marquis de Montcalm clearly knew what might happen after he and his Indian allies took Fort William Henry, and he failed his obligation to prevent the atrocity. He wrote a letter from "Camp on the Ruins of Fort William Henry" on August 15, 1757. His words disguised any mortification he may have felt at the violation of the terms of surrender:

> I cannot conceal from you that the capitulation has unfortunately suffered some infraction on the part of the Indians. But what would be an infraction in Europe, cannot be so regarded in America, and I have written with firmness to General Webb and to General Loudon, on the subject, so as to deprive them of all excuse for not observing the terms on a slight pretense.[46]

Thus, Montcalm expressed his belief that the standards of warfare differed from one continent to another—that acts that would be regarded as barbaric in France were permissible in America. Such an idea could be infectious. That French officers tried to rescue English prisoners, often at risk to their own lives, mattered little to those who remembered the "massacre at Fort William Henry." What Americans remembered was best expressed by the anonymous journalist at the fort—the French watched the massacre, he reported, "but their only business was to receive the plunder by the savages."[47]

British and American soldiers nursed a hatred for the Indians and a desire for revenge. The tragedy at Fort William Henry infected the Americans with doubt about the competence of their British leaders but, ironically, fear of the enemies provoked a surge of enlistments in the provincial forces.[48]

Loudon's expedition to Louisbourg came to nothing. It was July 10 before the ships from England met the American troops and rangers at Halifax harbor. Feeding an army of 12,000 in enemy country required the transport of great quantities of provisions. Soldiers went to work growing vegetables to feed themselves. Officers found a new use for the rangers—making hay to feed the horses. Each passing day made the supply problem worse.[49]

Rumor that a powerful French fleet had sailed for Louisbourg brought Loudon's expedition to an end. The British navy carried the army back to New York. The rangers arrived at Fort Edward to learn of the disaster at Lake George and the death of many comrades. Word of Webb's refusal to reinforce Monro passed through the ranks, but still Daniel Webb remained in command of the northern army.[50]

Soldiers in all eras have discussed among themselves the attributes and failings of their commanders. After the futile invasion of Nova Scotia and the debacle at Lake George, the provincials and the rangers had much to talk about. Braddock's defeat and Webb's timidity concerned them, but Loudon's decision to strip the northern defenses represented incompetence on a grand scale. Benjamin Franklin commented on Loudon's failure:

> On the whole, I wonder'd much how such a man came to be intrusted with so important a business as the conduct of a great army; but, having since seen more of the great world, and the means of obtaining, and motives for giving places, my wonder is diminished. General Shirley, on whom the command of the army devolved upon the death of Braddock, would in my opinion, if continued in place, have made a much better campaign than that of Loudon in 1757, which was frivolous, expensive and disgraceful to our nation beyond conception; … Loudon, instead of defending the colonies with his great army, left them totally expos'd while he paraded idly at Halifax, by which means Fort George [William Henry] was lost.[51]

While Franklin was among the first to recognize the failures of the British generals, he clung to the concept of "our nation." The British and the Americans, he believed, were one people, Englishmen, united by language, culture and law. The English constitution applied to all. But, he recognized the source of the leadership problem—"the means of obtaining and the motives for giving places." Promoting political generals, Franklin believed, led to failure.

8

THE MISBEHAVIOR SCOUT
A Set of Scoundrels

Robert Rogers noted that, in the autumn of 1757, one British officer arrived on the northern frontier who won the admiration and respect of the Americans. "In one of these parties [ranger missions], my Lord Howe did us the honour to accompany us, being fond, as he expressed himself, to learn our method of marching, ambushing, retreating, etc., and, upon our return, expressed his good opinion of us very generously."[1]

Howe, whose formal address was George Augustus, Lord Viscount Howe, was a thirty-three-year-old British colonel, brevetted to brigadier general. He would later be assigned to Major General James Abercromby, who was to be the new commander in chief for North America. Howe came with the highest praise from his fellow officers.[2]

Lord Howe made it his first priority to learn how the rangers fought. He hoped to create a body of British light infantry capable of holding their own beside the rangers. He ordered regular soldiers to lighten their loads, cut their hair and shorten their coats, and encouraged them to learn to soldier without needing to be constantly resupplied. A regular officer boasted, "No women follow our camp to wash out linen. Lord Howe has already shown an example by going to the brook to wash his own."[3]

Howe sought to break down the barriers between the regulars and the colonial troops. Americans in general, and John Stark in particular, admired him. But, Lord Howe was the exception among British officers, not the rule.[4]

In November 1757, Captain James Abercrombie, General Abercromby's aide, wanted to accompany a ranger mission to Ticonderoga. He was the same officer who had written to congratulate Rogers after the disastrous battle on snowshoes.

Rogers was too ill with scurvy to go on the mission, so he selected Stark to lead the rangers. Although, nominally, both Stark and Abercrombie were captains, under British army practice the regular army officer assumed command. Stark, the more experienced wilderness fighter, became the follower. John Stark, touchy by nature, apparently rebelled.

Another British officer went along as well, young Lieutenant Matthew Clerke, an engineer. It was a large force, three hundred men. They left Fort Edward and marched to Lake George and on into the forested hills east of the lake. Discipline broke down almost immediately. The rangers defied Abercrombie's orders; they even fired their muskets while on the march. The British captain was furious: "… all I could doe or say to the officers they could not prevent firing on our march." When they camped for the night, he claimed the sentries fell asleep.[5]

Near Ticonderoga they saw French soldiers in the distance. Abercrombie wanted to remain hidden in order to capture a prisoner. Instead, he wrote, "Captain Stark who was with me set up the Indian hollow [whooped like an Indian], upon which the whole party jumped up and yelled as if all hell had broken loose and all fell afiring at men running away. I did everything in my power to make them hold their tongues and behave as they ought to doe. I even knocked some of them down and damned their officers for a Set of Scoundrels."[6]

Returning to Fort Edward by the southern reaches of Lake Champlain, Captain Stark twice pretended that he "mistook South Bay for a beaver pond." Abercrombie wrote his final opinion of the affair in a letter to Lord Loudon: "… If Rogers had been with us we could not have failed but the rest of the Ranging Officers have no Subordination among them & not the least command of their men."[7]

The mission became known as the "misbehavior scout." No later account of the affair contradicts Abercrombie's report. Rangers fired their muskets in violation of their own rules; sentries slept on watch, or at least they appeared to sleep; they exposed their presence to the enemy. They behaved more like undisciplined louts than rangers. Yet, Abercombie was the only man in John Stark's long military career who claimed that Stark had no command of his troops.[8]

The whole affair seemed like a planned, deliberate attempt to foul up the mission and to embarrass the British officers, a plot probably concocted by Stark himself. The enlisted rangers would not have dared behave so badly without their captain's complicity. Perhaps the rangers enjoyed the farce. But Stark's participation in this fiasco damaged his military reputation, and the complaints of Abercrombie and Clerke threatened the standing of the rangers. Stark's performance was, at best, unprofessional.[9]

By late autumn in 1757, the rangers camped on the Island near Fort Edward, where the biting cold of the river valley chilled their blood. The companies of Stark and Buckley swelled the population. Officers could hardly have found a worse place for soldiers to spend a winter.[10]

The British strove to tighten discipline among the rangers. A prominent six-foot-tall whipping post stood on the parade ground. Here, recalcitrant rangers would suffer the lash under the eyes of their comrades, a staple of British army life. The whippings horrified the rangers, not out of fear, but because of the humiliation. One ranger said, "I was in mortal dread of the whippings. … I felt I could not survive the shame of being trussed and lashed before men's eyes."[11]

Inevitably, two rangers were whipped at the post, for stealing rum. Then they were locked in the guardhouse. On December 6 angry rangers gathered near the post. Someone produced an axe, and in a few moments the post fell. They then rushed the guardhouse to free their comrades. An officer interceded and tried to stop the growing mutiny. At Fort Edward the post commander, Colonel William Haviland, ordered the rioters jailed at the fort, out of reach of other angry rangers.[12]

Rogers initiated a court of inquiry for his men, but Haviland refused to release them to testify. Ranger witnesses would not testify against their own and, under questioning, they either evaded the queries or forgot the events. Rogers worried that some men might desert, and he told this to Haviland. The British colonel responded with sarcasm: "I answered, " he wrote, "it would be better they were all gone than have such a Riotous sort of people, but if he could catch me one that attempted it [desertion] I would endeavour to have him hanged as an example."[13]

⁂

Notwithstanding the growing hostility between the rangers and British officers, Rogers traveled to New York in January 1758 to meet Loudon, who did not yet know that he had been replaced by General Abercromby. The ranger wrote: "… upon my arrival was received by His Lordship in a very friendly manner." Loudon surprised Rogers by offering to form five new companies of rangers and asking Rogers to select the officers. If Colonel Haviland thought the British army could do without the rangers, Loudon and Howe knew otherwise.[14]

Rogers reported that he immediately "sent officers into the New England provinces, where, by the assistance of my friends, the requested augmentation of rangers was quickly completed, the whole five companies being ready for service by the 4th of March." Four of the companies sailed to Louisbourg to join General Jeffrey Amherst; the fifth joined Rogers.[15]

Rangers suffered from snow, cold and illness on the Island that winter. Then, on January 3, a sudden thaw caused the Hudson River to rise suddenly overnight and sweep over the Island. Some of the men's huts were waist-deep in water. Colonel Haviland reported, "most of the Rangers on the Island were floated out of their Hutts, and the greatest part of the firewood that was there Carried off."[16]

On January 28, 1758, Captain John Stark led a detachment of rangers from the island to the First Narrows on Lake George to test the condition of the lake ice and the depth of the snow.[17] It was a winter of deep snows. In February Lake George carried a blanket of snow between four and five feet deep. Men foundered to their armpits if they tried to walk without snowshoes.[18]

Their officers expected the rangers to be ready to fight no matter what the conditions, however, and planned a winter campaign against either Ticonderoga or Crown Point. Major Israel Putnam, of a Connecticut regiment, went out on February 28 with a small reconnaissance party. When he returned to Fort Edward, he discovered one man was missing; he had either defected or been captured. Since Rogers was getting ready to lead a large ranger force, 400 strong, the absent man worried Rogers. He confessed forebodings that the prisoner would betray them.[19]

Colonel Haviland made matters worse by reducing the number of rangers for the expedition to 180 men. Rogers wrote:

> I acknowledge that I entered upon this service, and viewed this small detachment of brave men march out, with no little concern and uneasiness of mind; for as there was the greatest reason to suspect that the French were, by the prisoner and deserter above mentioned, fully informed of the design of sending me out upon Putnam's return: what could I think to see my party, instead of being strengthened and augmented, reduced to less than half the number at first proposed I must confess that it appeared to me (ignorant and unskilled as I then was in politicks and the art of war) incomprehensible; *but my commander doubtless had his reasons, and is able to vindicate his own conduct.* [emphasis in the original][20]

Rogers wrote that paragraph to deflect blame from a disaster. He knew that Colonel Haviland was no friend to the rangers. Reducing the manpower of the expedition imperiled the safety of all its members. Haviland's decision was another British failure of leadership. Rogers was compelled to begin this mission with the knowledge that it would have to be carried out with exceptional prudence and caution.

The rangers left Fort Edward on March 10 without John Stark. They reached Sabbath Day Point on March 12, moving on bare ice after a thaw. Some rangers traveled on "scates."[21]

Rogers sensed that Indians were nearby. He moved the rangers off the ice into the mountains on the west. The snow was deep and the going was difficult. They moved north through the valley of Trout Brook, staying parallel with the stream. A ranger spotted Indians moving on the ice of the brook. Rogers prepared an ambush. They counted ninety-six of the enemy approaching, and they waited in hiding until Rogers acted: "I fired a gun, as a signal for a general discharge upon them."[22] A contemporary report written by Rogers told what happened next:

> We gave the Enemy the first Fire, upon which they retreated; my Party pursued them, and scalped about forty Indians in about one Quarter of an hour. We, imagining the Enemy Beat, Ensign M'Donald with his advanced Party strove to head them that none might Escape, but we soon found that the Party we had engaged, were only the Advance Guards of the Enemy; that their Main Body coming up in great numbers and joining them, occasioned my People retreating to their own Ground, where they stood and fought with the greatest Intrepidity and Bravery imaginable.[23]

The Canadians and Indians routed the rangers. For the second time in two years, Robert Rogers attacked without first knowing the enemy's strength, but in this action critical time was lost while he permitted a scalping party. Again his men fought courageously, but they suffered terrible losses. Some of them surrendered, relying on French promises of "good quarter," but were then slaughtered and scalped by the Indians. The official French report explained why no quarter was given: "… the Indians having discovered a chief's scalp in the breast of an officer's jacket, refused all quarter, and took 114 scalps; the opinion is only 12 or 15 men escaped."[24]

Ironically, given the rangers' terrible losses, the battle became famous for the legend of Robert Rogers's personal escape from the Indians. The tale had Rogers climbing a steep mountain along the west shore of Lake George and then sliding down a nearly vertical rock face (Rogers' Slide or Rogers' Rock) on the lake side to safety. The legend of the slide is probably false, but Rogers did escape.[25]

The survivors straggled south on Lake George. Rogers sent his strongest men ahead for assistance. On March 14, John Stark and rangers from Fort Edward met Rogers at Hoop Island. They brought food and three horse-drawn sleighs. By Rogers's own reckoning, 125 of his rangers were dead or missing, leaving 55 badly mauled survivors to reach safety at their base. A witness watched as the rangers entered the fort: "About 5' o'Clock I see ye Maj'r Com in Him Self Being in ye Rear of ye whol."[26]

ᏍᏍᏍ ᏍᏍᏍ

Despite their victory in this second battle on snowshoes, all was not well with the French. Montcalm noted that inflation in Canada made the prices for food and supplies soar. The population in Quebec swelled with French soldiers and Indians, creating a shortage of goods and food. The Marquis, accustomed to the high life of French nobility, complained that he could not afford to live the way he wished.[27]

Canada had suffered a crop failure in 1757. Food was rationed. Three ounces of bread sufficed for each person each day. Vendors sold horsemeat instead of beef. Relations with the Indians soured. Bougainville blamed the arrogance of French officers for the deteriorating alliance:

> First, I note that all winter only part of the Indians have come, proof of their coolness, since last year they were here all the time. Second, the English will perhaps succeed in detaching the Indians from our alliance and then La Belle Riviere [the Ohio River] is lost.[28]

Bougainville did not know yet that a smallpox epidemic had struck their Indian allies from the west. Still, nothing cooled the martial spirit of the French. Neither famine, nor inflation, nor disappearing allies weakened Montcalm's determination to hold what the French had won. On April 1, Bougainville observed a brilliant Canadian sky: "At nine in the evening there was an aurora borealis accompanied by a luminous band which crossed the sky from north-northeast to south-southwest. It ended on the south by a trail of fire which seemed to form a tail to it."[29] He thought it was an omen of good fortune.

9

DISASTER AT TICONDEROGA
They Fell Like Pigeons

The British replaced Loudon that winter. They ordered the new commander, Major General James Abercromby, to "lead in person the attack on Ticonderoga." They also made changes in the command structure; a junior regular officer no longer outranked a senior provincial officer. The presence of Lord Howe as Abercromby's second-in-command heartened the Americans.[1]

New Englanders enlisted in large numbers the next spring and marched through the mud to the Hudson River. Abercromby ordered the rangers to increase the number of their patrols to the French forts. In May, Rogers sent Captain Jacob of the Stockbridge Indians to the east of Lake George, and Captain Stark to the west side of the lake, with orders to "take if possible some prisoners near Carillon." Jacob came back with ten prisoners and seven scalps. Stark brought back six captives, four of whom had previously escaped from British custody.[2]

Lord Howe wanted to keep the intelligence flowing. He sent the rangers out again in June to search for landing places for a large army along the northern shore of Lake George. A French patrol engaged them in a fierce firefight.[3]

The Reverend John Cleaveland, chaplain of a Massachusetts regiment, arrived at Fort Edward with an infusion of fresh troops. The minister kept a journal. On July 1 he noted that he walked the sixteen miles to Lake George and got there "Something Fatigued" before sunset.[4]

Abercromby's army assembled along the south shore of Lake George near the charred ruins of Fort William Henry. Anticipating his need for all the soldiers he could muster, the general abrogated the terms of Colonel Monro's capitulation, calling it "null and void," and commanded, "all soldiers who were paroled are ordered to serve."[5]

The ranger camp lay about four hundred yards west of the fort's ruins. The general sought to enlarge their force and he ordered, "Such of the Provincial Troops as are willing and fit to serve with Major Rogers shall have an encouragement over and above their present pay."[6]

On Thursday, June 28, the bateaux for the voyage north arrived overland from Fort Edward. The following Sunday, roughly 15,000 troops crowded the landscape at Lake George.[7] Such an assemblage could not escape the notice of French and Indian scouts. They returned to Fort Carillon at Ticonderoga with exaggerated tales. Bougainville wrote:

The strength of the enemy increases every day … ; one thousand horses and a proportional quantity of oxen in use; depositions of prisoners unanimous on their intention to lay siege to Carillon and to start their movements early in July. Twenty to twenty-five thousand men destined for this expedition according to their report. This is our situation![8]

While the French worried, the English invoked heavenly assistance. That Sunday, Reverend Cleaveland noted, "There seems to be an excellent set of Chaplains in ye Camp." Chaplain Forbush preached that morning from Exodus 17, "upon Moses sending Joshua to fight against Amlick … and an excellent sermon he preached." Cleaveland held the afternoon service. The soldiers anticipated the battle to come, and there was much "Prayer and Supplication." The pastor noticed that, "there was remarkable attention in ye Assembly both parts of ye day."[9]

⚘ ⚘

French officers began to worry when the promised reinforcements didn't arrive at Ticonderoga. The western Indians failed to appear. Bougainville thought that those warriors who did come were far from helpful: "The small number of Indians that we have here, realizing the need we have of them are extremely insolent. This evening [June 30] they wished to kill all the General's hens. They forcefully take away barrels of wine, kill the cattle, and we must put up with it. What a country! What a war!"[10]

Montcalm knew that a crisis approached, and he took action. He sent out advance parties to the head of Lake George and to the falls on the La Chute River to slow the English advance and to convey an illusion of French strength. And he made a bold decision: rather than defend Ticonderoga at the fort itself, he would establish a line on the high ground about a half mile west of the fort. Montcalm went out himself on July 1, "… to select a battlefield and the place for an entrenched camp." It was a brilliant move. As Bougainville noted, "We lack man power, and perhaps time is also lacking. Our situation is critical. Action and audacity are our sole resources."[11]

At the highest point on the Ticonderoga peninsula, Montcalm began construction of a log and earth entrenchment that ran in zigzag fashion from near the La Chute River on the south toward Lake Champlain on the north. Frenchmen and Canadians, officers and enlisted men alike, worked around the clock with axes and shovels. They felled trees in a tangle in front of the lines, and they sharpened the tree branches until an attacker would have to pass through a jungle of spikes and limbs before reaching the French position. The work had to be completed quickly. "How to do it with so few people?" Bougainville asked himself on July 2.[12]

On Monday, July 3, General Abercromby issued the order to begin the enterprise. "The whole army to be victuall'd to the 9th July inclusive, as much as possible of that provision to be deliver'd out this evening, & the remainder tomorrow morning at day break." The daily ration for each man was to be one pound of pork and one pound of flour. That morning the general reviewed the assembled Connecticut regiments. They were ready to march to their boats at six o'clock the next morning.[13]

On the morning of the 4th, Abercromby played host to Reverend Cleaveland and several chaplains at his tent. Cleaveland reported that, "He treated us very kindly, told us that we would Teach ye people their Duty and to be Courageous." Abercromby then gave the clergyman a strange message to take back to the provincial soldiers. Tell them, he said "be courageous for the Cowards would go to Heaven." He treated them to punch and wine and sent them on their way.[14]

Cleaveland boarded a bateau by five o'clock the next morning, and thousands of soldiers filed down to the shore to join him. A rattle of drums signaled the first boats to shove off. Successive waves of boats followed with rangers in whaleboats taking the lead. It was a vast armada—900 bateaux, 135 whaleboats and artillery platforms covered the south end of the lake. When the fleet began to pass through the First Narrows, the vessels strung out over six miles from the first boat to the last.[15]

By late afternoon the whaleboats carrying the rangers reached Sabbath Day Point. Some men pitched tents and built fires to give the appearance they would spend the night. Most of the rangers lolled about and tried to rest. Here and there they found the bones of the Jersey Blues slaughtered there the year before.

Caleb Stark wrote that his grandfather, "had a long conversation with Lord Howe in his tent, seated with him upon the bear-skins which composed his camp-bed, respecting the mode of attack, and the position of the fort." The two men, from such different backgrounds, ate together. Howe ordered Stark to capture the bridge at the falls on the La Chute River the next morning.[16]

Lord Howe was unique among British officers; he deliberately cultivated good relations with provincial officers and men. He did so for the good of the service. Rufus Putnam, of Massachusetts, observed, "every soldier in the army had a personal attachment to him." Unlike other regular officers, Putnam praised Howe because, "his manner was so easy and fermiller, that you loost all that constraint or diffidence we feele when addressed by our Superiours, whose manners are forbiding."[17]

Late that evening the army took to the boats and rowed north to the end of the lake. They left fires burning at the point, hoping to draw French troops away from their destination. The woods were full of Montcalm's scouts; the subterfuge at Sabbath Day Point had not fooled them.[18]

At nine o'clock on the morning of July 6, the English army began to disembark at the north end of Lake George. The provincial soldiers anticipated a fierce battle there, but the landing was barely contested. A relieved Reverend

Cleaveland wrote, "the French only fired a few Small Armes w'ch did no Harm and then run off."[19]

Lord Howe urged a rapid advance toward the fort. He led a strong contingent of regulars, provincials and rangers in a wide sweeping movement toward the falls on the river. In thick woods they stumbled upon a French reconnaissance force, and a vicious firefight followed. A witness told the story:

> Lord How happen'd to be betwixt the head of the two Columns and the Lt. Infantry, who, immediately on the Fire of the Enemy advanc'd, and too boldly charging at the head of the Lt. Infantry receiv'd a shot under the left Breast which went thro' his Lungs, his Heart, & Back Bone, so that he died instantaneously to the unspeakable Grief of the whole Army.[20]

Howe's death profoundly affected his comrades. The army withdrew to the shore of Lake George. One soldier, Abel Spicer, reported that his regiment, "was very much broken to pieces and some came in and some was lost in the woods and came in next morning."[21] The English army of 15,000 far outnumbered the French defenders, but it was the English and Americans who became demoralized. British Major Thomas Mante declared, "In Lord Howe, the soul of General Abercromby's army seemed to expire." The provincial troops had no confidence in Abercromby, "an aged gentleman, infirm in body and spirit."[22]

Bougainville assessed the impact of Howe's death from the French perspective:

> The enemy suffered a considerable loss there in the person of Milord Howe, who was killed. ... He had above all in the greatest degree those two qualities of heroes, activity and audacity. He it was who projected the enterprise against Canada and he alone was capable of executing it. ... The disheartened English gave us twenty-four hours delay, and this precious time was the saving of us and of the colony.[23]

Activity and audacity—in a single day those qualities disappeared from the English army with the death of Howe, and they grew manifest in the French army in the person of Montcalm.

Abercromby did not attack on July 7. He spent the day preparing, thus giving the French time to complete their defenses. "The seventh we spent in reconnoitering the French lines before Ticonderoga and finding out the easiest approaches to them," wrote Lieutenant William Grant of the day's progress.[24]

On July 7, Captain John Stark and a detachment of rangers escorted two British officers to the top of Sugar Loaf Hill (Mount Defiance) to view the French positions. The mountain stood across the mouth of the La Chute River from the fort. Steep ledges and thick brush formed the formidable north slope of the hill facing the French.[25]

The two British officers with Stark were Captain James Abercrombie and Lieutenant Matthew Clerke, the same two men who had accompanied Stark on the "misbehavior scout" the previous November. The British had officers who were more experienced as military engineers than these two men, but those engineers were not available that day. Abercrombie and Clerke, by default, were left to determine the strength of Montcalm's defenses.

At the top of the mountain, the officers stood on ledges among wind-stunted trees and looked down at their enemies. A long stretch of Lake Champlain glistened in the sunshine beyond the fort. South of them the lake narrowed and wound like a river through wooded hills. A mile or so distant, down on the Ticonderoga peninsula, stood the massive fort and the new positions being hurriedly constructed west of the fort. With a telescope they could make out French soldiers swarming around the new log battlements. Abercrombie and Clerke decided that these raw emplacements, the new French lines, "could easily be forced, even without cannon, if they were attacked with spirit."[26]

Caleb Stark, Jr., believed that his grandfather disagreed with the regulars' assessment of the defenses. He claimed that John Stark "did not hesitate to say that the French had made formidable preparations for defence." If cannon could have been hauled into position on the mountain, and if their missiles could have reached the entrenchments, the English might have enfiladed and destroyed the lines. Stark's familiarity with the terrain and his combat experience qualified him to comment on the scene. But his history with these two officers insured that neither would listen to him.[27]

Another regular officer, Major Thomas Mante, wrote that the officers atop the hill disagreed about the strength of the French defenses. Mante criticized Clerke and Abercrombie, "whose duty it was exactly to inform themselves of these particulars." At least one officer, Mante wrote, considered the French lines a "well-finished work." That officer may have been Stark, but Mante did not identify the officer he cited. Clerke and Abercrombie looked at the French lines and thought that they saw "a flimsy construction, strong in appearance only," according to Mante. They advised General Abercromby accordingly.[28]

⁂

Lieutenant Clerke made a second trip to the mountain on the morning of July 8. According to Abel Spicer, "the engineer went with a guard upon a mountain against the fort to look and see if he could spy a good place to plant the artillery and he came back about 8 o'clock."[29]

General Abercromby decided to attack without placing cannon on the mountain. Weeks later he wrote a letter explaining his decision. He blamed his junior officers: "But before I undertook the attack we had the reports and Opinions of two very expert Engineers, who had been on that Ground at different Times before, and had seen the Ground & Works the preceding Night and that Morning."[30]

The general then suggested that he made the final decision under some pressure from his officers to proceed in haste:[31]

> And upon the report [from Clerke], all the principal Officers were Unanimously of Opinion, that the Attack should be forthwith made on the Entrenchments—And it was what the whole Officers and Troops earnestly wished for—Besides the Enemy were every Minute strengthening their Works, and every Hour Reinforcements were

coming up the Lake Champlain to them, in so much that they must have been 10 or 12000 strong before we could have brought up a small part of our Artillery against their Lines.

And if, after all this, the Attempt had not been made, what would have been said on all hands?[32]

Abercromby, of course, knew that Clerke and Abercrombie were not "two very expert engineers." Clerke has taken an outsized share of the blame for what ensued. In fact, he apparently did propose placing cannon on the flanks of the mountain. A map, drawn on July 7, showed a British battery at the base of the hill on the French left flank. That map may have been drawn by Clerke. Abercromby, unnerved by the wild estimates of French reinforcements and feeling pressure from his subordinates to act, attacked without placing artillery on the heights.[33]

All day on July 7 and during the morning on July 8, Montcalm and his soldiers worked to strengthen their entrenchments. "Even the officers, ax in hand, set the example, and the flags were planted on the works." The French slept at their posts overnight. By morning they were ready for the attack they knew was coming. The Marquis de Montcalm remained at the center, "to be within range of all parts."[34]

Despite Abercromby's fears, only 350 regulars arrived as reinforcements for the French forces. They could muster in total about 3,600 soldiers; they were far outnumbered.[35]

On the morning of July 8, British or American troops appeared on the slopes of Mount Defiance. While Montcalm's men sharpened branches on their "chevaux-de-frise," their enemies fired potshots at them from across the river, "which did not interrupt our work at all," Bougainville wrote; "we amused ourselves by not replying."[36]

Shortly after noon Abercromby's army moved to the attack. Thousands of redcoats, provincials and rangers marched up the gentle slope toward the lines in the July heat. The fighting began on the French left.

Captain Stark's company led the attack under the command of a lieutenant, not John Stark, who apparently was elsewhere. The rangers reached a point within three hundred yards of the French positions before they came under fire. The attackers faced a breastwork of logs at least eight feet high. The French fired down at them from concealed positions. The rangers rarely saw the enemy behind the logs, and then only brief glimpses of hats and faces. There were no targets to aim at.[37]

Abercromby's troops could try to take the positions by storm—a mad rush to engage the French in hand-to-hand combat—but to get there soldiers first had to thread their way through sharpened tree branches with musket balls whizzing past or striking home. Abel Spicer described the problem: "… the regulars pushed on as fast as possible and marched up to the breast works ten deep and fired volleys at the breast works, which was as high as the enemies heads, and they had holes between the logs to fire through, and the regulars ventured very near the breast works and they fell like pigeons."[38]

The attack was poorly coordinated, with a hot fight at one point and then at another. The British attempted to float cannon down the river to flank the French positions, but artillery fire from the fort drove them back.[39]

Abercromby stayed at a post near the waterfall, well back from the fighting. He ordered a frontal attack by all elements of his infantry. Captain Arnot wrote that, when the general heard a cheer from the provincial troops, he thought they had pierced the defenses, "(for he could not see what was a doing), … then the Whol Army was order'd to March up and attack (quite out of Breath from their Distance) which they bravely did but to no effect."[40]

British and American soldiers attacked again and again through the afternoon. On the far left of the attack, Highland Scots, the Black Watch, fought up a steep hill toward the French positions. Captain James Murray, wounded in the thigh, wrote to his brother that his men got within twenty paces of the trenches, "and had as hot a fire for about three hours as possible could be, we all the time seeing but their hats and the end of their muskets."[41] One witness said of the Scots: "They actually mounted the enemy's intrenchments. … They appeared like roaring lions breaking from their chains."[42]

Even Montcalm paid tribute to the Black Watch: "This column ... combined to charge repeatedly for three hours without being either rebuked or broken up and several were killed at only fifteen feet from our abbatis."[43]

The outnumbered French fought back with determination. The fact that the attacks were not simultaneous enabled them to shift men and resources from place to place and provided occasional respite from the struggle on a very hot day. The attackers, always on the move, could not rest.

Bougainville noted that each attacking column was supported by "light troops and better marksmen, who, protected by the trees, delivered a most murderous fire on us."[44] Montcalm's report of the battle to the French Minister of War identified the marksmen as rangers.[45]

A French battalion kept busy all afternoon replenishing the powder and ball from stores at the fort. They also hauled food and casks of water to the fighters. The log breastworks caught fire several times. When flames threatened to destroy the defenses, French soldiers scrambled over the walls to douse the flames.[46]

The attacks slowed and, by early evening, they stopped altogether. Abercromby's exhausted troops retreated under the cover of fire from the rangers. Montcalm had no way to know if or when they would come back again. The victors spent another night in their fortifications. The next morning Abercromby's army was gone. French soldiers buried the dead of both armies.[47]

After the battle, the British and Americans faced a night of horror. Those who could walk moved back to the landing place at Lake George. Abel Spicer wrote, "The roads was so full that a man could hardly walk without treading on them [bodies]." It was a black night, and the men stumbled along muddy paths in the forest. The units became all mixed up, and it was impossible to locate one's comrades. Rangers covered the rear of the retreat.[48]

The wounded and the dead lay where they fell. A member of the Jersey

Blues remembered that "the French were out plundering our dead and wounded with candles and lanterns." Two weeks later Montcalm wrote to Abercromby to tell him that the French had discovered seventy British wounded before the abbatis, but, "the delay of the night has been fatal to the wounded who remained there … the majority of them have died."[49]

In a letter to Pitt of July 12, Abercromby listed his casualties: "four hundred and sixty-four regulars killed, twenty-nine missing, eleven hundred and seventeen wounded; and eighty-seven provincials killed, eight missing and two hundred thirty-nine wounded, officers of both included." Abercromby had no way to accurately count his dead and wounded; he could determine only the number of missing. The French held total dominion over the battlefield afterward. Perhaps they provided the numbers to the English general.[50]

The night after the battle, British and American soldiers began to question the wisdom of their commander. Reverend Cleaveland thought it, "to be marvellous strange to order the entrenchment to be forced with Small Arms when they had cannon not far off." The chaplain became more perplexed the next day when he learned that Abercromby had ordered a retreat to the south end of Lake George. The troops, he said, were "all disgusted."[51]

By nightfall on July 9, most of the army had rowed the length of Lake George and reached the ruined fort. The soldiers now had time to talk, and their words expressed bitterness. "There was almost as many sorts of news as there was men," Abel Spicer wrote.[52] British regulars blamed Americans for the defeat. Captain Arnot wrote: "That these Numbers [of provincial troops] did not amount to what they promised is most certain; but the greater their Numbers, the greater the Evil; for of any sett of people in the Universe they are the worst cut out for war, the most stupid and most chicken-hearted sett of Mankind."[53]

General Abercromby shared the contempt for the Americans—an opinion he reached from the views of others, because he avoided the battlefield. In August he wrote his brother that, "no real dependence is to be had upon the bulk of the Provincials. … Their officers, with very few Exceptions, are worse than their Men. … I had but a nominal Army."[54]

The general's decision to remove his "nominal army" from Ticonderoga, though he still far outnumbered the French and still had the artillery to destroy their defenses, dismayed even his own regulars. His aide, Captain James Abercrombie, claimed that he wished to continue the battle. Abercrombie wrote to Sir Harry Erskine: "… I was for bringing up our Artillery next Day & attacking it [the French lines] in form. But others who have not seen half the service, & whose nerves are not quite braced for war, advised the contrary."[55]

Sir Harry forwarded Abercrombie's letter to Lord Bute, with the notation that it was from "Abercrombie the Engineer." The letter mentioned the reconnaissance at Mount Defiance with Clerke and Stark, but Abercrombie wrote only, "it was perceived the enemy was busy making an intrenchment." Historian Nicholas Westbrook pointed out that Abercrombie failed to acknowledge that he was one of the principal "perceivers" of that intelligence and thus bore responsibility for its misuse. Lieutenant Clerke became the scapegoat for General Abercromby's decision to attack without artillery, but Clerke could no longer defend himself; he had been killed leading an attack on the French left flank.[56]

Americans nursed their own grievances after the disaster at Ticonderoga. Cleaveland wrote on July 10, "This day where ever I went I found people, officers and soldiers astonished that we left the French Ground and lamenting the strange conduct in coming off."[57] The same day, Abel Spicer heard provincial officers talking: "Some of them said they would never go back again, some said they would be willing to if the regulars did not go."[58]

The battle at Ticonderoga left British and Americans thoroughly disgusted with each other. The days of cheerful cooperation, briefly inspired by Lord Howe, were over. John Stark left no record of his observations that day. He must have admired the courage and discipline of the regulars and the Black Watch, marching forward, rank on rank, into the hail of musket balls. He certainly noticed that Abercromby ordered the attack without artillery, without flanking maneuvers, without professional reconnaissance and without overall coordination. The battle was one more in a series of painful errors made by Stark's superiors; he learned from their mistakes.

10

THE TIDE TURNS
I Rejoiced That I Was an Englishman

Archibald Stark died a few days before the battle at Ticonderoga. The old man (he was sixty-five) must have known the end was near, for on June 22, 1758, three days before his death, he signed his last will and testament, in which he acknowledged that he was "weak in Body."[1]

Archibald left a third of the income from his estate to his wife, Eleanor. Almost everything else he divided equally among seven children. He made no provision in his will for his daughters Anna Stark Gamble and Mary Stark Conroy, who may already have received their shares as dower, and he named his sons William and John as executors of his estate.[2]

When word of his father's death reached him, John Stark left for home. He had to travel through forests that were particularly dangerous. Indians and Canadian partisans, emboldened by the French victory at Ticonderoga, patrolled the woods east and south of Lake George. William Stark probably accompanied his brother, and they reached home in August.[3]

They hired Matthew Patten to compile an inventory of their father's estate and appraise its value. Meanwhile, John rode off to Starkstown to court Elizabeth Page. Known in her family as Betsey, Elizabeth was twenty-one years old that summer. She had grown up on the frontier, and she had experienced her share of sorrow. Her mother died when she was five, and she was raised by a stepmother. Then, her brother Caleb was killed in the first battle on snowshoes. Life had toughened her to be a soldier's wife.[4]

The Stark family later handed down the story of John Stark's proposal to Elizabeth Page. He arrived at her home on horseback, and, "without dismounting, said, 'If you are ever to become my wife, Molly, you will have to come with me now.' She went." It seems likely that this romantic proposal was made with tongue in cheek. For the rest of their lives together, he persisted in calling her by his nickname for her—Molly. The wedding took place at her father's large home at Page's Corner on August 20, 1758.[5]

Their marriage was more than a joining of two families—it was a bonding between two historically alien cultures. When John Stark's parents arrived in the New World from Ulster, English colonists in Massachusetts spurned the Scotch-Irish immigrants. Now, less than half a century later, the daughter of a prominent English family wed a Scotch-Irish frontiersman of the most aggressive and rebellious sort. It was, by all indications, a happy marriage.

Matthew Patten kept busy that August appraising Archibald's estate. Patten and Thomas Hall met at Amoskeag on August 11 to perform their duties.[6] It took years before their findings were filed with the court. The assets amounted to £9,618, and the claims against the estate added up to £4,161. John Stark paid the appraisers £19 ¾ for their work, the payment made in beef.[7]

Three days after John and Molly married, Patten wrote a letter on John's behalf to Colonel John Goffe, who was at Albany recovering from an illness. The document has not survived, but Patten's diary entry about it suggests that he wrote it because Stark could not. Patten explained that it was a letter "by Capt. Stark."[8]

Abercromby's army suffered at Lake George. Smallpox struck the camp on July 12. Thereafter, Abel Spicer wrote in his diary about the alarming spread of the disease. Meanwhile, their officers worried about a French attack. Those soldiers who were well enough dug a trench and built a breastwork for defense. Indians ambushed a unit near Half Way Brook and left scalped and mutilated bodies.[9]

Morale sank to a new low. Twenty men were arrested for expressing disrespect for their officers and unwillingness to return to fight the French. Two men deserted from the Connecticut regiment and, on August 25, a British regular was hanged:

And he that was hanged did hang till sunset according to order and then was taken down and buried with all the clothes on that he had on when he was hanged … [including] a white cap. A regular never wears a white cap only when he is going to the gallows.[10]

To protect the hangman from the retribution of his fellow soldiers, the general officers had him escorted to Albany and released from further service. Discipline had deteriorated so badly that officers could not be sure they could control their men.[11]

In early August a large patrol of regulars, provincials and rangers left for the south end of Lake Champlain. Robert Rogers and Israel Putnam led the force, and Abel Spicer accompanied them. Spicer wrote, "Our officers shot at a mark thinking there was no danger."[12] Rogers and Putnam made a bet on their marksmanship and held a shooting competition, assuming that no enemies lurked nearby.

A Canadian and Indian party under the leadership of the partisan Marin heard the shooting and ambushed the Americans. After a firefight, Rogers's men drove off the attackers, but not before Indians captured Israel Putnam. They took Putnam to their camp where, without French officers to interfere, they might celebrate his capture in their traditional way. They stripped off Putnam's clothes, tied him to a tree and piled kindling around him, which they set ablaze. The more Putnam thrashed and squirmed, the more the Indians whooped and yelled. The noise brought Marin to the scene. The partisan rescued Putnam, who survived and returned to his troops in a prisoner exchange.[13]

Reverend Cleaveland seemed stunned by the army's bad fortune. Writing in his journal, he returned again and again to Putnam's capture and Rogers's folly in firing at marks. He finally concluded that, "this is a judg't of God upon us."[14]

But the French could not take advantage of English weakness. In early August both the Indians and the Canadian militia left for home. Bougainville traveled to Lake George under a flag of truce to parley with Abercromby. There would be no exchange of prisoners, however; they could not come to agreement. Nevertheless, Bougainville reported that he "was received and treated with the greatest politeness." Remnants of the gentlemanly etiquette of Continental warfare survived it seems, here and there, amidst the savagery of the American war.[15]

⊷ ⊶

That summer, while Abercromby suffered defeat at Ticonderoga, British generals Jeffrey Amherst and James Wolfe took the fortress at Louisbourg. Their achievement spread a wave of pride across the English-speaking world, where defeat had become commonplace. The victory won Amherst command of the army in America. London ordered General Abercromby to return home.

Amherst sailed to Boston and marched his conquering army across Massachusetts toward Fort Edward. Crowds of Yankees welcomed the British soldiers across the colony. Young John Adams, learning law at Worcester, was thrilled at the sight of the army. "I then rejoiced," he wrote, "that I was an Englishman, and gloried in the name of Britain."[16]

Soldiers at Lake George agreed with Adams. Reverend Cleaveland wrote, "This night General AMHERST arrived to the Camp to the no small Joy of the Army as they now expect their Destination either to Ticonderoga or Homewards." On October 6 generals Amherst and Abercromby reviewed the assembled troops at Lake George. Perhaps to demonstrate that British army discipline would continue, a black man then received fifty lashes before the regiments for the peculiar offense of "taking up Goods and Selling them for a quarter of the Price he gave for them."[17]

Military justice could take unexpected turns at the whim of the officers. A wayward soldier could not be sure what punishment to expect for his sins. A few days before Amherst arrived, a court-martial at Lake George sentenced several deserters to be hanged. On September 26 the condemned men marched to the gallows. Their hands were tied and nooses slipped around their necks. While a minister prayed for them, the hangman prepared to do his duty. At the last moment an officer arrived and read a proclamation of reprieve; they were set free. To come so close to death, only to survive by the caprice of a British officer, no doubt made an indelible impression on a man—and on all those who witnessed his terror.[18]

Amherst quickly improved the army's morale. He decided that the season was too far advanced for a campaign; on October 11 the general ordered that some of his force could go home. To preserve his modest navy for the campaign of 1759, Amherst ordered their whaleboats, galleys and bateaux to be submerged in the lake, with the intention of refloating them the next spring. On October 27, Abel Spicer noted, "every man left the lake."[19]

Amherst ordered the rangers to remain at Fort Edward for the winter. Rogers understood that their position had changed with the change of command. He wrote, "The headquarters were now fixed at New York, and I had new commanders to obey, new companions to converse with, and, as it were, a new apprenticeship to serve." He had dealt successfully with every commander he had served, and now he needed to adapt to Amherst.[20]

The general gave Rogers specific and emphatic instructions about one matter. Colonel Haldiman at Fort Edward passed on Amherst's words: "He recommended it in the strongest manner, that if some of the enemy should fall into your hands to prevent the Indians from exercising their cruelty upon them, as he desires prisoners should be treated with humanity."[21]

✵ ✵

While Amherst brought optimism to the northern army, one prominent American officer in the south remained disgruntled. George Washington resigned his commission at the end of 1758. He had soured on the British army. His biographer, Douglas Southall Freeman, wrote, "The more Washington dealt with the senior officers of the regular establishment, the less, in general, was his respect for their accomplishments."[22]

The officers he had commanded saluted him, giving him a letter they had all signed. They wrote, "Your presence only will cause a steady firmness and vigor to actuate in every breast, despising the greatest danger and thinking light of toils and hardships, while led on by the man we love." These officers were not Piedmont gentry—they were Virginia frontiersmen. Their respect had been earned. But Washington remained adamant that his career in the British military had ended. He went home to marry Martha Custis.[23]

Seeds of disenchantment with British leadership sprouted throughout the war zones. Provincial troops and officers wanted competent leadership, and they wanted justice. John Stark remained at home through the winter of 1758–59. He chose not to campaign with the rangers.

British officers blamed provincial troops for failures at Ticonderoga and elsewhere, but they knew they still needed the rangers. The high command in London understood the need. On December 29, 1758, William Pitt wrote to General Amherst:

> His majesty is further pleased to empower you, and has commanded me strongly to recommend to you, to keep up and raise, as considerable a number of Rangers, as may be practicable, for the various operations of the Campaign; and in particular that you do not fail to cause a body of the said Rangers amounting to not less than 600, to be sent with the forces to Cape Breton, for the expedition to Quebeck.[24]

That winter, John Stark assumed new family responsibilities. He was now a husband and a son-in-law, and he served as executor of his father's estate. His widowed mother needed him, too. The farm and sawmill at Derryfield also needed attention.

Most of Stark's siblings and their families lived in southern New Hampshire. Anna and William Gamble and their young daughter lived in Derryfield. William Stark and his wife, the former Mary Stinson, lived in Starkstown with their two sons. Archibald Stark, Jr., was a bachelor and served as a lieutenant with the rangers. The youngest son, Samuel, had just married Elizabeth Powers and they remained in Derryfield. Only Isabel lived far away. She and her husband, Hugh Stirling (another Scotch-Irishman), had moved to territory that would later be in Maine.[25]

Winter weather seized New Hampshire early in 1758. Patten reported that two inches of snow fell on November 10, and then it got worse: "This snow was followed by an exceeding cold turn of weather it froze up the River in a great many places said to be the Coldest turn for the time of the year Known in Remembrance." On November 27 there was a "violent wind."[26]

Patten recorded his activities and the changes in the weather throughout the winter. He spent many days transporting rye and corn to the mill to be ground. One day he pieced together a gunstock. He killed and dressed his hogs after the freeze, and then loaned his expertise as a carpenter in constructing the Bedford Meeting House. On January 29, 1759, Patten went to "Co Goffes and new drafted the Inventory of Archibald Starkes Estate and attest to the apprizement of the same." People called upon Patten to mediate their disputes in his capacity as justice of the peace. His diary reflected the diligence and care of a man who was trusted by his neighbors near and far.[27]

John Stark's life at home must have been similar. He probably divided his time between his mother's home at Amoskeag, and Molly's father's house at Page's Corners in Starkstown. John and Molly would live several years with Mr. Page after the war. People in Starkstown got to know the ranger well enough that they later sought his craftsmanship as a sawyer.

By spring it was time to return to duty. On March 1, Matthew Patten witnessed the "muster of Capt John Starks men" at Thomas Hall's tavern.[28] Some writers have placed John Stark at Fort Edward in February because Robert Rogers wrote that he used "Mr. Stark" as a messenger to General Amherst.[29] That "Mr. Stark," however, was probably John's younger brother Archibald, who travelled from Fort Edward to New York for Rogers. A more compelling indication of John's whereabouts during February is that, when he left New Hampshire in March, Molly was pregnant; their son Caleb was born on December 3, 1759, nine months hence.[30]

⁕⁂ ⁂⁕

John Stark's ranger company marched to Fort Edward in bitterly cold weather, but they missed the biggest fight that Robert Rogers encountered that winter. John's brother William, however, fought in the battle.[31]

On March 3, Major Rogers led a large force of rangers, regulars and provincials north under orders to reconnoiter the fort at Ticonderoga and bring back prisoners, if possible. According to Rogers the weather was "exceeding cold"; twenty-three men had to return to Fort Edward before they even reached Lake George. The rest arrived at Sabbath Day Point on the 5th, "almost overcome with the cold." Then Rogers led them across the ice and over the mountains to the shore of Lake Champlain. Across the lake they could see French soldiers cutting wood.[32]

Rogers wrote in his report, "I intended to Form my Ambuscade and Draw a Party out of the Fort by Scalping Stragglers With a Small Party and retire again to the main body." His tactic, to be sure, was to bait their enemies—not just by taking prisoners, but by scalping the prisoners they took while the French watched.[33]

The wood-cutting party appeared at an opportune time, and the rangers attacked them. French regulars reinforced the woodcutters, however, and forced the rangers into a fighting retreat. They crossed back over the ice on Lake Champlain and climbed into the mountains with several prisoners.[34]

The rangers struggled through deep snow the entire mission. Rogers noted that the long retreat "tired two prisoners we was oblidged to kill them." They camped in the frozen forest at Sabbath Day Point, where Rogers wrote to Colonel Haldiman, commander at Fort Edward, to warn him of possible attacks by way of South Bay. He ended his note with this observation: "Two-thirds of my detachment have frozen their feet (the weather being so severe that it is almost impossible to describe it) some of which we are obliged to carry." Several men lost their toes to frostbite.[35]

Still, the mission had succeeded. British engineer Lieutenant Brehm was able to view and map the positions at Ticonderoga. Colonel Haldiman wrote back his congratulations and sent "twenty-two slays" to bring in the frozen soldiers.[36] If the colonel was disturbed by Rogers's treatment of the prisoners, he remained silent about it.

General Amherst moved slowly. His army didn't even reach Lake George until late June. His new theatre commander, Brigadier General Thomas Gage, tried to plant seeds of distrust against the rangers in Amherst's mind. He wrote, "You will find them not very alert in obeying orders." He continued to slander the Americans: "The rangers have never been on a proper footing, & want to be new Modell'd." Gage instructed Haldiman to ignore the new ruling about the relative ranks of British and American officers: "… if You are forced to a decision, You must decide against the Officers of the Rangers as They certainly have no Rank in the Army."[37]

Gage, who never served with the rangers, wanted a British force to usurp their function, but he hedged his position. He foresaw "Light Infantry of the Regiment headed by a brisk Officer, with some of the boldest Rangers mixed with Them, to prevent their being lost in the Woods."[38]

Rogers knew nothing of Gage's machinations, but Amherst disregarded Gage's advice anyway. Amherst valued the rangers and intended to use them, come what may. When General Wolfe requested Rogers to assist in the attack on Quebec, Amherst ignored him.[39] Rogers went to Albany in May to see Amherst and "was very kindly received, and assured that I should have the rank of major in the army from the date of my commission under General Abercrombie."[40]

❧ ☙

Near the end of June, Amherst ordered Captain John Stark to lead three companies of rangers to Lake George. Rogers, with the remaining companies, stayed behind at Fort Edward. The British treated Lake George as enemy territory; they stationed no troops at the lake after the 1758 campaign. When, on June 21, Amherst's army advanced toward Lake George, they proceeded on high alert with the rangers in the lead.[41]

The army prepared for the mission against Ticonderoga. They re-floated some of the boats from the lake bottom, and they dug up armaments they had buried the past year. Construction crews began building a new fort, Fort George, on the rocky knoll where William Johnson's provincials had fought the French in 1755.[42]

Rangers went out to harass the enemy. They prepared an elaborate ambush on Lake George. A convoy of "fishing boats" floated north from Fort George to Diamond Island. At the same time, a detachment of rangers and regulars marched to a hidden position overlooking the boats. They planned to lure French and Indian patrols into attacking the fishermen on the lake, and thus draw them into a trap. John Stark led the fishing fleet. The orders read:

"Capt'n Stark will have a red Flag in his Batteau, and every Batteau must be near enough to call each other, and ready to follow Capt. Stark immediately, as he knows where the covering Party is posted."[43] But the fishing party apparently failed to lure an enemy attack, as no further mention was made of the mission.

Danger still lurked nearby, however. On July 2, a unit of the ever-unlucky Jersey Blues who were gathering bark near Fort George came under fire from Indians. Thirteen of the twenty Jersey soldiers were either killed or captured. Then, on July 5, a soldier shot an Indian near the fort itself, but the wounded warrior got away.[44]

Amherst enforced British discipline. Lemuel Wood, an enlisted man in a Massachusetts regiment, kept a journal in which he recorded graphic descriptions of the punishments meted out by British officers. Abraham Astin was convicted of theft and sentenced to 400 lashes. To impress the army, Astin "was brought forth and was striped 36 lashes at the head of each regiment [in] the army." All eleven regiments got to witness some part of his flogging. Astin's cohorts in thievery were pardoned, but officers ordered them to march from regiment to regiment so they would be compelled to witness the entire 400 bloody strokes.[45]

Three days later a court-martial sentenced a deserter to be shot in front of the troops. The condemned man knelt with his hands clasped before him in a prayerful position. Wood reported that the first volley killed the man, and the second volley "blowed his head all to pieces." On the 18th of July, another soldier received 400 lashes in the same piecemeal fashion as Astin's whipping.[46]

Such events, all happening in the space of one week, duly impressed young provincials fighting their first war. Whatever their motivations for enlisting had been, the hard truth was that their motivations mattered not at all; they would do the will of their officers or else suffer brutal punishments, with humiliation an intended part of the discipline. Such treatment appalled the Americans.

ൟ ൟ

Amherst's army began to move north on July 21, 1759. The boats cruised slowly. Frequent thunderstorms struck with the violence typical of the lake region; the army remained afloat all one night when strong winds riled the lake and made landing impossible. The rangers were the first to land at the north end of Lake George, muskets ready, but the French did not oppose the landing.[47]

Rangers moved quickly through the woods to scout the Ticonderoga peninsula. The sawmill at the falls was abandoned; "not a man there," Lemuel Wood wrote. Two of Amherst's regiments dug in scarcely half a mile from the fort. The army slept that night, disturbed only by the nervous firing of sentries. The next morning, smoke rose over the fort. The French had set fire to huts and sheds outside the walls. Americans and regulars took over the vacant remains of Montcalm's lines from 1758; the emplacements on the high ground now served to protect the attackers.[48]

On the slope beside the trenches, Montcalm had constructed a cross in celebration of the French victory. His enemies examined it; some of them remembered that day. Thomas Mante wrote, "Before this cross was sunk a deep grave." The French had carved a Latin inscription in the wood, translated as, "Soldiers and chief and rampart strength are nought; Behold the conquering Cross. Tis God the triumph wrought."[49]

The few French defenders remaining at the fort made a brave show. Their cannon fire killed and wounded several men. Amherst proceeded cautiously since he did not know the strength of his enemy. Emulating Montcalm at Fort William Henry, he ordered trenches dug to shelter his troops as they approached the fort.[50] Robert Rogers reported, "The General at this time had left several provincial regiments to bring the cannon and ammunition across the Carrying Place."[51] Amherst refused to repeat Abercromby's mistakes.

On the night of July 25, Rogers and sixty men crossed over to the east shore of Lake Champlain. He had orders to cut the boom, a floating blockade of logs chained together and strung across the water to prevent boats from moving past the fort. The rangers rowed one flat-bottomed boat and two whaleboats, hugging the eastern shore north past the cliffs until they reached the boom. They planned to use the dark night for cover as they sawed through the logs and cleared passage on the lake.[52]

Before they could begin, a fire broke out at the fort across the lake and an explosion rocked the scene. They could see French soldiers running toward their boats; the fleeing men were silhouetted by the flames behind them. Rogers attacked them.[53]

At about ten o'clock, a French deserter told Amherst that "a Match [fuse] was laid to blow the whole up."[54] Suspecting that his enemies had booby-trapped the great powder magazine in the fort, the general ordered his men to stay clear. The burning fuse reached its end at about eleven o'clock when the magazine exploded with a tremendous blast. Lemuel Wood heard it: "The noise of it was heard by our men at the landing place. It was very loud and shaking." Then, revealing a soldier's loathing for his enemies, Wood wrote, "It is generally thought in the army that the French, when they left the fort, bound their English prisoners to the magazine and left them to be blown up."[55]

Carillon, the French fort at Ticonderoga, had finally fallen. Amherst's battle plan had been thorough, and he had committed all his forces, but the victory was an anticlimax. The French had decided to sacrifice the fort months before. Bougainville had been in Paris to beg for resources for Montcalm. Colonial Minister Berryer had answered him, "Eh, Monsieur, when the house is on fire one cannot occupy one's self with the stable."[56]

The French government had decided to concentrate its flagging strength in Europe. Sending large reinforcements of troops by sea risked losing them all to the superior British navy. Bougainville returned to Canada with only a few hundred men. Montcalm would have to defend Canada with the resources he had. His intelligence agents had already informed him that he would face a two-pronged attack—one up the St. Lawrence to Quebec, the other from Lake Champlain. Montcalm decided to remain at Quebec.[57]

While Carillon burned, Rogers pushed his rangers in a race to catch the escaping French soldiers. The Americans rowed back across the lake in the glare of the flames and managed to capture about twenty men.

Regulars hauled the flag of Britain up the staff when the sun came up next morning. Fires still burned. Lemuel Wood toured the fortress, impressed by the massive structure. The explosion had done much destruction. When the powder magazine went up, Wood wrote that "the walls of the fort were so much damaged that 2 regiments would not repair it in a year."[58] Still, Amherst decided to repair it on the French plan, "which will save great expense & give no room for the Engineers to exercise their genius which will be much better employed at Crown Point."[59]

A party of rangers moved on to Crown Point, where they found the fort already in flames and the French gone. Rogers took possession of the ruins.[60] In the space of a week, General Amherst had captured both forts. He now held strong bases to consolidate English control of the Champlain Valley, but he had two forts to rebuild, and he had another engineering project in mind. Amherst intended to build a road across the Green Mountains to the fort named Number Four on the Connecticut River. He chose John Stark to lead that mission.[61]

The proposed route from Chimney Point to the Connecticut River was about seventy miles in a straight line. Stark measured the actual distance, with hills and valleys and curves, as seventy-seven miles. Some rangers had traversed the route before, but no trail existed in 1759. The way roughly followed two rivers—Otter Creek and its tributaries on the west slope of the mountains, and Black River on the east slope. The road would cross the gently rolling Champlain Valley, move up into foothills, and then pass over the spruce bogs of the high Green Mountains and descend deep "gulfs" or valleys to the Connecticut River at Wentworth's Ferry. The log stockade of the fort called Number Four stood across the river in New Hampshire.[62]

Stark and his force of two hundred rangers left on the route-marking expedition on August 8. Rogers recorded their return on September 9. "Capt Stark returned with his Party from No 4; fourteen of his men deserted, six left sick behind. He said he had made the Road & that there were no mountains or swamps to pass & as he came back it measured 77 miles. It may be much shortened."[63]

No one kept a record of the travails of this first mission over the mountains. The high number of desertions suggests that it was tough going. The rangers were in rugged, remote country, with no supply line for food and no chance to rest until the job was done.

Robert Webster, a Connecticut enlisted man, kept a journal of the second expedition to widen and improve the trail. His entries demonstrate just how tough the mission was. On October 26, Webster wrote, "Major Stark set out from Crown Point to go to Number 4 and to clear a road twenty feet wide. He had 250 men." Webster was the only source that put Stark in overall command of this second expedition. Major Zadoc Hawke actually led the second trip, with Stark as second-in-command. Nevertheless, Robert Webster's journal told the gist of the story.[64]

They built nine bridges during the first week out from Crown Point. They slaughtered cattle as needed, ate beef, and enjoyed "good health and high spirits." Bitter cold followed a snowfall on October 31, and by November 2 it was too cold to "stand about the road." Then the weather changed to rain and hail. By the second week they ran low on food. "Our bread is just about gone," Webster reported. "We haven't had but one biscuit a day four or five days."[65]

Thereafter, Webster's hunger pangs dominated his thoughts. They had reached the higher mountains and worked beside icy, boulder-strewn streams. The thick spruce forest kept the men in shade most of the day. The officers had to reduce the ration to one biscuit for four men. On November 11, Webster wrote:

> We are at work but we haven't any bread nor salt nor haven't had this for eight days. We live on fresh beef and water and some Chakabra leaf broth. The day before yesterday four of our party went from us sick to go to Number Four. … Our men are very weak living in this form. I am not well.[66]

Two days later they had no food at all. The men could no longer work. "It hasn't pleased the Major to give us any meat yesterday nor today," Webster noted, "as yet we lay still at present." Food was found by noon, however, and the men went back to work.[67]

The road builders reached the Connecticut River on November 16, where they ate a welcome meal of beef and turnips. Robert Wood reported no desertions during their three weeks on the trail. The rangers did arrest nineteen "Boston men" who had run away from the army, however. The road would require further work the following year, but Stark's men received their discharges.[68]

❧ ☙

In 1759 John Stark missed two of the most significant events of the campaign—Wolfe's forces took the fortress at Quebec, and Robert Rogers attacked St. Francis. It may have been the road assignment that prevented John Stark from joining Rogers, or it may have been his own scruples about attacking a people who had treated him well.

The rangers camped beside Lake Champlain at Crown Point when Stark's first road-building party returned in September. They knew another mission awaited, but Rogers kept them in the dark about their destination. Robert Webster noted that a rumor was passing around that they would raid a place called "Suagothel."[69] No ranger had ever heard of it. It may have been a name made up to preserve secrecy, or it may have been Webster's misspelling of some other location. Either way, the expedition began in an atmosphere of secrecy.[70]

John Stark was one ranger who had been to St. Francis, who knew the way there and back by two different routes, and who knew the layout of the town. Rogers would have found Stark's presence useful on the mission, and he probably sought him out before it began. But Stark remained at Crown Point, commanding the rangers there, when Rogers left for Canada.

If he and Rogers had talked about it, Stark would have learned that one goal of the rangers' mission was revenge. Amherst's orders to Rogers were explicit:

> Remember the barbarities that have been committed by the ene-
> my's Indian scoundrels on every occasion, where they have had an
> opportunity of shewing their infamous cruelties on the King's sub-
> jects, which they have done without mercy. Take your revenge, but

don't forget that tho' these villains have dastardly and promiscuously murdered the women and children of all ages, it is my order that no women or children are killed or hurt.[71]

Stark heard the tales from the survivors later: the epic advance through the swamps; the early morning attack and slaughter of the Indians, including women and children; the retreat through the wilderness; death from warriors and starvation; cannibalism; and finally, Rogers's brave effort to save the surviving rangers. Robert Rogers and his rangers are remembered for this famous mission, but it was not part of John Stark's war.

The army of General Wolfe fought the army of General Montcalm on the Plains of Abraham outside Quebec City on September 13, the same day Rogers left Crown Point for St. Francis. The British and Americans took Quebec, and it was the beginning of the end of French dominion in Canada. Word of the victory reached Crown Point on October 16. Robert Webster wrote, "We had some flying news that Quebec was taken and General Wolfe was dead and Montcalm."[72] The battle claimed the lives of both generals.

Quebec fell after a daring attack up the steep heights west of the city, led by Lord Howe's brother, Colonel William Howe. Before the final battle, Wolfe had tried to lure the French from the citadel. His troops had committed cruelties to bait their enemies, including killing and scalping a priest and several members of his congregation at St. Anne, Quebec. Wolfe had written an order that prohibited scalping, "except when the enemy are Indians, or Canads. dressed like Indians."[73]

The news from Quebec released Amherst from any obligation to proceed to Canada. He concentrated on rebuilding the two forts on Lake Champlain. It would be almost another year before Governor Vaudreuil of Canada would sign the articles of surrender of New France, but for most of Amherst's army the war was over.[74]

Matthew Patten noted that there "was a thanksgiving in the Province" at the news of the capture of Quebec.[75] Captain John Stark was ready to retire.

His grandson wrote that the conquest of Canada, "together with the jealousies of the British officers induced him to quit the service." Amherst learned of Stark's retirement and wrote to him to promise he would retain his rank if he wished to reenter the service. It was a promise Amherst didn't keep.[76]

Stark stayed at Crown Point, where he signed the ranger receipts in November 1759.[77] But, by Christmas, he was home in New Hampshire. Early in January, Matthew Patten borrowed £45 from Stark, to be repaid at 6 percent interest. The soldier was a civilian again.[78]

11

DOMESTIC INTERLUDE

Capt. Starks Mill

On December 3, 1759, the cries of a newborn echoed through the Caleb Page home in Starkstown, New Hampshire. Molly Stark's baby Caleb was named for his grandfather and for his Uncle Caleb, killed in the war. His grandfather so loved the child that he couldn't bear to part with him.[1]

The boy's father, John Stark, aged thirty-two, had been at war most of the past five years. He had earned the right to rest a bit, eat well, sleep warm and take stock of his life. Up in the rolling hills, John, Molly and the child settled in at her father's house. By the standards of the time, John was old to be a first-time father. He had not led a peaceful domestic life for nearly a decade, and he had not had a chance to become accustomed to married life. He had also missed years of the kind of investment Americans needed in order to prosper in 1760—the investment of labor.

In colonial New England virtually all young men toiled long hours, six days a week, building something. Even men educated for a profession worked with their hands as well. Matthew Patten, a surveyor, also farmed and labored as a carpenter. During the years that Stark fought the French and the Indians, Patten cleared his fields, built his walls and barns, bred his livestock, and increased his equity in life. Even John Adams, a lawyer, worked on his family farm in Braintree, Massachusetts.[2]

John Stark's portion in life was his inheritance from his father, and it was no small thing. But he had left undone much of the hard work of creating the farm and sawmills that would provide for his family. Now he needed to make up for lost time. Archibald Stark had taught his son a trade that would serve him well; John knew how to run a sawmill, and he knew how to build one as well. In October 1760 the proprietors of Starkstown proposed that he build a sawmill there on the understanding that, if it was completed in one year, he would be granted one hundred acres of land and the privilege of sawing lumber "by the halves"—that is, he could retain half the lumber he sawed in payment for his services.[3]

Stark went to work along a stream southwest of the Page home. Constructing a sawmill was complex and heavy work. If he was his own millwright, he had to solve the inherent engineering and hydraulic problems. First, he built a dam to create the millpond, then a sluiceway for a millrace or penstock, and then, after setting the mill on a solid stone foundation, hung the waterwheel to power his saw. The work was completed in a year, and John Stark entered upon his own lumber business.

As tobacco was to Virginia, and cod to Massachusetts, lumber was the mainstay of the New Hampshire economy in the eighteenth century. It was much in demand for local use, but it was also the principal export of the province. The Royal government viewed New Hampshire forests as repositories of naval stores. Tall pines for masts and spars, and timber for ship-building, were floated down the rivers to port towns.[4]

New Hampshire had a population of nearly 50,000 people by 1760, most of them living near the coast. Portsmouth was the principal city of the province and the financial center. Its harbor fostered shipbuilding and rope walks to rig the ships. The Royal Governor, Benning Wentworth, lived in Portsmouth. His wife died in 1760, and he promptly married his housekeeper, a woman young enough to be his granddaughter. He had served as governor since the birth of the province in 1741.

Wentworth and his family made a part of their substantial fortune importing wine and exporting timber. Governing also gave them the opportunity to make money from such public ventures as selling land they didn't own—land across the Connecticut River in the Hampshire Grants. The governor sold townships in what is now Vermont. He retained 500 acres in each township for future speculation. The first parcel he sold he named for himself—Bennington.

Lumbermen prospered in New Hampshire. Some farmers cut nearby woodlots as an adjunct to their agricultural work. Other men ventured deep into the forests north of the settlements seeking the big pines. Gangs of men cut and bucked the timber into log lengths, and oxen hauled the logs to water. One ship's mast was more than two feet in diameter and required thirty-two oxen to draw it out of the swamp. A witness remembered, "'Twas a notable sight."[5]

Men who searched the woods for suitable trees for rigging ships were said to have "gone a-masting." Such pines were so valuable to the British navy that their felling was illegal except on private land. The trees also had great value as sawn lumber, so a considerable trade in illegally cut pine trees flourished. Wentworth appointed a surveyor-general to cruise the forests and mark mast trees with the King's "broad arrow"—three cuts of an axe through the bark that resembled an arrowhead. These pine tree laws had been on the books for years, but they grew increasingly unpopular.[6]

At some point in 1760 or 1761, John and Molly Stark moved to his mother's house in Derryfield. Eleanor Stark may have needed care, or the sawmill and farm may have required attention. The reason for the move is unknown. John acquired his siblings' interests in the land at Derryfield.[7]

When his parents moved from Starkstown, young Caleb Stark remained with his grandfather. He would remain there for fifteen years, seeing his mother and father only occasionally. If Molly missed the child, she took some consolation when their second son, Archibald, was born in May 1761.[8]

Nature treated the province roughly during the decade after the war. Drought killed and stunted the crops for several years.[9] On May 15, 1761, fifteen inches of snow fell at Starkstown.[10] The following summer huge fires burned north of Derryfield. One fire burned for a month, blackening the forest all the way from New Hampshire to the coast of Maine.[11]

Indians were no longer a threat in the province, but the profusion of domestic animals actually increased the danger from wild animals. Towns established bounties on predators like wolves and bear.[12] In 1761, Matthew Patten spent an entire day tracking a bear. Two years later he lost a lamb to a bear.[13]

Nature also provided. The falls at Amoskeag still offered extraordinary fishing. Patten recorded his daily catch each spring, and he also noted when other men had good luck. The fishing began on May 25 in 1761, and Matthew stayed at it for a solid week. He caught "72 shad and a small salmon." A friend caught two salmon that weighed twenty-five pounds. One day, Patten landed ten large salmon "and a Storgion that weighed 94 [pounds] and was 6 feet & 2 inches in length and I had him."[14]

The war finally came to an official end on February 10, 1763, with the signing of the Treaty of Paris. Folks in New Hampshire were struggling with snow three and a half feet deep on the level. Word of the peace treaty didn't reach them for months. They finally held a "Thanksgiving" celebration on August 11.[15]

People as busy as Patten and Stark probably had little time to contemplate the meaning of the victory. They knew that it brought the end of the border wars with the St. Francis Indians, and they hoped that the lands west and north of their towns would be open for speculation and settlement. The unwelcome consequences were not so obvious. All the territory east of the Mississippi River, including Canada, was now ruled by the British, except for part of Louisiana. Along with a huge war debt, Britain now bore the additional expense of governing and maintaining the peace in a vastly larger territory. Ministers and members of Parliament pondered ways to finance the expenditures.

Many Americans prospered as trade and manufacturing grew. High-quality iron ore and endless forests for charcoal gave the colonists an advantage in iron production. England had no comparable ore beds or forests. The Iron Act passed by Parliament in 1750 had been an effort to reduce American competition in the industry, but the colonists still produced more and better iron and steel than the mother country.[16]

American-built ships sailed the oceans. With plenty of oak and pine, and with deep harbors, Americans outpaced the world in shipbuilding. New England fishermen dominated the fisheries along the Atlantic coast.[17]

The Royal government had tried to control American trade for decades. The Navigation Acts dated from the seventeenth century. Certain commodities produced in America could only be sold in England. It was a long list; sugar, cotton, tobacco, rice, molasses, rum, iron, coffee, hides, raw silk and lumber were among many other articles restrained by successive acts of Parliament. American merchants, planters and sailors had become adept at avoiding the regulations. Some even traded with France during the war. Transporting goods in violation of British law—smuggling—persisted.[18]

In 1764, Parliament passed a law with a long title, which read in part: an Act "… for more effectively preventing the clandestine conveyance of goods to and from the said Colonies and Plantations and improving and securing the trade between Great Britain and the same." The Crown sent its officer, Commissioner of Customs Henry Hulton, to Boston to enforce the act. Henry's sister, Anne Hulton, came to Boston with him. She was a prolific writer of letters to England in which she expressed her contempt for America and its smugglers and scoundrels. Her brother's mission, Anne wrote, "after combating with ye knaves in G [Germany], to find 'em out in America and ye West Indies."[19]

Henry Hulton was but one of many British agents charged with enforcing increasingly complex and onerous regulations in the colonies. The Crown's agents lived in a hostile environment. Anne Hulton's accounts of their experiences in Boston reflected the growth of tensions between the colonists and England. She recorded it all.

In 1763, King George III established the "Proclamation Line," which decreed that settlement west of the existing American colonies would not proceed beyond the headwaters of rivers flowing into the Atlantic Ocean. The British hoped that the limitation would prevent land speculators from intruding on Indian lands, but tensions remained on the frontiers. Pontiac's Rebellion broke out that very year in the Great Lakes and Ohio Valley regions, and the Crown realized that a military presence would be required to keep the peace.[20]

The American urge to move west grew after the end of the French and Indian War. The Crown granted some veterans parcels of land on the frontier. John Stark's brother-in-law, Lieutenant Hugh Stirling, moved his family to

a grant near the White Mountains at "Stirling's Location." The Stark brothers also received grants in northern New Hampshire and Maine. Perhaps as
settlement of his father's estate, John conveyed his land near Fryeburg, Maine,
to his sister, Isabel Stirling.[21]

Elsewhere, American frontiersmen ignored the Proclamation Line and
moved into the western portions of Virginia and Pennsylvania, even into the
Iroquois country of New York. White encroachment on their lands angered
the tribes; the Revolution would bring that anger to full boil.

The Stark family continued to grow. John, Jr., was born in 1763, and Eleanor
in 1765. Three generations lived in the small cape home with the family matri-
arch, Eleanor Stark. By 1765, John's sawmill on the Merrimack was in operation. It stood on the east bank at the head of the falls. During the previous
winter Matthew Patten had noted in his diary that he worked at "Amoskieg
Falls at a place out against Capt. Stark's Mill."[22] The broad and powerful Merrimack River provided a more dependable source of power than the tributary
stream that had powered his father's mill. Eighteenth-century sawyers relied
on the high water from spring snowmelt for most of their sawing. Loggers
cut timber through the winter and then floated the logs downriver after the
ice left the streams. John Stark's mill was, thus, advantageously sited for both
waterpower and lumber supply.

No description of his sawmill has survived. The typical New England
mill used a saw blade that travelled up and down in a timber frame, perpendicular to the log; it cut only on the down stroke. Water from a stream powered the mill, running through a penstock—an artificial channel that carried
the water to the wheel that powered everything. The sawyer worked beside
the carriage that held the log and impelled it toward the saw. The power
"turned on" by opening the sluice gate, and "turned off" by closing it. When
the stream froze the mill could not function. Men moved the logs onto the
carriage by muscle power. The water-driven works moved slowly. It was said
that "a man could sit on the log and eat his lunch while a single board was
cut off." The slow pace led to long days at work. Sawmills were noisy places

with heavy and unprotected moving parts—dangerous for grown men and no place for children.[23]

Compared with the crisp, dry air of the hill country, the riverbank could be a cold, raw place, subject to fogs and mists. The mill itself, while it may have been roofed, was probably only a shed that provided no shelter from the wind and spray. After years of campaigning in the bitter cold of the northern frontier, Stark now worked most days beside the river. He was contracting a debt to his health that would have to be paid.

The new year of 1765 began with two feet of snow on the ground. A heavy snowstorm on the 18th of January "drifted violently," according to Matthew Patten.[24]

That May, Patten caught forty shad one day, but had ten of them stolen. Theft became a common complaint in his diary. One day his lunch was stolen while he mowed hay. Another time a thief took his bridle and stirrups from his horse at a fair.[25] The thievery may have been a result of hard times after the war. A depression settled over America; it lasted several years and coincided with efforts by the British to tax the colonies. The two circumstances made a volatile mix.

Matthew Patten's diary was written in several successive volumes, each of which he faithfully headed, "A Day Book Continued From [date of previous entry]". But, on November 1, 1765, he broke this pattern and headed the new book, "NOVEMBER STAMP ACT".[26] It was one of the few times Matthew acknowledged events beyond his home neighborhood.

12

REBELLION BEGINS
That Nest of Locusts

The British government faced a fiscal crisis both from its war debt and a renewed need to keep troops in America. Pontiac's Rebellion began with an Indian attack at Detroit in May 1763. General Amherst still commanded some 6,000 men, but they were spread from Canada to Georgia. General Thomas Gage replaced Amherst. Great Britain faced the possibility of keeping a standing army in a land unfriendly to such a force.[1] How would the Crown pay for it? The government's view, by 1765, was that a portion of the expense should be borne by the colonists on whose behalf, the argument went, the expenditures were made. There had been a stamp tax in England for seventy years; why not impose such a tax on the Americans?[2]

Americans anticipated that Parliament would pass such a bill. The critical issue for the colonists was their lack of representation in the body that passed the Stamp Act. No tax passed in the British Parliament would be acceptable. Americans regarded themselves, for the most part, as entitled to all the rights of Englishmen. To be taxed without representation would violate those rights.[3]

The British Parliament passed the Stamp Act in the spring of 1765, with enforcement to begin on November 1—the cause of Matthew Patten's disgusted diary entry that day. Under the law every document, newspaper, advertisement, deed, bond—any legal, commercial or financial writing whatsoever—required revenue stamps to be affixed. The Crown appointed officers to distribute the stamps and collect the revenue. These agents quickly became the most unpopular men in the colonies.[4]

To enforce the act, Parliament enlarged the jurisdiction of the vice-admiralty courts wherein those accused of violations would be tried by a judge, and not by a jury of their fellow citizens. This point particularly galled citizens of New Hampshire, where men accused of cutting the King's pines were also tried in vice-admiralty courts. From the outset the Stamp Act outraged the colonists.[5]

Respected Americans took issue with the act. John Adams published an anonymous essay, "A Dissertation on the Canon and the Feudal Law," in which he wrote: "... Let it be known that British liberties are not the grants of princes or parliaments ... that many of our rights are inherent and essential, agreed on as maxims and established as preliminaries even before Parliament existed."[6]

Adams went on to draft the "Braintree Instructions"—a statement on behalf of his hometown that was adopted by many other Massachusetts towns. He stressed in the document that there must be "no taxation without representation" and that there must be trial by jury. Adams believed that the revolutionary spirit was born with the Stamp Act.[7]

George Washington wrote to his London business associates in September 1765. After complaining about the low price paid for his tobacco crop, he launched into a criticism of the Stamp Act, which he called a "direful attack" upon American liberties and "an ill-judg'd measure." He suggested that an American boycott of British goods might cause parliament to rethink the Act: "... many of the Luxuries which we have heretofore lavished our Substance to Great Britain for can well be dispensed with whilst the Necessaries of Life are to be procured ... within ourselves."[8]

Benjamin Franklin lived in London during the winter of 1766 and enjoyed a measure of respect from ministers and politicians. In February he permitted members of Parliament to question him as they deliberated whether to repeal the Stamp Act. They asked him why his regard for Parliament had diminished, and he answered, "... the new and heavy tax by stamps; [and] taking away, at the same time, trials by juries." One member threatened to use the army to enforce the act. Franklin responded: "Suppose a military force sent into America, they will find nobody in arms; what are they to do? They cannot force a man to take stamps who chuses to do without them. They will not find a rebellion; they may indeed make one."[9]

Rather than heed Franklin, Parliament made a show of responding to events in America that Britons regarded as outrageous. Reasoned opposition to the act might have succeeded, but mob action would draw a violent response. In Boston, stamp distributor Andrew Oliver was hanged in effigy. The mob broke into his home, smashed his windows, and then celebrated by burning his effigy.[10]

Similar acts by "Sons of Liberty" took place in Rhode Island and Connecticut. Gangs of men intimidated the stamp distributors in Pennsylvania, Maryland, Georgia and Virginia.[11] Not to be outdone, a mob in Portsmouth, New Hampshire, demonstrated against the stamp master, George Meserve, Esq., even though he had already resigned his commission. They burned his effigy alongside that of the devil. Meserve was compelled to demonstrate his resignation by making a public renunciation of the office.[12]

Riots and violence followed in many cities. In New York, rioters burned Governor Cadwallader Colden's coach and ransacked Mayor James's home. "Sons of Liberty" formed committees of correspondence to alert their brethren in faraway colonies.[13]

In London, William Pitt, the "Great Commoner," addressed Parliament and gave his counsel "that the Stamp Act be repealed absolutely, totally and immediately." Pitt knew of the reasoned constitutional arguments coming from the colonies. Members of Parliament listened to his advice, but they heard from their constituents in the business and financial communities as well. The boycotts and violence hurt these interests. The result was a division of opinion that the politicians couldn't bridge. They repealed the Stamp Act in 1766, but at the same time passed the Declaratory Act affirming their right "to legislate in all cases whatsoever."[14] What they gave with their right hand, they took away with their left.

The conflict subsided for a time. The immediacy of the Stamp Act was gone, but a vague threat of future impositions remained. Americans had taken baby steps in the direction of revolution. John Dickinson fanned the flames in his *Letters from a farmer in Pennsylvania: to the inhabitants of the British Colonies*. Dickinson was a Philadelphia lawyer as well as a farmer. He argued that the Stamp Act was a warning of worse tyranny to come: "we are taxed without our own consent, expressed by ourselves or our representatives. We are therefore—SLAVES."[15]

During the summer of 1767, the Starks endured a family tragedy. Three young children lived in their home—Archibald, John, Jr., and Eleanor, the youngest at just two years old (Caleb still lived with his grandfather). On June 20, Molly gave birth to another daughter. They named the baby, Eleanor Stark, Jr. Two months later, the baby's older sister Eleanor died.[16]

Giving two daughters the same name while both yet lived suggests that John and Molly knew that the elder girl would not survive for long. The baby may have been a consolation to her family before and after her sister's death. It remains unknown what illness or affliction carried off the toddler, but it would appear that her death was neither sudden nor unexpected.

John Stark's mother, also an Eleanor, died the next year.[17] Perhaps the old family home became unbearable to the grieving Molly, or the house may simply have been too small for the growing family, but John Stark built a new home a half mile north of his parents' house. He sited the house near the center of his large acreage and closer to the river. It was a two-story timber frame house with two chimneys. He built barns and sheds attached to the house on the windward side in the New England fashion, creating a sheltered dooryard on the east side. His farm of several hundred acres surrounded the home; it was not baronial in comparison to the Virginia plantations of Washington and Jefferson, but it was substantial by New Hampshire standards. Stark ranked fourth-highest among the fifty-three freeholders on the Derryfield tax list of 1766.[18]

Relations between the American colonies and the British government gradually and inexorably worsened. The repeal of the Stamp Act sent a message that united action by Americans might alter decisions in London. The question was whether that action was to be political and economic, or whether it was to be violent.

The war debt still pinched Britain. Chancellor of the Exchequer Charles Townshend proposed a new method of obtaining revenue from the colonies. The Townshend Act, passed in June 1767, established duties to be paid on imports into the colonies from Britain of paint, tea, glass and paper. In addition, colonial assemblies would no longer have the power of the purse over royal judges and governors. Instead, they would be paid by funds raised by the act. A companion bill gave jurisdiction over the act to the vice-admiralty courts, where judges without juries would decide the cases.[19]

New England reacted angrily to news of the Townshend Act. The Boston Town Meeting of freeholders expressed its common will to "rid the province of the need for importing these articles 'by the disuse of foreign superfluities.'" They began a "nonconsumption" movement—a boycott of the taxed goods.[20] Mobs in Boston intimidated the customs commissioners. General Thomas Gage, the same officer who had disparaged the rangers during the French and Indian War, sent British troops to Boston. Men who fomented the rebellious acts were threatened with trial in London.[21]

In Virginia, George Washington pondered the British act and the American response. He even considered a military response but, in 1769, he still favored the boycotts established in New England over force of arms. In April he wrote to George Mason, a member of the Virginia House of Burgesses:

> That no man sho'd scruple or hesitate a moment to use a–ms [arms] in defence of so valuable a blessing [American liberty], on which all the good and evil of life depends is clearly my opinion; Yet a-ms I wou'd beg leave to add, should be the last resource the denier [*dernier*, Fr., "last"] resort. Addresses to the Throne and remonstrances to parliament, we have already, it is said, proved the inefficacy of; how far then this attention to our rights & privileges is to be awakened or alarmed by starving their Trade and manufactures, remains to be tryed.[22]

Washington was willing to broach the subject of force even if he could not quite bring himself to spell out the word "arms." People already knew the economic effectiveness of the boycotts. Newspapers in England and America published an anonymous letter that revealed that the total revenues from the Townshend Act amounted to about £3,500, while the business loss to English merchants exceeded £7 million. People suspected that the letter had been written by Benjamin Franklin.[23]

Boston remained the hub of resistance in the colonies. The presence of British troops, placed there to control the populace, only increased the tension. Finally, on March 5, 1770, a group of men heaped abuse on a British sentry standing watch before the Customs House. A crowd gathered. A squad of redcoats marched up to support the sentry. The mob threw stones and snowballs. A British soldier fired his musket, and others followed suit. Five men fell dead. Boston firebrands labeled the event the "Boston Massacre."[24] Ironically, in April Americans learned that all the Townshend duties except the duty on tea had been repealed on that same day, March 5.[25]

The Starks welcomed another daughter, Sarah, in 1769. Caleb was now a boy of nine, still living with his grandfather in Starkstown, which had been rechartered and renamed Dunbarton.[26]

Matthew Patten continued to document daily life near Amoskeag. He made numerous visits to Captain John Stark, sometimes rowing across the Merrimack to pay interest on his debt or to do surveying jobs for the lumberman. He left a record of the weather conditions that New Hampshire folk dealt with between the wars. The winter of 1767–1768 seemed especially harsh, with twenty inches of drifting snow in November and high winds and bitter cold on New Years Day. By January 30, Matthew had to haul firewood through snow three feet deep, "with deep wadeing and fatigue." On September 5, 1768, there came a "great frost it kill'd the Corn potatoes and pumpkins &tc."[27]

John Stark became a justice of the peace.[28] Thereafter, he and Patten teamed up to mediate disputes in the towns of the Merrimack Valley. They spent years trying to resolve a conflict between men named Russ and McNeal. On May 30, 1770, Patten wrote, "I went to Russes along with Capt Stark and Lieut McNeal about their Controversie and went home with Stark and lodged there." Despite the length of the dispute, Patten never reported the outcome of their mediation efforts.[29]

Occasionally local events became big local news. On June 20, 1770, men gathered in a community effort to raise a bridge over the Piscataquog River near its mouth at the Merrimack. Something went wrong. "[T]here was six men throwed off the bridge and 3 of them very much hurt." Two days later, Patten wrote, "I made a Coffin for the Corps of Joseph Moor who died last night he lived after he got his hurt about 30 hours."[30]

The Boston trial of the British soldiers who had fired on the mob during the Boston Massacre began in October 1770. John Adams defended the redcoats. He knew his decision to take the case would draw criticism. Nevertheless, he provided his clients a strong, principled defense. A Boston jury acquitted all but two of the soldiers, evidently agreeing with Adams's summation: "Soldiers quartered in a populous town will always occasion two mobs where they prevent one. They are wretched conservators of the peace." Adams hinged his defense of the soldiers on the perceived mistakes of the British government. The two soldiers who were convicted of manslaughter suffered branding on their thumbs; the other six defendants went free.[31]

Mobs continued to roam Boston streets. In March 1771 a gang of "ruffians" tried to break into the home of Henry Hulton, commissioner of customs. His sister Anne described the experience: "I could imagine nothing less than that the house was beating down, after many violent blows on the Walls and windows, most hideous Shouting, dreadful imprecations & threats ensued." A stone tossed through a window narrowly missed Mrs. Hulton. Thereafter, the Hultons lived in fear of the mobs.[32]

New Hampshire lumbermen rebelled in 1772. Benning Wentworth's nephew, John Wentworth, had succeeded his uncle as governor. He also served as surveyor general, charged with the enforcement of the pine tree laws. His agents scoured the sawmills seeking, and often finding, illegally cut trees. Those who possessed the logs faced trial in Portsmouth.[33]

Most offenders settled with the surveyor general by paying a small fine. Angry loggers from the town of Weare defied the law; Weare was the town just west of the Page home in Dunbarton. Sheriff Benjamin Whiting of

Hillsborough County rode to Weare to arrest violators at Clement's mill. That night, at the local inn, black-faced men burst into the sheriff's bed-chamber, beat him and his deputy, and rode them both out of town.[34]

John Goffe took a militia unit to Weare to restore order and enforce the law. Justice of the Peace Matthew Patten followed:

> I set out to go to Hailstown on acct of a Number of men that Resqued a prisoner from the High sheriff on last Wednesday morn-ing and Abuseing the Sheriff and cutting one of his horses Ears off the Militia was Raised and sent up   they went up yesterday and I went within a few Rods of John Smiths in Goffstown and I met the high Sheriff & a number comeing home and I turned about and came home.[35]

Other New Hampshire lumbermen defied the pine tree law, but John Stark's name does not appear among them. Perhaps, like Goffe and Patten, his public position as justice compelled him to abide by a law he probably detested. Patten and Goffe did their duty, but in years to come they became confirmed rebels.

⁂

In May 1773, Parliament passed the Tea Act, intended to help the struggling East India Company. The act gave the company a monopoly on the impor-tation of tea in America, allowing it to sell tea in the provinces at a price lower than that obtained by smugglers. The East India Company established warehouses for tea in the major ports. Colonial merchants became alarmed. On December 28, Major General Haldiman of the British army in Boston (the same Haldiman that commanded at Fort Edward during the French and Indian War) wrote to the Earl of Dartmouth:

> I conceive that the fear of an Introduction of a Monopoly in this Country has induced the mercantile part of the Inhabitants to be very industrious in opposing this Step of the Honorable East India

Company under the Sanction of Parliament, and added Strength to a Spirit of Independence already too prevalent.[36]

Though merchants opposed the act, the core reason for colonial anger was a matter of principle; Parliament had no right, the Whigs reasoned, to legislate any monopoly upon the Americans and, most of all, no right to collect a tax on the tea. It was the same objection triggered years before by the Stamp Act. Once any tax legislated by Parliament was accepted by the colonists, they reasoned that a precedent would be set for further taxes. The committees of correspondence drummed up opposition throughout the colonies.[37]

The East India Company quickly loaded ships with chests of tea bound for Charleston, Philadelphia, New York and Boston. Company agents faced public hostility in New York and Philadelphia, and they declined to bring the tea ashore. They locked the tea in warehouses in Charleston. But, in Boston, Governor Hutchinson was determined to deliver the cargoes to distributors despite the opposition of Bostonians.[38]

On December 16, 1773, dozens of "Indians" marched through the narrow streets of Boston. When they arrived at the public wharf, they confronted English ship captains. One participant, George Hewes, remembered the scene:

It was now evening, and I immediately dressed myself in the costume of an Indian, equipped with a small hatchet, which I and my associates denominated the tomahawk, with which, and a club, after having painted my face and hands with coal dust in the shop of a blacksmith, I repaired to Griffin's wharf, where the ships lay that contained the tea. When I first appeared in the street after being thus disguised, I fell in with many who were dressed, equipped and painted as I was, and who fell in with me and marched in order to the place of our destination.[39]

The "Mohawks," as some called them, accomplished their mission without violence and with superb organization. Ship captains delivered the keys to the holds, and Americans removed the chests and chopped them open. They cast a small fortune in tea leaves into the harbor. Yankees in rowboats beat the floating tea with their oars to insure its ruin. No one was hurt.[40]

News of the "Boston Tea Party" reached England with the next packet boat. Loyalists wrote to friends and family, each narrating version of events without sympathy for American interests. Anne Hulton wrote to Mrs. Adam Lightbody of Liverpool: "… but really the times are too bad & the Scenes too shocking for me to describe them." Then, she described them: the commissioners of the customs, she reported, "were obliged to seek refuge at the castle." She had heard that a man was tarred and feathered by a mob; "They say his flesh comes off his back in stakes."[41]

Scores of such letters must have reached England from America, and the reports no doubt were passed on to members of Parliament. Aroused by such pressure, the members debated how to deal with the colonists.

American Whigs now began to call themselves "patriots." They held a much more favorable view of the tea party. Men who would not approve of mob action under normal circumstances hailed the "Mohawks" of Boston. The day after the event, John Adams noted in his diary, "There is a Dignity, a Majesty, a Sublimity in this last Effort of the Patriots, that I greatly admire." It was, he thought, "an Epocha in History"—a turning point—and wondered what retaliation they could expect from the British:

> What Measures will the Ministry take, in Consequence of this?—Will they resent it?—Will they punish us? How? By quartering Troops upon us?—by annulling our Charter?—By restraining our Trade? By sacrifice of Individuals, or how.[42]

In fact, men in London debated several measures anticipated by Adams, including closure of the port of Boston and annulment of the Charter of Massachusetts. Parliament voted to pass both measures in the spring of 1774. Prime Minister Lord North advocated stern measures for "blocking up the use of the harbours."[43] In debate a Mr. Van of the House of Commons vented, "I am of opinion that you will never meet with that proper obedience to the laws of this country until you have destroyed that nest of locusts"—the Boston radicals.[44]

Friends of America in England tried to dampen the fury of their compatriots. Edmund Burke understood the American opposition to the act. He predicted that military force would be necessary to carry out such policies, but he doubted that force would succeed. As for America, Burke predicted, "a great many red coats will never be able to govern it."[45]

In the space of a few weeks, Parliament passed, and King George approved, a palette of legislation intended to punish Boston, tighten control of all the colonies, and send a message of determined strength. The Boston Port Bill, the Massachusetts Government Act, the Administration of Justice Act and the Quartering Act, taken together, became known in the colonies as the "Intolerable Acts."[46] Even George Washington, who disapproved of the Boston Tea Party, bristled at these laws. He wrote, "the Ministry may rely on it … that the cause of Boston the despotick Measures in respect to it I mean now is and ever will be considered as the cause of America." If conservative men like Washington felt that way, achieving a "proper obedience" to British law would be difficult.[47]

King George ordered the British army to be prepared for intervention in America. During the summer of 1774, military exercises in England demonstrated that such preparation was underway. Sergeant Roger Lamb noted in his memoirs that General Sir William Howe conducted light infantry maneuvers at Salisbury, England, viewed by "His Majesty himself." Lamb believed the maneuvers were "well adapted for the service in America."[48]

That spring, Matthew Patten and John Stark met to settle a matter between John Goffe and Captain Karr. Unable to resolve the case, they agreed to meet again at McGregore's tavern on May 2. Patten and Stark occasionally repaired to McGregore's to drink a mug of toddy. The proprietor also sold them rum by the gallon. When they gathered on May 2, Captain Karr declined to agree to the decision of the justices, and they postponed their deliberations once again. The combination of arbitrations and tippling seemed to prolong their cases.[49]

The citizens of Bedford and Amherst had elected John Goffe to represent them in the Provincial Assembly. During the spring of 1774, the assembly considered matters that Governor John Wentworth deemed illegal, like the appointment of a committee of correspondence. When the assembly voted to concur "in all salutary measures that may be adopted by them [other colonies]", Wentworth prorogued the assembly (adjourned their meetings without date). The representatives then met illegally to choose Nathaniel Folsom and John Sullivan as delegates to the new Continental Congress to be held in September.[50]

In recognition of the importance of such an event as a Continental Congress, the New Hampshire Committee of Correspondence called for a fast throughout the province on July 14 to coincide with a similar observance in Massachusetts. Mr. Houston, Pastor of the Meeting in Bedford, refused to observe the occasion. A disgusted Matthew Patten rowed across the river to Derryfield that Sunday to worship in another preacher's congregation.[51]

A consignment of East India Company tea reached Portsmouth in September. Governor Wentworth prudently ordered the offensive cargo shipped on to Halifax, Nova Scotia. There would be no tea party in New Hampshire.[52]

On September 19, 1774, Matthew Patten began a strange narrative in his diary. He had been to a town meeting that evening where he learned that several men intended to "visit" a Mr. Atherton in Amherst. These men, he wrote, "Insisted on my going with them and they told me that I must and Should go and that if I did not they would Viset me on which I said I would go." The next day, Patten reported:

> I went to Amherst and about 300 men assembled and chose a Committee who went to Mr. Atherton and he came to the people at the Court house and he Signed a Declaration and Read it to the people who accepted it   he Invited them to go to Mr. Hildreth's and Drink what they pleased   the people Dispersed about Midnight without Doing any Out Ragious act   I stayed till morning.[53]

Mr. Atherton harbored Loyalist sentiments, and the "visets" contemplated by the mob threatened him, and Patten, with some punishment, perhaps tar and feathers. The "Declaration" was a form of loyalty oath to the patriot cause. The dark side of the American Revolution had come to the Merrimack

Valley—neighbor against neighbor, brother against brother. Mr. Atherton was but one of thousands of Americans treated to such "visets."

That Matthew Patten's fellow townsmen would threaten him to induce his cooperation (and perhaps lend a tinge of legality to their actions) illustrated how far civil society had broken down by 1774. Patten was a respected public official whose judgment was sought by men all over the region, but he was not immune from mob action.

Things boiled over in December. Paul Revere, of Boston, warned New Hampshire patriots that British troops were on their way to Portsmouth to secure the militia armaments there at Fort William and Mary. John Sullivan, a lawyer from Durham, New Hampshire, and John Langdon, a wealthy Portsmouth merchant, led a raiding party to the fort and removed the cannon, small arms and most of the powder kept there.[54]

Governor Wentworth accused Sullivan and Langdon of treason and rebellion, and he threatened to arrest them.[55] The Provincial Congress at Exeter paid lip service to the need to "support the laws," but they proceeded to appoint both Sullivan and Langdon as delegates to the Continental Congress of 1775.[56]

⁂

Representatives of all thirteen colonies except Georgia rode to Philadelphia in the fall of 1774 to attend the congress. They debated how to respond to the harsh treatment meted out to Americans by Parliament and the Crown. The result of their deliberations was truly revolutionary.

In Massachusetts, Dr. Joseph Warren had drafted a platform known as the "Suffolk Resolves," and the congress at Philadelphia adopted the Suffolk Resolves in their entirety. The colonies went on record to declare: that the Intolerable Acts were unconstitutional and should be defied; that tax receipts be withheld from Crown officers; that the Quebec Act establishing the Roman Catholic faith in Canada threatened the Protestant religion; that militia officers be elected by each town, and not appointed by the royal governors; and that there be no commercial intercourse with Great Britain or its other dependencies. John Adams wrote a further declaration for the congress, adding a provision for the right of jury trial and protesting the presence of the British army. Though the Resolves advocated a "defensive" posture, they strongly suggested that armed resistance was possible.[57]

The Continental Congress established an "Association" of colonies, a loose arrangement, with committees of safety empowered to enforce congressional declarations and to serve as the executive power in place of the royal governors—a form of interim revolutionary government.[58] Such measures made no provision for, and allowed no tolerance for, the thousands of Americans who remained loyal to the Crown.

General Thomas Gage, acting governor of Massachusetts and commander of the British army in America, responded sternly. He called for a large increase in the number of troops, and he enlarged the scope of the Intolerable Acts to cover all of New England. His edict cut off New Hampshire from trade and excluded her sailors from the Atlantic fisheries. As he tightened the noose, Yankee patriots grew more militant.[59]

In February and March of 1775, the antagonists stalked each other. Redcoats marched into the countryside outside Boston. John Hancock and the committee of safety decided when and where their militia would respond to these incursions. Farmers and mechanics left their work at a moment's notice to meet the British, but no shots were fired. The maneuvers gave the Americans experience in the field and improved their response time to calls to action.[60]

The committee of safety decided that weapons and powder should be stored outside Boston, far from British strength. To that end a depot was established at Concord, Massachusetts, several miles distant from the redcoat forces. Concord gave an additional advantage to the rebels—the town was surrounded by active and aggressive militias, including those from New Hampshire.[61]

Archibald Stark home, Derryfield (now Manchester), New Hampshire, where John Stark grew up. Photograph by the authors.

Caleb Page home, Starkstown (now Dunbarton), New Hampshire, where Elizabeth "Molly" Stark grew up. The home is still a private residence. Photograph by the authors.

John and Molly Stark home, Manchester, New Hampshire. The home burned in the nineteenth century. Postcard 1905. Collection of the authors.

A period engraving of Robert Rogers. By G.N. Raspe, 1778, published in Geschichte der kriege in und ausser Europa, *Courtesy the Library of Congress.*

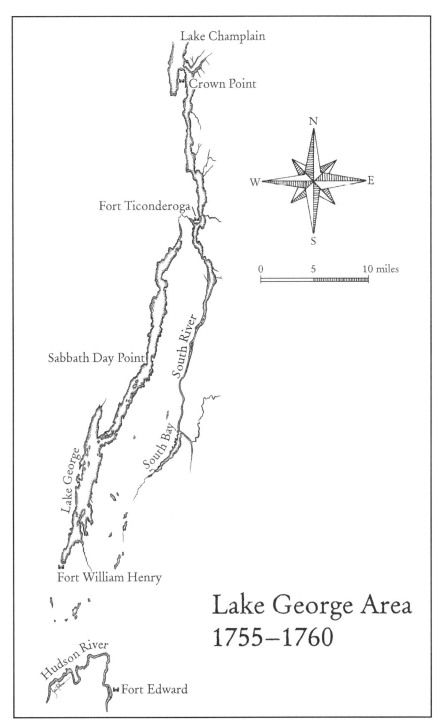

Lake Champlain

Crown Point

N

W   E

S

0   5   10 miles

Fort Ticonderoga

South River

Sabbath Day Point

South Bay

Lake George

Fort William Henry

Lake George Area
1755–1760

Hudson River

Fort Edward

Lake George Area, 1755–1760. Map by Julie Polhemus.

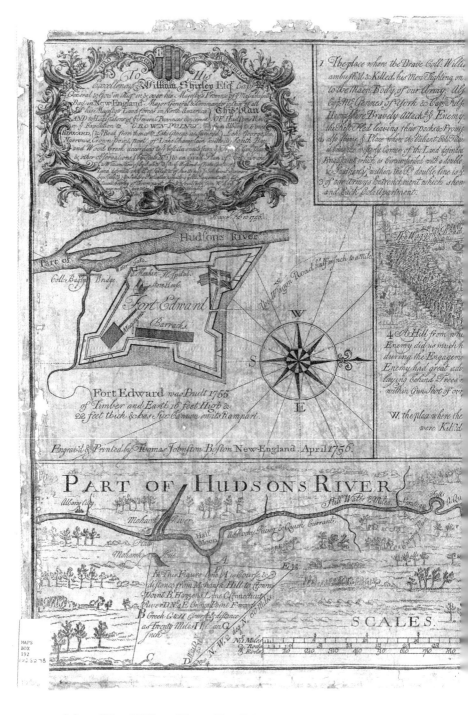

Map of Fort William Henry, Fort Edward, and Part of Hudson River.

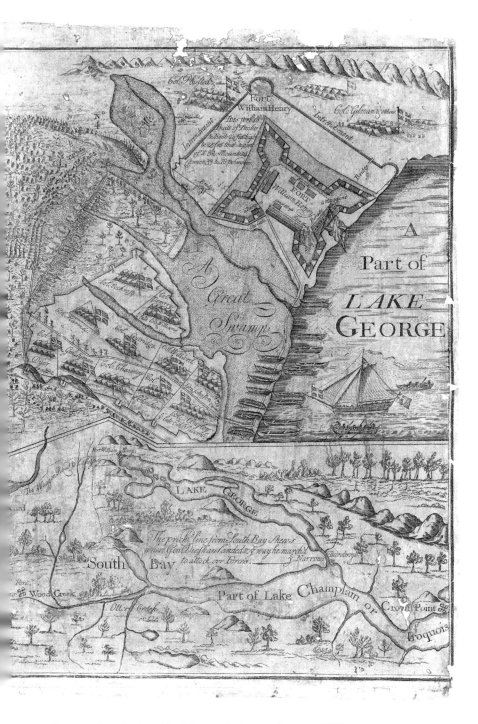

Engraved and printed by Thomas Johnston, Boston, 1756.

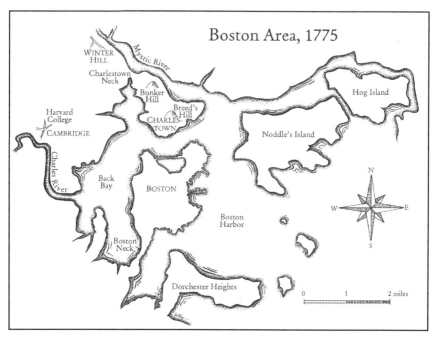

Boston area, 1775. Map by Julie Polhemus.

The Death of General Warren at the Battle of Bunker's Hill, June 17, 1775.
Oil on canvas by John Trumbull, courtesy of the Connecticut Historical Society, Hartford, Connecticut.

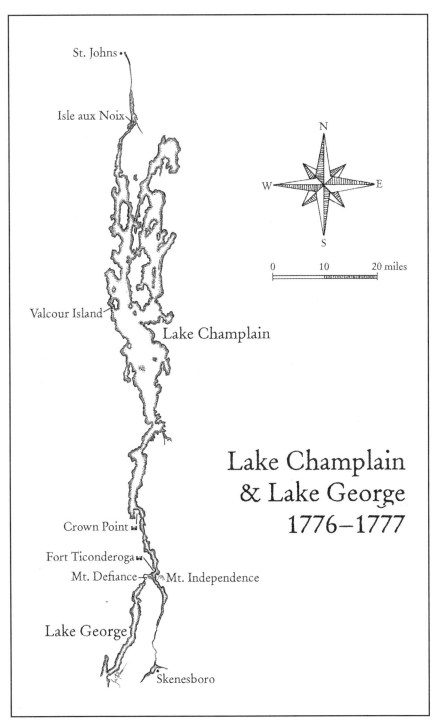

Lake Champlain and Lake George, 1776. Map by Julie Polhemus.

Fort Ticonderoga from Mt. Independence. Photograph by the authors.

Fort Ticonderoga from Mt. Defiance. Photograph by the authors.

The reconstructed Fort Ticonderoga as seen today, courtesy Fort Ticonderoga.

Walloomsac River from the area of Stark's Bridge. Photograph by the authors.

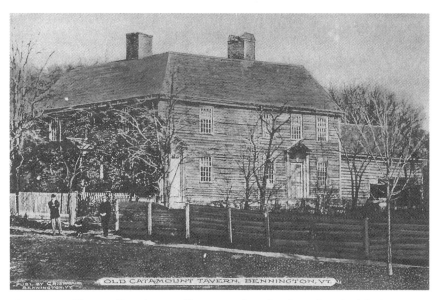

Catamount Tavern, Bennington, Vermont, where Stark conferred with the Vermont authorities. The tavern burned in 1871. Postcard 1909. Collection of the authors.

This map drawn by Lt. Desmaretz Durnford, an engineer with the British army at the Battle of Bennington, is a primary source of information about the battle and battlefield. North is to the right, rather than at the top. The map was engraved for John Burgoyne's A State of the Expedition from Canada, as Laid Before the House of Commons... published in London in 1780.

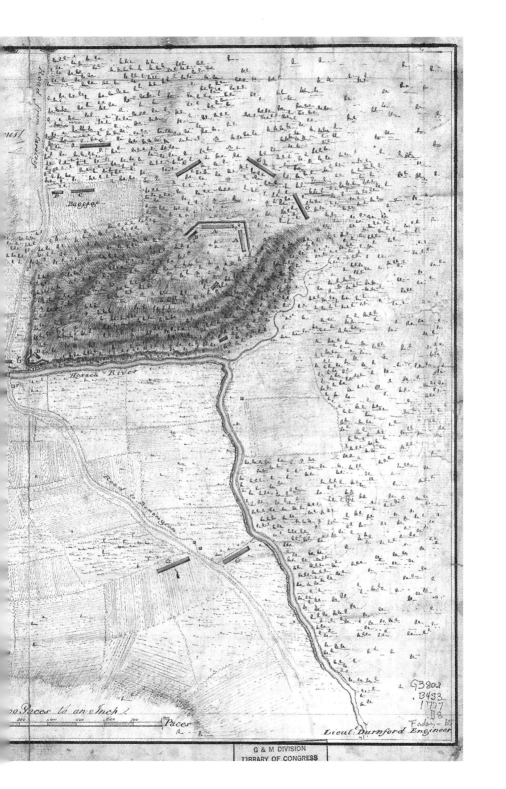

Baggage

Hosack River

Paces to an Inch

Paces

Lieut: Durnford Engineer

The Battle of Bennington, August 16, 1777. *Oil on canvas by Alonzo Chappel (1828–1887). Collection of the Bennington Museum, Bennington, Vermont. Chappel was a prolific painter of American history scenes and personages. The*

captured German dragoons at left are portrayed in uniforms of a later era than the Revolution, but the painting nicely depicts the high mutual regard between Stark (on horseback) and his troops.

Prisoners Taken at Bennington Battle, August 16, 1777. *The men on horseback are (l. to r.) Col. Samuel Herrick, Col. Seth Warner, General John Stark, and an unidentified man. The First Bennington Meetinghouse and Walloomsac Inn are*

in background. Large painted mural on canvas, by Leroy Williams, Collection of the Bennington Museum, Bennington, Vermont.

MAJOR GENERAL JOHN SULLIVAN,
A distinguish'd OFFICER in the CONTINEÑTIAL ARMY.
Publish'd as the Act directs 22 Aug.t 1776 by Tho.s Hart.

Major General John Sullivan, a distinguish'd officer in the Continental
Army. *Publish'd as the Act directs by Thos. Hart, 1776 Augt. 22, London.*
Courtesy Library of Congress.

Henry Dearborn at age 54, engraving by artist Charles Balthazar Julien Fevret de Saint-Mémin, 1770–1852, Published in Washington, D.C., 1805. Courtesy Library of Congress.

The Surrender of General Burgoyne *by John Trumbull, painted in 1822. The central figure, General Horatio Gates, refuses to accept Burgoyne's sword, customarily offered as a token of surrender. General Daniel Morgan stands to the right of Gates. This painting hangs in the rotunda of the United States Capitol in Washington, D.C.*

Braunschw. Dragoner Reg^{in.}

A soldier of the Prinz Ludwig Dragoon (heavy cavalry) Regiment, 1777, from
a series of period watercolors by a Brunswick officer. They marched as infantry,
knee-high horseman's boots exchanged for shoes and black cloth gaiters. They
retained their dragoon swords on campaign, unwieldy weapons for a man on foot.
Their coats were medium blue with yellow facings. Freidrich Baum was the Lt.
Colonel of this regiment.

John Stark

General John Stark *by Alonzo Chappel, engraved and published in* National Portrait Gallery of Eminent Americans, Vol 1, *Johnson, Fry & Company, New York, 1862. Collection Ron Toelke.*

The Stark Monument that Thoreau saw from the river. Courtesy of the Manchester (N.H.) Historic Association.

Part II

The American Revolution

13

First Actions

Raw, Undisciplined, Cowardly Men

General Thomas Gage had commanded the British Army in North America for twelve years since he replaced General Amherst in 1763. When he succeeded Governor Thomas Hutchinson as military governor of Massachusetts, he became a soldier facing a politician's nightmare. He had to navigate the strait between determined opposition in Boston and hard orders from London. A great outcry arose when London compelled him to close the Port of Boston. Gage understood the strength and breadth of colonial opposition to British policy, while his superiors in London did not. He wrote to England: "If force is to be used at length, it must be a considerable one, for to begin with small numbers will encourage resistance, and not terrify, and will in the end cost more blood and treasure."[1]

Parliament resisted his calls for more troops. Many English politicians viewed Americans with contempt. Speaking in the House of Commons, the Earl of Sandwich scoffed at the colonists: "They are raw, undisciplined, cowardly men," he said. "Believe me, my Lords, the very sound of a cannon would carry them off … as fast as their feet could carry them."[2] A British marine, Major John Pitcairn, encouraged the Earl's prejudice in a letter: "I am satisfied that one active campaign, a smart action, and burning two or three of their towns, will set everything to rights. Nothing now, I am afraid, but this will ever convince these foolish, bad people that England is in earnest."[3]

Goaded from all quarters, Gage believed he must act. He decided to move against the armory at Concord. He issued secret orders to muster 700 picked men, grenadiers and light infantry. Obese Colonel Francis Smith and Major John Pitcairn commanded the force. Americans learned of the "secret" plans. As the British troops began to row across the Charles River, Paul Revere and William Dawes were already spurring their horses toward Lexington and Concord to rouse the militia and to warn patriot leaders Samuel Adams and John Hancock.[4]

On Sunday, April 19, someone fired the shot that started the American Revolution. Each side blamed the other. News of the encounters at Lexington and Concord spread quickly. New England towns relied on their meeting-house bells for news; bells rang for worship, tolled for mourning and, rarely, called out to their communities in times of danger. Now they sounded the tocsin, and Yankee militia homed in on the British column like hornets whose nest had been kicked. Redcoats and patriots died in the firefights at Lexington and Concord, but the most blood was shed during the British withdrawal toward Boston. Major Pitcairn's soldiers made a forced march under constant fire from farmers shooting from behind walls, trees and buildings.

The British and Loyalists recounted tales of Yankee atrocities. Hugh, Earl Percy, one of the officers on the march, wrote to Gage of the "cruelty and barbarity of the Rebels who scalped and cut off the ears of some of the wounded men who fell into their hands."[5] The stories told in Boston grew even grimmer. Anne Hulton wrote, "The Troops went on to Concord & executed the business they were sent on, & on their return found two or three of their people Lying in the Agonies of Death, scalp'd & their Noses and ears cut off & eyes bored out—Which exasperated the Soldiers exceedingly."[6]

But the diary of British Lieutenant Frederick MacKenzie reported no such scalping or mutilation. His troops were angry at being attacked from all sides, he said, and "the soldiers were so enraged at suffering from an unseen enemy that they forced open many of the houses from which the fire proceeded, and put to death all those found in them." In addition MacKenzie wrote, "Many houses were plundered by the soldiers, notwithstanding the efforts of the officers to prevent it. I have no doubt this inflamed the Rebels, and made many of them follow us farther than they would otherwise have done."[7]

Patriots heard an entirely different account of the day than their British and Loyalist contemporaries, one which tended to confirm MacKenzie's diary entry. The "Official Patriot Account," written on April 26, 1775, and addressed to "the Inhabitants of Great Britain," reported:

Let it suffice to say that a great number of the homes on the road were plundered and rendered unfit for use; several were burnt; women in childbirth were driven by the soldiery naked into the streets; old men, peaceably in their houses were shot dead; and such scenes exhibited as would disgrace the annals of the most uncivilized nation.[8]

The Massachusetts Committee of Safety, on April 28, wrote to the towns begging for men to "defend our wives and children from the butchering hands of an inhuman soldiery."[9]

Horsemen galloped out in all directions, carrying news of the events. Ezra Stiles, at Providence, Rhode Island, learned of the fighting at eight o'clock the next morning. He heard that 1,500 redcoats had attacked the patriot militia.[10] Experience Storrs, in Mansfield, Connecticut, "heard ye Mallencolly Tidings of an Engagement." He called up the militia under his command.[11]

Each side believed the stories of their foe's atrocities, and the stories inspired action. Those who wanted the pot to boil rejoiced. Samuel Adams and John Hancock escaped across the fields on April 19 ahead of the British. Adams turned to Hancock and said, "What a glorious morning this is. I mean for America."[12]

Some patriots held a more sober view of the day. That evening John Adams wrote, "When I reflect and consider that the fight was between those whose parents but a few generations ago were brothers, I shudder at the thought, and there's no knowing where our calamities will end." Fifteen years earlier John Adams had "gloried in being an Englishman." Now, he found himself torn.[13]

Up in Bedford, New Hampshire, Matthew Patten "Rec'd the Melancholy news in the morning [April 20] that General Gages troops had fired on our Contrymen at Concord yesterday." His son John and two nephews gathered their kit to leave for Massachusetts the next day. Patten's daughters stayed up all night baking bread for the young militiamen.[14]

Word of the fighting reached John Stark across the river in Derryfield. Years later his son-in-law, Benjamin Stickney, set down the old soldier's recollection of that day: "He was found at work at his saw mill at Amoskeag Falls; he stopped his mill and went to his house, took his musket and three dollars in his pocket and without any coat that he might not be encumbered, he went off to meet his little band."[15]

Stark left a family of seven at Derryfield. Molly had borne three more children since 1769—Sarah, Elizabeth and Mary. They, together with Archibald, John, Jr., and Eleanor, all lived at home with Molly. Caleb remained in Dunbarton with his grandfather, Mr. Page. The Starks expected another child later that year. John had plenty of reasons not to go to war.[16]

On the march south the "little band" following Stark grew until, according to Stickney, a thousand volunteers arrived at Cambridge behind their leader. He reported to the Massachusetts Committee of Safety, in whose service his regiment enlisted. On April 26, Stark's men elected him colonel by a show of hands.[17]

John Patten, with his cousins and other men from Bedford, Goffstown and Derryfield, arrived to join Stark's troops. They were commanded by John Goffe's son-in-law, John Moore (or Moor), Stark's second-in-command. Their numbers grew as they neared Cambridge.[18]

Angry Americans descended on the towns around Boston, spoiling for a fight. General Gage wrote to the Earl of Dartmouth to describe the consequences of the foray to Concord: "The whole country was assembled in Arms with Surprizing Expedition and Several Thousand are now Assembled about the Town threatening an Attack and getting up Artillery."[19]

Many of the American volunteers had no prior military experience. They marched off to war of their own free will and, when they found no fight awaiting them, they marched home with the same blithe spirit. John Patten was home by May 1, and Captain Moore drilled his men in Derryfield on May 2. New Hampshire patriots had yet to instill the discipline of professional soldiers in their militia.[20]

❧ ❧

Boston contained a mixed population of British soldiers, Loyalists, patriots and those of no particular political persuasion. They shared one characteristic—the sense of being besieged. Rebel forces faced them, spread in a great arc around the city. Anne Hulton described her fears:

> The next day [April 20] the Country pourd down its thousands, and at this time from the entrance of Boston neck at Roxbury round by Cambridge to Charlestown is surrounded by at least 20,000 men, who are raising batteries on three or four different Hills. We are now cut off from all communication with the Country & many people must soon perish with famine in this place.[21]

Gage himself took a grim view of British prospects. "The situation these wretches have taken in forming the blockade of this town is judicious and strong," he admitted in a letter to Lord North. But the government ignored his plea for reinforcements. With no means to feed his men and animals except by ship, Gage knew he was in a hard place.[22] To make matters worse, HMS *Cerberus* sailed into Boston harbor on May 25 carrying Generals Howe, Burgoyne and Clinton. Gage would have to command under the watchful eyes of three ambitious men who wished to supplant him.[23]

Colonel Stark's troops camped at Winter Hill in Medford, about three miles north of Cambridge. Stark established his headquarters at the home of Isaac Royal, a Loyalist who had vacated the premises.[24] The New Hampshire soldiers were ill-equipped for a military campaign. They lacked uniforms, weapons and medical supplies. On May 18, Stark wrote the New Hampshire committee requesting weapons, "as no arms are to be procured here at present." He explained that men without muskets were a drain on the army and must return home before they ate up scarce rations to no purpose. Eventually the weapons arrived, but no blankets or medicine. Stark was forced to write to Exeter again requesting the missing items.[25]

It now became apparent that there would be an awkward relationship between American politicians and American soldiers, and it would be especially awkward in Stark's case. The New Hampshire Council appointed its own leader, Nathaniel Folsom, to "take General Command of the men that may be raised or are already raised in this Gov't for this session." Folsom was a militia officer with military experience. His appointment was a foretaste of innumerable political appointments by American politicians, decisions that would enrage Washington's officers throughout the Revolution. Folsom, it turned out, was no friend of Stark.[26]

New Hampshire organized Folsom's command into a brigade, consisting of three regiments. Colonel James Reed and Colonel Enoch Poor would lead two regiments, "leaving the other colonelcy open for Col. Stark if he should see fit to resign his commission under the Massachusetts Government."[27] A more sensitive man would have perceived that the New Hampshire representatives already disapproved of him, but Stark was too busy to pay attention to matters back in Exeter.

Patriots denied the British army provisions from the countryside; wheat, corn, apples, bacon and mutton entered Boston only by boat. Those farmers who might have been tempted to profit from the urgent needs of the British were intimidated or barred by American soldiers. The quest for meat led the British to two islands northeast of Boston. Horses, cattle and about 400 sheep were pastured on Noddle's Island and Hog Island; English troops made frequent forays there to round up stock. The islands were uninhabited spits of sand and marsh separated from the mainland by a wide tidal waterway that could be forded at low tide. The committee of safety decided to tighten the American grip on Boston by removing the livestock from the islands.[28]

On May 27, Colonel John Stark led 600 New Hampshire troops across the knee-deep inlet toward Hog Island. Horses hauled two four-pound cannons behind them. By early afternoon they had driven most of the sheep north toward Chelsea on the mainland. Stark then moved across another tidal reach to Noddle's Island and drove off a number of cows and horses. Then, a detachment of British marines appeared and fired on the Americans.[29]

General Gage sent 100 regulars to reinforce the marines, and a running firefight began. The Americans retreated toward Hog Island. Meanwhile, a British schooner, a sloop and twelve barges with swivel guns moved into the channel to cut off the Americans. The schooner *Diana* had no room to maneuver in the shallow water; she made an easy target for New Hampshire marksmen.[30]

Stark managed an orderly withdrawal across the marshes. When the British advanced and fired by platoons, the Americans shot back from ditch banks and whatever cover they could find. The redcoats took several casualties, but Stark's men made it safely back to the mainland.[31]

The *Diana* became bottled up in the shallow water off Noddle's Island. Her crew had intended to prevent an American retreat, but they were now themselves cut off. Sailors and marines attempted to tow her out with rowboats. Israel Putnam led a party of patriot reinforcements against the ship. They fired from shore at first; then, Putnam waded into the water and attacked. The British fled in the small craft, leaving the *Diana* with "Blood running out of the scuppers." Patriots stormed aboard amid dead and dying sailors and removed twelve swivel guns. Then they packed hay beneath the stern and set her ablaze.[32]

Americans won the "Battle of Chelsea," as it became known, without losing a single man killed and with only four wounded. Stark and Putnam achieved the main goal—the removal of the livestock. They also destroyed or damaged two British naval vessels and routed the enemy. Reports of British casualties varied widely; one claimed just two marines died, but in Boston a witness "stated … that he saw sixty four bodies landed at Long Wharf after the engagement."[33]

John Stark used ranger tactics against his old allies in his first engagement. His New Hampshire men fired from cover with accuracy and then withdrew in order, without panic, against regular troops. That a confrontation over pasturage should become so bloody revealed that there was mutual animosity between these foes. Putnam and Stark shared the hostility toward the British.

Two days later, John Stark sent the New Hampshire Committee of Safety, "a return of the men who have enlisted in the service of the province of New

Hampshire (now under my command)."[34] The committee in Exeter had apparently previously requested the muster roll. This second roll never reached Exeter either. On May 31 the Provincial Congress became irritated by the colonel's failure to communicate. They resolved, "That Coll John Stark be sent for, that he is desired to attend this Congress and to give account of his conduct relative to the army, to this Congress as soon as may be, in order that the same may be properly commissioned."[35]

Stark rode to Exeter to appear before the congress. When he had first led volunteers to Cambridge after Lexington and Concord, his unit had been pledged to the service of Massachusetts. Now, it was understood, the regiment was to be a New Hampshire force and the question to be answered was, what priority would the regiment have? Would it be the "First" or the "Second" regiment? The answer would determine the seniority of the commander of the regiment, a matter of first importance to John Stark.[36]

In the New Hampshire Congress, Stark argued that he had more military experience and greater seniority than either Folsom or the other colonels, and that his should be the First Regiment. A legend arose that Stark addressed the group and asked them, "if they had any way of making a child that was born to-day older than one that was born six weeks ago." Then, the story goes, he stalked out of the room.[37]

The New Hampshire Congress voted to commission him colonel of the "1st regiment in New Hampshire for the defence of America."[38]

Stark's regiment at Medford contained several experienced and capable officers, and some who were green but popular. Lieutenant Colonel Isaac Wyman, of Keene, had been a delegate to the January convention that chose representatives to the Continental Congress. He had fought with a provincial regiment in the war with France, and his men thought well enough of him to elect him their leader. Major Andrew McClary was a giant of a man and brave to a fault. Captain Isaac Baldwin, like Stark, had served with Robert Rogers. Major John Moore, John Goffe's son-in-law, came from a military family. Captain Henry Dearborn, a physician, had little soldiering experience, but he was a natural soldier who rose high in the ranks of the army and kept a journal through his many campaigns.[39]

Overall command north of Boston fell to the Massachusetts Committee of Safety. With Samuel Adams and John Hancock serving in Philadelphia, Dr. Joseph Warren led the committee. He was a widower with four young children who abandoned his medical practice to be a revolutionary. Known for his fairness and his humanity, Warren believed that a leader's place was in the thick of the action. He appeared wherever his compatriots were in danger. He also believed that civil political authority must control the military, "otherwise our soldiery will lose the ideas of right and wrong, and will plunder, instead of protecting the inhabitants." The doctor's conviction arose from an enlightened and growing American belief that civil authority should actually be civilized. If not, then neither the government nor the military would have any moral strength and the power of persuasion would be lost.[40]

General Artemas Ward was the military commander at Cambridge. He made his headquarters in a mansion near Harvard College, where the students had been sent home. Beneath Ward, General Israel Putnam led the Connecticut troops. He was short, blunt and pugnacious, and he advocated aggressive war. Colonel William Prescott of Massachusetts supported Putnam's measures. Like Putnam, Prescott had fought in wars since the battle of Louisbourg in 1745. Both subordinates had more experience than Ward, and they tried to sway their commander.[41]

On June 16, 1775, unknown to the American officers and soldiers on the front lines near Boston, the Second Continental Congress at Philadelphia unanimously elected George Washington commander in chief of the American "continental army." At the moment that army consisted only of militia from New England. Washington accepted the role without bombast. He rose in Congress and spoke briefly: "… I beg it may be remembered, by every gentleman in this room, that I, this day, declare with the utmost sincerity, I do not think myself equal to the command I am honored with." He did not depart to take command at Cambridge until June 23. The war did not wait for him.[42]

14

Bunker Hill
Good God How the Balls Flew

Twice in two months Yankee farmers clashed with British regulars, and twice they drove them back to Boston. They burned a navy warship, disabled another, took prisoners, and now they dominated the countryside. On Lake Champlain, Benedict Arnold and Ethan Allen captured Fort Ticonderoga. At both Noddle's Island and Ticonderoga, the Americans captured cannon to augment their weaponry.

General Gage tried to command under the watchful and ambitious presence of Howe, Clinton and Burgoyne. As the rebel noose tightened, he seemed powerless. Back in England, where the worst was not yet known, critics in high places attacked him. Lord George Germaine, Secretary of State for the Colonies, agreed with the critics. Gage, he said, "finds himself in a situation of too great importance for his talents."[1]

Germaine now believed that General William Howe, with his experience of the American style of warfare in which "our light troops were taught to separate and secure themselves by trees, walls or hedges …" could "… teach the present army to be as formidable as that he formerly acted with."[2]

The British high command and the government in London suffered from a handicap—the ideas of the ministers took weeks to reach their commanders in America, while knowledge of events in America took weeks to reach London. In the meantime Yankee radicals could stir up a great deal of trouble.

General Gage decided to address the Americans in a way he hoped would stem the rebellion. On June 12, 1775, he issued a proclamation in which he labeled the patriot leaders "incendiaries and Traitors" and the actions of New England militias as "outrage," "cruelty" and "lawless tumult." This would be the last chance, he warned, to avoid further bloodshed, and he offered to pardon all who laid down their arms—except Samuel Adams and John Hancock. Those who scorned this amnesty, Gage threatened, would be treated as "Rebels and Traitors."[3]

Several thousand New England soldiers, including many who had already risked their lives at Lexington, Concord or Noddle's Island, greeted Gage's offer with contempt. If his words had any effect, it was to confirm the rebels in the course they followed. They had the upper hand, and both sides knew it. Gage, having made his threat, now had to back it up.[4]

The patriots placed their forces in a semicircle around Boston. The city was almost an island anyway, hemmed by the harbor and the Charles River; only Boston Neck permitted access to the country, but rebels choked that off. Two elevated sites, one south of Boston and one north, threatened the British as potential artillery strongholds. Dorchester Heights commanded the southern aspect, while Bunker Hill, across the Charles River in Charlestown, dominated the north side of the city. Gage decided to occupy both high points to deny them to the Americans, but rebel spies learned his plans almost as soon as they were made. On June 15 the Committee of Safety unanimously resolved to secure Bunker Hill.[5]

Charlestown and its two hills, Bunker and Breed's, sat on a leaf-shaped peninsula connected to the mainland and to the roads to Medford and Cambridge only by a narrow stem called Charlestown Neck. The Mystic River flowed past the northeast shore of the peninsula, and the Charles River bounded the west and south shores. The British fleet dominated the water; American cannon on Bunker Hill might threaten Boston, but royal warships could destroy American artillery positions. A combination of naval gunfire and redcoat flankers could have cut the leaf from the branch. An anonymous British officer recognized this advantage: "By this movement we shut them up in the peninsula as in a bag, their rear exposed to the fire of our cannon and if we pleased our musquetry. In short, they must have surrendered instantly or been blown to pieces."[6]

Seen from across the broad Charles River from Boston, the village of Charlestown occupied the near left of the peninsula, with little Breed's Hill behind it. The highest point, Bunker Hill, lay back nearest Charlestown Neck, fronted by a long stretch of meadow that rose up from Marston's Point at the near right. Charlestown and Breed's Hill were within cannon range from Boston. Naval artillery could reach the rest of the peninsula.

The decision to fortify a position near Charlestown unnerved General Ward. Suppose, he thought, the British did not intend to occupy Bunker Hill, but instead planned a feint; that would leave Ward's main force at Cambridge vulnerable. While Ward pondered, Israel Putnam acted. He sent Connecticut troops to Charlestown and paraded them in sight of the British. Dr. Warren tried to mediate between the two generals. He told Putnam, "I admire your spirit, and respect General Ward's prudence. We shall need them both, and one must temper the other."[7]

Finally, on June 16, Ward ordered Colonel William Prescott to build a redoubt at Bunker Hill. He had not given much thought to his order. He sent Prescott off without enough men, food, powder and ball to hold the position. He made no provision for reinforcing Prescott. He named no overall commander to coordinate the positions and movements of troops from three different colonies. Ward may even have sent this force without a map that identified the hill they were meant to occupy.[8]

At about 6 o'clock that Friday evening, Colonel Prescott ordered his men to parade at Cambridge. They were to bring one day's provisions, a blanket and their weapons. The militia column started for Charlestown at dusk, and as darkness settled they reached a hill they thought was their destination. It was Breed's Hill. They had marched right past Bunker Hill.[9]

Amos Farnsworth, a soldier in the regiment, wrote in his diary: "… marched to Bunker Hill and begun their intrenchment and careed it on with the utmost vigor all night." The men dug a trench "of about ten rod long and eight wide, with a breast work of 8 more."[10]

At first light on June 17, the sight of the little fort caused a shock among the British. Lord Rawdon wrote in a letter that, if the Americans had perfected the battery, it could have "probably destroyed the greater part of Boston."[11]

Prescott's men had a greater shock; with daylight, they realized their danger, for they could see the Charles River and "about 8 ships of the line and all Boston fortified against us." It was unclear whose error placed them on the wrong hill as easy targets for British artillery. Peter Brown, one of Prescott's soldiers, described their feelings: "The danger we were in made us think there was treachery, and that we were brot here to be all slain, and I must and will venture to say that there was treachery, oversight or presumption in the conduct of our officers."[12]

Artillery from Boston, and Admiral Graves's cannon on HMS *Lively* opened fire on Prescott's earthworks shortly after five o'clock in the morning. The roar of the cannons roused Boston. The city, the river and the Charlestown peninsula formed a vast amphitheater in which spectators and participants alike could view the gathering battle. Bostonians looked across the water at tiny figures of men—Americans defying British gunfire. Patriot militia on the hills behind Charlestown saw white puffs of smoke from Gage's guns in the city, then heard the report, then waited for the shot to reach them. The conflict would play out in full view of America's third-largest city.[13]

In Medford, three miles distant, John Stark could plainly hear the cannonade. Still, for several hours he received no orders to march. Later in the morning, Ward commanded him to send a part of his force as reinforcements for Prescott. Stark complied. "Upon this," he wrote, "I was ordered by the general to send a detachment of two hundred men, with proper officers to their assistance; which order I promptly obeyed, and appointed Colonel Wyman to command the same."[14]

Stark probably sensed that his entire regiment might soon be called to the fight. He had commanded small units in battle before, but never a regiment. In the 1750s the men he commanded were his peers, his age group. Now his ranks included the sons and grandsons of his friends—the sons of Matthew Patten and John Goffe, and Goffe's four grandsons, along with John Moore. On this day, too, Stark's eldest son, Caleb, made his first appearance as a soldier.[15]

Caleb, like most young New Englanders, was drawn to action by the news of Lexington and Concord, but his grandfather resisted his pleas to join the fray. Finally, temptation triumphed.

> … the young man resolved to go at all events; and having secretly collected his clothing in a valise, without the knowledge of the family, and before day-light on the morning of June 16, 1775, he mounted a horse which had been given him by his grand-father, and with a musket on his shoulder, started for the American camp.[16]

John Stark registered only mild surprise when his son appeared at Medford and told him he wanted to fight. The colonel assigned the boy to Captain Reid's company. It was the beginning of a long and distinguished military career.[17]

Stark became anxious to learn how matters stood near Charlestown on the morning of the 17th. He and Major McClary rode to the Neck to see for themselves, and what they saw convinced them that their regiment would soon be wanted. They quickly returned to Winter Hill to prepare. On their way back they encountered Isaac Wyman and his 200 soldiers "lying down to rest." Stark angrily sent them on toward the battle, but Stark's son-in-law, Benjamin Stickney, wrote, they "went to the right where Stark saw no more of them until after the action."[18]

At Bunker Hill and at Breed's Hill, farm boys from Massachusetts and Connecticut had a clear view across the water to Boston. British cannon fire ceased; men rested in the hot sun and watched rows of barges move to the waterside on the city shore—twenty-eight boats in all. Columns of red-coated regulars marched down to the quay and climbed into the boats. A stately procession of barges rowed across the Charles, oars dipping into the water in unison. Bright sunlight flashed on muskets and bayonets. When the regulars landed on the Charlestown shore, the boats returned to Boston for more soldiers.[19]

Prescott's men had almost completed their earthworks when the cannons resumed firing, killing and wounding men within the parapet. By now the men confined in the "fort" knew they were squarely in the sights of the British artillerymen.[20]

Captain Thomas Knowlton's Connecticut reinforcements arrived and took up positions on Prescott's left, "behind a fence half of stone and two rayles of wood," as Lieutenant Dana described it. There was a large gap in the American lines on their left between Knowlton and the Mystic River. The Yankees watched a second wave of barges move slowly across the river with their cargo of redcoats and their field commander, General Howe.[21]

Up on Bunker Hill, behind the American lines, scores of militiamen gathered, but no officer commanded them to march down to reinforce the front line. They waited and watched. General Putnam put some of them to work fortifying Bunker Hill, "in order," he said, "to secure the line of retreat across Charlestown Neck." Putnam was the ranking officer on the scene, but he never took overall command of the Americans. Prescott and Knowlton acted independently, as did John Stark when he arrived.[22]

⁂ ⁂

Stark faced an immediate problem at Medford—his men were "destitute of ammunition," in Henry Dearborn's phrase. Why that should have been so, with battle plainly imminent, Dearborn never explained, but the responsibility belonged to the regiment's colonel. Stark corrected the failure before he was called on to march.[23]

The officers distributed a gill cup of powder to each man, with fifteen balls and one flint. The soldiers returned to their quarters, where they made up "their powder and ball into cartridges with the greatest possible dispatch." Those men who had no cartridge boxes carried powder horns and ball pouches into battle.[24]

Dearborn wrote that they began the movement to Bunker Hill at about one o'clock.[25] Other sources claimed that orders arrived to march "urgently" at two o'clock.[26] Stark and Dearborn, both on foot, led the column of New Hampshire fighters, who went to the battlefield clad in workday clothing.[27]

The booming cannons grew louder as they neared Charlestown Neck. A Massachusetts soldier, Samuel Blachley Webb, wrote to his brother to describe his own arrival at the battleground:

> We pushed on and came in to the field of Battle. Thro the Cannon-adeing of the Ships, Bombs,—Chain Shot, Ring Shot & Double headed Shot flew as thick as Hail Stones,—but thank Heaven, few of our men suffered, by them, but when we mounted the Summit, where the Engagement was,—good God how the Balls flew. I freely Acknowledge I never had such a tremor come over me before.[28]

At Charlestown Neck, Stark found the way to the battlefield blocked by two regiments of men who feared to brave the artillery fire sweeping the isthmus. Samuel Blachley Webb identified these men as the reinforcements who never entered the battle but "lay sculking the opposite side of the Hill."[29] Major McClary cleared a path through the mob, and the New Hampshire regiment passed through.[30]

John Stark led his men across the Neck through the cannon fire with Henry Dearborn walking beside him. Alarmed by the deliberate pace set by his commander, Dearborn "suggested the propriety of quickening the march of the regiment that it might sooner be relieved from the galling fire of the enemy." Dearborn wrote that Stark responded, "With a look peculiar to himself, he fixed his eyes upon me and observed with great composure, 'Dearborn, one fresh man in action is worth ten fatigued ones,' and continued to advance in the same cool and collected manner."[31] This was not bravado; Stark knew from experience that a marksman who was out of breath usually missed his target. He intended that his men hit what they aimed at.

They found General Israel Putnam on Bunker Hill, but Putnam did not give orders to the fresh troops from New Hampshire. On his own, Stark recognized the gap in the American line to the left of Knowlton's troops and marched his regiment down the hill to fill the vacancy.[32]

On Stark's orders, Captain John Moore led his company down to the beach along the Mystic River and began building a stone wall for his marksmen to shelter behind. The rest of the regiment took positions behind a rail fence. They faced downhill, across a new-mown meadow. Henry Dearborn described the position:

> Part of the grass having recently been cut, lay in windrows and cocks on the field. Another fence was taken up—the rails run through the one in front, and the hay mown in the vicinity suspended upon them from the bottom to the top, which had the appearance of a breast work, but was in fact, no real cover to the men; it, however, served as a deception to the enemy.[33]

Lines of British regulars advanced up the hill from their landing place on the Charles River, marching straight toward Dearborn. Beside them, down on the Mystic River beach, light infantry from the Royal Welsh Fusiliers, marching in column four abreast threaded the waterside, headed directly toward Captain Moore's company. The Fusiliers enjoyed a reputation for gallantry, but most of these men lacked combat experience. Behind them soldiers of another storied regiment, the 4th Foot or "King's Own," marched in measured step toward the New Hampshire farmers.[34]

John Stark walked out toward the advancing redcoats to a point where he judged his men could shoot accurately; he stopped and drove a stake into the ground. Then he called out to his troops, "There, don't a man fire till the redcoats come up to that stake; If he does I will knock him down."[35]

On the hill beside the beach, Henry Dearborn watched British soldiers approach him through the grass under a blazing sun. Each trooper carried a heavy pack along with his musket and ammunition. They came, Israel Potter remembered, in "a deliberate march with a slow step."[36]

As the British gathered their forces, Admiral Samuel Graves asked General Howe if he wanted Charlestown burned to force the rebels out of the cover of the houses. Howe agreed. Navy ships and the battery on Copps' Hill in Boston commenced firing red-hot cannonballs and carcasses (combustible missiles) into Charlestown and, perhaps helped by human incendiaries in the streets, quickly set the town ablaze.[37] One American surmised, "It is supposed that the enemy intended to attack us under the cover of the smoke from the burning houses, the wind favoring them in such a design."[38] The sight angered rebel soldiers. Afterwards one witness wrote: "It was a pretty town! But now there is not one house left standing! It is nothing but a heap of ruins. … All America will avenge our cause."[39]

Captain Moore's troops, crouched behind the stone barricade on Mystic beach, waited with hearts pounding, watching the attackers come nearer. The urge to open fire must have been strong, anything to keep these disciplined-looking soldiers in their smart uniforms as far away as possible. But Moore's men held their fire until the leading redcoats reached their commander's stake in the ground. Then they rose up and "gave such a deadly fire as cut down every man of the party opposed to them." Behind the shattered Welsh Fusiliers the soldiers of the King's Own advanced over the bodies of their comrades, and they fell in their turn. Survivors fled down the beach. Later, John Stark would say, "The dead lay as thick as sheep in a fold."[40]

Officers of the two British units from the Mystic beach attack tried without success to reform their ranks to attack the New Hampshire sharpshooters again. A witness watched the officers "use the most passionate gestures & even to push forward ye men with their swords."[41]

⚜ ⚜

As General Howe developed his attack, three other generals watched from Boston. Burgoyne, who was an aspiring writer, described the tableau:

> And now ensued one of the greatest scenes of war that can be conceived: if we look to the height, Howe's corps ascending the hill in the face of the intrenchments and in a very disadvantageous ground was much engaged; to the left the enemy pouring in fresh troops by the thousands, over the land; and in the arm of the sea our ships and floating batteries cannonading them; straight before us a large and noble town in one great blaze—the church steeples, being timber, were great pyramids of fire above the rest; behind us, the church steeples and

heights of our own camp covered with spectators of the rest of our army which was engaged; the hills around the country covered with spectators; the enemy all in anxious suspense; the roar of the cannon, mortar and musketry; … and the reflection that, perhaps, a defeat was a final loss to the British Empire in America, to fill the mind—made the whole picture, and a complication of honour and importance, beyond anything that ever came to my mind to be witness to.[42]

Up in the meadow, behind the rail fence, Stark's men waited for the long line of attackers moving toward them. Then, like Moore's company, they opened fire. Henry Dearborn reported that their shooting was so accurate that the balls were fatal, "especially to the British officers." Dearborn emphasized that his troops intended to kill "every officer they could distinguish in the British line."[43]

Lord Rawdon, a grenadier lieutenant, related what it was like to face such a hail of musketry: "The Americans rose up and poured in so heavy a fire upon us that the oldest officers say they never saw a sharper action."[44] To observers in Boston it looked like "a continual sheet of lightning" flashing from the American positions.[45] Dead and wounded men littered the field. The sound of the guns reached miles away to Braintree, where Abigail Adams listened. "The constant roar of the cannon is so disturbing," she wrote to her husband John, "that we cannot eat, drink or sleep."[46]

The attackers withdrew, but within minutes General Howe reformed his lines and came at the rebels again. Once more a terrible roll of musket fire drove the British back toward the river. For a minute William Howe, a combat veteran, stood dazed in the midst of his fallen men; it was, he said, "a Moment I never felt before." One of the fallen was Colonel James Abercrombie, the officer who had accompanied John Stark on two fateful scouting missions near Ticonderoga. Abercrombie died a week later.[47]

Reinforcements rowed across the Charles River from Boston while both armies waited for a third attack. Now the Americans realized that they had run low on powder and ball. Back at Bunker Hill, hundreds of men milled around or dug new defensive positions. Some feared to enter the fray; others received no orders to advance. Prescott, Knowlton and Stark desperately needed their ammunition, but they were never resupplied.[48]

When the regulars started forward for a third time, they concentrated on Prescott's redoubt and prepared for a bayonet charge. The Americans could hold them off no longer; redcoats burst over the breastworks.[49]

A musket ball killed Dr. Warren, one of the bravest firebrand leaders of the revolt. He fought as a common soldier this day, but his enemies recognized him. One wrote, "He died in his best cloaths, every body remembers his fine silk-fringed waistcoat."[50]

Prescott's men tried to escape from the redoubt, but many were caught. General Howe wrote that, once the position was taken, "Thirty of the Rebels not having time to get away were killed with bayonets in it." The American officer, Samuel Webb, painted a more vivid picture of the killing: "After they entered our Fort they mangled the wounded in a Most horrid Manner—by running their Bayonets thro them,—and beating their Heads to pieces with the britches of their Guns."[51]

The American commanders could not fight without ammunition. Prescott, Knowlton and Stark each ordered withdrawal. Massachusetts and Connecticut troops passed to the rear first, covered by New Hampshire sharpshooters. Then, "Col. Stark drew off his regiment in such order that they were not pursued."[52] Burgoyne remarked on the American withdrawal. He called it, "no flight: It was even covered with bravery and skill."[53]

After the regiment passed Bunker Hill and crossed Charlestown Neck, Stark questioned whether the British were in pursuit. Major McClary volunteered to go back to reconnoiter. He walked across the Neck, saw the redcoats digging in on Bunker Hill, and started back to rejoin his men, his third trip through the artillery barrage that day. A cannon ball fired from a ship killed him. He was one of about 450 Americans killed or wounded that day.[54]

Israel Putnam, the highest-ranking American officer at the battlefield, played an obscure role in the battle. Several accounts placed him on or near Bunker Hill, in the rear, with detachments of potential reinforcements who did not enter the fight. All of these soldiers carried needed arms and ammunition. Years later Henry Dearborn wrote a monograph in which he criticized the performances of both Putnam and Ward that day:

> Gen. Ward, then commander in chief remained in his quarters in Cambridge, and apparently took no interest or part in the transactions of the day.
>
> No general officer except Putnam appeared in sight, nor did any officer assume the command, undertake to form the troops, or give any order, that I heard. Except Col. Stark, who directed his regiment to reserve their fire on the retreat of the enemy until they advanced again.[55]

When Prescott led his Massachusetts troops on the retreat past Bunker Hill, he confronted Putnam. Two men, both ministers, signed affidavits that Prescott asked Putnam, "Why did you not support me, General, with your men, as I had reason to expect, according to agreement?" Putnam answered, "I could not drive the dogs up." Prescott responded, "If you could not drive them up, you might have led them up."[56]

ఆక్ష్ ఈస్ణ

The British won possession of the Charlestown peninsula at a terrible cost; their officers reported staggering losses. Lord Rawdon wrote celebrating the victory, but, he allowed, "Our loss is very great." That loss was almost half the soldiers who entered the action: 1,054 dead or wounded out of a total force of 2,300.[57]

General John Burgoyne corresponded with Lord Stanley. The day, he wrote, "ended with glory … but the loss was uncommon in officers for the number engaged."[58]

General Gage admitted to Lord Barrington, Secretary of State for War, "These people shew a spirit and conduct against us they never shewed against the French."[59]

General Howe, who would later command the British Army in America, gave his opinion about "the fatal consequences of this action—92 officers killed and wounded—a most dreadful account." His final judgment: "The success is too dearly bought."[60]

An anonymous British officer admitted, "We went to battle without reconnoitering the position of the enemy." He believed the navy alone could have driven the rebels from the peninsula with artillery. Even better, "Had we intended to have taken the whole rebel army prisoners, we needed have only landed in their rear and occupied the high ground above Bunker's Hill." The officer blamed Gage for the slaughter. Much like Abercromby's soldiers at Ticonderoga, he thought, "the brave men's lives were wantonly thrown away."[61]

Both armies suffered from failure of leadership, but the British suffered worse. When news of the battle reached England, the government fired Gage. Howe replaced him. On June 19, before news of Bunker Hill reached Philadelphia, the delegates in Congress there chose Israel Putnam and Artemas Ward as major generals of the Continental Army.[62] They retained their new ranks even after Congress learned about the battle. The field officers—Prescott, Knowlton and Stark—whose cool leadership saved this newborn American army, received no notice from Congress.

15

BOSTON FALLS
New Lords New Laws

George Washington arrived in Cambridge with his aides on July 2. He wanted to examine his command immediately. Ward and Putnam rode with him to show him their positions around Boston. The following day Ward formally transferred command to the Virginian. It annoyed Washington that Ward could not supply a "return" that numbered the troops under the various commanders. It was the first of many annoyances he found with New Englanders.[1]

The tall, imposing general impressed the soldiers. His black servant, Billy Lee, accompanied him everywhere, riding beside him and carrying a telescope by a shoulder strap. The general intended to make an impression; he advocated to his junior officers, "Be easy … but not too familiar lest you subject yourself to a want of that respect, which is necessary to support a proper command."[2] A more egalitarian style suited the New England farmers, most of whom elected their own officers from men like themselves—men like John Stark. They respected Washington, but he did not yet claim their affection.

His soldiers would have loved him even less if they knew of the contempt he felt for them. Within a few weeks he wrote a letter to his cousin, Lund Washington, overseer at Mount Vernon, that the soldiers he commanded "are an exceeding dirty and nasty people." He felt particular loathing for their officers: "… generally speaking the most indifferent kind of People I ever saw." But, he admitted, if properly led, the Yankees might yet make effective soldiers.[3]

On July 4, Washington issued his first General Orders to the army. He identified his principal lieutenants—Major Generals Charles Lee, Artemas Ward, Philip Schuyler and Israel Putnam—and he commanded that "due Obedience" be paid to them. In the absence of congressional commissions for the other officers, they were to continue serving in their present capacities. He told the soldiers that they were "now the Troops of the United Provinces of North America; and it is hoped that all Distinctions of Colonies will be laid aside." Washington warned of an insidious enemy that would come to haunt his army: "No person is to be allowed to go to a Fresh-water pond a fishing or on any other occasion as there may danger of introducing the small pox into the army."[4] No one knew for certain where this dreaded plague came from.

Thousands of young New Englanders, provincials whose first loyalty had always been to their own provinces, now found themselves led by a haughty Virginian who harbored a poor opinion of them. Antagonisms stirred, particularly when troops from outside New England arrived. If these men were united in their will to rebel, sharing that goal with others who dressed and spoke differently was a new experience. The capacity of young men of different backgrounds to form alliances with each other needed to be developed or the army could not function. Even in Congress, John Adams felt a "strong Jealousy" toward New England. Adams understood the need for unity:

> But America is a great unwieldy Body. Its progress must be slow. It is like a large Fleet sailing under Convoy. The fleetest Sailors must wait for the dullest and slowest. Like a coach and six—the swiftest horses must be slackened and the slowest quickened, that all may keep an even pace.[5]

On June 19, Colonel Stark wrote to the New Hampshire Congress to give his account of Bunker Hill. He reported that he had lost fifteen killed or missing in his regiment and forty-five men wounded, but he was "well satisfied that where we have lost one, they have lost three." He concluded the letter by requesting that all deserters from his command found in New Hampshire be returned to him.[6]

Three days later General Nathaniel Folsom, member of the Provincial Congress and the brand new commander of all New Hampshire troops, wrote two letters to the committee of safety. In the first he outlined what he had learned of the action at Bunker Hill. He also complained that Stark had not yet given him a return of his regiment. In his second letter, also dated June 23, Folsom reported that Stark "absolutely refused to comply" with his order to provide the return. Colonel Stark, he complained, "does not intend to be under any subordination to any person appointed by the Congress of New-Hampshire to the general command of the New Hampshire troops." According to Folsom, John Stark told him in person that "he [Stark] could take his pack and return home."[7]

Folsom's letter assumed that Stark's insubordination would lead to his loss of command of the regiment, and Folsom thought he knew who should take Colonel Stark's place—Lieutenant Colonel Isaac Wyman, the same man who, according to Stark, led two hundred men away from the battle at Bunker Hill. In Folsom's view, Wyman "has behaved prudently, courageously and very much like a gentleman."[8]

General Folsom enjoyed a short-lived command. Another politician, lawyer John Sullivan, lobbied the Continental Congress for the position. By the end of June, he succeeded. Despite his having never led troops in so much as a skirmish, Congress made Sullivan a brigadier general. By July 10 he commanded the New Hampshire units near Boston.[9]

Stark never recorded his thoughts on being superseded, first by Folsom and then by Sullivan. It was perfectly in character for him to be insubordinate to Folsom. He may well have threatened to go home, but he stayed and commanded his regiment through 1775 and beyond. That American legislative bodies made a practice of appointing political favorites to high military rank troubled many officers, but it infuriated John Stark.

By midsummer, diseases struck the American camps around Boston. The soldiers called the afflictions "putrid fever" or "camp fever"—ailments now known as dysentery, typhus and typhoid. They resulted from inadequate sanitation, polluted drinking water and open sewers. The longer an army remained in one place, the more likely it would suffer these diseases. The Americans remained camped around Boston for a very long time.[10]

There was a limit to each individual soldier's time, however; most enlistments ran out by New Years Day of 1776. Washington faced the possibility that in six months his army would simply evaporate. He would have to convince men to reenlist during the autumn, at the very time when many of them felt they needed to be home on their farms for the harvest.

The officers tried to infuse order and discipline in the army. Some British and Tories called the American troops "rabble in arms." Washington may have agreed. He applied a firm hand. Reverend William Emerson described the general's measures:

> There is a great overturning in camp as to order and regularity. New lords new laws. The Generals Washington and Lee are upon the lines every day. New orders from his Excellency are read to the respective regiments every morning after prayers. The strictest government is taking place, and great distinction is made between officers and soldiers. Everyone is made to know his place and keep it, or be tied up and receive not 1000 but thirty or forty lashes according to his crime. Thousands are at work every day from four till eleven o'clock in the morning. It is surprising how much work has been done.[11]

Whipping posts had been anathema to Stark and the rangers during the war with France. Now, an American general was applying British discipline to American soldiers. In the face of short enlistments, the measures seemed risky. Many factors threatened retention, not least the shortage of every necessity from food to gunpowder. Washington continually wrote to politicians begging for help; to John Hancock he pleaded, "But my situation is inexpressibly distressing to see the Winter fast approaching upon a naked Army, the time of their Service within a few Weeks of expiring, and no Provision yet made for such important Events." Unless Congress and the colonies acted rapidly, the general thought, "the Army must absolutely break up."[12]

There were those, however, who thought the army could do more. The war could not be won simply by besieging Boston. Canada lay north of the colonies, ripe for a political and military second front.

❧ ❧

On June 27, 1775, only ten days after Bunker Hill, Congress voted to send a strange message to General Philip Schuyler: "… if General Schuyler finds it practicable and that it will not be disagreeable to the Canadians, he shall immediately take possession of St. Johns, Montreal and any other parts of the country."[13]

That a decision of such magnitude should be left to the discretion of a military officer reflects the murkiness of the idea in the first place. It probably seemed to the delegates in Philadelphia that Canada was much like Pennsylvania or Virginia—a vast wilderness populated by people who might wish to throw off British control. If so, perhaps an American military presence could encourage Canadians, most of them French, to join the revolt. It was a strategy born of ignorance.

Within a month Schuyler organized an expedition and placed forces at Fort Ticonderoga. His subordinate, Richard Montgomery, arrived a few weeks later; when Schuyler became ill, Montgomery took command. Their flotilla set out on Lake Champlain on August 28. The Americans had learned that the British were building ships to take control of the lake. Schuyler and Montgomery hoped to destroy the nascent fleet. Lake Champlain seemed to point straight at Canada.[14]

❧ ❧

Colonel Benedict Arnold sought to lead the second attack wing—a daring strike through the forests of Maine and Quebec. The plan entailed transporting 1,000 troops by ship from Boston to the Kennebec River, paddling or poling upriver in bateaux, crossing the height of land into Quebec, floating down the Chaudiere River to the St. Lawrence, and attacking the fortress at Quebec City. Only an officer of Arnold's great ambition and energy would consider leading such an epic mission. Washington appointed him commander.[15]

Arnold's force didn't leave Boston until mid-September. In an era when military campaigns took place only in relatively warm months, it was a late start toward a cold country. By the time the expedition reached the Maine wilderness, it had run out of both provisions and luck. Struggling through dark forests and swamps, the soldiers nearly starved en masse. Isaac Senter wrote that, on October 27, they boiled the meatless jawbone of a hog into a kind of soup. Four days later his fellows ate "water stiffened with flour." That same day they devoured a companion—their dog.[16]

Finally, on November 8, Arnold's starving legion reached the south bank of the St. Lawrence. Across the river, high on a cliff, stood the fortress city. It presented a mighty challenge for the exhausted Americans, but few of them doubted that their strong-willed commander would take up the challenge.

At Boston the two armies lay within sight of each other, indulging in occasional skirmishes and nuisance firing. Disease attacked both sides; starvation stalked the British. Morale suffered. When a regular attempted to desert by swimming across the Charles, redcoats caught him and hanged him.[17]

That August an English officer wrote home to express his "abhorrence of the inhuman service we are upon, and of the shocking outrages that have been committed." He described the diet of the regulars—salt beef and salt pork—"as hard as wood, as lean as carrion." He condemned the behavior of his own army. The Americans, he thought, deserved revenge.

> If we hear a gun fired upon the [Boston] Neck we are all under arms
> in a moment, and tremble lest the Provincials should force their way
> into the town and put us all to the sword for our cruelty at Lexington and setting fire to the large, ancient and flourishing town of
> Charlestown. Certainly our conduct at both places was alike inhuman and unjustifiable; and if heaven punishes us for it, it is no more
> than we deserve.[18]

The feelings of the anonymous officer surely represented a minority opinion in the British army, but Americans would have agreed with him, and they would have added a complaint about the mistreatment of American prisoners.

Soldiers captured by British forces at Bunker Hill were jailed in Boston like common criminals, not prisoners of war. Gage regarded them as felons "destined for the cord."[19] When stories of the prisons reached Washington in August, he lodged a written protest with General Gage. He insisted that the customs of warfare "are universally binding," and he closed with an ultimatum: "If Severity and Hardship mark the Line of your Conduct, (painful as it may be to me) your Prisoners [those in American hands] will feel its Effects." Washington asked Gage for a prompt response.[20]

Gage declined to offer military honors or humane treatment to the rebels. In his view the commissions of American officers were invalid since they were not derived from the Crown and, thus, he would not treat these prisoners as officers. Gage's contempt insulted and angered Washington. He wrote another letter insisting that British "Officers and Soldiers have been treated with a Tenderness due to Fellow Citizens." Once again the American commander warned, "I shall now, Sir, close my Correspondence with you, perhaps forever. If your Officers who are our Prisoners receive a Treatment from me, different from what I wished to shew them, they, & you, will remember the Occasion of it."[21]

Ethan Allen gave the King's government ample opportunity to rethink their policy toward American prisoners. They captured Allen near Montreal in September 1775, put him in irons, and shipped him off to England to face charges of treason. He wrote a narrative of the treatment he and others received on the voyage. Thirty-four prisoners were confined in a dark, twenty-by-twenty-two-foot space. They all used the same two "excrement tubs" and suffered from lice, disease and thirst. Once in England, the government considered the possible negative effects of a public trial and shipped Allen back to America.[22] Perhaps for the first time, the possibility of retaliatory executions dawned on them. If so, it did nothing to improve conditions awaiting American prisoners.

In October the British Navy struck at seacoast towns to punish the rebels and to find food for the hungry army in Boston. Sixteen vessels appeared off

Bristol, Rhode Island. A message from Captain James Wallace of HMS *Rose* demanded that the leading citizens of the town appear before the captain aboard his ship. When the Rhode Islanders refused the invitation, the fleet opened fire. The British threatened to continue the bombardment unless the Americans delivered 200 sheep and 30 fat cattle.[23]

The people of Bristol responded that their livestock had been driven off and they could not possibly supply so many animals. The captain relented. He reduced his price for not leaving Bristol in ashes to 40 sheep—a price the townspeople paid.[24]

The following week another British squadron, commanded by Captain Mowat, hove to off Falmouth (now Portland, Maine). Mowat advised the town that he had "orders to execute a just punishment on the Town of Falmouth" and gave the people two hours "to remove without delay the human species out of said Town."[25]

True to his word, at nine o'clock he opened fire on Falmouth, a barrage consisting of "balls, from three to nine pounds weight, bombs, carcasses (incendiary shells), live shells, grapeshot and musket balls." The shelling lasted nine hours and destroyed most of that part of Falmouth that lay on the hillside facing the harbor—139 dwellings, the new courthouse, the public library and St. Paul's Church. Sailors and marines came ashore and torched other buildings.[26] Washington, advised of Captain Mowat's orders, assumed that "the same desolation is meditated upon all the Towns on the Coast."[27]

While Stark served on garrison duty near Boston, Robert Rogers appeared near the American camp. He was now a retired British officer with a pension from the Crown and, because of that, he aroused suspicion wherever he went in America. He visited political and military leaders on both sides seeking a commission—but only a commission that paid well. It was well known that he had only recently been released from debtor's prison in England.

In Philadelphia in September 1775, John Adams noted in his diary, "The famous Partisan Major Rogers came to our Lodgings to make Us a Visit." The note betrayed the lawyer's distaste for the old ranger.

He [Rogers] thinks We shall have hot Work next Spring. He told me an old half Pay Officer such as himself, would sell well next Spring. And when he went away, he said to S.A. [Sam Adams] and me, if you want me, next Spring for any Service, you know where I am, send for me. I am to be sold.[28]

Two days later, on September 23, Rogers visited Adams again and gave the rebel leader an ambiguous message, "Said he had a Hand and an Heart: tho he did not chose by offering himself to expose himself to Destruction."[29]

The Committee of Safety in Philadelphia ordered Rogers arrested and detained. Congress released him when he gave his word that he would not fight against Americans.[30] Rogers made his promise and rode north into New York. He passed through Albany, examined "land grants" in the Mohawk Valley, and stopped at Dartmouth College to offer a grant to the college president Eleazar Wheelock, who distrusted the major from the start. Wheelock wrote to Washington to express his suspicion that Rogers already served the British. Rogers then travelled on to visit his wife and son in Portsmouth.[31]

In December, Washington ordered General John Sullivan to interview Rogers when the ranger arrived near Boston. Sullivan wrote a skeptical report to Washington: "What may be his secret designs I am unable to say." He advised his commander to issue no travel passes to the major: "... should he prove a traitor, let the blame centre on those who enlarged him."[32] Rogers was not permitted within the American camp.

Rogers did reach Medford, near John Stark's quarters. Caleb Stark believed that they met and that Rogers advised his grandfather to sell himself to the highest bidder. The colonel answered, Caleb wrote, "that no proffers of rank or wealth could induce him to abandon the cause of his oppressed country."[33] If this encounter really happened, it was the last time the old friends ever met. Before long, Rogers accepted a British commission leading a Loyalist unit.

❦❦

At year's end the soldiers in Stark's regiment had not been paid in several months. Colonel Samuel Hobart was paymaster for all the New Hampshire regiments. Because virtually every farmer and merchant in the service relied on his own labor for his family's livelihood, the absence of wages caused real hardship. The men blamed the paymaster. On December 30 a group accosted Hobart in his quarters, demanding their pay. They hauled him away, took him before Stark, and stated their grievances. Stark underestimated the gravity of their mutinous acts. He admitted later that he "threw out some warm and illiberal reflections on some of the members of the [New Hampshire] Congress," and he declined to punish his rebellious soldiers.[34]

Hobart complained to his political superiors in Exeter, who passed the complaint on to General Washington. A Court of Inquiry looked into the matter, but dismissed the case when Stark signed a "confession" in which he accepted responsibility for failing to punish the soldiers and for his heated language directed at the politicians. He wrote that he was "sincerely sorry."[35]

Patriots quickly came to believe that British soldiers were not their only enemies, nor even their most dangerous enemies; they regarded Loyalists as the worst of their foes. For the most part the Tories were unrecognizable, indistinguishable from the rebels themselves. They wore no uniforms, carried no flags, and lived in the midst of their enemies. Their proximity made them seem more dangerous than the redcoats themselves. The divide between Americans grew wide; it separated neighbors and families.

Benjamin Franklin's Loyalist son, William, the boy who had aided his father's electrical experiments, served as Royal Governor of New Jersey. William's teenage son, Temple, accompanied his grandfather to Paris when Benjamin became the minister to the French Court; the separation hurt William, and the breech between Benjamin and William became final. William wrote to Lord Dartmouth, the Colonial Secretary: "No attachment or connection shall make me swerve from the duty of my station." His father agreed. Politics came before family.[36]

Loyalties also divided the Stark family. William Stark, John's brother and fellow officer in the rangers, offered his services to the American cause early in 1776. He applied to lead a regiment along the Canadian frontier. The New Hampshire committee appointed another man in his stead. William returned to Starkstown, now Dunbarton, carrying a grudge. Finally, he wrote to General Sullivan: "It is the land of my nativity shall I stay and bare the Scorn teamly [tamely] or Shall I go and Seek Bread elsewhere is the great Question." William had answered the question by the end of 1776. The British gave him a lieutenant colonel's commission, and he left for Long Island. He died there, after a fall from a horse. John Stark is supposed to have commented that dying was the best thing that William ever did.[37]

The enmity between patriots and Loyalists grew extreme. In New Jersey, in the Carolinas and in central New York, vicious civil wars raged, even when the main armies were engaged elsewhere.

※　※

The two wings of the Canadian expedition linked up on December 2 when Montgomery and Arnold met at Point aux Trembles. Together they commanded only slightly more than 1,000 soldiers. The fortress on the cliffs over the St. Lawrence presented a formidable obstacle.[38]

On the snowy night of December 30, the attack began. Montgomery led a column of men on the western approach, passing along the river toward the lower town. Arnold approached his target from the east. British sentries discovered the attackers and opened fire, killing Montgomery at once. Arnold fell with a ball in his leg. Both parties faltered and fell back. The clash killed ten Americans and wounded forty more. The redcoats captured as many as four hundred patriots, including Henry Dearborn and Daniel Morgan. Just as the death of Lord Howe at Ticonderoga disheartened his troops, Montgomery's loss demoralized the Americans.[39]

The failure at Quebec ended American hopes of forging an alliance with the Canadians. Quebec would remain a dangerous staging point for the Crown.

※　※

In early 1776, Americans were conflicted about the purpose of their rebellion. Did they want reconciliation or independence? The question split the rebels into two camps.

The strongest voice for independence came not from the army, nor from the leaders in Philadelphia; it came from a recent immigrant from England, a corset maker and pamphleteer, Thomas Paine. His argument expressed in *Common Sense* appeared in January 1776 and roused patriot Americans. The clarity of his reasoning and the power of his prose moved men from all levels of society.[40]

After King George's proclamation of August 23, 1775, the focus of the rebellion had shifted from Parliament to the Crown. In his proclamation the King intervened personally, declaring that rebellion against the Crown constituted treason. He gave Americans reason to view hereditary monarchy, not Parliament, as their main enemy. Thomas Paine seized on precisely that point as the foundation of his argument for independence. He declared that there was "no truly natural or religious reason" for the "distinction of men into kings and subjects."[41]

Paine ridiculed the idea of "hereditary succession." Few successor monarchs inherited the virtues of their forebears. "One of the strongest natural proofs of the folly of the hereditary right of Kings, is that nature disapproves it, otherwise she would not so frequently turn it into ridicule by giving mankind an ass for a lion."[42]

After proclaiming the commercial advantages of independence, Paine opened the door to a glimpse of American exceptionalism—that a free and independent America would be a beacon to people everywhere:

O ye that love mankind! Ye that dare oppose not only the tyranny but the tyrant, stand forth! Every spot of the old world is overrun with oppression. Freedom hath been hunted around the globe. Asia and Africa have long expelled her. Europe regards her like a stranger, and England hath given her warning to depart. O receive the fugitive, and prepare in time an asylum for mankind.[43]

First printed in Philadelphia, *Common Sense* was quickly reprinted throughout the country; eventually over 100,000 copies reached eager readers. John

Adams, who was widely suspected of being its author, admired the pamphlet but had misgivings. He wrote to Abigail that he thought Paine was "a better hand at pulling down than building." But Paine inspired Adams to set down his own *Thoughts on Government*. The corset maker gave voice to the higher ideals of the revolutionaries, and he pushed them toward independence.[44]

John Stark remained with the army through the winter of 1775–1776. Back home in Derryfield, Molly gave birth to another son, Charles. She was, for now, the sole parent to their children; the winter must have seemed endless to her.[45]

Washington and his officers had faced the prospect of losing many soldiers to short-term enlistments at the end of 1775. A surprising surge of enlistments filled the ranks with volunteers, however, and new soldiers marched in from the south.[46]

Colonel Henry Knox raised spirits in January when he arrived in Framingham with forty-three cannon and fourteen mortars taken from Fort Ticonderoga. His teamsters drove oxen that hauled the artillery on sledges across the Hudson River and over the Berkshire Mountains. Washington placed the array of cannon at strategic points on the high ground and waited for the right moment.[47]

The army struggled with new experiences. New England troops predominated around Boston. They were hometown militias filled with men who knew each other. Then, new units arrived from Pennsylvania and Virginia and other colonies. Some of these soldiers were frontiersmen who carried long rifles instead of muskets. They distrusted strangers, and the Yankees seemed strange to them. The southerners came from a slave tradition; some of Colonel Glover's Marblehead sailors were freed black men. Before long Americans were fighting each other.[48]

A brawl broke out between groups of soldiers. General Washington rode up to the mob, and he and Billy Lee spurred their horses into the middle of the men. Washington dismounted and, in the words of one witness, "rushed into the thickest of the melee, with an iron grip seized two tall, brawny, athletic, savage-looking riflemen by the throat, keeping them at arm's length, alternately shaking and talking to them."[49] Other combatants paused to watch their commander subdue the two men; then they broke and ran. The riot ended, but sectional distrust remained.

Early in March the Americans occupied Dorchester Heights. The ground was too frozen to dig trenches, so the soldiers built makeshift defenses. They worked at night or out of sight from the city. A British colonel wrote, "The rebels at the same time made a battery within point-blank cannon shot of our lines and with such caution that we could not discover that it was intended for a battery."[50]

By the time General Howe discovered his peril, the patriots had begun a cannonade of Boston. One rebel soldier remembered, "The last fortnight before Howe evacuated Boston, we kept up a smart cannonading every night from twelve o'clock till sunrise." The shelling caused havoc in the city. "The shells were thrown in an excellent direction, they took effect near the centre of the town and tore several houses to pieces; the cannon was unusually well fired."[51]

Howe decided to take the new American positions by amphibious attack, but the weather intervened when, "so high a wind arose that it was impossible for the boats to take to sea." The general recognized that the Dorchester Heights batteries posed an unacceptable threat to his forces; he would have to evacuate Boston. He told his officers that lack of provisions forced them to sail to Halifax rather than New York.[52]

Redcoats began to assemble in the streets of Boston at 3:00 AM on March 17. They marched down to the docks and boarded the navy vessels. "Every vessel which they did not carry off they rendered unfit for use." By nine o'clock the British ships set sail.[53]

American soldiers watched the grand fleet cruise out of the harbor with a mixture of exaltation and disbelief. Samuel Larrabee remembered the scene in his pension application sixty years later: "The drums beat to arms from Dorchester Heights all around to Cambridge, and we instantly left our fort and hastened to our regiment."[54] His unit marched rapidly to the gates of Boston and, by noon, they occupied the State House. The streets were quiet. Word of the evacuation spread quickly in the countryside. Abigail Adams wrote her husband, "I think the sun shines brighter and the birds sing more melodiously."[55]

John Stark learned of the British departure that morning. Soon he made his way to Bunker Hill with Colonel Reed and Captain James Wilkinson. Wilkinson wrote later that the three men examined the battlefield, the rail fence and the stone wall on the beach along Mystic River. "I paced the distance to the point from whence the British light infantry, after three successive gallant charges, were finally repulsed." Stark and Reed described the action to him "in a manner so simple and so clear" that Wilkinson imagined he could see the events of that June day.[56]

They examined Prescott's redoubt and walked through the blackened ruins of Charlestown. Then they rowed across the river and followed a narrow, winding street into Boston. The British had warned the residents to stay in their homes during the embarkation, and the streets still remained empty and silent. The three American officers found the quiet "death-like." Stark, Reed and Wilkinson had all had smallpox; the disease was too common in the city to risk exposing men who had not survived the illness.[57]

Washington rode into the city the next day. There were no parades, no cheers, no celebrations. He went to church and prayed. The British had departed. Washington did not know where they went, but he guessed and feared their target was New York.

16

RETREAT FROM CANADA

Not an Army, but a Mob

Horatio Gates, the patriot army's adjutant general, signed an order command-ing John Stark to lead two Continental regiments to Norwich, Connecticut, and there await further orders. The order was dated March 16, 1776, the day before the British evacuation of Boston.[1] American officers knew in advance that Howe intended to leave Boston, but they didn't dare release many troops until he actually set sail. Stark led one of the advance units of the army and left Boston on March 20.[2]

Gates's order specifically warned Stark to prevent "all pillage and maraud-ing and every kind of ill-usage, or insult to the inhabitants of the country."[3] This was the first time an American army would travel across a wide stretch of its own territory. Rebel leaders knew that many in the population had yet to decide where to attach their loyalty. A disciplined, well-behaved soldiery would advance the patriot cause; a "rabble in arms" would not.

While Washington considered how to defend New York, events in Can-ada altered his plans. Chaos had overwhelmed the northern campaign. It took months for Americans to comprehend the full scale of the disaster. That spring, Congress still believed that the Canadian adventure could succeed. John Hancock, president of Congress, wrote a letter in January to the inhab-itants of Canada promising, "And if more considerable forces should become necessary, they shall not fail being sent."[4] He urged Washington to send four fresh battalions.[5]

To complement the military strategy, Congress authorized a unique dip-lomatic mission to Canada. Commissioners were to travel through the wilder-ness to encourage a proposed alliance. Benjamin Franklin, age seventy, would lead the delegation. Samuel Chase, Charles Carroll (a Catholic), and Carroll's cousin, John Carroll (a Jesuit priest), rounded out the commission. They faced a formidable challenge just getting to their destination.[6] Franklin feared he might not survive the journey: "I have undertaken a fatigue that at my time of life may prove too much for me. … So I sit down to write a few friends by way of farewell."[7]

All the members of Franklin's entourage reached Canada safely, but to no purpose. The Canadians not only resisted American efforts to lure them into the rebellion, they actively opposed them. Multiple Yankee defeats at Quebec and elsewhere had convinced Quebec's people that their future lay with England. One Jesuit priest did not counterbalance the effect of an army of anti-Catholic Protestants.[8]

Obedient to the wishes of Congress, Washington chose regiments to be sent north and appointed General John Sullivan to lead them. But, he wrote Congress, "The securing this post [New York City] and Hudsons River is to us also of so great importance that I can not at present advise the sending any more troops hence." By the end of April, Sullivan's regiments started north up the Hudson River. They included the New Hampshire troops of Colonel Stark.[9]

❧ ❧

John Stark travelled in a different direction. On May 6 he surprised his wife and children at Derryfield. The next day, Matthew Patten crossed the Merrimack to visit him: "I went with my bror [brother] Sam'll to see Col John Stark who came from New York yesterday," Patten noted in his diary on May 7. Matthew probably sought news of his sons John and Bob who served with the New Hampshire troops.[10]

It was strange that Stark should be at home at a time when his troops were on the move to a new campaign. Patten shed no light on the reasons for the "furlough," but Sullivan must have approved it for he did not criticize the colonel. In order to rejoin his regiment, Stark had to travel again the only path to Lake Champlain from New England—his own Crown Point Road. Caleb Stark later reported that his grandfather rejoined the army at St. Johns in Quebec.[11] Sullivan himself didn't embark for Canada until May 27, and Stark may have accompanied him.[12]

The New Hampshire regiments had sailed north in advance of their commanders. Most of the soldiers had not yet had smallpox; they didn't know they were heading into a full-blown epidemic.[13]

Colonel Reed's regiment, with Caleb Stark as adjutant, left Ticonderoga on May 5. They had a physician with them, Dr. Lewis Beebe of Sheffield, Massachusetts, brother-in-law of Ethan Allen, and a diarist. Beebe noted that the soldiers rowed the boats in "a hard snow storm" the day they set out. Reed and the doctor spent the several days of the voyage engaged in conversation.[14]

For a few days Beebe narrated a pleasant travelogue, until he met the remnants of the American army at Sorel:

> … but our army were so Scattered in beseidging the town, besides great numbers sick with the small pox, that they were able at the alarm, to embody on the grand parade only 250 men, when it was thot expedient to mak a retreat, tho great numbers were wholly unable to make their escape and were left to the mercy of the Britons. And those who Come safe to Sorrell were obliged to leave all their baggage and bring nothing away but the cloaths upon their backs. No person can conceive the distress our people endured the winter past, nor was it much less at the time of our retreat.[15]

While the army tried to survive, the diplomats also faced disappointment. The mission led by Franklin failed to sway the French-Canadians to the American cause, and the commissioners made their way back through the wilderness.

The great distance between the American armies, and the confusion and ignorance that distance fostered, now struck hard. Rather than reinforcing a victorious invasion force in the midst of a joyful populace, as Congress imagined, Sullivan's forces defended a defeated and plague-ridden skeletal force in a hostile land. Moreover, the British had been reinforced by a strong cadre of General Riedesel's German troops from Brunswick, whose ships reached Quebec City on June 1. The Germans got their first look at the Americans two days later when Dr. Julius Wasmus, their regimental surgeon, saw a column of prisoners: "… they are very shabby," he wrote in his journal, "and do not look like soldiers."[16]

General Wooster, temporary American commander, convened a council of war at Chambly on May 30. Stark attended the meeting, at which the assembled officers concurred that the army should remain in Canada. The next day, Wooster departed for home and Sullivan replaced him. John Sullivan held no optimistic notions about Canada. He wrote to John Hancock: "… no one thing is right. Everything is in the utmost confusion and almost everyone frightened at they know not what." Congress had been duped. "I am extremely sorry to inform you," he told Hancock, "that from the officers whose business it was to give Congress the true state of matters, Congress has not, as I believe, received anything like it." The northern army "has dwindled into a mobb without even the form or order of regularity."[17]

Despite the poor condition of his forces, Sullivan ordered an attack on Three Rivers on the opposite bank of the St. Lawrence. John Stark opposed the mission "as hazardous and imprudent and after delivering his opinion obeyed implicitly the orders of his commander."[18]

The attack failed. Hundreds more Americans became prisoners of Sir Guy Carleton's augmented army. Captain John Lacey of Pennsylvania wrote: "On the night of the 13th [of June] a council of war was held at gen. Sullivan's head quarters, at which it was decided that it was advisable for the whole of the American armey to evacuate Canada and to … make a stand at Ticonderoga." If true, Lacey's statement suggested that a decision had already been made to abandon Crown Point.[19]

The Americans struggled to mount an orderly withdrawal from Canada. In the midst of the suffering and strife of the retreat, some American soldiers remembered one unusual fact—the British commander, General Sir Guy Carleton, had behaved with singular humanity toward American prisoners. Benedict Arnold wrote, "The prisoners are treated politely and supplied with everything the garrison affords." Many of the American captives suffered from smallpox. Carleton ordered his men to "convey them to the general hospital where proper care shall be taken of them."[20]

Sullivan found it necessary to try to instill some discipline in the remaining effective soldiers. They were dirty, hungry and exhausted. His order of the day for June 11 threatened punishment for any soldier who appeared on parade "dirty, with a long beard, or his knee-breeches open." His men began the retreat from Sorel on June 14.[21]

Those men who were strong enough either rowed or poled boats upstream on the Richelieu River (also known as the Sorel River), the waterway from Lake Champlain to the St. Lawrence River. Others marched along the shore. In some places rapids reduced the river depth, and soldiers had to drag the boats with ropes, straining against the combined weight of the current and the boats with their cargo of sick men, arms and baggage. Charles Cushing wrote to tell his brother of their trials:

> After refreshing ourselves with a little breakfast, we were obliged to assist in getting the batteaus, cannon, and other stores, above the lower Rapids; and then it is as much as twenty men can do to tow a loaded batteau up the river in many places. After our party had drawn over two batteaus, two pieces of cannon and all their tents and baggage and put them on board, we set off with three or four boats up the river. In some places the men were obliged to wade up to their middle. ... During this fatigue, the men had but little to eat but pork and flour and lake water to drink.[22]

Several weeks after the retreat, John Stark wrote to Congress on another matter, but he included a synopsis of his responsibilities during the withdrawal: "In our retreat from Sorel, I brought up the rear to Crown Point, was left with a great part of the stores and about 30 men only to assist me, and the Regulars very often within five miles of us."[23]

They reached Chambly on June 15, with General John Burgoyne's redcoats close behind. Sullivan ordered men to torch the sawmills, row galleys and schooners along the river. They also burned what they could of the massive stone Fort Chambly, "down to the walls." Rebels were leaving the south end of the town as the British entered the north end.[24]

The troops of Sullivan and Benedict Arnold met at St. John and continued south together. Arnold's men had crossed the St. Lawrence from Montreal and marched overland. Arnold agreed that the Canadian adventure should end and patriots should "secure our own country before it is too late."[25]

South of St. Johns, there were too few able men and too few boats for the task of moving the army, with all its invalids, up (south on) the lake. The sick were sent ahead to Isle aux Noix near the north end of the lake.[26] The boats then returned to St. Johns to be reloaded. Two men rowed each boat the twelve miles to the island and back.[27]

Caleb Stark was among the last to leave St. Johns, as Americans torched everything of military value. He later wrote a deposition about the burning of the mansion of Moses Hazen. "The roof had been entirely covered with lead," he wrote, "but was ripped off by the American troops to make musket balls which they stood in great need of." Hazen himself evacuated St. Johns in the same boat with Caleb.[28]

Without boats to pursue them, the British gave up chasing the Americans at St. Johns. Roads existed on which they might have overtaken parts of the fleeing army; they far outnumbered the rebels. But they let Sullivan, Arnold, Stark, and the remnants of their commands escape.

⁂

Isle aux Noix (Nut Island) in the Richelieu River was a low, swampy plain about a mile long and quarter mile wide—a miserable place in the June heat. The island's population of desperately ill men grew daily. The simplest medical help was unavailable, and well men could only watch as the sick suffered and died. When Dr. Lewis Beebe arrived, he told of the horror there:

> Language cannot describe nor imagination paint, the scenes of misery and distress and continually groaning, & calling for relief, but in vain! Requests of this nature are as little regarded, as the singing of Crickets, in a summers evening. The most shocking of all Spectacles was to see a large barn Crowded full of men with this disorder, many of which could not See, Speak or walk—one nay two had large maggots an inch long, Crawl out of their ears, were on almost every part

of the body. No mortal can ever believe what these suffered unless they were eye witnesses.[29]

An affliction now almost extinct, smallpox gave its sufferers unspeakable tortures. Excruciating headaches and back pain accompanied by high fever led to a rash of sores in the mouth and nose. The rash was an irruption of raised pustules that spread on the victim's skin and often became confluent (where the pustules ran together and converged over each other), creating a single oozing mass with a horrible stench. The rash scabbed and crusted. It might take as long as ten to sixteen days for death to ease the suffering.[30]

The Americans on Isle aux Noix dug a great pit. Each day the dead were rolled into the hole and covered with a layer of earth and left to rot. The next day, fresh bodies were added to the layers.[31]

On June 20, Matthew Patten's son John died of smallpox on the island. His father didn't learn of his death for a month, when he wrote a diary passage in memory of his son: "He was shot through the left arm at Bunker Hill fight and now was lead after suffering much fatigue to the place where he now lyes in defending the just Rights of America to whose end he came in the prime of life by means of that wicked Tyrannical Brute (Nea worse than Brute) of Great Britain he was 24 years and 31 days old."[32]

On June 20, Sullivan ordered all the sick to be moved south to Crown Point. Healthy soldiers remained on the island until the invalids had been encamped in tents and huts on the east side of the lake at Chimney Point. John Stark, immune because of his prior illness, was among the last to leave the pestilent island.

By July 2 most of the army had reached Crown Point. Most of the soldiers that were well made camp on the west shore in hopeful isolation from the diseased men. Stark's regiment, however, remained across the lake at Chimney Point.[33] Dr. Beebe noted that death visited both shores of the lake: "Buried 4 this day, 3 belonging to our Regt. On the other side, they generally Lose more than double to what we do here."[34]

Sullivan arrived after midnight on July 2 to find that morale had broken down. A court-martial met on July 4 to try several men and officers for various misdemeanors. Soldiers had quarreled with each other, visited "grog shops," and in one instance "pulled down a guard house."[35]

The Americans made no effort to improve the fortifications on either side of the lake. According to Beebe, the old fort "has tumbled to ruin and decay." The doctor faulted the leadership: "The Genls. have their hands full in riding about the camp—prancing their Gay horses."[36]

Hot, steamy weather continued without relief, broken some days by strong thunderstorms. "This is a remarkable Cuntry for thunder and lightning," Beebe wrote, "this is the 9th day since my arrival here, during which time we have had it severely every day." He thought for a while that the cases of smallpox had dropped off, but on July 3 he noted sadly, "Death visits us almost every hour."[37]

Some men reached their breaking point. Engineer Jeduthan Baldwin hoped to be discharged, but while he waited he agonized, "I am heartily tired of this Retreating, Raged [ragged], Starved, lousey, thievish, Pockey Army in this unhealthy country."[38]

John Trumbull, son of Connecticut's governor, arrived at Crown Point where, "I found not an army, but a mob, the shattered remains of twelve or fifteen fine battalions ruined by sickness, fatigue and desertion and void of every idea of discipline or subordination."[39]

Morale suffered further with news that Congress planned to replace Sullivan with General Horatio Gates. Whether he intended it or not, Washington may have nudged Congress toward this move when he wrote of Sullivan that he displayed "a little tincture of vanity … an over desire of being popular, which now and then leads him into some embarrassment."[40]

Sullivan, stung by the loss of his command, responded on July 6 by writing to his superior, General Schuyler, "… surely my honor calls upon me to leave the service after a person is put over me without any impeachment of my conduct." He threatened to resign his commission.[41] Schuyler, who was at Crown Point with Sullivan, answered the next day, assuring his subordinate that his character as an officer remained "unimpeached" but granting Sullivan leave to depart if he wished.[42]

Most of Sullivan's officers thought he had performed well under difficult circumstances, and they told him so in an address presented in his honor at Crown Point on July 8. Notably, even colonels from Pennsylvania, like Wayne and De Haas, joined in expressing admiration for the general. His subordinates agreed with Sullivan that holding Crown Point was essential. Sullivan wrote to Schuyler, "The Officers & Soldiers under my command Seem to think with me that this place [Crown Point] must be fortified and never given up." Sullivan was the sole general officer in the theater who held that conviction, but Colonel John Stark agreed with him.[43]

The decision to replace Sullivan worried Dr. Beebe. "Genl. Gates, Superceding Genl. Sullivan, I find gives universal uneasiness to all the New England officers, and most likely will finally cause them to resign their commissions; then we Shall be in a fine pickle to meet the enemy." Beebe's diary entry went on to describe the effect on proud officers of being "superceded": "… they will tell you they can be of no further service to their Country." He called this attitude a "spirit of pride and ambition" and believed it would "yet prove our ruin." Beebe, of course, had Sullivan in mind, but his analysis applied to most American officers.[44]

On July 6 the five generals of the northern army met at Crown Point to consider a critical question—whether to remain at Crown Point or to move the army south to Ticonderoga and the wooded hillock across the lake from the fort. Generals Schuyler, Arnold, Gates, De Woedtke and Sullivan debated the question. A determining factor seemed to be whether the hill on the Vermont shore could be defended.[45]

Schuyler had ordered twenty-year-old John Trumbull to examine the wild promontory across from Ticonderoga to determine its merits. He and Colonel Wynkoop, commander at the fort, determined that the hill "was admirably adapted for a military post."[46] Trumbull gave his report at Crown Point.

If the general officers had not already concluded to abandon Crown Point, Trumbull's opinion convinced them. The engineer, Jeduthan Baldwin, had not yet examined the new ground, but the commanders made their decision without his advice. The minutes of their council stated their reasoning:

RESOLVED: That under our present circumstances the Post of Crown Point is not tenable; and that, with our present force, or one greatly superior to what we may reasonable expect, it is not capable of being made so this summer.

RESOLVED: That it is prudent to retire immediately to the strong ground on the east side of the Lake, opposite to Ticonderoga, with all the healthy and uninfected troops; and that the sick and infected with the small pox be removed to Fort George; ...[47]

Without consulting the field officers, the generals ordered this decision to take effect. John Stark, who had attacked the forts at Ticonderoga and Crown Point during the war with France and who probably knew their defensive capabilities better than anyone, was thunderstruck. He was not alone.[48]

On July 8, twenty-one colonels of the northern army signed a "Remonstrance" directed to General Schuyler, in which they vehemently disagreed with the decision. Stark's was the first signature on the document. The colonels cited seven reasons for their position, of which the first four made the strongest statement. First, they could defend Crown Point from any enemy force. Second, they could maintain naval superiority from Crown Point, but not from Ticonderoga. Third, the existing fortifications at Crown Point would be difficult to retake from the British, once given up. Fourth, if the British held Crown Point, they would have easy access by road to the New England settlements—using the road built by Stark's men in 1759.[49]

There was not much difference in the physical condition of the two forts; they were both in ruins. Crown Point burned in 1773, leaving only the stone walls, and Ticonderoga had been blown up by the French. The hill across the lake from Ticonderoga, which the generals proposed to fortify, was a "howling wilderness" according to Bayze Wells, a Connecticut officer stationed there.[50]

At Ticonderoga the terrain on both sides of Lake Champlain was dominated by a high mountain on the west shore south of the La Chute River. It had been named Sugar Loaf Hill, but was newly renamed Mount Defiance. No such high ground threatened Crown Point. In addition, the lake north of Crown Point was a broad expanse of water with plenty of maneuvering room for sailing vessels and plenty of coves and rivers for hiding from British warships. Lake Champlain was narrowest at Crown Point, making passage difficult in the face of cannons at the fort.

Schuyler wrote a reply to his colonels on July 9 in which he brushed off their views. Rather than explaining the thinking of the generals, he wrote, "The reasons which induced the council of General officers unanimously to give their opinion to remove the main body of the Army from Crown Point, I cannot conceive myself at liberty to give without their consent."[51] This was an astonishing statement to make to the men expected to carry out the mission, men who would ordinarily be consulted on such a question.

Philip Schuyler was a New Yorker. Most of the officers who signed the Remonstrance were New Englanders. No colonels from Pennsylvania had signed it. Schuyler knew there was bad blood between the officers of the two regions of New England and the Mid-Atlantic. He wrote Washington: "… disorder and discord reign triumphant."[52] Colonel Hastings of Pennsylvania bluntly told Gates, "we shall be happier and act better, if the eastern and southern troops are in distant brigades."[53] Schuyler blamed the New England officers for the schism. He may have believed their Remonstrance amounted to carping.

It may have been the perceived need to isolate those ill with smallpox from the rest of the army that motivated the general officers to abandon Crown Point. If so, they owed that explanation to their field officers.

George Washington, who had never visited either fort, agreed with Stark and the other colonels. He had read the Remonstrance and Schuyler's response to it. He wrote to the president of Congress and to Gates on July 19 to express his disapproval of the abandonment of Crown Point. The decision, he said, "… surprised me much; and the more I consider it the more striking does the impropriety appear. The reasons assigned against it by the Field Officers in their remonstrance coincide greatly with my own ideas and those of the other General Officers I have had the opportunity of consulting with, and seem to be of considerable weight—I may add, conclusive."[54]

Washington advised Congress that he believed the British would occupy Crown Point as soon as the Americans left and, thus, all chance for naval superiority on Lake Champlain would be lost. Despite his disappointment, he refused to reverse the decision, however, "lest it might increase the jealousy and diversity of opinions which seem already too prevalent in that Army, and establish a precedent for the inferior officers to set up their judgement whenever they would in opposition to those of their superiors, a matter of great delicacy, and that might lead to fatal consequences, if countenanced; though in the present instance I could wish their reasoning had prevailed."[55]

17

INDEPENDENCE

Now We Are a People

The generals lost no time once they made the decision to abandon Crown Point. They sent engineer Jeduthan Baldwin to Ticonderoga on July 7 along with twenty-six carpenters with orders to repair the fort and commence building boats at Skenesborough at the south end of the lake. During the next weeks Baldwin and his cadre of shipwrights and carpenters worked furiously to prepare for a British attack.[1]

Meanwhile, smallpox continued to ravage the soldiers at Crown Point and Chimney Point. Deputy Adjutant General John Trumbull described the men's plight: "I found them dispersed, some few in tents, some in sheds, and more under the shelter of miserable brush huts. … I can truly say that I did not look into a tent or hut in which I did not find either a dead or dying man." He counted a total complement of 5,200 men, of whom 2,800 were too ill to function—more than half. The first task facing the army was to move all those invalids, overland and by boat, to Fort George at the south end of Lake George.[2]

Before the evacuation of the sick, John Stark's nephew and namesake, William's son, sixteen-year-old John Stark, died of smallpox at Chimney Point.[3] The adjutant of the First New Hampshire Regiment also died that summer. Caleb Stark, age sixteen, replaced him and earned a promotion to lieutenant.[4]

The withdrawal to Ticonderoga began in earnest on July 10 and continued for a week. Men rowed boats to two destinations—some carried New England troops to the wooded hill on the eastern shore; others ferried Pennsylvania regiments to the peninsula below the fort. The latter troops camped around the ruins and on the hillsides near the old French Lines.

Late at night on July 19, a cloudburst struck the area, "one of the most severe showers of rain, ever known," according to Dr. Beebe. The storm drowned at least two sick soldiers from a Pennsylvania unit at Ticonderoga. Beebe related, "One man having the small pox bad, & unable to help himself, and being in a tent alone, which was on ground descending; Current of water came thro his tent in such plenty, that it covered his head." Beebe denounced officers who would take such poor care of their soldiers.[5]

Men billeted near the French Lines discovered the horrors of the previous war. Erosion over the past eighteen years had disinterred the dead of General Abercromby's failed attack. Colonel Anthony Wayne described the scene: "… the ancient Golgotha or place of Skulls—they are so plenty here that our people for want of Other Vessels drink out of them, whilst the soldiers make tent pins out of the shins and thigh bones of Abercrombies' men."[6]

Colonel John Stark commanded the brigade at the new encampment on the eastern shore. John Trumbull examined the site again, this time with Wayne and Baldwin, and they agreed with his description of the hill as an admirable defensive position:

> At the northern point, it ran low into the lake, offered a good landing place; from thence the land rose to an almost level plateau, elevated from fifty to seventy-five feet above the lake, and surrounded on three sides by a natural wall of rock, everywhere steep, and sometimes an absolute precipice sinking to the lake. On the fourth and eastern side of the position ran a morass and deep creek at the foot of the rock, which strengthened that front, leaving room only, by an easy descent, for a road to the east, and to the landing from the southern end of the lake. We found plentiful springs of good water at the foot of the rock. The whole was covered with primeval forest.[7]

The hill had no name. Scores of men leveled the primeval forest with axes and saws. They built a stockade near a good spring on the hilltop and constructed roads to connect huts, gun emplacements, and a hospital, all spread across a broad expanse. While digging into the hillside, the soldiers killed "a vast number of rattlesnakes." When the news of the signing of the Declaration of Independence arrived, Jeduthan Baldwin began to call the hill, "point Independency" or "Mount Independency." Mount Independence it remained.[8]

On July 28, Colonel Arthur St. Clair read the entire Declaration to the assembled troops after worship services. He closed the reading by adding, "God Bless the free independent states of America," and the soldiers erupted with cheers. A witness recorded, "It was remarkably pleasing to see the spirits of the soldiers so raised, after all their calamities; the language of every man's countenance was, Now we are a people; we have a name among the States of the world."[9]

On July 20, Dr. Beebe made a brief entry in his journal: "… three New Brigadier Genls. appointed." One of them, according to the doctor, was John Stark. Beebe was wrong; Stark received no promotion.[10] John Sullivan's promotion to major general had left a vacancy at the brigadier level to be filled by a New Hampshire officer. Congress promoted Colonel James Reed, leader of the Third New Hampshire Regiment. Stark, commander of the First New Hampshire, believed the promotion should have gone to himself, as the first in line. The slight was particularly galling to him because Colonel Reed had been stricken with smallpox months before and was never again able to serve in any military capacity.[11]

Stark was furious and wrote a letter of protest to Congress. In it he reviewed his considerable military experience in two wars and pointed out an unwelcome truth—that politics determined promotions: "… there are so many officers in the Continental army promoted before me that neither seniority or merit intitles them to and that never was in an army until they joined the Continental service." Unfortunately, the statement applied as well to many of Stark's superior officers, men like Nathanael Greene and John Sullivan, who were bound to resent his words. Not content with prodding the politicians, Stark delivered an ultimatum: "… I hope the Honorable Congress will take it into consideration and either give me my rank in the army or give me leave to retire to my family." Congress took no action on his demand, but the delegates remembered the tenor of his words.[12]

Stark remained in command of the Third Brigade, nominally superior to Colonels Maxwell, Winds, Wynkoop and Poor. Wynkoop's regiment was removed from Stark, however, and placed under the command of Colonel Poor, perhaps testament to the fact that Wynkoop could be as difficult as Stark.[13]

Relations between the soldiers from New England and the soldiers from Pennsylvania remained testy. Colonel Anthony Wayne's orderly book contained repeated criticisms of the troops over on Mount Independence. On September 3 the entry read, "The Gen'l sees with concern the dilatoriness with which the public works are carried on Mount Independence at a time when our friends and countrymen are engaged with the enemy." A few days later Wayne noted, "The Gen'l is surprise at the negligence and carelessness of the guard on Mount Independence." Such reports reflected directly on the colonel in command, John Stark.[14]

Insubordination arose within Stark's own brigade. One incident gave rise to a general court-martial with a peculiar result set forth in Wayne's orderly book:

> Captain Newland try'd at a General Court Martial of which Colonel Poor was President for damning and otherwise abusing Colonel Stark the Court are of the opinion that the charge is fully supported but judge at the same time that the satisfaction offer'd Colonel Stark at the time of the abuse was sufft. [sufficient] & thereby acquit him from his arrest.[15]

What constituted Stark's "satisfaction"?—an apology perhaps, or did Stark thrash Captain Newland? The orderly book never answered the question, but the entry reflected one more instance of failure of discipline among Stark's troops. Wayne was creating a written record that would be of no help to John Stark.

Militia units from Connecticut and Massachusetts arrived at Mount Independence. The encampment grew to great size, rivaling the populations of America's largest cities.

In August, Matthew Patten received a frightening message; his son Bob had fallen ill with smallpox and had been taken to the hospital at Fort George. Matthew was still grieving from the loss of his son John at Isle aux Noix. He borrowed enough money to make the weeklong journey to Lake George, where he found that his son had recovered and had returned to Mount Independence. Matthew followed, noting in his diary that on August 16, "I arrived at Tyconderoga and tarried at Col Starke and his other field officers until the 22ⁿᵈ in the morning which time I set off for fort George and Bob with me on Furlow. We were two days comeing over Lake George and September first we arrived home."[16]

American officers anticipated a British attack. Sullivan had tried to destroy the enemy's naval capability during his last days in Canada when his troops had burned every boat they found. When Sergeant Roger Lamb of the British army arrived at St. John on the heels of the fleeing Americans, he found "all the buildings in flames, all the craft and large boats the enemy could not drag up the rapids of Chamblee, with some provisions were also burnt."[17]

By September 30 the British had built a new fleet capable of engaging the Americans, including the ship *Inflexible*, two schooners, a flat-bottomed radeau, a gondola, twenty smaller vessels and many bateaux. Sergeant Lamb noted on October 1, "Our little squadron was put under the command of Captain Pringle, and is now ready to sail."[18]

Meanwhile, Benedict Arnold raced to build an American fleet at Skenesborough (now Whitehall) at the southern tip of the lake. Loyalist Philip Skene owned sawmills and a forge there, and the rebels put them to use. General Schuyler had recognized the potential of the site early and ordered boats to be constructed there even before the retreat from Canada.[19] At the end of August, Colonel Jeduthan Baldwin could report: "… we double mand [manned] our Smith's fires and workt in all the Shops both night & Day to get the Shiping riggd & the Artillery mounted."[20]

Arnold and Baldwin had their hands full. Shipwrights laid down the keels and lapped the planks on the craft at Skenesborough. Then crews rowed the hulls to Ticonderoga where the boats became naval vessels. Workers stepped the masts on each craft from atop a cliff beside the lake on Mount Independence. Then, sailors swarmed aloft to fix the standing and running rigging. (Standing rigging supports the masts, while running rigging raises and lowers the sails.) Finally, each boat was armed and equipped for war. Baldwin felt overwhelmed:

> … I have the intire direction of all the House & Ship Carpenters, the Smiths, Armourers, Roap makers, the Wheel and Carriage makers, Miners, Turners, Coalyers, Sawyers and shingle makers, which are all together 286, besides the direction of all the fateaging parties, so that I have my hands & mind constantly employed night & Day except when I am a Sleep & then sometimes I dream.[21]

Arming the ships proved to be hazardous duty. A practice firing of a mortar went awry when a shell exploded prematurely. "[I]t was a great wonder no man was kild," Baldwin wrote. A few days later a cannon went off while the weapon was being charged and "killd the gunners mate   he was blown into many pieces and scattered on the water."[22]

While the northern army awaited its confrontation with the British, news arrived of Washington's defeat at Long Island. Baldwin copied the information into his journal: "… we again hear that 1200 Regulars & 600 provencials were killd. In the battle on Long Island."[23] Baldwin's troops kept preparing for the conflict in a gloomy context; the rebel army now seemed to be on the brink of defeat.

Washington personally commanded the other corps of the American army at New York. He had faced a daunting challenge—Manhattan Island was almost surrounded by navigable water, and the world's most powerful navy might appear any day at many locations. The Americans needed to defend both Manhattan and Long Island, and that required the general to divide his army into two parts, separated by the East River. Then, he could only wait.

On June 29 the British fleet had appeared, so many masts and sails that one observer said, "I declare I thought all London was afloat."[24] The ships anchored, and General Howe's soldiers lined the decks. Blue-coated Hessians climbed into landing boats alongside their British allies.[25]

On Long Island, John Sullivan, newly promoted to major general, had replaced the ailing Nathanael Greene as commander of the left wing. He needed to defend a series of four approaches to Brooklyn, passes through a height of land that ran from west to east. Sullivan stationed troops at three of them. The fourth, Jamaica Pass, the most easterly approach, remained undefended.[26]

Beginning on August 22, Howe's troops landed on the south shore of Long Island. A Tory farmer led them through Jamaica Pass. They emerged on the flank and in the rear of Sullivan's soldiers and proceeded to roll up the patriots into the Brooklyn defenses. With the East River at their backs, the Americans were trapped.[27]

Washington tried to rally his retreating soldiers. "I will not ask any man to go further than I do," he told them. "I will fight so long as I have a leg or an arm."[28]

Some 1,000 Americans were killed, wounded, or captured.[29] Rebel soldiers feared being captured. One officer described his feelings: "The opinion we had formed of these troops [Hessians] determined us to run any risk rather than fall into their hands; and finding after our struggles no prospect of escaping, we determined to throw ourselves into the mercy of a battalion of Highlanders."[30]

The Highlanders would have accorded the rebels no mercy, however, as one British officer explained in a letter: "The Hessians and our brave Highlanders gave no quarter; and it was a fine sight to see with what alacrity they despatched the Rebels with their bayonets after we had surrounded them so that they could not resist." The same officer told how the British induced the Hessians to these measures: "We took care to tell the Hessians that the Rebels had resolved to give no quarter to them in particular, which made them fight desperately and put all to death that fell into their hands. You know all stratagems are lawful in war."[31]

By August 29, Washington faced a terrible choice—keep his force in Brooklyn and risk surrendering thousands of soldiers, or withdraw across the

East River to Manhattan and risk destruction by British naval gunfire. He chose to cross the river that very night. Washington's chief intelligence officer, Benjamin Tallmadge, recalled the danger of that decision: "To move so large a body of troops, with all their necessary appendages, across a river a full mile wide, with a rapid current, in the face of a victorious, well disciplined army nearly three times as numerous as his own, and a fleet capable of stopping the navigation so that not one boat could have passed over, seemed to present most formidable obstacles."[32]

The withdrawal of the army from Long Island required utmost secrecy. If the British discovered the movement, they could destroy the army. To achieve secrecy Washington ordered universal silence. Private Joseph Plumb Martin recalled the suspense: "We were strictly enjoined not to speak, or even cough, while on the march. All orders were given from officer to officer, and communicated to the men in whispers. What such secrecy could mean we could not divine.[33]

Nature aided the Americans. Colonel Glover's Marblehead sailors rowed the first units across under cover of darkness. At dawn, fog shrouded the river and concealed the movements all morning long. A northeast wind barred Admiral Richard Howe's ships from sailing up the East River to interfere.[34] Colonel Tallmadge watched the last boats leave the Brooklyn shore: "… I think I saw Gen. Washington on the ferry stairs when I stepped into one of the last boats that received the troops."[35] Washington saved what he could after the defeat on Long Island—an army of over 9,000 men with their weapons.[36]

During August and September, Jeduthan Baldwin had laid out artillery redoubts at Ticonderoga and Mount Independence. He noted that Gates and several senior officers examined and approved his work. But Baldwin never mentioned any effort to occupy or fortify the highest hill in the vicinity— Mount Defiance.[37]

When John Trumbull wrote his autobiography years later, he stressed his efforts to convince his superiors of the advantages of occupying Mount Defiance. He wrote, "I had for some time, regarded this eminence as completely overruling our entire position." Other officers scorned his opinion, claiming that the mountain was "at too great a distance to be dangerous." When Trumbull raised the question at dinner with General Gates, he was ridiculed. But Gates gave Trumbull permission to experiment. Trumbull oversaw the firing of two cannons, one from Mount Independence and one from Fort Ticonderoga. Trumbull claimed that both shots stuck the mountain, the ball from the fort near the summit.[38]

But the officers found other reasons to deride Trumbull's ideas. They insisted the summit was "inaccessible to the enemy." This time the young adjutant took Benedict Arnold and Anthony Wayne on a hike. They climbed the mountain from the lake, its steepest side. Once on top, the officers could see the truth: "… when we looked down upon the outlet of Lake George, it was obvious to all, that there could be no difficulty in driving up a loaded [gun] carriage."[39]

Trumbull claimed that he wrote a "memoir" to Generals Gates and Schuyler urging them to occupy and fortify Mount Defiance. Long afterward he could find no such document in the papers of either general, and he had kept no copy. The generals ignored the mountain in 1776 and again in 1777. As at Crown Point, however, there was one officer who had reason to know the tactical possibilities of that high ground from actual combat experience—John Stark—but if anyone sought his views, the record is silent.[40]

Before Arnold's navy could set sail to fight the British on Lake Champlain, Arnold needed to establish who commanded it. Gates had ordered him to take command on August 7.[41] Ten days later Arnold wrote to Gates to complain of a problem with Commodore Jacobus Wynkoop, who believed Schuyler had previously given him the fleet. Arnold wrote, "He [Wynkoop] refuses to be commanded by any one, and imagines his appointment (which is by General Schuyler) cannot be superseded." The commodore refused to turn over control to Arnold without a direct order from Gates.[42]

Wynkoop wrote to Arnold: "I find by an order you have given out, that the schooners are to go down the lake. I know no orders but what shall be given out by me, except sailing orders from the Commander-in-Chief. If an enemy is approaching, I am to be acquainted with it, and know how to act in my station."[43]

Arnold responded heatedly, "You surely must be out of your senses." To ensure that Wynkoop would not mistake his meaning, Arnold told the commodore that if his orders were disobeyed, "I shall be under the disagreeable necessity of convincing you of your error by immediately arresting you."[44] Gates backed Arnold and ordered Wynkoop "instantly" placed under arrest.[45]

Wynkoop's hopes to command the fleet probably never stood much chance against the aggressive energy of Arnold. The Dutchman didn't help his prospects when, on August 10, he convened a council of war to consider what action to take about a fleet of sails he had spied with his telescope. Closer examination revealed that the "fleet" was a flock of white gulls.[46]

With Arnold in charge, the little navy set forth on Lake Champlain to challenge the British. His orders from Gates required much interpretation: "… it is a defensive war we are carrying on, therefore no wanton risk or unnecessary display of power of the fleet is at any time to influence your conduct." On the other hand he instructed Arnold, "you will act with such cool, determined valor as will give them [the British] reason to repent their temerity."[47] Some officers, given such ambiguous orders, might be forgiven for acting timidly—not Benedict Arnold.

After several tentative probes on the lake and after weathering a dangerous storm, Arnold anchored his ships in the narrow waterway between Valcour Island and the New York shore. He reported to Gates that his ships were "as near together as possible, & in such form that few Vessels can attack us at the same Time, & then will be exposed to the fire of the whole fleet."[48]

Arnold's tactic was the naval equivalent of a fighter backing himself against the ropes, gambling that he could punch hard enough to avoid destruction. The Americans could escape to the north, but only if the wind blew from the south. The first element of the gamble was whether the British fleet would pass east of the island before they discovered the American ships. If so, they would have to beat back against the prevailing wind in order to engage the Americans. The British obliged, cruising south past the island before turning back. On October 11 the two armadas met.[49]

The American ships rode at anchor in a curve nearly a mile long across the channel west of Valcour Island. The largest and most dangerous of the British ships were square-rigged and difficult to sail upwind. The outgunned Americans could stay in the fight only if the English could not use all their strength.[50]

Lieutenant Bayze Wells fought under Arnold and recorded what he saw: "… the Battle lasted Eight hours Very hot." Arnold later calculated he lost about sixty men killed before the badly mauled Americans sought to escape. Wells wrote: "After dark orders was Given for our fleet to Retreat to Crown-point   accordingly we Did and Come by them undiscovered."[51]

It was a miraculous escape. The British had anchored far enough out in the lake to permit the Americans to drop south along the shore without being discovered. British Lieutenant James Hadden praised the American withdrawal in his journal: "All the enemies vessels used oars and on this occasion they were muffled. The retreat gave great honor to Gen. Arnold, who acted as admiral to the Rebel fleet on this occasion."[52]

Arnold did not escape for long. The enemy discovered his absence and pursued, catching slower vessels one by one. Arnold, aboard the *Congress*, led a squadron into Arnold Bay on the Vermont side, where he ordered his sailors to abandon and burn their ships, "Arnold being the last man who debarked." He refused to strike the colors and scuttled his fleet with the flags flying.[53]

The surviving Americans walked south along the lake until boats sent to their rescue reached them. They arrived back at Ticonderoga "about Sun Set" on October 14.[54] At Ticonderoga, Jeduthan Baldwin noted grimly, "… our fleet Destroyed, only 5 out of 16 Return'd." Americans burned the remaining buildings at Crown Point and left the smoking ruins to the British—"a Mellancholly Sight that was Seen at Ticonderoga," Baldwin wrote, "but we may Expect a more Mellancholly seen [scene] to morrow or Soon."[55]

Americans expected a British attack at Ticonderoga that fall. Baldwin kept his men busy fashioning a boom across the lake between the fort and Mount Independence to prevent ships from getting past the artillery emplacements. Gates approved the engineers' plan to build a bridge over the boom to enable soldiers from either shore to reinforce those on the other side.[56]

Toward the end of October, false alarms called out the army to several musters. Rumors flew. "Some say they will attack this post," Dr. Beebe wrote on October 22, "others that they will return to Canada."[57] The Americans now lived in huts with fires to warm them; the British lived under canvas. Beebe thought "the cold nights must be very uncomfortable in their present situation." Trumbull calculated the American strength at more than 13,000, "principally however militia."[58]

Americans watched as redcoats rowed small boats around the lake north of the defenses while their officers took soundings with weighted ropes to measure the water's depth. Their activity seemed to point to a naval attack. Gates and Stark conducted a dialogue about British strategy. Stark reportedly told the general, "My opinion is, that they will not fire a shot against this place this season; but whoever is here next must look out."[59] Stark believed it was too late in the season for the British to take advantage of a victory, if they should succeed. Their fleet would soon be frozen in lake ice, and they had no means to provide for the army with their base far away in Canada.

British General Sir Guy Carleton soon tested Stark's thesis. On October 28 sails appeared, and drums sounded in the American camps. "[T]he whole army presented a terrific blaze of fire arms issuing from every quarter to prepare for battle, which was momentarily expected to commence."[60] Rebel cannons belched smoke to ward off the ships.[61] Troops from Mount Independence rowed across the lake to reinforce the Pennsylvanians.[62] But the show of sails was Carleton's last salute for 1776. A few days later, scouts confirmed that the British had left Crown Point and sailed north, bound for Canada.[63]

A redcoat, Sergeant Lamb, confirmed that Stark had been correct: "Some of our vessels came within cannon shot of the American works at that place [Ticonderoga]. But the strength of that garrison and the season of the year restrained us from making any attempt, at that time on Ticonderoga."[64]

Benedict Arnold's little navy lost the battle of Valcour Island, but they won the campaign. The weeks it took the British to build a powerful fleet, and then more weeks to find and destroy Arnold's flotilla, used up the available time. The Canadian campaign was finally over.

18

Retreats and Defeats
Times That Try Men's Souls

After Carleton's fleet departed, thousands of American soldiers prepared to leave Mount Independence and Fort Ticonderoga. So many men on the move required considerable planning and logistical support. The units left in sequence, not all at once. As early as November 6, Colonel Wayne's Pennsylvanians, "was Drumed out of Camp by order of the Genl." This was not the drumming out of a malefactor, but a ceremony of honor.[1]

Dr. Beebe noted the departure of the New Hampshire troops on November 14. The invalids headed home. Beebe feared that many of them would never live to see their families. The fit soldiers left for Fort George the next day without knowing where they would go next.[2] John Stark went home with the invalids; he was in Derryfield by November 24.[3]

Stark's reasons for going home after a six-month absence were personal, not medical. He had left Molly with six minor children, and Molly was again pregnant. The two oldest boys, Caleb and Archibald, were in the army. Only John, Jr., at age thirteen was old enough to be much help to his mother. The others were too young: Eleanor, nine; Sarah, seven; Elizabeth, five; Mary, three; and Charles, a baby. Benjamin Franklin Stark would be born in January. None of the children would have been capable of running the sawmill, which probably stood silent for the duration of the war. The economic hardship from John Stark's absence was real. His family depended on his officer's wages but, in 1776, Molly had no means of getting her husband's pay unless he or an emissary handed it to her.[4]

Stark had other business at home as well. He brought with him wages owed young John Patten, who had died before drawing his pay. The colonel had also advanced John Patten money to clothe himself after the debacle in

Canada. Matthew Patten visited the Starks in Derryfield on November 24 to settle his son's accounts. Stark paid Patten £1 11s. plus "one farthing over" for the difference in the accounts. Matthew stayed overnight with the Starks because a "great snow storm" prevented him from recrossing the river.[5] The two friends had time to sit by the fire and talk of their sons—Caleb Stark, Archibald Stark and Bob Patten; all three boys were with the army, risking disease and violent death.

It was a brief interlude with his family. Stark's regiment marched down the Hudson, crossed the river at Esopus, and passed through the Minisink Valley on the way to Pennsylvania. The colonel left home to join his troops. Orders had arrived that made clear that Washington desperately needed help.

Washington's troops at New York suffered one defeat after another. The British overwhelmed militia troops at Kip's Bay and followed up by pushing the Americans to the north edge of Manhattan. Fort Washington surrendered on November 15. A few days later the British crossed the Hudson and took Fort Lee in New Jersey. Nearly 3,000 Americans became prisoners as a result of these actions alone. A desperate attempt to establish an American base in Westchester County failed after the battle of White Plains. Plagued by desertions and expired enlistments, the American army crossed the Hudson and began a painful retreat across New Jersey.[6]

Thomas Paine, traveling with the army, called this "the times that try men's souls," in *The American Crisis*. He wrote the first of his *Crisis* pages, according to tradition, "with a drumhead for a desk and a flickering campfire for light."[7]

After the loss of New York, the behavior of the combatants began to define what kind of war the revolution would be. What began as an angry reaction to an army of occupation had grown into a war for independence. Random British cruelty at Lexington and Bunker Hill expanded to the starvation of thousands of American prisoners at New York and the intentional murder of wounded and captured rebels at Long Island. But, in December 1776, there was still an ambiguity about the conflict. British leadership faltered at conducting all-out war, and Washington doubted the commitment of his own countrymen.

During the summer, the Howe brothers had written letters to members of Congress suggesting reconciliation. Franklin responded quickly: "It is impossible we should think of submission to a government that has with the most wanton barbarity and cruelty burnt our defenceless towns in the midst of winter, excited the savages to massacre our farmers, and our slaves to murder their masters, and is even now bringing foreign mercenaries to deluge our settlements in blood."[8]

The Howes persisted. They released one captive, General John Sullivan, to deliver a letter to Congress inviting a parley. John Adams rose in the chamber to oppose any meeting. Sullivan, he said, is "a decoy duck, whom Lord Howe has sent among us to seduce us into a renunciation of our independence."[9] In September, however, Adams joined Franklin and Rutledge in a futile council with British Admiral Richard Howe at Staten Island.[10]

British officers took a dim view of their commanders' efforts at peacemaking. Some even hinted that treason lay behind the Howe brothers' actions. Sir George Collier, a naval commander, waxed sarcastic over the failure to stop the American retreat from Long Island. Washington, he wrote, "was certainly very deficient in not expressing his gratitude to General Howe for his Kind behavior towards him."[11]

American officers harbored their own ambivalence about the war. Some advocated "hard war," in which all means might be used. Before the army left New York, the Americans understood that the British would benefit from the housing and Loyalist support available there. General Nathanael Greene urged the destruction of New York. He told Washington that Tories owned most of the city and, thus, "We have no very great reason to run any considerable risk for its defence." On September 5, Greene advised Washington to burn the city, but Congress refused to authorize arson, and the army left the city unburned.[12]

Then, in the early morning hours of September 21, the Fighting Cocks, a tavern near the Battery, caught fire. A strong south wind fanned the flames northward over wood-shingled roofs; the blaze roared through the town until it reached a firebreak of green pasture on the outskirts. A mile-long strip, nearly a quarter of the city, lay in charred ruins. General Howe, of course, blamed the rebels.[13]

Had Congress permitted, Washington would have burned New York as a military necessity. He wrote his cousin and overseer, Lund Washington: "Had I been left to the dictates of my own judgement, New York should have been laid in Ashes before I quitted it." He denied any responsibility for the fire, but he regretted that a more thorough conflagration had not been ordered. "This in my judgement may be set down among the capitol errors of Congress." The Americans could easily have destroyed the entire city when they occupied it, which is strong evidence that the actual fire was not their doing. Washington simply thanked good fortune. "Providence or some good honest fellow, has done more for us than we were disposed to do for ourselves," he wrote.[14]

The morning after the fire, a young American officer, Captain Nathan Hale, fell into the hands of the British. He wore the clothing of a schoolmaster, his occupation in civilian life, but carried papers that suggested he was an American spy.[15]

Nathan Hale was twenty-one years old and a recent graduate of Yale College. Although he had no military or espionage experience, he had volunteered to enter enemy territory at Long Island and New York City to spy on British positions. On Long Island he met a man more experienced in deception—Robert Rogers.[16]

A Connecticut Tory with the improbable name Consider Tiffany either witnessed or learned of the meeting of Hale and Rogers, which took place at a tavern. Tiffany reported that the two men were strangers to each other, but in the convivial taproom atmosphere they struck up a conversation. After a while, Tiffany wrote, Rogers "suspected that he [Hale] was an enemy in disguise." Pretending to be a rebel sympathizer, Rogers induced the younger man to confess that he was a patriot spy.[17]

Rogers had recently taken command of a Tory unit, the Queens American Rangers, but he probably suspected that the British trusted him only slightly more than the Americans did.[18] He feared that his word alone would be insufficient to convict young Hale, so he arranged to meet him again, this time in company with other Loyalists to corroborate Hale's admission. Tiffany wrote: "… Capt Hale repaired to the place agreed on, where he met his pretended friend, with three or four men of the same stamp, and after being refreshed, began the same conversation as hath already been mentioned."[19]

At some signal given by Rogers or one of his comrades, "a company of soldiers surrounded the house." They seized Hale and took him to Manhattan where General Howe questioned him. The young captain readily confessed he was a spy, and Howe summarily ordered that he be hanged.[20]

At the gallows the next morning, Provost Marshall William Cunningham took charge of the execution. He refused Hale's request for a clergyman and a Bible. A British witness, Captain MacKenzie, praised the condemned man's courage. "He behaved with great composure and resolution," MacKenzie wrote, "saying he thought it the duty of every good officer to obey any orders given him by his Commander in Chief."[21]

Hale's body was left hanging there for several days afterward. British soldiers mocked the dead man by suspending a board beside him, on which was painted the image of a soldier with words printed to identify the figure—"General Washington."[22]

In late November, while the main American army retreated across New Jersey, a skeletal force of 600 men from the regiments at Ticonderoga and Mount Independence marched south through the forests and mountains near the Delaware River in New York. It was a long walk for footsore men. Many of them suffered from "camp itch," an inflammation around the groin and upper thighs. Marching aggravated the condition; weeping sores appeared that made a man's breeches stick to his thighs.[23]

Private William Chamberlin of Stark's continental regiment remembered the journey through the backcountry. Only six or seven men from his company reached Pennsylvania; they had numbered seventy-six in Canada. The weather grew bitterly cold. Chamberlin wrote, "our shoes scarcely sufficient to keep our feet from the frozen ground without wrapping them in rags, the allowance of provision being poor, fresh beef without salt to season it."[24]

John Stark rejoined the Ticonderoga regiments during the march. General Gates had planned a route west of the settlements and, thus, the units were without news of the war, including the location of Washington's army.[25] Gates's aide, Major James Wilkinson, who had viewed Bunker Hill with Stark in March, described the conditions:

> In this sequestered valley we were thrown out of the ordinary current of intelligence, and cut off from all authentic information respecting the adverse armies. The winter had set in with severity: our troops were bare of clothing: numbers barefoot and without tents, provisions or transport of any kind. The men and officers sought shelter wherever they could find it in that thinly settled tract. We were halted on the 11th [of December] by a heavy fall of snow, which increased the General's anxiety for information from General Washington, and to relieve his solicitude, I volunteered my services to find him.[26]

Washington was at Brunswick on December 1, keeping his army barely one jump ahead of the enemy pursuing him. Alexander Hamilton's artillery company held off the redcoats across the Raritan while the rebels withdrew. Lieutenant James Monroe estimated that only 3,000 men remained with the American army. The British, on orders from Lord Cornwallis, halted at Brunswick, but the Americans slogged on to Princeton. Some officers and soldiers took shelter in a college building, Nassau Hall.[27]

Expiring enlistments continued to winnow the American force. "We are in a terrible situation," one soldier wrote, "with the enemy close upon us and whole regiments … leaving us."[28] But, Washington told Colonel Joseph Reed, "I will not despair." He intended to cross the Delaware River and find winter refuge in Pennsylvania. On December 7 the lead elements of the army reached the river. Washington remained behind to supervise the work of the pioneers, "tearing up bridges and cutting down trees to impede the march of the enemy."[29]

Cornwallis resumed his pursuit. His advance troops reached Princeton on December 7 and paused at the college, where they admired "A remarkable excellent library." Other redcoats came along and "spoiled and plundered a good library," in the words of a British sergeant.[30]

Princeton seemed to bring out the worst in the King's soldiers. They tore down fences and houses for the boards, sawed down fruit trees for spite, and burned a gristmill.[31] Where no man was at a home, it suggested to the regulars that the missing man was a rebel soldier, so they killed all the livestock. They raped women and girls.[32] The regulars and the Hessians committed these acts in open defiance of Howe's specific orders—"The Commander-in-Chief calls upon the commanding officer of corps to exert themselves in preserving the greatest regularity and strictest discipline in their respective quarters, particularly attending to the protection of the inhabitants and their property in their several districts."[33]

American soldiers collected boats along the Delaware to ferry the army across. The crossing took days in the small boats. The artist Charles Wilson Peale, a militia lieutenant from Philadelphia, watched. "All the shores were lighted up with large fires," he wrote, "boats continually passing and repassing full of men, horses, artillery and camp equipage." Peale thought it looked "rather the appearance of Hell than any earthly scene." The soldiers he saw were so dirty and bedraggled that he failed to recognize his own brother James.[34]

Eventually the army regrouped on the west bank. Men scoured the navigable length of the river for seventy miles to obtain boats and to deny them to the British. Cornwallis would have no means to attack the rebels until the Delaware froze hard from shore to shore.

Washington hoped for reinforcements. General Lee and his corps were nearby, but they were agonizingly slow in arriving. General Gates and his men were out in the wilderness somewhere. Meanwhile, soldiers left camp daily, their obligations terminated.

Then, word of General Lee's capture by Tarleton reached camp. Washington told the dismal story to Lund Washington in a letter on December 17: "Our only dependence now is upon the speedy enlistment of a new army. If this fails, I think the game will be pretty well up."[35]

On December 14, Howe ended his pursuit of the American army and ordered his campaign closed for the year. It was a remarkable piece of luck for Washington. The enemy stationed troops at a string of posts stretching across New Jersey. Three regiments of Hessians manned the garrison at Trenton.[36] Cornwallis sought permission to sail home to England, and Howe accommodated him. Howe intended to spend the winter in comfort in New York in the company of his mistress, Mrs. Loring, the wife of his commissary of prisoners, Joshua Loring.[37]

Washington knew nothing of these British plans. He thought they might still build a flotilla to follow him into Pennsylvania, or perhaps they would march across on the ice once the river froze. He strove to be ready for an attack. The Americans established a headquarters at McConkey's Ferry, about eight miles upriver from Trenton, with Washington's quarters at the home of William Keith.[38]

The American commander lived in a maelstrom of anxiety and uncertainty. He composed himself by thinking about home—Mount Vernon. He wrote a letter to his overseer, instructing him to plant locust trees "thick enough for their branches to interlock." He suggested that Lund purchase another mare for Mrs. Washington's chariot. Then, reality intruded on his thoughts and he warned the overseer to ready his papers for instant removal in the event "the Enemy's Fleet should come up the [Potomac] River."[39] Like many of his rebel compatriots, George Washington knew that his penalty for losing this war might be a trip to the gallows.

His officers compounded the pressure on the commander in chief. On the morning Lee was captured, Washington obtained a letter Lee had written to Horatio Gates. "Entre nous," Lee wrote, "a certain great man is most damnably deficient."[40] Lee had been removed from action, but Gates was equally disloyal to Washington. He declined to participate in any offensive campaign in December; he intended to go to Philadelphia; he felt ill. In truth, he wanted to convince Congress that he should replace Washington as supreme commander. When he arrived at Philadelphia, he discovered that Congress, fearful of a British attack, had fled to Baltimore.[41]

Once all the parts of the American army came together along the west bank of the Delaware, there would be no more than 5,000 effectives to confront the British and Hessians and, after New Years, most of them would be gone, their enlistments over. The soldiers lacked clothing, blankets and shoes. Many of them had been marching for weeks, travelling hundreds of miles without proper food or shelter. The enemy might strike them any day.

Two senior officers had already demonstrated their disloyalty to Washington, and it remained unclear how far down the chain of command that sentiment reached. Congress had removed itself to safety, severing or extending the lines of communication with the man running its war. Washington might have despaired; instead he resolved to attack.

19

Crossing the Delaware

The Dauntless Stark

John Stark arrived in the American camp with Horatio Gates and the New Hampshire regiments on December 20. Lee's men came in with Sullivan. Nathanael Greene, Henry Knox and John Glover were already present. None of them knew of the bold plan working in Washington's mind.[1]

Dr. Benjamin Rush, a fiery member of Congress, visited the commander in chief on the evening of December 23. He found the general "much depressed." While they talked, Washington absent-mindedly moved a quill pen across a paper on the table in front of him. A puff of air in the room sent the paper sailing to the floor near Rush, who looked down and read the words scratched on it—"Victory or Death."[2]

That same evening Washington wrote to his aide, Colonel Joseph Reed, who was on a mission downriver: "Christmas-day at night, one hour before day is the time fixed upon for our attempt on Trenton. For Heaven's sake keep this to yourself, as the discovery of it may prove fatal to us."[3] The general had already ordered rations for three days to be cooked. The countersign for the attack, he declared, would be "Victory or Death."[4]

On Christmas Eve, Washington rode to General Greene's headquarters at the Merrick house for a council of war. He knew when and where he wanted to strike, and the council's purpose was to assign roles to the officers. Six general officers and four field officers attended. Colonel Henry Knox and Colonel John Glover learned that they would lead the amphibious part of the expedition, loading the boats and getting them across the Delaware.[5]

Then, according to Stark's son-in-law, Benjamin Stickney, Washington called Colonel Stark into the room and told him the plan. Stickney wrote that Stark said to his commander: "Your men have long been accustomed to place dependence on spades, pickaxes and [illegible] for safety; but if you are ever to establish the Independence of the United States you must teach them to put confidence in their fire arms."[6]

The other officers in the room must have held their collective breath while Washington eyed the tactless colonel. The commander in chief and his troops had fought five battles in the past six months. But Washington responded calmly, "That is what we have agreed upon: we are to march tomorrow for the attack of Trenton; you are to command the right wing of the advanced guard and Gen. Greene the left."[7] As it turned out, General Sullivan would command the right wing; Stark and his men would serve as the point of Sullivan's spear.

The Hessians at Trenton watched great chunks of ice float down the Delaware and hoped for a total freeze-up. They dreamed of wintering in Philadelphia, America's largest city, with warmth, women and spirits. Grenadier Johannes Reuber noted in his diary that the ice was not strong enough to cross; "We will have to be patient."[8]

The Germans worried about an attack. Their commander, Colonel Johannes Rall, kept them on constant alert, but Trooper Reuber thought the Americans would be unable to mount an offensive. Still, there were continual reports that the rebels planned something. Apparently a spy lurked somewhere in the American camp, close enough to a senior officer that Rall received accurate intelligence that the Americans planned to attack Trenton. The report elicited the Hessians' abiding contempt for the rebels. Rall burst out, "Old women's talk." Then he boasted, "These clod-hoppers will not attack us, and should they do so, we will simply fall on them and rout them."[9]

For all his braggadocio, Rall remained on the alert; his troops could get no rest. One of them wrote: "We have not slept one night in peace since we came to this place. The troops have lain on their arms every night and they can endure it no longer." On Christmas night exhaustion led the Hessians to relax their vigilance just once. That night a winter storm with snow, sleet and high winds bore down on Trenton. One officer cancelled a regular nightly patrol on the outskirts of the town. It seemed absurd to imagine that the hapless Americans could manage an attack in such weather.[10]

⁂

Late in the afternoon of Christmas day, American troops formed up at parade and then, instead of returning to their tents and huts, they marched toward the river. One of Washington's aides described the scene: "It is fearfully cold and raw and a snowstorm setting in. The wind is northeast and beats in the faces of the men. It will be a terrible night for the soldiers who have no shoes. Some of them have tied old rags around their feet; others are barefoot, but I have not heard a man complain."[11]

James Wilkinson left General Gates in Philadelphia and returned to follow the army's march. He had no difficulty trailing the soldiers. "There was a little snow on the ground," he wrote, "which was tinged here and there with blood from the feet of the men who wore broken shoes."[12]

Soldiers huddled together along the riverbank waiting for their turn to cross. Colonel Glover's Marblehead sailors, the same men who had rescued the army from Long Island, crewed the flotilla. They poled and rowed "Durham" boats—large, shallow-draft vessels that were normally used to haul iron ore, grain and produce downriver to the ports. Soldiers stood as the boats crossed the swift, black current, with slabs of ice banging into the hulls. It was slow work rowing 2,400 men to the eastern shore with all their arms, horses and provisions. The sailors made the trip several times in the failing light.[13]

Washington ordered passages from Thomas Paine's writings read aloud to put heart into the men. They listened as an officer intoned, "The summer soldier and the sunshine patriot will, in this crisis, shrink from the service of their country; but he that stands it now deserves the love and thanks of man and woman."[14]

All the officers had orders to attach pieces of white paper to the backs of their hats so that their men would know which leaders to follow, and so that the officers would remember to lead from the front. Men gathered around wind-blown fires for warmth as the booming voice of Henry Knox called units to the boats.[15]

The floating ice slowed the bulky craft. The sailors kept at their task, hour after hour, through the night. Washington waited on the Jersey shore, wrapped in a cloak as the night slipped by. The mission was hours behind schedule; a pre-dawn attack was now impossible. The army still had to march nine miles through the storm.[16]

With so much on his mind, Washington now confronted a political problem. James Wilkinson walked up to him and handed him a letter. Wilkinson reported that Washington said, "'What a time is this to hand me letters!' I answered that I had been charged with it by General Gates. 'General Gates! Where is he?' 'I left him this morning in Philadelphia.' 'What was he doing there?' 'I understand him that he was on his way to Congress.' He earnestly repeated 'On his way to Congress!'"[17]

Washington understood the implications of Wilkinson's message. Gates, like Lee before him, openly opposed his commander and dared to shirk a vital mission in order to lobby politicians for a promotion. But Washington had no time to dwell on such matters this Christmas night.

The entire army was across the river by four in the morning. Then, columns of soldiers began the slippery march south through snow and mud. The storm had freshened into a howling nor'easter, but at least the wind struck the men in their backs. Two men who dropped out to rest froze to death where they lay.

Sputtering torches mounted on cannons threw narrow circles of light into the black night. Washington on horseback rode beside his men, occasionally stopping to exhort them, "Press on, press on, boys."[18] A Connecticut soldier remembered his commander pass by and say, "Soldiers, keep by your officers. For God's sake, keep by your officers." The soldier was struck by the general's "deep and solemn voice." The same man witnessed a close escape by Washington: "While passing a slanting, slippery bank his Excellency's horse's hind feet both slipped from under him, and he seized the horse's mane and the horse recovered."[19]

At Birmingham, about halfway to Trenton, the River Road branched off to the right. Washington and Greene led one corps to the left, down the Pennington Road. Sullivan, with Stark's troops in the lead, followed the River Road. Sullivan's soldiers discovered that snow and ice had wet the priming powder on their muskets, rendering them useless. Advised of the problem Washington sent an aide, Samuel Blachley Webb, to Sullivan with a message: "Use the bayonet. I am resolved to take Trenton."[20]

The planned attack on Trenton included three separate units crossing the river: Washington led the main force; militia General James Ewing and 800 men were to cross at Trenton Ferry, just below the town; and 1,800 Philadelphia Associators (Pennsylvania militia) intended to come over even farther south. River ice and strong wind kept both of the latter maneuvers from happening. Washington had no way to know that his attack would be made without the support of those units.[21]

Once Sullivan's men disappeared down the road, communications between the officers became haphazard. Aides on horseback carried messages with information that might arrive too late to be useful. The plan was for the two corps to strike Trenton at the same time, but the operation was already hours late. Achieving a coordinated attack seemed unlikely. Sullivan halted his columns in the woods for a few minutes, as he had been ordered, to allow for the greater distance to be travelled by Greene's forces. By 7:30 AM the Americans were still two miles from Trenton. They had lost the protective cover of darkness, but the swirling storm kept them hidden.[22]

John Stark's New Hampshire regiment moved at a snail's pace. Darkness, the icy road and cumbersome artillery pieces combined to slow the tired and freezing men. A young fifer, John Greenwood, remembered: "… we began an apparently circuitous march, not advancing faster than a child ten years old could walk, and stopping frequently, though for what purpose I know not."[23] During the halts the men tried to clear the moisture from their muskets by squibbing—firing charges of powder and wadding through the barrels.[24]

Local farmers and a company of forty New Jersey soldiers guided Stark's column nearer Trenton. They approached two buildings near the road—a small house used as a picket post by the Hessians, and the manor house of General Philemon Dickinson known as the Hermitage. At 8:00 AM they heard the sound of shooting from General Greene's direction. Almost immediately,

Stark's men encountered Hessians from the picket house and a company of Jagers at the Hermitage.[25]

Stark's men fought with fixed bayonets, charging the astonished Hessians and chasing them into the streets of Trenton.[26] A Washington aide wrote that, while Greene attacked on the Pennington road, "Colonel John Stark from New Hampshire in the advance on the river road, was driving Knyphausen's men pell-mell through the town."[27] By a combination of good planning and good luck, both wings of the army struck as one.

Henry Knox had insisted on hauling eighteen cannons to Trenton despite the challenges posed by the river and the weather. Both Greene and Sullivan ordered their artillery into action when they reached the town. The Germans, aroused by the shooting, ran into the streets and tried to mount a defense. American cannons caught them in a crossfire, broke up their formations and sent them running for cover. American infantrymen rooted them out where the cannons couldn't reach them.[28]

In addition to dragging his own artillery to the fray, Knox had planned to capture enemy guns and use them against the foe. Each wing of the attack contained "a detachment of artillery without cannon"—men equipped with the tools and the knowledge to load and fire whatever weapons came their way.[29] James Wilkinson described how a future president used this tactic:

> … Captain William Washington, who, seconded by Lieutenant James Monroe, led the advanced guard of the left column, perceiving that the enemy were endeavouring to form a battery, rushed forward, drove the artillerists from their guns, and took two pieces in the act of firing. These officers were both wounded in this charge; the Captain in his wrist, the Lieutenant through the fleshy part of his shoulder. These particular acts of gallantry have never been noticed … .[30]

The musket ball that struck James Monroe sliced an artery; he nearly bled to death. Dr. Riker, a local doctor who had just volunteered to help the Americans, clamped the artery and saved the young man's life. Meanwhile, American gunners turned the captured battery on the Hessians.[31]

Sullivan's soldiers drove the enemy into Trenton. Henry Knox watched as, "The hurry, fright and confusion of the enemy was [not] unlike that which will be when the last trumpet shall sound."[32] Wilkinson remembered how the shocked German auxiliaries reacted to Stark's onslaught: "The enemy made a momentary shew of resistance by a wild and undirected fire from the windows of their quarters which they abandoned as we advanced." And Wilkinson watched "the dauntless Stark, who dealt death wherever he found resistance, and broke down all opposition before him."[33]

Colonel Rall tried to rally his men, riding his horse among them. As usual, American marksmen targeted officers, and Rall made himself conspicuous. Two musket balls struck him in the side. His soldiers lifted their mortally wounded leader from his saddle and carried him into a church.[34] One young trooper thought Rall's loss meant the loss of the battle: "… when he was shot there was not an officer who had the courage to take up the half-lost battle."[35]

Dead and wounded Hessians filled the streets of Trenton. "The sight," one American remembered, "was too much to bear. I left it soon." Some rebels collected souvenirs from the bodies; others passed by in a kind of trance. Private Greenwood's regiment marched up to a large gathering of German prisoners, five or six hundred, standing at parade. "When we reached the end of their line," he wrote, "we were ordered to wheel to the right, which brought us face to face six feet apart." Victor and vanquished stood looking at each other, the first time either had the opportunity to see their enemies as men. Johannes Reuber thought, "I must confess that we thought too slightingly of the rebels who thus far had never been able to resist us."[36]

Washington found the dying Rall, who offered his sword in surrender.[37] One of Washington's aides watched while, "He [Rall] asked that his men might be kindly treated. Washington promised that he would see they were well cared for."[38] Hessian Private Reuber admitted, "A promise was given and it was kept."[39]

The American commander could report to John Hancock that his force had captured 23 officers and 886 men, and he thought not more than 30 of the enemy had been killed, "as they never made any regular Stand."[40] No

Americans died except the two men who froze to death; only four were wounded.

The officers debated pressing the attack elsewhere, but Washington resisted. He ordered a withdrawal back across the Delaware that night to the camp in Pennsylvania. He worried that strong enemy detachments from Princeton and Burlington might still attack his exhausted force. The condition of his army was made worse by the "liberation" of forty hogsheads of rum. A considerable number of patriot soldiers were dead drunk.[41]

⁂

Back across the Delaware in Pennsylvania, American officers still faced the same problem that confronted them before Trenton—the majority of enlistments would end at the New Year. The victory at Trenton would lead nowhere if the army evaporated. While Washington pondered his options, surprising news arrived—1,800 Philadelphia Associators had crossed the river into New Jersey under General John Cadwalader. They were looking for a fight.[42]

Washington saw an opportunity and convened a council of war at the home of Widow Harris on the evening of December 27. He told his assembled officers about the Associators' bold action, and he told them what Cadwalader hoped for: "If we can drive them from West Jersey, the success will raise an army by next Spring." The idea clearly appealed to the commander in chief. Some officers objected that their troops were ill-clad and exhausted, but the council approved a plan to join Cadwalader.[43]

This time the army embarked at multiple points up and down the river. A heavier accumulation of ice made the crossing even more difficult. Some men could walk across the layers of river ice, but horses, cannon and provisions still required boats. Most of the combined forces had reached Trenton by December 30, where they waited for orders.[44]

A Sergeant "R.," whose last name has been lost, described the scene: "At this trying time General Washington, having now but a little handful of men and many of them new recruits in which he could place but little confidence, ordered our regiment to be paraded, and personally addressed us, urging that we should stay a month longer. … The drums beat for volunteers, but not a man turned out." The general, never willing to admit defeat, tried again. Sergeant R. wrote:

> The General wheeled his horse about, rode in front of the regiment and addressing us again said, "My brave fellows, you have done all I asked you to do, and more than could be reasonably expected; but your country is at stake, your wives, your houses and all that you hold dear. You have worn yourselves out with fatigue and hardships, but we know not how to spare you. If you will consent to stay only one month longer, you will render that service to the cause of liberty and to your country which you probably never can do under any other circumstances."[45]

His plea was reinforced by an offer to pay a bonus of ten dollars in coin to each man who stayed. One by one, the men of Sergeant R.'s regiment stepped forward, "nearly all who were fit for duty in the regiment." The army had no cache of dollars to distribute, however. Washington begged Robert Morris in Philadelphia to find the funds and, somehow, Morris raised the cash and sent it to Trenton.[46]

Other officers pleaded with their men to stay and fight, and they dangled the bonus as bait. General Thomas Mifflin mustered some New England regiments. He managed to obtain reenlistments, which the soldiers acknowledged by raising their muskets in the air.[47]

Colonel John Stark needed to convince his own New Hampshire men. William Chamberlin approached Stark and asked for a discharge. The colonel answered that "he had not orders to give a discharge. ... He said we must wait a day or two as he could give no discharge until orders arrived." Stark was stalling for time. On January 1 the men were free to go, and their commander had no power to stop them.[48]

Stark addressed his soldiers, and an officer reported what he said: "He told them that if they left the army all was lost, reminded them of their deeds at Bunker's Hill and other occasions." Then the plain lumberman bet his farm. He "assured them that if Congress did not pay them their arrears, his own private property should make it up to them. He proposed a re-enlistment of six weeks, and such was his influence and popularity that not a man refused."[49]

The Hessian debacle at Trenton convinced General Howe that he needed Cornwallis; he cancelled Cornwallis's furlough and ordered him back to Trenton. Cornwallis moved quickly south toward the American army, collecting the scattered garrisons as he went and combining them into a formidable force. But, conditions had changed. The brutality of the occupiers and Washington's recent victory inspired a legion of partisans who took pleasure in killing redcoats from ambush. One Hessian wrote, "a fright came over the army. … Since we had thus far underestimated our enemy, from this unhappy day onward we saw everything through the magnifying glass."[50]

Rage mixed with fear among the Hessians. The late Colonel Rall's former commander, Colonel von Donop, "went thro' the Ranks and declared openly to his men that any of them who would take a Rebel prisoner would receive 50 stripes, signifying to them that they were to kill all the Rebels they could without mercy."[51] Such actions would invite retribution.

But, Washington's orders expressly prohibited cruelty to prisoners. He explained this decision in a letter to Robert Morris on January 1:

> I advised the Council of Safety to separate them [Hessian enlisted men] from their officers and canton them in the German Counties. If proper pains are taken to convince them, how preferable the Situation of their Countrymen, the Inhabitants of these Counties is to theirs, I think they may be sent back in the Spring, so fraught with a love of Liberty and property too, that they may create a disgust to the Service among the remainder of the foreign Troops and widen that Breach which is already opened between them and the British.[52]

Washington seemed to believe that simply allowing the German prisoners to live as Americans lived would convert them.

Cornwallis and a combined force of British and Hessians arrived on the outskirts of Trenton on January 2. The outnumbered Americans now had their backs to the river. Skirmishes broke out on the road to Princeton and quickly spread into Trenton. As darkness approached, Major Wilkinson watched the fighting: "I could distinguish the flames from the muzzles of our muskets." The British pushed the Americans beyond the Assunpink Creek, where they dug in.[53]

One of the American soldiers at Trenton was a sixty-two-year-old Presbyterian minister, John Rosbrugh, commander of a Pennsylvania militia company. Someone stole his horse, and he found himself trapped by enemy soldiers in the streets of the town. They caught him, and they followed Colonel von Donop's orders. They stabbed him with bayonets "and mangled him in the most shocking manner," according to John Witherspoon, president of the College of New Jersey at Princeton. A contemporary newspaper reported, "After he was thus massacred, he was stripped naked and … left lying in an open field."[54]

The Americans massed artillery behind the creek, which ran high with snowmelt. The stream could be forded at one or two places or it could be crossed on a bridge; rebel cannons sighted in on these crossings. The British attacked in small units and were thrown back. Washington's army held its ground until nightfall ended the action.[55]

That evening, Cornwallis rejected advice to continue the assault into the night. One of his officers, Sir William Erskine, told him, "My Lord, if you trust these people to-night you will see nothing of them in the morning."[56] Erskine believed the Americans would run away under cover of darkness.

Washington conducted his own war council that night. He sketched out their situation to his officers, told them they would probably lose a pitched battle, and admitted there was no good avenue of retreat. Then he asked for their advice. Once again the American officers reached a bold consensus— rather than retreat they would strike the British rear at Princeton.[57] Washington, who desperately needed success, wrote, "One thing I was sure of, that it would avoid the appearance of a retreat." Instead, he thought, the move would "give some reputation to our arms."[58]

Some rebel officers had reached a level of determination and defiance that bordered on the fanatic. On New Years Day, Dr. Benjamin Rush dined with General Hugh Mercer and heard him say that he "would not be conquered, but that he would cross the mountains and live among the Indians, rather than submit to the power of Great Britain in any of the civilized states."[59] A popular army camp song of the day shared Mercer's passion:

> With the beasts of the wood
> we will ramble for food
> and live in wild deserts and caves,
> and live poor as Job
> on the skirts of the globe,
> before we'll submit to be slaves.[60]

That night a hard freeze set in. Washington ordered a corps of 400 men to remain in the positions at Trenton to give the appearance that his whole army remained there. They lit great bonfires and walked about in the open so that the enemy could see an active encampment. None of the 400 knew the destination of the army; if some were captured, they could not give accurate intelligence to the British.[61]

At one o'clock in the morning, the American army departed for the back road to Princeton. Henry Knox watched his artillery caissons, wheels muffled, move out on the journey. "Our troops marched with great silence and order," he wrote. A January thaw had turned the roads to mire during the previous day, but the weather changed suddenly. "The roads, which the day before had been mud, snow and water, were congealed now, and had become hard as pavement and solid." The Americans moved all the way around to the rear of the British army in the darkness without being discovered.[62]

By early morning the army reached Stony Brook, just southwest of Princeton. Brigadier General Mercer led a detachment to seize and hold the bridge over the brook, hoping to delay Cornwallis if he returned to defend the college town. By chance a unit of British regulars spotted Mercer's soldiers, and a skirmish ensued that grew rapidly into a fierce battle. Fighting raged through an apple orchard. The redcoats pushed the Americans back until Washington arrived and took command himself. He rode into the midst of the gunfire and rallied the Americans. He led them on a chase of the fleeing British, yelling, "It's a fine fox chase my boys!"[63]

Mercer lay wounded, surrounded by redcoats. "Call for quarter, you damned rebel," one soldier demanded. Instead, Mercer drew his sword. The swarm of British soldiers repeatedly stabbed the general with bayonets. Mercer died of his wounds nine days later, but he was able to tell his story. Other wounded Americans suffered similar treatment that day, dying from bayonet wounds and blows from musket butts delivered when they were defenseless.[64]

No record remains to tell what part John Stark played that day at Princeton. He probably rode with General Sullivan's troops, who marched directly into the town while the battle went on to the southwest. British soldiers took refuge in Nassau Hall and shot at the rebels from the windows. Captain Alexander Hamilton placed a battery facing the building and opened fire, while Captain James Moore led a frontal attack on the main door. The enemy quickly surrendered.[65]

At Princeton the wounded lay where they fell. No organized system existed to care for them; their survival depended on the charity of those who found them. An elderly Princeton resident opened his home to two injured British troopers who were carried in on the shoulders of American fighters. The old man wrote, "They were both Used very tenderly by the Rebels (as they call them). … three of them [Americans] Stayed with the wounded men near an hour after the others were gone."[66]

Cornwallis left a surgeon and five privates to care for his wounded after his army departed. Washington left the Americans to the chance care of the neighborhood. Both armies were gone by late afternoon, the British to Brunswick and the Americans toward Morristown in the northwest hills.[67]

Dead soldiers littered the bloody ground of Princeton in the aftermath of the battle. When the army moved on, a New Jersey miller, Captain John Polhemus, remained behind, he wrote, "to secure stores and bury the dead with the assistance of a small guard, which they did by hauling them on sleds to great holes and heaping them in."[68]

On January 7, 1777, George Washington wrote an order for his troops. He composed it with the memories of Trenton and Princeton fresh in his mind—the murder of John Rosbrugh, the mutilation of General Hugh Mercer, and many more reports of enemy atrocities. He knew of the prison ships where men died of disease and starvation, and he had seen the ravages of the countryside with his own eyes. He knew of the anger that burned in his soldier's hearts—the desire for revenge. To Lieutenant Colonel Samuel Blachley Webb, his aide, he wrote: "You are to take charge of [211] privates of the British Army. … Treat them with humanity, and let them have no reason to Complain of our Copying the brutal example of the British army in their Treatment of our unfortunate brethren."[69]

Washington understood that he fought a political struggle. Force alone could not win the Revolution. The winner must capture the hearts of the people. His audacious gambles at Trenton and Princeton—small victories though they were—brought support and converts to his cause. Washington and John Adams thought the strategy would win over some enemies as well. It was a strategy of equal parts idealism and pragmatism.

Meanwhile, the British hardened their military methods. Royal Marine John Bowater wrote, "I am certain that our troops will act with less humanity this campaign than they did in the last." The influence of the Howe brothers was nearing an end. The rebels clearly sought no reconciliation with England. While some British officers favored a sterner war, others recognized waning support from the population. Lord Bute's son, Colonel Charles Stuart, informed his father: "We planted an irrevocable hatred wherever we went, which neither time nor measure will be able to eradicate."[70]

20

The Road to Bennington

Our Friend John Stark

The remnants of the Continental Army wintered at Morristown, New Jersey. An officer's wife found the place charming, "a very clever little village … in a most beautiful valley at the foot of five mountains. It has three houses with steeples which gives it a very consequential look."[1] A revolving population of militia, coming and going, gave the impression that the army was larger. A determined attack could have destroyed Washington's force that winter, but the British rested.

Recruiting new soldiers became an essential duty for American officers. Accordingly, John Stark made his second journey of the winter between New Jersey and New Hampshire, several hundred miles of bad roads, poor lodgings and bitterly cold weather. Because of the threat from the British and Loyalists near Manhattan, he took the longer route, well west of the Hudson River. At home Stark would have the opportunity to reacquaint himself with his young family, some of whom probably didn't remember him. He had never met his youngest, the baby, Benjamin Franklin Stark.

The practice of American soldiers going home when their time was up, no matter how much the army needed them, was a custom that weakened the military from 1755 onward. It was not, however, just a problem of losing malcontents and malingerers, the worst of the lot. The bravest and most aggressive soldiers of the Continental Army thought it perfectly natural to go home when their contractual obligations came to an end. The Marblehead sailors of Colonel John Glover, men who had saved the army at Brooklyn, ferried it across the Delaware on Christmas night, and then fought valiantly at Trenton, would not stay to fight at Princeton. Their time was up and they went home. Nothing could induce them to reenlist.[2]

The best officers made the best recruiters. Young men would sign on the drumhead if they admired their leaders. That winter Benedict Arnold, in Rhode Island, tried to gather a force to attack occupied Newport. John Stark worked at recruiting in the Merrimack Valley. He had been successful at raising troops his entire career, but he found it difficult this time. Times were grim at home. Hard money was scarce, and paper money was worthless. Men needed to stay home to feed their families.

Young men, teenagers, bachelors and the poor became the likeliest targets for recruiters. Those without military experience could most easily be persuaded to join. Others, like Private Joseph Plumb Martin, who had lived the soldier's life in 1776, were reluctant to do it again. In the spring of 1777, officers and sergeants visited Martin to sign him up. Once he had reenlisted, he had time to think about it, however. "I began sorely to repent," he wrote, and he reneged on his obligation. The recruiters came back, and young Martin signed up again. He reflected sorrowfully that he had become "the scapegoat for them."[3] The early fire of patriotism had cooled for Martin and for many young men like him.

❧ ❧

After the battle of Princeton, Congress decided to strengthen its authority over the military. It prohibited Washington from appointing general officers, reserving that power to itself. Washington had advised the delegates of the number of generals of various grades he required to conduct the war. Presumably, promotions to those ranks would be based on seniority in the ranks below. Congressmen had other ideas. They would promote men based on "due regard" for seniority, competence and the "quota of troops raised, and to be raised, by each state." These standards meant, effectively, that politics would control promotion. If a state had four men competent for promotion, only two would advance. If a state had no men competent for promotion, at least two would advance, and not necessarily in order of seniority. In an army staffed by officers who were exquisitely sensitive to their "honor," such political meddling invited trouble.[4]

Trouble quickly arose in Connecticut. Israel Putnam and Joseph Spencer already held commissions as major generals from that state. Connecticut's troop quota would be lower than some other states so, by political reasoning, that meant that major generals must be selected from other states. Of the five new major generals selected by this method, none could match the acknowledged military ability and achievements of Benedict Arnold of Connecticut. Congress bypassed him, however, and he was furious.[5]

Washington was appalled, but he could do nothing. He wrote to Arnold: "I confess I was surprised when I did not see your name in the list of Major Generals, and was so fully of opinion that there was some mistake in the matter, that I (as you may recollect) desired you not to take any hasty steps." There was no mistake, however, and Washington could only express his mystification and condolence. The troop quota standard would prevail, he told Arnold. "I confess this is a strange mode of reasoning, but it may serve to shew you that the promotion which was due to your Seniority, was not overlooked for want of Merit in you."[6] Arnold was bitter; he refused to be consoled.

John Stark had been angry in 1776 when Colonel James Reed, an invalid, had been promoted above him. Congress now appointed Enoch Poor as the new brigadier general from New Hampshire even though he was junior to Stark. Historians ever since have been unanimous in their condemnation of this promotion: Bancroft called Stark "the best officer from that state"; Trevelyan wrote, "Congress, enamored of mediocrity, ignored his [Stark's] claim for recognition."[7] Stark, it seemed, had few political friends in either Philadelphia or Exeter.

Washington anticipated that Poor's promotion would cause trouble. He wrote Poor on March 3 to advise him of his new commission; he also told him, "I am apprehensive that your Promotion will cause Colo. Stark to resign, should you find this to be the case, let the oldest Lieutenant Colo. in the Line of your State, be appoint'd to the Command of his Regiment. ... This should not be mentioned if my doubts prove groundless."[8] Washington knew his man—Stark resigned.

John Stark rode directly to Exeter and, on March 22, presented his written resignation in person to the "Council & House of Representatives." It was a peculiar act since, as a Continental officer, his commission came from Congress. His one-paragraph statement reviewed his service, then declared that he was "extremely grieved that I am bound on Honour to leave the service,

Congress having tho't fit to promote Junr officers over my head; so that least I should show myself unworthy of the Honour conferred on me & a want of that Spirit which ought to glow in the Breast of Every officer appointed by this Honble House, in not suitably resenting an indignity … ."[9]

To John Sullivan, Stark sent a more pithy explanation: "an officer who would not maintain his rank, was unworthy to serve his country."[10] The members of the New Hampshire House of Representatives passed a resolution thanking him for his service, and Stark went home to Derryfield.[11]

Congress continued to infuriate American officers. The American commissioner to France, Silas Deane, sent foreign military officers to Philadelphia with the expectation that Congress would commission them; it served diplomatic interests to do so. Thomas Conway, a French officer of Irish descent, became a brigadier general. French aristocrat Phillippe du Coudray arrived expecting to be made commander of all American artillery. An exasperated Washington wrote to Congress to explain that Henry Knox was invaluable in that position. He predicted that, if du Coudray superseded him, Knox "would not think himself at liberty to continue in the service."[12] The phrasing of Washington's letter demands attention—"would not think himself at liberty to" means something other than "would be too proud to." The pressure on a man of honor, as the commander in chief understood, would be overpowering; only a poltroon would ignore such an insult.

When General Sullivan learned that du Coudray had been promised a major general's commission, he wrote to John Hancock, president of Congress, "if this Report be True I Shall be under the Disagreeable necessity of Quitting the Service."[13] Nathanael Greene and Henry Knox followed suit. Congress took no action on their resignations. The wholesale departure of general officers was avoided, however, when, on September 15, du Coudray drowned trying to ford the Schuylkill River on horseback.[14]

Washington understood his officers' motivations. Honor propelled them just as it had propelled him to resign in 1758. He also understood the need to cultivate the French and to welcome the skill and resources they brought to the American cause. In August he dined with a new American major general, the Marquis de Lafayette, age nineteen. The young Frenchman served in an honorary capacity, without authority to command troops and without compensation. Washington would come to believe that, for this man, Congress made the right decision.[15]

King George III approved a new British plan for the 1777 campaign, a plan presented to him in person by General John Burgoyne. Burgoyne was a favorite of London society. He wrote plays, gambled at cards and socialized with the nobility. With the King's blessing, the War Ministry gave command of the northern wing of the army to Burgoyne; he replaced General Carleton, who had lost favor by his failure to take Ticonderoga the previous year.[16]

Burgoyne hoped to split the American rebellion in two and destroy it piecemeal. His plan called for British troops, much augmented by Canadians, Brunswick Germans, Indians and Loyalists, to move south out of Quebec on Lake Champlain, seize Crown Point, Ticonderoga and Fort Edward, and then attack Albany. General Howe would come up the Hudson to join him. A third force under Colonel Barry St. Leger would strike toward Albany through the Mohawk Valley. These combined forces would divide New England from the "southern" states. The plan relied on overwhelming concentrated force. Burgoyne's army would have to live off the land.[17]

The invasion army set out from Quebec on June 17, with over 8,000 men. Baron Friedrich Adolph von Riedesel commanded the German contingent. He set off with high confidence in the mission, so much confidence that he brought his wife, Baroness Frederika Riedesel, and their three young daughters on the expedition. The Baroness kept a diary.[18]

A German surgeon, Julius Wasmus, accompanied the army. He served in the regiment of Lieutenant Colonel Friedrich Baum. Like Baroness Riedesel, Wasmus also wrote a journal in which he carefully recorded both what he saw and what he heard. One of his first entries, made on June 5, 1777, described Colonel Baum as a martinet who told a subordinate, "If a bateau goes ahead of my bateau, its commander shall be arrested even if he is a Captain of the Cavalry."[19]

Burgoyne's army took a month to reach the vicinity of Fort Ticonderoga. The general traveled on a ship, the *Maria*. Most troops crammed into hundreds of bateaux. They paused at Crown Point, where the houses and fort had been reduced to burned ruins. The men already suffered from lack of bread. The weather was hot, broken only by fierce thunderstorms "such as I never experienced in Germany," Wasmus wrote. He shuddered from his encounters with rattlesnakes and copperheads; "I cannot describe how afraid, even terrified, I have been of them." Mosquitoes and black flies tortured the men. Wasmus reckoned they had travelled 250 miles from their base at Three Rivers.[20]

They sighted Ticonderoga on July 3. The surgeon noted, "The enemy has hoisted a red flag on the fort to express that they would rather lose their lives than their freedom." Burgoyne expected a long siege and brought up his artillery to confront the American cannons on both sides of the lake. Redcoat infantry units fanned out west of the old French Lines and approached Mount Defiance.[21]

His Indian allies had been displaying violent moods, and the general tried to quell their actions. When he stopped paying bounties to the warriors for scalps, Wasmus wrote, "they became ill-disposed towards us for they used to get two piasters for every scalp." Burgoyne sought to tighten control over the Indians on the eve of the assault on Ticonderoga; he forbade selling rum to them. "This is very good," the surgeon thought, "for when they are drunk they scalp both friend and foe."[22]

Sergeant Roger Lamb remembered Burgoyne's war message to his troops before the assault: "This army embarks tomorrow, to approach the enemy. ... During our progress occasions may occur, in which nor difficulty, nor labour, nor life, are to be regarded. This army must not retreat."[23] With a supply line stretching all the way to the St. Lawrence River, the general expected a difficult fight, but he was confident there would be a generous welcome from Loyalists and his force would prosper on food and forage from American farms.

※ ※

American General Arthur St. Clair commanded no more than 2,300 men at Ticonderoga. St. Clair admitted that they were "ill armed, naked and unaccoutered."[24] He believed their only hope for holding Lake Champlain was a massive infusion of militia, even though he could barely feed the men already stationed there. The northern commander, Horatio Gates, remained at Albany and did nothing to strengthen St. Clair's hand.

Over on Mount Independence, a unit of Seth Warner's Continental Regiment, Vermont Green Mountain Boys, camped alongside a New Jersey regiment. The Vermonters boasted a long history of fighting, mostly with sheriffs from New York. As the British approached Ticonderoga, St. Clair dispatched Warner to plead for more men from the Vermont convention delegates then meeting at Windsor. Warner rode off to Rutland after sending a letter to Windsor alerting them of the need for militia and cattle to feed the troops. He closed his message with a pointed jab at "sunshine patriots": "I should be glad if a few hills of corn unhoed should not be a motive sufficient to detain men at home, considering the loss of such an important post might be irretrievable."[25]

Seth Warner had begun his fighting career as a partisan in the Vermont hills, defying the claims of New York land speculators in the Hampshire Grants. Warner, like his cousins Ethan Allen, Ira Allen and Remember Baker, owned land purchased from New Hampshire. When New Yorkers claimed superior title, New York's colonial officers tried to enforce the claims by ejecting Vermont farmers. They met determined, and sometimes violent, resistance from the Green Mountain Boys; most of these men lived near Bennington and Manchester, Vermont. Stephen Fay's Catamount Tavern high on the hill in Bennington was their unofficial headquarters. Ethan Allen, with his booming voice, led the talking for the Vermonters; Seth Warner led the fighting.[26]

Warner was a very big man for his times—six feet two inches tall. While Ethan Allen and Benedict Arnold led the assault on Fort Ticonderoga in 1775, Warner captured Crown Point. Another Vermonter, Samuel Herrick, took the Tory stronghold at Skenesborough. Later in the year 1775, Congress established a Vermont regiment of the Continental Army with the resolution, "that Seth Warner be appointed lieutenant Colonel of Green Mountain Boys."[27]

His regiment joined Montgomery's failed campaign in Canada, but the men went home when their enlistments expired in December. Warner went home with them, but only briefly. He answered the call for reinforcements after the defeat at Quebec and led a regiment north on the lake ice in January. They experienced disease and defeat with the rest of the American army. To save lives, Colonel Warner defied the order forbidding self-inoculation against smallpox. He told his soldiers, "I do not wish to countermand the General Orders but if you should take it [inoculation] in the Thigh and Diet [die] for it, it would be much better for you and they [army commanders] will not find out."[28] Defiance of authority came naturally to the man.

Warner and Stark met on the retreat from Canada. Descendants of both men credited them with guarding the rear of the desperate army. Colonel Warner's son Asahel told his story: "My father brought up the rear and would not leave one sick man behind, and pressed every Frenchman that had a horse, and a Cart, to go and Carry his sick soldiers (those who had the Small Pox) and they Retreated until they came to Ticonderoga."[29]

By July 5, Warner was back at Mount Independence with a fresh contingent of 500 men. He found that St. Clair had prepared his defenses. A bridge and a log boom stretched across the lake from the fort to the Vermont side, placed there in the hope of halting British navigation south of that point. Mount Defiance remained unoccupied. The Americans waited for Burgoyne's next move.[30]

The British sent a work party to hack out a road up the southwest side of Mount Defiance. Then they began hauling two twelve-pound cannon up its slopes, "tho their getting there was almost a perpendicular ascent, and drawn up by most of the cattle belonging to the army."[31]

Burgoyne's soldiers accomplished in a day what no officers previously had imagined could be done (with the possible exceptions of John Trumbull and Tadeusz Kosciusko). Many of Burgoyne's men expressed astonishment that the Americans had not fortified the mountain. The Americans had underestimated the British, as Sergeant Lamb wrote, "The Americans vainly imagining that the difficulty of the ascent would be sufficient to prevent the British troops from taking possession of it."[32] Surgeon Wasmus noted, "From the mountain, Ticonderoga could be shot at and I cannot understand why it had not been occupied by the enemy."[33]

The sight of artillerists manning cannons atop the mountain jolted St. Clair. Although the British had not yet fired any shots with their artillery, the general ordered the evacuation of Fort Ticonderoga and Mount Independence. The British learned the Americans were gone at daybreak the next day. Lieutenant Digby of the British army wrote, "… on the night of the 5th they set fire to several parts of the garrison, kept a constant fire of great guns the whole night, and under the protection of that fire and clouds of smoke they evacuated the garrison, leaving all their cannon, ammunition and a great quantity of stores."[34]

The Americans departed in two groups. A flotilla of boats carrying the wounded and sick, together with several cannons, left the fort at three o'clock in the morning. Twelve hours later they arrived at Skenesborough at the head of the lake. The British quickly broke through the boom at Ticonderoga and pursued the Americans. Dr. James Thacher, escaping with the patients, wrote, "Burgoyne himself was at our heels. … All our cannon, provisions and the bulk of our baggage, with several invalids, fell into the enemy's hands."[35]

The main body of Americans, led by St. Clair, struck out overland toward the mountains of Vermont. British and German regiments followed them. Seth Warner commanded the last three regiments that reached Hubbardton in the foothills, and he decided to camp there. His men held a strong position overlooking the road their pursuers would follow to reach them.[36]

The action began at dawn on July 7 when General Fraser's redcoats marched up the hill toward the Americans. Warner's men and Colonel Francis's Massachusetts regiment gave the enemy a hot fight for an hour before Riedesel's Brunswick auxiliaries arrived and forced Warner's soldiers to retreat across a wheat field and up Pittsfield Ridge. With the Germans as reinforcements, the British pursued the scattering Americans into the forest. Warner called out to his running soldiers to separate and meet him in Manchester.[37]

Caleb Stark fought in the battle, and he ran with the rest of the Americans. Patrick Cogan, quartermaster of their regiment, wrote to John Stark to tell the story of Hubbardton. He blamed St. Clair for the whole affair. As for the ordinary soldiers, he wrote, "some behaved and some did not." They all scattered through the woods and headed for Manchester as fast as they could, stealing oxen for food, "without cloathes, victuals or drink & constantly wet." Cogan maintained a soldier's grim humor about their trials. "Caleb and I," he wrote, "are just as our mothers bore us without the second shirt, the second pair of shoes, stockings or coats—but however it's all in the Continental." Then, Cogan wrote a strange allusion to a father-son conflict: "Caleb does vastly better than he ever did with you."[38]

The events of these two days, July 6 and 7, damaged morale in the northern army. The loss of Ticonderoga particularly astounded the soldiers. Doctor Thacher reported: "The conduct of General St. Clair on this occasion has rendered him very unpopular, and subjected him to general censure and reproach; there are some indeed, who even accuse him of treachery." Thacher also believed General Schuyler acted badly in being absent from Ticonderoga "during this critical period."[39]

Disapproval of the generals grew as word of the loss of the fort spread. John Adams said, "We shall never be able to defend a post until we shoot a general!" Adams wanted Gates in command. Philip Schuyler's defenders argued in vain that it was Horatio Gates who ignored John Trumbull's advice to fortify Mount Defiance. Of the three generals who shared the blame for Ticonderoga's loss, Gates fared the best. He replaced Schuyler.[40]

The news from Lake Champlain and Vermont shocked New England. Warner and the survivors of his Green Mountain Boys reassembled at Manchester. The Vermont convention remained in assembly at Windsor, where the delegates strove to gather muskets and ammunition. They appointed a council of safety to act as an interim government until elections could be held, and they empowered the council to take military action if necessary. The presence of redcoats in Vermont precipitated a flood of refugees moving south. On July 15 the Vermonters wrote their counterparts in New Hampshire, asking for help.[41]

Vermont's artfully drawn plea struck a responsive chord in New Hampshire. Ira Allen, secretary of the Vermont Council of Safety, wrote the letter: "… the defenceless inhabitants [of Vermont] are heartily disposed to Defend their Liberties … and make a frontier for your State with their own." However, if Vermont were conquered, he suggested, "You will naturally understand that when we cease to be a frontier your state must take it."[42]

The New Hampshire House of Representatives met on July 17 to consider the emergency. Deserters from St. Clair's army had spread distrust of Continental Generals Schuyler and St. Clair throughout New England. The members of the House met in an atmosphere of defeatism; they needed to act, but the treasury was bare. They had no funds to raise an army. Then, Speaker of the House John Langdon rose and spoke:

> I have a thousand dollars in hard money. I will pledge my plate for three thousand more. I have seventy hogsheads of Tobago rum which will be sold for the most they will bring. They are at the service of the state. If we succeed in defending our firesides and our homes I may be remunerated. If we do not then the property will be of no value to me. Our friend John Stark, who so nobly maintained the honor of our state at Bunker Hill, may safely be entrusted with the honor of the enterprise and we will check the progress of Burgoyne.[43]

The New Hampshire Committee of Safety immediately organized an expedition to aid Vermont but, as yet, it existed only on paper. They proposed two brigades of militia. They hoped Stark would consent to command both with the state rank of brigadier general. But they made their plans without his consent. A messenger rode to Derryfield to seek his answer.

The committee's order anticipated that Stark might refuse: "That in case the said John Stark Decline accepting the said service, that then Col. Benjamin Bellows be appointed to the said office & command."[44] Stark had always maintained a prickly relationship with Exeter politicians. In this case they specified that he "be always amenable for their conduct to the General Court or Committee of Safety for the time being." The New Hampshire authorities intended from the beginning that Stark would act independently, without responsibility to Continental officers or to Congress in Philadelphia.[45]

Historians and biographers have written extensively ever since claiming that John Stark's subsequent actions stemmed from his own animosities and prejudices—that he allowed his personal resentments to govern his decisions. This notion is false. Josiah Bartlett, who was a member of the body that appointed Stark and a member of the committee of safety that instructed him, wrote in September 1777: "As to the State giving such orders to Genl Starks, because he had not the rank he thought himself entitled to (which seems intimated) I can assure you is without foundation and I believe never entered the mind of any of the Committee of safety who gave the orders." New Hampshire gave Stark an independent command, Bartlett wrote, because "Surely every State has a right to raise their militia for their own Defence against a Common Enemy and to put them under such Command as they shall think proper."[46] That the Continental Army had abandoned Fort Ticonderoga particularly distressed the New Hampshire Committee of Safety, whose president branded that failure "probably criminal." New Hampshire men believed that they could best provide their "own defence."

Stark rode to Exeter to accept the command in person. Caleb Stark wrote, "He informed them that he had no confidence in the commander of the northern army [he meant Schuyler]; but if they would organize a brigade to be by him commanded, to hang upon the left wing and rear of the enemy, with full authority to direct their operations according to his own judgement, without responsibility to any other authority other than their own body, he would again take the field."[47] These conditions, as it happened, conformed exactly to the aims of the New Hampshire authorities. President Weare, of the House, ordered Stark to "march into the State of Vermont and there act in conjunction with the Troops of that State or any other of the States or of the United States or separately as it shall appear Expedient to you for the protection of the People or the annoyance of the enemy."[48]

Militia officers fanned out across the state carrying the news of Stark's command. Over the next six days towns enlisted militia companies and sent them off to their commander. In Concord, Colonel Gordon Hutchins recruited an entire congregation of men from a church at the conclusion of Sunday services.[49]

Similar scenes took place in other towns. One man remembered, "I enlisted … as soon as I heard that Stark would accept the command of the state troops." In Salisbury, Captain Ebenezer Webster, Daniel Webster's father, recruited more than a third of the town's eligible men. In all, 1,492 New Hampshire men signed up to fight.[50]

The new brigades marched to a rendezvous at Fort Number Four at Charlestown along the Connecticut River. Brigadier General Stark, with his new aide, John Casey, reached the old fort by July 25, where they tried to assemble the mountains of equipment, armaments and provisions for the mission. Casey wrote a letter for his commander on July 30 requesting supplies. The letter, perhaps dictated by Stark, reveals an unusual idiom, likely Stark's own speech pattern. After writing several perfectly clear English sentences, the writer turned to the subject of rum: "… as there is but little Rum in the Store here if some could be forwarded to us it would oblige us very much as there is none of that article in them parts where we are agoing." John Casey either suffered a brief lapse in his diction or he quoted his commander accurately.[51]

Seth Warner wrote directly to Stark on July 24, "urging the necessity of your speedy assistance." The New Hampshire commander quickly sent 700 men ahead to Manchester, where they joined the Vermont troops by August 2. The next day, Stark and the rest of his force started up into the Green Mountains. On August 6 he camped at Peru, with the dark bulk of Bromley Mountain looming in the west. That night he wrote to the commander back at Number Four, asking him to "forward with all convenient speed all the rum and sugar." On August 7 the last of the New Hampshire militia filed down the long hill into Manchester with John Stark riding at their head.[52]

Portly Benjamin Lincoln, a new major general in the Continental Army, awaited the militia's arrival in Manchester. Lincoln had written a brief note to Stark the day before, telling him he had a message for him from General Schuyler and that he was preparing to march Stark's troops to the Hudson as

Schuyler had requested. The New Hampshire troops stood in formation, ready to follow Lincoln's orders, when John Stark arrived. He promptly changed their destination. He told Lincoln "that my orders was not to put myself under the Command of the Continental Troops." Instead, he told Lincoln he would take his force to Bennington in compliance with the wishes of the Vermont Committee of Safety.[53]

Stark reported his meeting with Lincoln to his superiors in New Hampshire and asked them "not to put me under the Command of those officers on whose account I quitted the army, Lest the remedy should prove worse to me than the disease." He closed the letter with a familiar complaint: "Rum at this place is Twenty Shillings a Quart, from which you Can form a judgement Gent. how much we can afford to drink."[54]

General Lincoln didn't argue with Stark. Instead he wrote to Schuyler, complaining that Stark was "exceedingly soured. ... It is a fixed point with him [Stark] to act there as a separate corps and take no orders from any officer in the northern department, saving your honor [Schuyler], for he saith they were all either commanded by him the last year or joined the army after him."[55] Schuyler forwarded Lincoln's letter to Congress, where the members had not yet been advised of the nature of the New Hampshire orders under which Stark operated.

The formation of New Hampshire volunteers stood at parade rest and watched the two generals converse at Manchester. Then they fell out and prepared to follow their new orders from John Stark. Rumors flew through the ranks. Captain Peter Clark wrote his wife: "A few minutes after I finished my letter there was a considerable turn in affairs by reason of Gen. Stark arriving in town. The orders we had for marching [to the Hudson] was given by Gen. Lincoln. What passed between Lincoln and Stark is not known, but what we can gather together Stark chooses to command himself."[56] General Stark then commanded his men to march to Bennington.

⁂

General Schuyler's Continental troops had retreated southward as Burgoyne's army advanced toward the Hudson River. The Americans slowed the march of their enemies; they felled trees across the trails and destroyed bridges. Redcoat Sergeant Lamb observed, "The face of the country was likewise so broken with creeks and marshes, that there were no less then forty bridges to construct, one of which was over a morass two miles in extent."[57] Schuyler also warned fleeing settlers to burn their crops and scatter their livestock.[58]

The main British force reached Fort Edward on the Hudson River on July 20. The rebels had "demolished" the settlement before they left, but two houses remained intact. General Burgoyne shared a red-painted house with General and Baroness Riedesel and their daughters. They dined together out-doors under the trees, eating bear meat, which the Baroness found "of capital flavor." Bear meat was an emergency ration, for Madam Riedesel wrote, "We were often put to it to get anything to eat."[59] If the generals went hungry, the whole army went hungry.

Burgoyne's Indian allies frightened the German surgeon, Wasmus. He believed these naked warriors not only scalped their victims, but ate them too. He feared the British officers had no control over the Indians.[60]

On August 1, Wasmus reported that the Indians had murdered a young white woman, Jane McCrea. Two warriors seized her. Then they argued between themselves and became enraged. One man struck her with a toma-hawk. He scalped her, stripped off her clothing and left her body in the woods. Back at camp, her killer displayed her long, beautiful hair to his shocked Euro-pean allies.[61]

Burgoyne was horrified. He told General Simon Fraser that he intended to punish the murderer, but the next day the assembled Indians threatened to leave unless he pardoned the killer. Burgoyne relented. News of the atrocity and of the tepid British response to it spread across the region, provoking fear and anger.[62]

The British needed to obtain food for their hungry soldiers and horses for the footsore German dragoons, who marched in high boots through the wilderness. Burgoyne wrote an order sending a detachment east, across the Green Mountains to the Connecticut River. He intended to "try the affec-tions of the country."[63] A Loyalist, Philip Skene, a retired colonel from the British Army, told Burgoyne that the countryside swarmed with Loyalists just waiting for their chance to fight for the King. Skene had served in the French war and then settled on a grant of more than 30,000 acres at the south end of Lake Champlain that was known as Skenesborough. He had much to lose if the British lost the war. Burgoyne believed Skene's predictions of abundant local Tory support.[64]

General Riedesel disapproved of the ambitious scheme, but Burgoyne forged ahead.[65] He selected Lieutenant Colonel Baum to command the expedition. When the troops were almost ready to march, Burgoyne changed his orders, instructing Baum verbally through an interpreter to march instead to Bennington.[66] Tory informers reported a large supply depot in the Vermont town, and they said it was lightly guarded. Bennington was much closer to the army, and reinforcements could be sent quickly if needed. Philip Skene would accompany Baum, who spoke no English, to interpret and advise.[67]

Baum's force, between 700 and 800 strong, moved out on August 11. He led a mixed body of over 400 Germans, 50 redcoats, and between 200 and 300 Tories, together with Canadians and Indians. Horses hauled two three-pound artillery pieces.[68] The Germans slogged through the hot day carrying heavy packs and swords.[69] Wasmus marched with the dragoons as the medical officer for the mission. He anticipated a successful raid on the supply depot, "After we have driven off the scattered corps of Americans who are at Bennington."[70]

Had John Stark not defied General Lincoln at Manchester, only local militias would have stood in Baum's path. If Generals Schuyler and Lincoln disapproved of Stark's independent action, and if his decisions annoyed Congress, as they did, one important observer would have approved of his strategy—General George Washington. The commander in chief had written Schuyler on July 22: "You intimate the propriety of having a body of men stationed somewhere in the Grants [Vermont]. The expediency of such a measure appears to me evident. … It would keep him [Burgoyne] in continual anxiety for his rear … and would serve many other valuable purposes."[71]

If Burgoyne should be so foolhardy as to send a detachment of a few hundred men into Vermont, Washington thought, it might be cut off and destroyed by the American force. Such a victory "would inspirit the people and do away much of their present anxiety. In such an event, they would loose [lose] sight of past misfortunes, and urged at the same time by a regard for their own security, they would fly to Arms and afford every aid in their power."[72]

Like a playwright staging a great drama, Washington imagined the scenes to come in the next weeks. His foresight lacked only the casting of the actor for the lead role. That actor took the stage on his own initiative.

21

THE BATTLE OF BENNINGTON
A Continual Clap of Thunder

The Americans converging on the little town of Bennington looked like a collection of farmers on a hunting trip. The men wore the same garb they worked in every day on their farms or in their shops—"small clothes, coming down and fastening just below the knee, and long stockings with cowhide shoes ornamented with large buckles. ... They had shirts of homespun, and on their heads was a large, round-topped and broad-brimmed hat."[1]

Many of the soldiers were just boys, carrying the primitive muskets they hunted with at home. A witness reported, "Instead of the cartridge box a large powder horn was slung under the arm, and occasionally a bayonet might be seen bristling in the ranks."[2] Older men stiffened the mix, veterans of the French and Indian War, even some rangers.

Someone called upon Stark's old allies, the Stockbridge Indians, to scout for the Americans, but they arrived too late to be of help.[3] Not counting Colonel Seth Warner's Continentals, who were still up in Manchester, more than 1,500 patriots assembled at Bennington, most of them militia. There were companies from Massachusetts and New York in addition to the volunteers from New Hampshire and Vermont.[4] Seth Warner himself was at Bennington; he was a crucial asset to the Americans because he knew the landscape intimately. While the forces gathered, Stephen Fay's Catamount Tavern served as the meeting site for the council of safety and the American officers.[5]

Only a few days before, General Schuyler had written to Washington from Stillwater on the Hudson complaining that he lacked the manpower to stop Burgoyne. "Our continental force is decreasing," he wrote, "and not a man of the militia now with me, will remain above one week longer."[6] Schuyler did not yet know that volunteers were swarming to Stark's camp.

On August 13, Baum's heavily laden soldiers took twelve hours to march from the Hudson to Cambridge, New York, near the Vermont border. Their road was a hilly, rugged track, and the trek on the hot day exhausted the dragoons. Baum's men liberated cattle and chickens from the farms they passed, but the farmers had driven off their horses. The officers could not control the band of Indians with them; they looted homes and farms and sent a jolt of fear through the countryside.[7]

The Americans in the countryside saw no distinction between German auxiliaries from Brunswick and Hesse. The Hessians at Long Island and New Jersey had earned a reputation for pillage, rape and brutality. Newspapers carried accounts of Hessian cruelty at Long Island including the murder of prisoners with bayonets. Whether deserved or not, this reputation attached to Burgoyne's Brunswickers as well.[8]

Refugees streamed away from the raiders. "Beds and bedding were hastily thrown into the wagon, and the family on top of them drove off toward Bennington."[9] One young mother, Sarah Rudd, always remembered her terror as she told of "my flight on horse-back, and in feeble health, with my babe and two other small children and my eldest daughter running on foot by the side of me." Sarah's husband, Lieutenant Joseph Rudd, had marched off to fight under Stark.[10]

That night the invaders camped near Cambridge. A rumor spread through the camp that British Colonel St. Leger had taken Fort Stanwix, the American stronghold in the Mohawk Valley. The German surgeon Wasmus doubted the talk. "Without a doubt, this is only being spread to inspire our men with courage, for who would want to bring us this news here in the wilderness?"[11] The rumor was untrue, and St. Leger had yet to encounter Benedict Arnold and the continentals he led.

Baum's force broke camp and set out for Bennington at five o'clock the next morning, August 14. They reached the gristmill at San Coick by breakfast time.[12] Baum sent a report to Burgoyne that he had driven off enemy soldiers from the place and seized "Seventy-eight barrels of very fine flour, one thousand bushels of wheat," and sundry provisions.[13]

The Germans captured five Americans who gave them startling news—1,500 rebel soldiers, and perhaps more, waited at Bennington. Baum passed this intelligence on to Burgoyne, adding that the Americans were supposed to leave the area "on our approach." The German officer advised that his unit had gained volunteers, who were "flooding in hourly and want to be armed."[14]

When John Stark learned from refugees that enemies approached, he ordered Colonel William Gregg to march toward Cambridge with 200 men "to make discoveries." It was Gregg's detachment that the Germans encountered at the San Coick mill. When Gregg ordered a withdrawal, one of his men volunteered to stay behind to burn the bridge over Little White Creek. Eleazor Edgerton, a carpenter by trade, was well known locally for being "beloved by children." He managed to damage the bridge seriously enough to delay Baum's passage.[15]

Gregg brought back the first intelligence that a large enemy force with regular troops was advancing on Bennington. Stark moved his forces to a height of land west of Bennington overlooking the winding Walloomsac River, in full view of Baum's troops. Stark later wrote: "Our little army was immediately drawn up in order of battle, upon sight of which the British halted and commenced intrenching on very advantageous ground."[16] Stark hoped to draw the enemy into battle on the plain beside the river, where the Americans' superior numbers gave them an advantage. But the German commander withdrew his men to a steep hill north of the river, where they built timber fortifications on the stony soil. When Stark realized he could not bring them to an engagement, he moved back toward Bennington and made camp.[17]

Small parties of rebels harassed the Germans and British near the bridge across the Walloomsac. A musket ball killed a Mohawk chief. British, German and Indian fighters gave the dead warrior a funeral service, firing three volleys in salute as his body was lowered into the grave. Wasmus sensed that the Indians were both angry and demoralized; "they wanted to depart for Canada tonight," he wrote.[18]

American marksmen patrolled the woods near the enemy positions. A British officer, Captain McKay, voiced anger that Baum did not attack immediately. "I cannot understand," he told Wasmus, "how one can entrust a detach-ment to such a man as Lieut. Colonel Baum, who has no military experience at all, cannot take proper measures, particularly here in the wilderness." As darkness fell, Wasmus found that McKay's words troubled him. He knew that Baum had posted no sentinels. Even the inexperienced doctor thought that was foolish.[19]

Both armies settled down for an uneasy night. Both commanders had sent for reinforcements. A detachment of Green Mountain Boys started south from Manchester, but their commander, Colonel Seth Warner, was already at Stark's side.

The Americans outnumbered the German-British force two to one. Baum could have constructed strong defensive positions on the hill, where his men might hold off the rebels until help arrived. Instead, he spread his forces between three main positions, so distant from each other that no dependable communi-cation could be maintained between them. If the Americans could get accurate intelligence about these positions, they could attack them piecemeal.[20]

The road west from Bennington threaded the Walloomsac Valley and crossed the river on a trestle bridge at the foot of Baum's hill. A small unit of British regulars deployed at the bridge with one of the two cannons. Canadi-ans, a few Germans, and Baum himself also remained near the bridge. They faced south and east across the Walloomsac River toward Stark's forces.

At the top of the hill, several hundred yards up from the bridge, Bruns-wick dragoons manned a breastwork of earth and logs. Steep ground sur-rounded their position on three sides, and they built their defenses to defend against the direction that afforded the easiest access, north and west.[21] The convex shape of the hill made it impossible to see the bridge from the hilltop. Surgeon Wasmus remained with the dragoons on top of the hill.[22]

Across the river, on a small rise, two hundred Loyalists occupied a redoubt to cover the roads there. They were commanded by Colonel Francis Pfister, a retired British officer who lived nearby. Behind their position a steep hillside dropped toward the river. These Tories were about 1,000 feet from the units at the bridge. The Indians remained with the baggage and horses, west of the hill. None of Baum's positions connected with any other; in military terms, all the flanks were "in the air."[23]

Heavy rain started to fall on the morning of the 15th, rendering the muskets of both armies useless. Wasmus became increasingly uneasy as he watched; "the inhabitants living around here come and go through our camp; they will surely give the enemy information about our weakness."[24] Philip Skene had assured Baum that these Americans were Loyalists who wished to join his forces. In fact, many of them served as amateur spies for Stark, providing information about enemy numbers and location.

Meanwhile, rebels crept through the dripping woods, hiding behind trees and sniping at their enemies. They picked off thirty Canadians and Indians from ambush. Baum sent out patrols to monitor American movements but, according to Wasmus, all patrols reported that they "have not seen anything in particular up to tonight."[25] Such poor intelligence could only have come from scouts who feared to venture far from their lines.

The rain fell all day and into the night. Soldiers on both sides bedded down in the wet on the night of the 15th. Americans took shelter under leaky brush and bark huts. John Stark slept in a settler's cabin nearby.[26]

At about one o'clock in the morning, someone woke Stark by banging on the cabin door. Outside stood a wet and angry minister of the Lord, Parson Thomas Allen of Pittsfield, Massachusetts. He had driven a horse and buggy from Berkshire County at the head of a militia company. Allen was a militant Christian and an active member of his local militia. He could not wait for morning to confront the American commander. According to Caleb Stark, his astonished grandfather listened while Allen stated his case: "The people of Berkshire have often turned out to fight the enemy, but we have not been permitted to do so. We have resolved that if you do not let us fight now, never to come again."[27]

The general could be a stern disciplinarian, and here a subordinate had addressed him in an insulting manner—a subordinate who had the temerity to wake him from a sound sleep. Perhaps Parson Allen's calling protected him, for Stark answered him in good humor: "Would you go now in this dark and rainy night? No; go to your people; tell them to take rest if they can; and if God sends us sunshine to-morrow and I do not give you fighting enough, I will never call on you again."[28]

The parson went away satisfied, and Stark went back to bed.

The next morning, August 16, Stark conferred with his field officers. In addition to Seth Warner, they were: Colonel Samuel Herrick of the Vermont Rangers; Lieutenant Colonel Moses Nichols, a physician from Amherst, New Hampshire; Colonel David Hobart of Plymouth, New Hampshire; and Colonel Thomas Stickney of Concord, New Hampshire. There were other field officers, but these men would lead the attack. With the intelligence gathered from local farmers who had strolled about Baum's positions, the Americans knew where to find the enemy. They also learned that Baum had moved one of his two cannons to the top of the hill.[29]

Stark had witnessed the suicidal frontal assaults mounted by Abercromby at Ticonderoga and Howe at Bunker Hill, and he rejected the tactic. He divided his force into four units: one, under Nichols, would swing wide to the east and then north in the hills to attack the dragoons on the hilltop; the second, under Herrick, would march west and north around the Germans to join Nichols in the attack; a third detachment led by Hobart and Stickney would approach the Tories in their little fort overlooking the roads from the south. Stark and Warner would confront the central position by the bridge. If coordination and secrecy could be achieved, Baum would find his scattered forces surrounded.[30]

The rain stopped by noon, the sun came out, and the day grew hot and sultry. Nichols and Herrick moved out first, leading their men to the flank attacks. It would take them much longer to get into position. Hobart and Stickney told their men to put cornhusks in their hats so they could distinguish each other from the Tories.[31]

Stark ordered his men in the center to march around in a wide circle, repeatedly parading a portion of their ranks in plain view of Baum's troops, "to amuse the Germans," Stark told them.[32] He hoped to impress the enemy with the illusion of a large number of rebels.

Warner and Stark rode their horses toward the enemy positions to take a closer look. Both armies watched the two officers spur their mounts closer and closer to the Walloomsac. Then, German artillerists touched off a cannon in their direction, and the shot whistled past them. The two men galloped back to the American lines, where Stark called out to his soldiers, "Those rascals know I am an officer. Don't you see how they honor me with a big gun as a salute!"[33]

With no communication between the units of the rebel force, achieving a coordinated attack would be difficult. The two flanking parties needed several hours to get into position. The soldiers led by Hobart and Stickney separated into two units and took different paths toward the Tory redoubt. Finally, they all reached their destinations, where they waited for a signal.

A militiaman from Berkshire County, who had marched with the flankers to the hilltop, remembered that his unit reached their jumping-off point "and there, pursuant to orders, sat in silence until a signal (the firing of two muskets) was given, when the American army, upon three sides of the British encampment, made a simultaneous attack."[34] It began with a tremendous roar. John Stark thought that the noise produced by the battle resembled "a continuous clap of thunder."[35]

Baum's men, who knew an attack was coming, nevertheless were stunned when it came. Hunkered down behind their timber barricades, they could not see the Americans approach. Patrols that morning had reported no enemy activity near them. Baum, himself, operated within a cone of ignorance. Surgeon Wasmus noted, "The strangest of all was that our commander did not know where we were standing. He had not visited us in these past three days." Runners carried messages from one unit to another by threading their way through woods infested with Yankees.[36]

The Indians might have served as scouts but, Wasmus reported, "All the Savages came onto our mountain, lay down behind the trees and refused to go forward against the enemy."[37]

On the hilltop, the German dragoons felt the first shock of American-style warfare. The disciplined Brunswickers crouched behind their breastworks to load their weapons; then they stood up together to fire a volley. Wasmus watched, horrified: "But as soon as they rose up to take aim, bullets went through their heads. … Thus in a short time our tallest and best dragoons were sent into eternity."[38] American sharpshooters killed all the enemy artillerists by the bridge and on the mountain.

The German doctor set up his field surgery behind a giant oak near the dragoon redoubt, where he tried to bandage wounds. Several Indians crowded into the shelter with him, knocking him down and lying on top of him. The dragoons began to run, and their surgeon followed them. Rebels shot at him. He fell down with musket balls snapping over him. An American soldier dragged Wasmus to his feet and pointed a bayonet at his throat.[39]

The attackers scrambled over the log walls of the dragoons' defenses. One soldier, David Holbrook, recounted that he and his militia comrades fought "without form or regularity, each American fighting according to his own discretion."[40]

Another Yankee, Thomas Mellen, wrote that the Germans fired by platoons and were soon hidden by the smoke. Mellen agreed with Holbrook that the Americans fired "each on his own hook, aiming wherever he saw a flash."[41] Few of the militia troops carried bayonets or cartridges; they loaded their muskets with loose ball and powder poured loose from powder horns. The action at the hilltop ended quickly. Vermonter Silas Walbridge reckoned that the fighting there lasted thirty minutes, at most, before the Germans took to their heels. Another Vermonter, Jessee Field, believed it happened even faster—that the Americans entered the fortification within five minutes of the first shot.[42]

Once the rebels took the entrenchments, the struggle became a foot-race, with the Germans trying to escape and the Americans pursuing, all of them running downhill. The dragoons, with heavy swords, were no match for the lightly clad Americans. "Many were killed and taken in going down the hill, and others on the flat upon the river," Jessee Field remembered. He also stressed that the Americans fought as individuals. "Every man seemed to manage for himself," he wrote, "and being by chance attached to a squad either under some leader or without any would attack any party that would come in their way."[43]

The Yankees killed enemy soldiers who tried to run away, but spared those who surrendered. Surgeon Wasmus, a bayonet pointed at his neck, addressed his captor as my "*freund und bruder*" (friend and brother). The American understood, put down his weapon, and "made a friendly face and was so human that he urged me to drink from his wooden flask."[44]

Down by the river, Stark's men quickly overwhelmed the British and Canadians at the bridge and captured the cannon positioned on the steep hillside behind the bridge. Nearby, a musket ball slammed into Colonel Baum's abdomen, a mortal blow that caused the Brunswick commander hours of suffering before he died.

⚜ ⚜

The men led by Colonels Hobart and Stickney had proceeded toward the Tory redoubt by different paths. One unit had pressed head-on through fields of corn and flax; the other had circled around to the left and approached the little fortress from the side, where Colonel Joab Stafford led a detachment through a deep, brushy ravine. Some men on each side of this particular engagement knew each other; Tories and patriots came from the same communities. Unlike the other confrontations on the Bennington battlefield, where the foes were from different countries, this particular clash was a mini–civil war.[45]

Fiery Parson Allen seized a leading role in the attack. He stepped up on a log, in full view of the Tories, and called out to them to switch sides—to join the patriots. A moment of silence followed. Then a voice from the redoubt called out, "There's Parson Allen. Let's pot him." Allen jumped down from the log as musket balls flew around him.[46]

The attackers in the ravine remained hidden from the Loyalists until they were near at hand. One Tory remembered: "We had not expected, however, that they would approach us under cover; but supposed we should see them on the way. We did not know that a little gully which lay below us, was long and deep enough to conceal them; but they knew the ground, and the first we saw of the party coming to attack us, they made their appearance right under our guns."[47] At the same time Stafford's attackers appeared almost behind the Loyalists.

The shocked defenders rose to fire down at the rebels in the ravine and, in standing, they exposed their upper bodies to marksmen out in the flax field. A deadly volley struck them. The Tories scrambled out over the walls and fled. A patriot yelled, "Come on, my boys! They run! They run!" A musket ball struck Joab Stafford in the foot, but he fought on, hopping on one leg.[48]

With the redoubt in rebel hands, the Loyalists escaped toward the river, splashed across it, and tried to clamber up the steep bank on the opposite side, where they were easy prey for patriot sharpshooters.[49] Some Americans chased the fleeing men. One Tory jumped over a rail fence with shots flying around him. He looked back and saw "a tall, rawboned fellow, running like a deer, only a short distance behind, and gaining on me every step he took." The Loyalist threw away his musket to lighten his load; fear spurred him on. But his pursuer would not quit. "I supposed he must be in a terrible passion, or he would not have taken such extraordinary pains to overtake me; and even if he should spare my life and do me no injury, in that solitary spot, I did not know what to expect from the rebels."[50]

The terrified Loyalist ran straight toward a high bank along the river. "A frightful precipice," he called it. He ran right out over the precipice and dropped through the air into the stream, where his legs sank deep in the muddy bottom. The rebel chasing him followed him over the cliff, and he too became stuck in the river bottom. Side-by-side, they struggled to escape the mud. The Loyalist managed to break free, and he got away. He never knew what became of the fierce patriot in the river. "A man who has never been frightened as I was," he wrote, "with the expectation of instant death, cannot easily imagine how he will run, or how much he can do, to get out of danger." During the entire chase and the struggle in the river, neither man spoke a word to the other.[51]

The familiarity of the foes at the Tory redoubt fueled the ferocity of the combat. One New York patriot wrote, "the bigger part of Dutch Hosack

[Hoosick] was in the battle against us." Hoosick was the community just west of the battlefield. Colonel Stafford of the militia encountered an elderly man in his ranks as they prepared to attack. He advised the old man to remain behind, but the elder replied, "Not till I've had a shot at them first captain, if you please." Stafford wrote that the old man's long hair "shone as white as silver."[52]

Years later some historians embellished the savagery of the fight at the Tory redoubt. Chandler Potter, the New Hampshire historian, wrote: "The tories expected no quarter and gave none—fighting to the last like tigers. They were completely surrounded in their fortifications, and the work of death was finished with bayonets and clubbed muskets. Hobart and Stickney saw the work thoroughly done."[53]

Veterans of the battle remembered no such brutality. A burial pit near the redoubt held either thirteen or eighteen bodies, according to the accounts of two men who watched the interment of the dead. One soldier in Colonel Stickney's regiment wrote, "I saw thirteen Tories, mostly shot in the head, buried in one hole."[54] He didn't report whether they were shot in the front or the back of their heads. They may have been those who stood up to fire at the attackers in the ravine and, thus, became easy targets. Austin Wells, who also claimed to be an eyewitness to the burial, said, "seventeen bodies were thus thrown in here, this being the number of tories left dead upon the hill [the redoubt] on the day of the battle."[55] Tory Colonel Pfister numbered among those who received a fatal wound in the attack.

One patriot, William Clement, of Stickney's regiment, carried a musket with a bayonet attached. When he charged the fortress, a Tory thrust a bayonet at him. He parried the blow, and then drove his own bayonet through his foe's eye and into his head, killing him. The bayonet broke off and remained in the Loyalist's body when he was buried. Clement declined to remove it, saying he would never touch it again. No other account of a Tory dying by the bayonet appeared in the narratives about Bennington. Clement's victim died in combat—not as a result of being denied quarter.[56]

✦ ✦

Yankees pursued Baum's fleeing soldiers; they took prisoners and pocketed plunder from captives. Those Germans and British who refused to surrender either escaped into the woods or were shot. Some Americans pursued them for miles.[57] One narrator reported that his father, then a boy of fourteen, saw several German soldiers "shot after they had ceased firing."[58]

Taken back to the hilltop by his captors, Wasmus treated the German wounded until a rebel officer ordered him to care for the American casualties. Many patriot soldiers carried canteens filled with rum or a mixture of rum and water; Wasmus thought many of these men were drunk—he called them "dumb" Americans. Someone picked Wasmus's pockets and stole some of his surgical instruments. Despite his disdain for his enemies, he noted that they were "well-shaped men of very healthy appearance and well-grown; better than the Canadians." It seemed that General Stark made a poor impression on the German doctor, however, who described him as "one who in attire and posture was very similar to the tailor Muller in Wolfenbuttel," back in Germany, meaning that Stark appeared to be a very ordinary man.[59]

Wasmus saw many prisoners like himself, but he found it difficult to believe that no Indians had been captured. Of his countrymen he wrote, "Many had been killed or wounded in their flight; all the rest had been taken prisoner." He saw Loyalist prisoners being taken away: "Like cattle, they were tied to each other with cords and ropes and led away; it is presumed they will be hanged." All the prisoners prepared to be marched off, they knew not where, when, a little after five o'clock, "we heard cannon and volley firing in the direction of Sancoick. This was the Breymann Corps. that had been designated for our aid but unfortunately had arrived too late."[60]

When Breymann's relief column reached San Coick, they encountered a scattering of refugees from Baum's defeat. These soldiers told various tales of what had happened, none of which alerted Breymann that the Americans had totally destroyed Baum's force.[61] Philip Skene, who accompanied the reinforcements, assured Breymann that all was well. To demonstrate, Skene rode forward to talk to some men that he assumed were Loyalists on a nearby hillside. He wrote, "I galloped up to them, at the distance of 100 yards and desired them to halt; some did—I then asked them if they were for King George, they immediately presented and fired confusedly, hit my horse but missed me."[62]

Breymann's sudden appearance surprised the Americans, who were not prepared to fight his compact force; many rebels were exhausted from the heat and exertion, while others were scattered around the countryside hunting fleeing enemies. Colonel Herrick tried to rally men to resist. He rode past young David Holbrook and his companions and called out, "Boys, follow me." Holbrook and others ran behind Herrick some two miles until they saw Breymann's detachment. Herrick galloped back for more men. Holbrook was tired out. He and his comrades "ran behind a haystack and rested until the British army came along and then went out from behind the stack and discharged their pieces at the enemy and ran."[63]

Breymann's force drove the few Americans back toward the earlier battlefield. The Germans stopped several times to fire musket volleys at the rebels, who were too far away to hit. One veteran remembered how the Germans' brass kettle drums glittered in the sunlight.[64]

Stark and Warner arrived. Then, the Vermont troops from Manchester marched onto the scene just in time to stiffen the resistance. Teamsters hauled a captured cannon to the front, but no American knew how to fire it. One report claimed that Stark himself loaded and fired the weapon to show his men how to do it.[65]

American officers prepared a counterattack. David Holbrook watched as "an old man, with a Queen Anne's sword and mounted on a black mare, with about ninety robust men following him in files two deep, came up. ... And, just as the old man had got his men to the spot and halted, his mare fell, and he jumped upon a large white oak stump and gave the command." At the same time, Holbrook wrote, he heard Colonel Seth Warner, in a voice "like thunder," order, "Fix bayonets. Charge." The old man jumped off the stump and led his company against the Germans.[66]

Yankee soldiers, commanded by a Sergeant Luttington, overran an enemy cannon and killed its crew. Then they "caught hold of the limber and whirled about the piece and fired it at the enemy and the blaze overtook them before they had got ten rods and mowed down a large number of them."[67]

Stark recognized the good fortune that brought Warner's Continentals at just the right moment. He wrote Horatio Gates later: "Luckily for us, that moment Col. Warner's regiment came up fresh, who marched on and began the attack afresh. I pushed forward as many of the men as I could to their assistance."[68]

Philip Skene appeared again, riding a fresh horse. He waved his sword in the air and tried to rally Breymann's men for a counterattack. Someone shot this horse out from under him. Skene then "cut the traces of an artillery horse, mounted him and rode off."[69] The German counterattack came to nothing, and Breymann led his surviving soldiers away from the field. It had taken them thirty-one hours to march twenty-four miles; had they arrived sooner, the outcome of the battle might have been different.[70]

Darkness fell. Patriot soldiers wanted to chase after the retreating Germans, but Stark called them back. He feared they would shoot each other in the gloom. "With one more hour of daylight," he wrote, "we should have captured the whole detachment."[71]

The Americans marched back toward Bennington in a long line of exhausted soldiers and prisoners. Stark met a weary young man by the roadside and ordered him to help haul a captured cannon. The boy pleaded that he was too tired, but Stark told him, "Don't seem to disobey; take hold and if you can't hold out, slip away in the dark."[72]

A soldier stopped Seth Warner and told him, "Your brother is killed." Warner dismounted and walked over to a lifeless form on the ground. In the gathering darkness, Seth "stooped and gazed in the dead man's face and then rode away without saying a word." The dead man may have been Seth's brother Daniel, who fought at Bennington, but it remains unclear whether he died there. In John Stark's battle report to General Gates, he singled out Warner and Hobart for their "great service" and their "superior intelligence and experience."[73]

At some time, late in the battle, Stark must have dismounted and left his horse for a few moments. When he returned, the horse was gone—stolen. In his letter to General Gates a few days later, he said simply, "I lost a horse in the action," a statement that led some to believe his horse had been shot from under him.[74]

After an unsuccessful search for the animal, Stark posted an advertisement to the *Connecticut Courant*: "Stole from me the subscriber, from Wallomscock, in the time of the action the 16th of August last, a brown mare, five years old, with a star in her forehead. Also a doe skin saddle, blue housing trimmed with white, and a curbed bridle." Stark's posting closed with an expression of contempt for the "sly, artful, designing villains" who stole his horse.[75]

It was no army horse that John Stark lost that day—it was his horse, a mare that he knew well, even her age and her markings. And she wore the tack her master had selected and paid for himself. That he wanted her back badly enough to advertise for her in a Connecticut newspaper seems a small thing, but it reveals how personal the Revolution had become. Those who risked their lives, their health and their property for the American cause could expect no recompense for their losses. It was their burden and their spur.

Rebel fighters in the Bennington battle felt a personal stake in the outcome, and they fought accordingly. By rough count, 200 of the invaders lay dead, with more wounded and hundreds of them captured. About thirty of Stark's men died.[76] Judged by the number of casualties, the battle was small compared to other great contests of the war. But the combat that day reduced John Burgoyne's strength by as many soldiers as the later, bloodier contests at Freeman's Farm or Bemis Heights—only here, at Bennington, most of those soldiers became prisoners, not corpses. Measured by that standard, the fight along the Walloomsac River was a big battle indeed.

22

A Storm Gathers at Saratoga

The Fate of America May Be Determined

When the roar of the guns ceased, twilight descended on a landscape littered with dead and dying men. The survivors were exhausted, soaked in sweat, and numb from a day that, for most of them, was unlike any day they had ever experienced. They functioned as best they could amid the carnage. Somewhere in the woods nearby, fugitive Loyalists hid or thrashed through the brush trying to evade capture.[1]

Men and horses clogged the road to Bennington the evening after the battle on August 16, 1777. Captured cannons and ammunition wagons crowded the militia companies. The soldiers plodded eastward, bone-tired, hungry and thirsty. Some men were too drunk to walk.[2] Guards walked beside a sullen mob of prisoners. The captives with the most to fear, the Loyalists, staggered along, roped together "like cattle."[3]

General Stark estimated that he held 700 prisoners. A few days later a more accurate count revised the number to 651, of whom 155 were Tories. All these captives presented a staggering problem to the Americans, who had no means to feed and house them.

A soldier escorted Julius Wasmus, occasionally grasping the doctor's arm, showing off to his comrades. The Americans were in high spirits. A cart carrying Colonel Baum rattled past the German captives. "He was shot through the abdomen," Wasmus wrote, "and was crying and begging that the cart should go slow but the men did not understand our language." Soldiers carried the mortally wounded man into a house, but they refused to let the doctor stay with him.[4]

They took Wasmus to another house and put him to work dressing the wounds of Germans and Americans alike. Wasmus watched as an American major clowned, prancing around wearing a dragoon cap and sword. But, when a British officer informed the major that a soldier had stolen Wasmus's possessions, the major quit fooling and made the soldier return the items.[5]

The prospect of being prisoners of the Americans terrified the Germans. "To all appearances, we live here under a nation extremely enraged, whose language none of us understands; each one is asking what will become of us."[6]

The victors kept Wasmus and some of the captured officers in Stephen Fay's Catamount Tavern, a large wooden building with a mansard roof, up the street from the crowded meetinghouse where most of the enlisted prisoners had been locked. The tavern must have been particularly grim that night because Fay's eldest son, John, had been killed in the battle.[7]

Somehow the Americans managed to feed at least some of the prisoners that evening, and that calmed fears, the doctor reported: "… we were cheered up a little when we were regaled tonight with beef, pork, potatoes and punch; we were greatly pleased. 'Well', everybody said, 'I am satisfied if we will not be treated any better or worse during our imprisonment.'"[8]

After they had eaten, a tall American came into the room and sat down next to Wasmus. It was Seth Warner. The Vermonter returned some of the surgeon's instruments along with his journal and his receipt book. Warner kept some of the lancets, the doctor wrote, "as something very peculiar." Wasmus closed his account of this terrible day by writing that the American officers "behaved with extreme politeness and civility toward us, but we could not understand each other."[9]

***

Most of the captives in Bennington were billeted in an overcrowded meetinghouse. There was barely room to stand; makeshift beds had been created with loose boards laid over pews so that the wounded had room to lie down. That evening one of the boards broke with a loud crack, provoking panic that a floor had given way and men might be crushed. Some prisoners rushed to the door. The outnumbered guards feared a breakout. They fired their muskets through the door, killing two men and wounding another.[10]

The gunfire brought Americans on the run, led by Parson Allen brandishing a "naked sword." Several armed men followed him. Allen confronted surgeon Wasmus and his frightened companions, who were walking in the street. "He [Parson Allen] first started to strike us and push us, the detachment cocked their triggers and wanted to shoot." Allen struck one of the Germans many times with his sword. Then, someone behind Wasmus wrapped his arms around the German doctor and spoke to the Americans in English. "Thereupon the men calmed down and did not shoot." Wasmus could not understand what was said, but he recognized the man who grasped him and saved his life—it was the same American major who had returned his possessions the day of the battle. The major also rescued his companion who had been struck by the sword. "I have never seen a man so enraged as this noble pastor," Wasmus wrote. Yet all of the sword blows had been made with the flat of the weapon; remarkably, the victim's coat "showed no hole." Parson Allen, the Christian soldier, credited the "God of armies" for victory that day.[11]

The next morning, August 18, General Stark visited the prisoners. He ordered the captured baggage to be arrayed on a field near the Presbyterian meetinghouse so that they could walk about and claim their own property. He even sent a purloined watch to Wasmus, thinking it belonged to him. The presence together of British and German prisoners demonstrated that the Americans harbored different attitudes toward the soldiers of the two lands. "One can see," the doctor wrote, "that the Americans nourish great hatred against the English inasmuch as they treat them with much more contempt than us."[12]

Most of the prisoners began the long march south and east to Boston. The Germans, Canadians and British signed a parole—a promise "that we would not desert nor talk in any way about the affairs of the war with the inhabitants of the country." Wasmus marveled at the friendliness of the people they encountered. "We understood no English, but they treated us like friends."[13] This stood in marked contrast to the rude treatment complained of by British soldiers.[14] Both fared better than the Tories, however, who marched off to jails in various states, including the notorious Newgate prison in Connecticut. They were, in the eyes of their captors, traitors.

General Riedesel was an unhappy man after Bennington. Many of his Brunswick troops had been killed or captured, and he blamed Burgoyne. Riedesel had not been in favor of his men's mission to Bennington before they left, thinking Baum had too small a force; he now viewed the entire expedition as a disaster. He wrote in his memoirs:

> This unfortunate affair [Bennington] caused a sudden cessation of all our operations. Our boats, provisions—in fact nothing was received from Fort George. The army, therefore, could not proceed further, and the despondent spirits of the enemy became suddenly so elated, that its army grew daily stronger.[15]

News arrived that Lieutenant Colonel Barry St. Leger had abandoned the siege of Fort Schuyler (formerly Fort Stanwix) in the western Mohawk Valley and had retreated to Canada. Tryon County Militia under General Nicholas Herkimer had marched toward the fort to attempt to raise the siege, but the regiment ran into an ambush at Oriskany. The slaughter that resulted convinced General Schuyler to send Benedict Arnold with 900 Continentals to reinforce the troops at the fort. Even with Joseph Brant's Iroquois as his allies, St. Leger could not prevail over the combined American forces. Two key elements of Burgoyne's invasion had collapsed, and General Howe had failed to appear, leaving the main body exposed.[16]

These two defeats, Riedesel thought, "raised the spirits of the enemy so amazingly, that the militia poured forth in crowds from the provinces of New Hampshire and New York."[17] American Lieutenant Colonel Henry Dearborn, in camp by the Hudson, mirrored Riedesel's pessimism with his own optimism. On August 19 he wrote, "General Gates takes Command of the Northern army this Day which I think will Put a New face upon our affairs." The next day he celebrated "the Glorious News" of Stark's victory. Over the next weeks, Dearborn hailed the arrival on the Hudson of Daniel Morgan and Benedict Arnold, and of the legion of fighters who came with these officers, all of whom "appear in high spirits."[18]

The promotion of Gates over Schuyler contributed to the high spirits. Yankees had no confidence in Schuyler. The New York general's strategy had been successful, however. Earlier in the summer he realized that his smaller force of about 4,500 men could not stop the British. He compensated by staging orderly withdrawals and denying the invaders the use of roads, crops and livestock. Burgoyne's advance bogged down, his troops ran short of food, and his horses grew lean from lack of forage. By September the British and Germans were stuck far from their base with no hope of reinforcement.[19]

When Gates arrived and took command, he convened a council of officers, but he did not invite Schuyler to the meeting. General Schuyler accepted his demotion manfully, stayed in camp and remained a loyal soldier. He wrote later, "I thought it my duty to remain with the army."[20]

American troop strength multiplied until more than 10,000 men gathered north of Albany and awaited orders. Some of the soldiers had volunteered because they wanted to serve under Gates. But General Nathanael Greene understood that Schuyler and others had created the climate for Gates to succeed. Gates appeared on the scene, Greene wrote, "just in time to reap the laurels and rewards."[21]

Caleb Stark served as adjutant in Colonel Joseph Cilley's New Hampshire regiment, which was in camp beside the Hudson. He was not yet eighteen, but young Stark was already a veteran of Bunker Hill, Canada, Ticonderoga and Hubbardton. When Horatio Gates learned that Caleb was in camp, he sent for him.[22]

Gates congratulated the boy on his father's victory at Bennington, and then asked, "Don't you want to see your father?" The question was more than a friendly overture. Gates knew that John Stark served New Hampshire and owed no obedience to Continental officers. Gates wanted Stark's militia to occupy an exposed position on the east side of the Hudson River; Stark had been slow to respond to requests. Gates thought Caleb might convince his father to join the Continental forces. Specifically, the general told Caleb to ask for "the artillery he has taken for the brush I soon expect to have with Burgoyne."[23]

A replacement was found for the adjutant job, and Caleb rode off with a party of soldiers "to open communications with General Stark." They passed through devastated countryside on the way to San Coick, a wasteland of deserted farmhouses, ruined crops and the carcasses of butchered livestock.[24]

Father and son held a brief reunion at San Coick, where Stark was trying to recover from illness. Then Caleb rode back west to prepare for the coming battle. He could tell Gates that his father had already given orders for his troops to march to the American camp at Stillwater. John Stark knew, however, that his men did not intend to remain there.

⚔

Stark wrote to Gates on September 7 to explain that his New Hampshire troops had enlisted for two months, and only for two months. "One more difficulty," he wrote, "the men's time is nearly out and it is out of my power to detain them, not with my utmost endeavor to persuade them to the contrary." He could not even give his "utmost endeavor"; he lay in bed, he told Gates, "in the greatest agony and pain."[25] The precise nature of his ailment remains unknown, but he complained of poor health periodically for the rest of his life.

Colonel Samuel Ashley commanded the New Hampshire militia while Stark recovered. On September 12, Jeduthan Baldwin watched 800 of "Gen'l Starks" cross the Hudson to the encampment at Stillwater. Two days later Baldwin noted that Stark himself reached the American camp.[26]

On September 13, Burgoyne's army crossed the river on a temporary bridge, which was removed once the British and Germans all reached the west bank. Now both armies faced each other on the same side of the Hudson.[27]

Gates tried unsuccessfully to convince Stark's troops to stay and fight, but the New Hampshire farmers would not be swayed. They had served their enlistments, and they needed to go home to bring in their crops. They started the trek home, and they kept marching even when the first loud peals of gunfire reached them from Freeman's Farm. John Stark headed home with them.[28]

James Wilkinson, aide to Gates, wrote to General St. Clair: "The celebrated General Stark, the Bennington hero, by way of gilding his reputation and finishing his character, left the camp at a time when we hourly expected an engagement, and on the day before the action."[29] Had he waited to comment for a few days, Wilkinson might have written a more charitable letter.

Before he left Stillwater, Stark wrote a letter to an as-yet-unknown offi-cer in New Hampshire who, he expected, would command two newly enlisted regiments from the state. He urged him "to hasten your troops to join the army without loss of time. It is probable the fate of America may be deter-mined in a few days. Your exertions in this will get you everlasting Honour, and Neglect to the contrary."[30] Stark knew a battle loomed. Without soldiers to command, he left for home, clearly recognizing the honor he would forfeit without a command at this critical time. But, men in New Hampshire had other plans for him.

23

STARK'S KNOB

They Go There To Serve under Genl Stark

The two great clashes at Saratoga known as the Battle of Freeman's Farm and the Battle of Bemis Heights were among the largest and most complex conflicts of the war. John Stark played a peripheral but important role at the very end of those clashes, which are treated here in synopsis.

Horatio Gates commanded the Americans. He had the good fortune to command perhaps the most competent assemblage of senior officers present at any contest in the Revolution; Benedict Arnold, Daniel Morgan, John Glover, Thaddeus Kosciusko, Henry Dearborn, John Stark, and many others fought there.

The Battle of Saratoga played out in two conflicts separated by almost three weeks of heavy skirmishing. Gates and Kosciusko set the stage by creating a fortified position on the high ground west of the Hudson River known as Bemis Heights. Gates's defensive strategy was to stop Burgoyne at the narrow pass between the heights and the river. Arnold wanted to attack. He and Gates argued; their dispute grew into a quarrel, then a festering wound.

Meanwhile, without a command, John Stark still had very personal reasons to care deeply about American fortunes at Saratoga. Caleb served as adjutant in the First New Hampshire Regiment commanded by Colonel Joseph Cilley. His unit would be in the thick of the fighting both days. Stark's old friend Henry Dearborn commanded light infantry attached to Morgan's riflemen.[1]

On September 19, Burgoyne ordered a flanking movement west of the American positions on the heights. Arnold urged Gates to send Daniel Morgan's Virginia riflemen into the woods in front of the British. Morgan was a big, rugged man, a former teamster. Like Stark, he had fought alongside the British in the war with France and, like Stark, he had no use for them. His back bore the scars of 499 lashes laid on because he slugged a redcoat officer.[2] Now he ordered his backwoodsmen to target British officers. When his men became scattered in the woods, he called them back with a turkey call.[3]

While Morgan stymied the flankers, Arnold ordered a charge into the center of the enemy line. General Riedesel reinforced the position and stopped the American counterattack. The battle at Freeman's Farm ended in a bloody draw. The British lost 600 killed, wounded or captured; the Americans lost over 300. In his report of the action to Congress, Gates gave Arnold no credit.[4]

Dearborn and his light infantry fought in the thick of the fray. He exulted in his journal: "On this Day has Been fought one of the Greatest Battles that Ever was fought in Amarrca, & I Trust we have Convinced the British Butchers that the Cowardly Yankees Can & when there is Call for it, will, fight."[5]

Burgoyne's army rested and hoped for reinforcements that would never come. Desertions and illness reduced his forces; starvation became a real threat. Meanwhile new arrivals of militia and Continentals strengthened the American army.

On October 7, British troops under General Simon Fraser tried again to flank the American left wing. James Wilkinson reported the movement to Gates and suggested a counterattack. Gates reportedly replied, "Well, then, order on Morgan to begin the game." Gates remained in the rear, well back from the "game" that would be known as the Battle of Bemis Heights.[6]

General Fraser rode in front of his redcoats to inspire them. Morgan ordered a rifleman to target the British leader. On his third try the marksman fired a ball through Fraser's abdomen. The general lingered many hours in the presence of the horrified Baroness Riedesel before he died. Several other British officers fell to the accurate shooting of the Virginians. One of Dearborn's men wrote that Morgan "astonished the English and Germans with the deadly fire of his rifles."[7]

Gates had relieved Arnold from active command as a result of their quarrel, but the fiery Arnold refused to sulk in his tent. He appeared on his horse in the midst of battle and saw an opportunity. He galloped the length of the firing lines in the killing field between the armies to lead an attack on British fortified positions. Astonished Americans rose to follow him. One soldier thought, "He seemed inspired with the fury of a demon."[8]

Sword in hand, Arnold led an attack on a position known as the Breymann Redoubt. A musket ball slammed into his left thigh, into the same leg that had been wounded at Quebec. Arnold's soldiers captured the redoubt and killed its commander, Lieutenant Colonel Heinrich von Breymann, whose reinforcement column had arrived late at Bennington.

Dearborn, Cilley and Scammel led attacks on the enemy. New Hampshire men seized a strongpoint, where Caleb Stark took a ball through his left arm.[9] With smoke swirling around him, Colonel Cilley sat astride a captured cannon, waving his arms in victory. Bemis Heights cost the Americans 150 soldiers killed, wounded or captured, while the British and their auxiliaries lost about 600 men.[10]

Burgoyne withdrew his army to the village on the Hudson known as Saratoga (now Schuylerville). The Americans pressed them so closely that they considered leaving their sick and wounded behind. On the 9th of October, the forward elements of the British retreat learned that Americans were already behind them, "employed for the purpose of preventing all retreat."[11] John Stark led the Americans blocking Burgoyne's escape.

⁂

The previous month, back in New Hampshire, Stark had found that the committee of safety wanted him to lead the new levy of militia to aid Gates. The committee wrote him on September 10 asking him, "not to think of leaving the Command at a Time when your Continuance is so Essentially Necessary, the Committee have assured the Men that are to March, that they go there to serve under Genl Stark, and they will go forward with that Expectation."[12]

The New Hampshire authorities had radically changed their outlook since the summer; where before they had insisted on an "independent command," free from the meddling of Continental officers, now they intended their troops to serve under General Gates. Stark himself had urged that these men "join the army." He accepted the state's commission again and quickly marched the two undersized regiments westward to Fort Edward, where he would try to bottle up the British army.[13]

During the night of October 12, Stark and his troops crossed the Hudson River. They took up positions near the river on the only avenue of retreat available to Burgoyne. Stark placed artillery on a small hill a little west of the river—a lump of black rock known thereafter as "Stark's Knob." British scouts soon discovered this force in their path, and their report convinced Burgoyne that there was now no escape.[14]

On October 13 a council of British and German officers decided to seek surrender terms from the Americans. Gates's offer, or "convention," allowed the defeated troops to return to their home countries on the condition that they agree not to take up arms against America. That Gates consented to this arrangement shocked his own officers. Even General Riedesel admitted that he viewed this arrangement with "great amazement."[15] When the defeated army stacked arms, every German regiment retained its colors; the Baroness sewed them inside bedding to safeguard them.[16]

Gates did not want American troops to witness the surrender ceremony; he wished to minimize the humiliation to the King's troops. Lieutenant William Digby of the Shropshire Regiment remembered the events of the day:

> I shall never forget the appearance of their [American] troops on our marching past them; a dead silence universally reigned through their numerous columns, and even then they seemed struck with our situation and dare scarce lift up their eyes to view British troops in such situation. I must say their decent behavior during the time (to us so greatly fallen) merited the utmost approbation and praise.[17]

Baroness Riedesel also was compelled to ride through the American camp in a calash (light carriage) with her three small daughters. She dreaded the experience. But, she wrote later, "I observed, with great satisfaction, that no one cast at us scornful glances. On the contrary, they all greeted me, even showing compassion on their countenances at seeing a mother with her little children in such a situation."[18] General Schuyler greeted the baroness, arranged for a meal for her family, and invited them all to stay with his family in Albany. At her husband's urging, she accepted. Schuyler also played host to Burgoyne at Albany, apparently forgiving him for burning his Saratoga home to the ground.

⚔ ⚔

John Stark's grandson Caleb wrote that his father and grandfather visited the American headquarters after the surrender. He claimed that American officers met the British senior officers, including Burgoyne, who chatted with Stark about their service in the French War.[19] The gathering, as described by the grandson, had the air of a tea after a hard-fought cricket match, where the players gather to socialize—a gathering of like-minded aristocrats. John Stark, Daniel Morgan and John Glover were no aristocrats; it is hard to imagine them rubbing shoulders with British officers, particularly given their eagerness to shoot them.

The men in the ranks socialized, too, in a manner of speaking. British Sergeant Lamb wrote: "During the time of cessation of arms, while the articles of capitulation were preparing, the soldiers of the two armies often saluted and discoursed with each other from the opposite banks of the river." He wrote of two Irish soldiers—one in the British army, the other in the American—who recognized each other's voices and dashed to the middle of the river to hug each other. They were brothers who, as Lamb noted with irony, had just been "engaged in hostile combat against each other's life."[20]

Lamb found little to celebrate in his new role in the convention army. Americans treated him badly, he reported, on the march to Boston and afterwards. "The people of New England appeared to indulge a deadly hatred against the British prisoners," he remembered, but he told of no incident of the hatred having deadly results. When Congress later broke the convention agreement and refused to allow the repatriation of Burgoyne's army, the British were marched on to Virginia instead of boarding ships for home. Lamb responded to this bad faith by escaping to New York, where he was welcomed by Major John André. Lamb chose to stay and fight.[21]

Surgeon Wasmus and the corps of Brunswickers from the Bennington defeat made the same march to Boston, but they encountered an entirely different welcome. "They [New Englanders] were very good people who took us in and treated us like brothers." One host gave the German doctor a shirt to replace his worn garment. An American woman stayed up all night to nurse a grenadier with a broken leg. Wasmus wrote, "Take note, you Germans, and learn to treat your friends as well as the inhabitants of New England treat their enemies!"[22]

Loyalists captured at Bennington and Saratoga faced a darker future. Patriots regarded them as criminals and traitors; many Tories were returned to their home jurisdictions for punishment. Schuyler ordered Loyalists from the Bennington battle sent to Albany, since most of them were New Yorkers.[23] Some Vermont Tories languished in a Bennington jail. The following winter they were herded out on the roads to trample down the snowdrifts like beasts of burden. Unluckiest of all were those men who passed months in the Simsbury, Connecticut, copper mine known as Newgate Prison.

One Loyalist tried to avoid the fate of his brethren by adopting a new persona. Ignoring his own history as British officer and owner of the manor at Skenesborough, he signed his parole, "Philip Skene, a poor follower of the British army."[24]

24

ALBANY

They Do Very Well in the Hanging Way

While the Northern Army celebrated the victory at Saratoga, Washington's troops in Pennsylvania suffered two setbacks. On September 10, Howe's redcoats attacked the Americans at Brandywine, forcing Washington to retreat to the north. He could no longer defend Philadelphia, and the British took the city.

On October 4 the Americans attacked the British at Germantown; they used a complicated pincer movement, but the two elements became lost in a fog and failed to converge at the critical time. In the chaos that followed, rebel soldiers shot at each other. Washington tried to put a positive slant on the fiasco when he reported to Congress; he wrote, "the day was unfortunate rather than injurious."[1]

Gloom pervaded Congress. The members had been forced from Philadelphia and now sat at York, Pennsylvania. Many of them understood one fact— Gates had won; Washington had lost. Some believed Gates should relieve Washington as commander in chief. Dr. Benjamin Rush actively campaigned for the change. He wrote to Patrick Henry: "The northern army has shown us what Americans are capable of doing with a GENERAL at their head. The spirit of the southern army is in no way inferior to the spirit of the northern. A Gates, a Lee or a Conway would in a few weeks render them an irresistible body of men."[2] Rush asked that his letter be destroyed, but the fiery Henry forwarded it to his compatriot from Mount Vernon.

Another rival, Thomas Conway, was an Irish-born officer in the French army. Congress made him a major general in the American army. When Washington learned of this appointment, he wrote to Richard Henry Lee; the decision was "as unfortunate a measure as ever was adopted. … it will give a fatal blow to the existence of the army."[3]

Conway had earned Washington's contempt by lobbying for rank among the politicians and by loose talk about American officers. There were twenty-three brigadier generals in the army, all of them senior to Conway. Washington anticipated that the foreigner's promotion over them would precipitate a rash of resignations. Congress promoted him anyway.[4]

Meanwhile, Washington acquired a copy of a letter from Conway to Horatio Gates that contained insulting language: "Heaven has been determined to save your Country; or a weak General and bad Councellors would have ruined it." The commander in chief promptly confronted Conway, quoting this statement.[5] He also advised General Gates that Conway was a "dangerous incendiary," a fact Gates knew firsthand.[6] When the correspondence between the two generals became public, talk of Gates superseding Washington ceased.

Only a few malcontents in Congress ever seriously considered replacing Washington. The backbiting subsided, but the controversy caused by Gates and Conway left vestigial damage. Washington knew he could not trust some of his subordinate officers, but he could not always be certain which officers. John Stark, a New Englander who had previously shown a preference for Gates over Schuyler and who had already resigned once from the army, must have been suspect. Washington betrayed no overt signs that he distrusted Stark, but subsequent events made clear he did not regard Stark as one of his own.

John Stark returned to Derryfield by way of Bennington in the late autumn of 1777. His brother-in-law, James McColly, led a string of "blooded" horses the general had purchased for his own account.[7] Congress had approved Stark's promotion to brigadier general on October 4, but news of his promotion probably didn't reach him until he arrived home. His commission charged him to obey the orders of Congress "or Commander-in-Chief for the time being of the Army of the United States."[8] John Hancock's letter of congratulations accompanied the commission. John Stark's contribution to his country's cause had finally been recognized, but the news came with the uneasy awareness that he owed allegiance to two separate chains of command. Congress and

Washington did not always agree on the best way forward; Stark's orders carried an inherent conflict.

On December 4, Matthew Patten noted that the New Hampshire authorities had proclaimed that date a day of "Thanksgiving through the State." Patten made no record of John Stark's homecoming. The arrival of the hero of Bennington provoked no stir—no parade, no honors. The general spent a few private days with his young family. The older boys, Caleb and Archibald, remained with the army.[9]

In the meantime Congress tinkered with the command structure by naming Horatio Gates to head a Board of War. The monumental problems of supply, armaments, pay, forage and a host of other mundane matters required an extensive administration. The politicians thought General Gates was the man for the job. Gates now believed he had authority to carry out his own war strategy, independent of Washington. Thus, an officer like Stark might find himself beset by conflicting orders from Washington, Gates, or Congress itself.[10]

Congress passed a resolve in December to "destroy the enemy's shipping at St. John's and elsewhere on Lake Champlain."[11] They appointed James Duane to deliver secret instructions personally to General Stark commanding him to raise and supply troops for the mission. Stark was to pay his volunteers "double continental pay and rations, during the expedition, in consequence of the inclemency of the season and the importance of the service." Duane wrote to Stark from the "Manour Livingston" to arrange a meeting in Albany as soon as possible. They met there before the 14th of January 1778, and General Stark immediately began recruiting Vermonters and other frontiersmen for the mission.[12]

Later that month, Gates changed the order of Congress; Lafayette would command the operation, Conway would be second-in-command, and Stark would report to both foreign generals.[13] Without complaint, Stark wrote to Lafayette on February 7 asking how many troops he should enlist and where they should rendezvous. His letter demonstrated that he knew nothing of Gates's plan for the expedition. Rather than expressing resentment at being upstaged by two French officers, he closed his letter with, "I shall leave no method untried to meet your expectations."[14]

Horatio Gates had changed more than the leadership of the enterprise; he had changed the mission itself. He envisioned "an irruption into Canada" with a far more ambitious goal than burning a few ships. He believed that Lafayette's presence and leadership would secure the loyalty of the French-Canadians throughout Canada.[15]

Washington disapproved of the whole affair. But, because he liked and admired Lafayette, he did not actively oppose the Canadian adventure. He had more pressing concerns—the survival of his army through the Valley Forge winter.[16]

The young Marquis de Lafayette arrived in Albany to find that his mission was in chaos. He wrote Washington, "What business had the Board of War to hurry me through the ice and snow? … Well, the first letter I receive at Albany is from General Stark who wishes to know what number of men, for what time, for what rendez vous I desire him to raise."[17] Lafayette had expected that Stark would already be on his way to Canada. When Congress learned of this confusion, they cancelled the mission. Stark was left with the problem of paying the volunteers he had already enlisted.

Lafayette was still in command at Albany. He toured settlements in the Mohawk Valley and Tryon County, and he ordered a stockade built at a particularly vulnerable place called Cherry Valley.[18]

Back in Albany, the Marquis became acquainted with a young Loyalist lawyer, Walter Butler, who languished in the Albany jail. Something about the prisoner's bearing and speech impressed the French general. Butler's father was John Butler, leader of a troop of Loyalist rangers. Walter had been captured at German Flats in 1777 and only escaped hanging at the hands of a military tribunal when General Philip Schuyler, who knew his family, had him transferred to Albany. Some sources state that Lafayette convinced the Albany authorities to accept Butler's "parole"—his word that he would not try to escape. Walter was moved to a private residence, from which he quickly fled.[19]

With the Marquis de Lafayette commanding in Albany in January 1778, General Stark seemed to be in a soldier's limbo; he went home to Derryfield. When Congress abandoned the Canadian expedition, Lafayette had no mission that matched his expectations; by spring, he was at Valley Forge with Washington. Gates became the commander of the Northern Department, and Stark returned to Albany on May 18 to serve under Gates.[20]

Even before he settled into his new post, John Stark seemed confident enough that he would be based in Albany that he applied for membership in Master Lodge Number Two of the Albany Free Masons. After his presentation to the membership and a vote, he was admitted "by unanimous consent of the members present and was initiated accordingly." He paid a £5 initiation fee.[21]

He followed in the footsteps of many of his Revolutionary peers, including Washington. Freemasonry became a vital part of the Enlightenment experience and a common bond among diverse elements of American society. There was no social hierarchy in Masonry other than "personal Merit."[22] Some of the first steps of the rebellion were taken in the "Long Room" of St. Andrews Masonic Lodge on the second floor of the Green Dragon Tavern in Boston, where Paul Revere, Dr. Joseph Warren and John Hancock hatched secret plans.[23]

Benjamin Franklin, another Mason, once wrote, "The only secret about Masonry is that there is no secret."[24] Franklin obviously didn't know all that transpired at the Green Dragon Tavern, but his statement was a reaction to widespread suspicion of Masonry and of its rites that were practiced outside public view. Back in 1738, Franklin had found it necessary to explain to his mother that the Masons were, "in general a very harmless sort of people; and have no principles or Practices that are inconsistent with Religion or good manners."[25] The old diplomat even attended lodge meetings in Paris, between visits with his lady friends.[26]

Enlisting in a peaceful brotherhood seemed out of character for John Stark, a man who was often rude, not religious, and far from harmless—and in Albany, of all places. He had detested Albany ever since his captivity at St. Francis, and the letters he wrote in 1778 showed that familiarity with the city had failed to soften his heart. Probably an advisor, perhaps his aide Archibald

Stark, suggested that joining the Albany Masons might serve as an olive branch offered to the natives before he inevitably clashed with them. In all his subsequent correspondence about the people he encountered there—"Tories, peculators and militia poltroons"—the general never mentioned the Masons.

Command at Albany amounted to a mandate without the means to perform the task. The Mohawk Valley and the Champlain/Lake George waterways were two arrows pointed at Albany—invasion avenues that John Stark knew could be used again. His grandson Caleb wrote: "For this service he had very few reliable troops, and was obliged to depend for support, at times, upon the militia.[27] The Tories and Iroquois knew that Burgoyne's defeat ended their hopes that England would control the New York frontier; this knowledge provoked them to desperate measures.

The Iroquois Confederacy occupied the vast territory west of the New York settlements and had benefitted temporarily from the British victory in the French and Indian War. The Proclamation Line protected Indian country from encroachment by American settlers. The Revolution ended that fragile security. Farmers and adventurers tested the boundaries, and the war divided the Confederacy. Most of the tribes sided with the British and Loyalists; the Oneida allied with the rebels. Bands of Tory partisans, supported by British regulars from Fort Niagara, made common cause with the Seneca, Cayuga, Onondaga and Mohawk tribes. The divisions were not always that neat but, in general, the Iroquois had chosen sides, and now they acted on their choice.[28]

Thayendanegea, a Mohawk more commonly known by his English name, Joseph Brant, played a pivotal role in convincing the pro-British Iroquois to act. Educated at Eleazor Wheelock's Indian school, Brant crossed easily between the two worlds, Indian and white. He joined a Christian church and became a Freemason. His sister Molly married Sir William Johnson, and that powerful connection gave the young Mohawk access to the highest levels of colonial society.[29]

Brant fought under Johnson in the war with France. Then he sailed to England, where he experienced gracious treatment by fashionable society. When he returned to America in 1776, he travelled among the Iroquois, spreading his message that the American rebels endangered the freedoms and the lands of his people. Brant was a natural leader; the warriors listened to him.[30]

He found Loyalist allies in Colonel John Butler and his son Walter. The colonel led a large contingent of Tories known as Butler's Rangers. Some of his followers daubed themselves with war paint and wore Indian garb when they attacked remote farms and settlements in New York and Pennsylvania.[31]

The Indian warriors appeared suddenly out of the forest when they attacked. They wore loincloths and moccasins, with their skulls shaved except for a scalp lock on the tops of their heads. They carried muskets and hatchets and used them to deadly effect. An Indian war party inspired terror.[32]

Before long, Butler's rangers provoked similar fear. Walter Butler had been well known in Albany, where he had briefly practiced law. The Butlers and the Indians adopted a strategy that sought to destroy the granary of the Revolutionary army.[33] The river valleys and uplands of central New York contained excellent farmland. John Stark called it "the best country for bread in America, which is much wanted for the use of the army."[34] To relieve the pressure on the farmers, Stark had only a handful of Continentals and whatever New York militia could be mustered. The latter had already earned the general's scorn: "… you know there is no dependence to be put in them," he told Gates.[35]

Brant struck at Cobleskill, New York, on May 30, 1778. His raiders lured the small detachment of Continental soldiers posted there into a trap and killed most of them. When five Americans took refuge in a house, Brant's men burned it down, roasting the soldiers alive. They burned houses and barns and took few prisoners. One victim "had his body cut open and his intestines fastened around a tree several feet distant."[36]

Stark wrote to militia General Ten Broeck two days later asking for his help. He advised Ten Broeck: "The Indians and tories have made a descent upon a place called Cobuskill, about forty miles from this place, and destroyed some part of it. A party of continentals, posted not far off, attacked them; while a company of militia poltroons looked on, excepting six, who behaved well."[37] Stark expected little from Ten Broeck, however; as he wrote to Gates, "I have applied to Gen. Ten Broeck for his militia, and he has promised to assist me as soon as church is over."[38] It was an early indication that John

Stark, a combat officer, might be out of his element in an administrative post. Requesting "militia poltroons" from a militia general displayed characteristic Stark diplomacy.

⁂

In the midst of Stark's frustration, a letter arrived from Washington that must have further darkened his mood. General John Sullivan was preparing to attack Rhode Island and had requested Stark's assistance. Washington wrote:

> Sir: In a letter from Major General Sullivan of the 1st. Instant [May] he complains of wanting assistance in his command, and begs that you may be desired to take post with him this campaign; you will therefore be pleased to join him as soon as possible.[39]

This order created a dilemma for Stark—a direct result of the multiple chains of command. Congress had posted him in Albany. Did Washington's order outweigh the mandate of Congress? Clearly, John Stark would have preferred to serve in an active military campaign with Sullivan, with actual soldiers to command. He wrote Washington: "Had it been the pleasure of Congress to have ordered me to that station [Rhode Island], I should have thought myself very happy to have served a campaign with that worthy officer; and would still be happy to join him, if it could be for the public good."[40]

He then expressed his unhappiness with his job at Albany, "with nothing to do but guard the frontier; with no troops but militia. … I can not obtain any great advantage to the public, nor honor to myself." Nevertheless, Washington's order was inconsistent with the order from Congress, and Stark knew that the will of Congress was supreme. He wrote, "But I shall cheerfully obey any orders that are entrusted to me, and proceed wherever Congress shall think I may be of most service."[41] It must have been a painful letter to write—to decline a posting he preferred, and to remind the commander in chief that Congress outranked him.

Stark's letter crossed with a brief message from Washington that indicated he had not been aware of Stark's prior order from Congress and that he now understood that Stark must remain at Albany.[42] This brief correspondence between the two generals betrayed no ill feeling between them. It should have demonstrated Stark's willingness, even eagerness, to serve under General Sullivan, a man with less military experience and ability.

Duty at Albany presented a host of petty problems the general had not met in his previous service. He had to deal with politicians regularly. The Committee of Safety of Tryon County, west of Albany, complained that they had insufficient manpower to defend their territory because they had failed to enlist the number of troops ordered by the governor. They asked Stark to make up the deficiency. He declined. "[Y]ou may blame yourselves for it in large measure," he wrote them.[43]

The mayor and aldermen of Albany pressed him to withhold Continental troops Gates had ordered him to send to Fishkill, New York, and he felt compelled to keep a regiment at Albany.[44] He explained matters to Gates: "Murders and robberies are daily committed in the adjacent counties by our internal enemies [Tories]. … By letting these infamous villains [remain] at large, we should greatly endanger our most valuable friends."[45]

Stark's letters to Gates revealed the depth of his animosity toward Loyalists. He told Gates, "I should be glad to have Colonel Ethan Allen command in the Grants [Vermont], as he is a very suitable man to deal with tories and such like villains."[46]

Ethan Allen approved of Stark's harsh rhetoric. "I hear you are doing very well with some of them," he wrote. Grandson Caleb Stark explained that "doing very well" meant that Allen thought Stark was hanging Loyalists.[47] The general let the Vermonter believe the rumors. He replied that he would cooperate with Allen "in purging the land of freedom from such most infamous and diabolical villains."[48]

Stark could not have ordered the execution of Tories without the order of a military tribunal, however, and no such proceeding occurred during his tour of duty. In a letter to the president of the New Hampshire Congress, Stark implied that civilian authorities, perhaps a committee of safety, ordered such hangings. His letter revealed how many men died by the noose. "They (the people) do very well in the hanging way. They hanged nine on the 16ᵗʰ of May; and on the 5ᵗʰ of June, nine; and have one hundred twenty in jail, of which, I believe, more than half will go the same way." He did not clarify what crimes beyond being Loyalists justified such a purge, but he seems to have approved of the measure. A vicious kind of civil war raged across the entire northern region, from Vermont across the Iroquois lands in New York. Stark finished his letter to New Hampshire on a plaintive note: "So you may judge of my situation, with the enemy in my front and the devil in my rear."[49]

John Stark wrote one letter that implied that summary execution, without any tribunal, would be a proper end for a certain kind of Loyalist—those who masqueraded as Indians when they attacked white settlers. He concluded a letter to Colonel Ichabod Alden on August 15: "Should your scouts be fortunate enough with any more of these painted scoundrels, I think it not worth while to trouble themselves to send them to me. Your wisdom and your scouts may direct you in that matter." Caleb Stark later wrote an annotation to the letter in which he explained that "painted scoundrels" were Loyalists dressed as Indians, and that Colonel Alden's men should "knock them in the head."[50] By implication, then, a Tory fighter dressed like an American might be entitled to a notch higher standard of justice than one dressed like an Indian; the norms of warfare might vary with the enemy.

Stark pursued Tories with zeal, but he remained rational about them. It was difficult to distinguish Loyalists from Whigs absent some overt action or speech to confirm their allegiance. Local committees of safety pressed for loyalty oaths. Sometimes the authorities rounded up people they assumed were "disaffected" based on flimsy evidence. Stark tried to convince the committees to be more judicious. When Vermont officers presented him with several citizens slated for banishment, the general interrogated one man and found "no crime against him worthy of banishment." He wrote the accusers, "I hope your Committee do not banish every body on so slight an accusation, for if every one should be banished for such slight crimes, I am afraid there would be but few left."[51]

The Committee of Safety at Bennington captured eight New York Loyalists and sent them to General Stark, who accepted responsibility for them. The Albany committee asserted jurisdiction over the men, but Stark, assuming that his authority reached into Vermont, refused to release the prisoners to the Albany delegation. He shipped them down the river to General Gates accompanied by a letter: "I send you by the bearer eight of those people called tories, who have been so inimical to their country that the council of our good friends at Bennington have thought proper to send them as a present to their friends, to obey their laws and worship their gods in future."[52]

Stark's independent action infuriated Governor George Clinton of New York, who posted angry letters to Washington and to Congress. "I flatter myself," he wrote, "that your Excellency will not fail calling Gen. Stark to account for his unwarrantable conduct in this instance."[53] Clinton also complained to John Jay of "this atrocious insult on the civil authority of this state."[54] Washington referred the whole matter to Congress, where it was tabled for further consideration. This ended the affair, but Washington remembered Clinton's anger at Stark.

Tory and Indian raids continued on the frontier, and Stark could do little to protect the settlers with the manpower allotted him. The raiders could strike anywhere. Early in July, Butler led an attack on the Wyoming Valley of Pennsylvania, where they overwhelmed the militia and killed many people. Then they torched the homes and barns. Shocked Americans called it the "Wyoming Massacre."[55]

On July 14, Stark wrote to Washington to request Continental troops as reinforcements. Washington sent Lieutenant Colonel William Butler (no relation to the Loyalist Butlers) with Pennsylvania soldiers along with a cadre of Morgan's riflemen.[56] Stark thanked his commander and suggested a strategy for the border war: "I think that the western frontiers will never be at peace until we drive an army into the Indian country, and drive the nefarious wretches from their habitations, burn their towns, destroy their crops, and make proclamation that if they ever return they shall be served in the same manner."[57] In 1779, Stark's plan would be exactly what Washington ordered.

Several commanders recognized the importance and vulnerability of Cherry Valley. Colonel Peter Gansevoort had successfully defended Fort Stanwix against invaders in 1777; in 1778 he sought to command at another post, perhaps the fort at Cherry Valley.[58] But Gansevoort was an Albany Dutchman who spoke English with an accent.

Instead, Colonel Ichabod Alden and his Seventh Massachusetts Regiment were chosen to defend Cherry Valley. It is unclear who selected Alden for the post; it may have been Lafayette, Gates or Stark. Stark was aware of the significance of Cherry Valley, writing that it was a post that "covers all the Mohawk River and stops all passage from Unadilla (the Indians' strongpoint) to that place."[59] Colonel Alden, a descendant of the pilgrim who wouldn't speak for himself, proved to be thoroughly incompetent.

By midsummer, Horatio Gates was writing to Stark about Alden's shortcomings: "Colonel Alden's behavior is exactly what it was last year. Be assured he shall be made to answer for his conduct."[60] Gates didn't specify what that conduct was. The Massachusetts colonel had established a peculiar defensive strategy at Cherry Valley. He named the new stockade Fort Alden, after himself, and then proceeded to insure that the enclosure protected no one. There were no living quarters within the stockade; soldiers were quartered in private homes around the neighborhood. Alden's plan assumed that the troops would have plenty of time to repair to the stockade if Cherry Valley were attacked. Once safely within the walls, however, the defenders had no fire steps from which to shoot either muskets or cannon at attackers. Alden himself resided in comfort with the Wells family, outside the walls.[61]

Washington was familiar enough with Alden that he expressed his preference for Lieutenant Colonel William Butler over the Massachusetts colonel, but he knew that the prerogatives of rank protected Alden from summary removal. On August 5, Washington wrote to Stark: "If Colo. Alden is with his Regiment, and forms a junction with Lt. Colonel Butler, he must command of course, except Colo. Alden could by any means be put upon some other service. If the thing could be managed it would be very agreeable to me, as I place great dependence upon Colo. Butler's Abilities as a Woodsman."[62] By "Woodsman," Washington meant "Indian fighter."

Stark's answer suggested that he knew of Alden's poor performance and that he planned to remove the patrician officer when he could. However, some impediment seemed to restrain Stark from taking the final step. On August 10 he replied to Washington: "I shall find some method to remove Colonel Alden so that Butler may have the command, and Alden be satisfied."[63] It remains unclear why anyone would care if an incompetent officer would need to be satisfied, but no American officer took the initiative to remove Alden from the Cherry Valley command.

⁂

Lieutenant Colonel William Butler's early success with his Continental troops against the Indians promoted a false sense of security. He led a raid on the Indian town of Onoquaga along the Susquehanna River in October. His troops waded waist-deep across the river to burn the dwellings and destroy the corn crop.[64] Their feat prompted Stark to gloat a bit in a letter to Washington written on October 28. He predicted, "They [the Continentals] have put it entirely out of the power of the enemy to do our frontier any serious injury for the remainder of the campaign."[65]

Barely a week later, on November 6, the commander at Fort Stanwix learned that "Young Butler" (Loyalist Walter Butler) planned to lead an attack against "Charevalley." It was accurate intelligence gleaned by an Indian in a council at Tioga. Within two days Colonel Alden heard the warning, but he took no action to prepare for an attack, assuring the people of Cherry Valley that his scouts would give them adequate warning of a raid.[66]

Butler and Brant learned that Alden and his soldiers remained scattered around the community, so the attackers split their forces to strike the various targets. The American scouts failed to warn the settlers. The raid came as a complete surprise. People fled, some into the woods, others to the stockade. A warrior brained Alden with a hatchet as he tried to escape from the Wells house. Joseph Brant tried to restrain the Senecas, but they murdered women and children freely, ranging through Cherry Valley burning and looting. It took two days for them to finish their work, and their cruelty shocked even the British.[67]

When the raiders had left and help arrived, word of the atrocities spread. The *New-Jersey Gazette* printed an account of the attack: "The enemy killed, scalped, and most barbarously murdered, thirty-two inhabitants, chiefly women and children." The newspaper went on to name the dead soldiers and to count the dwellings burned. Then it gave the details:

> They committed the most inhuman barbarities on most of the dead. Robert Henderson's head was cut off, his skull bone was cut out with the scalp. Mr. Willis' sister was ripped up, a child of Mr. Willis', two months old, scalped and arm cut off, and many others as cruelly treated.[68]

Whether all the gruesome facts were exactly as the paper printed them is unclear, but the massacre had indeed been barbarous and the newspaper coverage insured that all America would know of it. The ripples from the story spread in both space and time and darkened the reputations of Joseph Brant and Walter Butler.

John Stark's judgment that the frontier would be safe from "serious injury" for the rest of the year proved tragically wrong, but the most serious error in judgment had been leaving Colonel Ichabod Alden in command at Cherry Valley. That Gates and Washington both knew Alden should be replaced suggests that they shared some of the responsibility for the consequences, and General Edward Hand had already replaced Stark in Albany when the attack took place. But, blame flows downhill, and John Stark's esteem in Washington's eyes suffered.

George Washington seems to have formed a negative opinion of John Stark even before Cherry Valley. As with many judgments the commander in chief had to make, it was formed at long distance, with the prompting of parties like Governor Clinton, who had their own motives. In Stark's case, the commander in chief used inaccurate information. Washington never communicated this opinion to officers beyond his own headquarters. The only surviving evidence of his disfavor exists in a few lines crossed out of a draft of a letter to Governor George Clinton of New York on September 25, 1778. Clinton had asked for more troops, and Washington wrote that he would try to send some soldiers. Then he added these lines, which were crossed out of the draft:

> I am far from being satisfied myself with the present command to the Northward [Stark], but some peculiar circumstances render it very difficult to effect a change without introducing a good deal of uneasiness and confusion in the Army should Genl. Stark be called down to it. You are, I dare say, acquainted with his Resolution to obey no Officer, now a Brigadier, who was a junior Colonel, and from his promotion, not taking place in course, there are several in that situation. He has for that reason been generally employed in some separate command.[69]

This letter was in the handwriting of Tench Tilghman, Washington's aide, but the sentiments expressed, even if redacted, must be assumed to be those of his commander. Stark's "Resolution," as the letter worded it, amounted to a restatement of General Lincoln's report of what he claimed passed between Stark and himself in Manchester, Vermont, in 1777—that Stark told him he refused to take orders from "any officer … commanded by him last year or [who] joined the army after him."[70]

By the autumn of 1778, John Stark had several times given Washington reason to know that Lincoln's accusation was either false or no longer true. Stark had returned to Saratoga to help bag Burgoyne. He had expressed eagerness to serve under Sullivan, who had limited military experience, and under Lafayette, who was little more than a boy. It may be that Washington read those lines in his letter, realized their unfairness and, despite his desire to placate Clinton, crossed them out.

The commander in chief's subsequent decisions proved that he was not overly concerned about calling Stark to join the main army. On October 19, 1778, Washington ordered him to join General Sullivan at Rhode Island, adding, "your influence near the seat of war will enable you to render more essential service there, than where you are now."[71]

25

THE LAST SIGNIFICANT BATTLE IN THE NORTH

Give 'em Watts Boys

While Stark struggled with the many problems of the northern department in Albany, American fortunes elsewhere improved during the summer of 1778. Patriots could celebrate the second anniversary of independence that July in the knowledge that General Washington had commanded a successful encounter against the British army at Monmouth Courthouse in New Jersey. A few days later the French fleet arrived off the coast to challenge the British Navy. Americans could now play the chess game at sea as well as the British. Hard challenges remained ahead, but the United States still survived.

In consultation with the French, Washington decided to mount a joint attack on the British base at Newport, Rhode Island, on Aquidneck Island in Narragansett Bay. General John Sullivan commanded a force on the mainland opposite the island. Generals Greene and Lafayette commanded the two wings of the army under Sullivan. An infusion of militia from New England would give them adequate manpower for the mission. Stark's popularity with the New Englanders and his proven ability to attract recruits convinced Washington to send him to Sullivan.[1] General Edward Hand relieved Stark at Albany in October.

A combined land and sea attack, mounted by forces of two different countries with different languages, required skill, diplomacy and luck; Sullivan possessed none of these. He quarreled with the French; the British fleet arrived unexpectedly; and, on August 12, a powerful storm damaged the ships of both navies. Admiral Jean Baptiste Charles Henri, Hector, Comte d'Estaing, following orders from Paris, sailed to the West Indies. He left Sullivan barely able to withdraw his troops to safety. Colonel Israel Angell, a Rhode Islander commanding a regiment in Greene's corps, noted in his diary, "the french fleet Left us to day bound to Boston and I think left us in a most Rascally manner."[2]

Stark arrived to find disgruntled Americans, both officers and enlisted men, encamped at various points around Narragansett Bay. They chafed under Sullivan's temper and arrogance. On December 22, for example, he ordered all military musicians to march to Providence through a snowstorm for a gala. The order infuriated some of his subordinates. Angell reported: "Major Huntington put himself in a most violent passion on the matter Swore the order was a dam'd rascally one if the Genl. did give it."[3]

Stark travelled back to New Hampshire to recruit volunteers. He avoided a terrible winter on the coast. A blizzard known as the "Hessian storm" struck after Christmas; soldiers on both sides died of exposure. Two American privateers, the *General Stark* and the *General Arnold,* wrecked on the shore, and their sailors froze to death.[4]

The storm must have been a coastal nor'easter, for Matthew Patten recorded no bad weather for that period in interior New Hampshire. On January 15, 1779, he wrote, "General Stark and his Wife and son Archibald came to see us."[5]

When Stark returned to Rhode Island in the spring of 1779, he found Horatio Gates in command. Washington had ordered an expedition to punish the Iroquois, and he had offered Gates the opportunity to lead it. Gates declined, however, so he and Sullivan traded places.

Stark served as second-in-command to Gates; he was the only brigadier present. For a few days Caleb was not available to handle his father's correspondence, leaving the general to write his own message to Gates: "The enemy laned [landed] this morning and Sirprayesed [surprised] a gard. …The enemy moved off with all the Speed they coud in the great Persipation [precipitation] and ar gone I shall be up in the evening and give you an account of the hole."[6]

The warm season in Rhode Island, from April to October, passed with little fighting. The British kept to the island town of Newport, and the Americans manned outposts on the shore of the bay within sight of the enemy. Stark and Colonel Israel Angell became friends and often took their meals together. On one occasion they rode to Providence to serve on a court-martial. Angell would prove to be an aggressive combat commander in Stark's mold.[7]

Out at sea the two navies jockeyed for position. The British feared they might become trapped at Newport and prepared to evacuate their army. As usual the Americans quickly learned of their enemy's plans; in late October, soldiers and civilians watched from the shores of the bay for the happy event to take place. Angell wrote: "there was Some hundreds of people out of the Country, on the hill looking out to See the fleet go off." Before leaving, British soldiers torched their barracks, their fortifications, even the lighthouse.[8]

Across the water, Angell reported, Americans burned an effigy of Count Donop, the former commander at Newport, even though he was already dead. They raised a liberty pole in celebration, "near fore score feet high." Just after sunset on October 26, they watched the white sails of the British ships leaving Newport harbor.[9]

Soldiers rowed General Stark and his aide, Major Caleb Stark, across to Newport. Caleb's own son, Caleb, wrote that "General Stark took possession of Newport and placed guards in the street to prevent plunder and preserve order."[10] The next day Israel Angell arrived and wrote, "I road with the General Round all the Enemy Lines where I Saw Some of the Beautifullest works that I Ever Saw in my life."[11] Newport harbor provided an anchorage for the French fleet for the remainder of the war.

⚜   ⚜

During the spring of 1779, while John Stark waited out the British at Rhode Island, General John Sullivan prepared his expedition against the Iroquois. It was intended to be an attack in three parts: General James Clinton would push west along the Mohawk River, while Colonel Daniel Brodhead would move up the Alleghany River from the west. Sullivan planned to march his main force north from the Wyoming Valley in Pennsylvania. They hoped to converge in the heart of Iroquois country.[12]

Among Sullivan's officers were veteran New Hampshire soldiers like Joseph Cilley and Henry Dearborn, along with one young man from Derryfield—

Lieutenant Archibald Stark, age eighteen, who served as Dearborn's aide. The force assembled at Easton, Pennsylvania, in June. It was a large corps for a protracted wilderness mission, about 4,000 men, and it moved slowly.[13]

New York Colonel Goose Van Schaik set the stage for Sullivan in April by destroying an Onondaga village near Fort Stanwix. His men killed twelve warriors and captured several women who were planting corn. The Indians accused Van Schaik's soldiers of raping the women. General Clinton, brother of New York Governor George Clinton, had specifically warned Van Schaik against such behavior: "Bad as the savages are, they never violate the chastity of any women, their prisoners. … It will be well to take measures to prevent such a stain upon our army." In the minds of the Iroquois, the stain had already spread.[14]

On June 23, Sullivan's army reached the Wyoming Valley, the desolate scene of the 1778 Tory and Indian attack. The Americans made camp and awaited the arrival of supply wagons. Henry Dearborn led a group of officers on an inspection of the scene of what became known as the Wyoming Massacre of the year before. They found bodies with skulls crushed by tomahawks. Dearborn observed "some skettling Indians skulking about us."[15]

Sullivan postponed a celebration of the Fourth of July to the next day, a Monday. Dearborn noted that thirteen "Patriotick Toasts were Drunk," twelve of them celebrating the new country, its leaders and its high ideals. Then they all raised their glasses to one more, very different toast: "Civilization or Death to all American Savages." With lurid images of the Wyoming attack fresh in their minds, and remembering Washington's orders, Sullivan's soldiers prepared themselves for their mission.[16]

The army marched north along the Susquehanna River, moving slowly with flanking parties on either side. They expected attacks, but none came; the Indians retreated before them, leaving deserted villages and acres of standing corn. The Americans destroyed both homes and corn. Finally, on August 29, the expedition encountered a combined force of Loyalists and Iroquois, about 1,000 men, near Newtown. Sullivan routed them, but the survivors disappeared, taking their dead and wounded with them. The Americans lost three dead and thirty wounded. For the next month Sullivan found little opposition; the Indians had retreated to Fort Niagara.[17]

Several American soldiers on the expedition kept journals. They reported, week after week, as they made war on corn and vegetables, burned fields and stacks of fodder, and destroyed houses. Lieutenant William Barton noted that, on September 13, Lieutenant Boyd led a scout away from the main force. They killed two Indians and were in the act of scalping them when a large body of Iroquois surprised them. The next day, Barton's unit found Boyd's body, beheaded and mutilated, with "A great part of his body … skinned, leaving the ribs bare."[18] Henry Dearborn described the same scene, closing with, "… from which we are taught the necessaty of fighting these more than divils to the last moment rather than fall into their hands alive."[19]

Two weeks later, Colonel Durbin's men came across two Indians, an old woman and a young crippled man. Durbin ordered that they be spared and that a house be left standing to shelter them. Lieutenant Barton told what happened: "… some of the soldiers taking an opportunity when not observed set the house on fire, after securing and making the door fast. The troops having got in motion and marched some distance, the house was consumed together with the savages, in spite of all exertions."[20]

The mission was complete by September 30, when Sullivan's army reached Tioga. "We now have finished our campaign," Dearborn wrote, "and gloriously too."[21] They had lost no more than 60 men out of 4,000, and their accomplishments merited a celebration. Lieutenant Archibald Stark attended the party and logged minutes of the occasion: "Dance at head quarters; the Oneida sachem was master of ceremonies."[22]

Sullivan's officers and soldiers carried a high charge of emotion on their mission against the Iroquois, and the feeling lasted from beginning to end. Still, the mission failed of its purpose; Butler and Brant returned the next year to scourge the Mohawk Valley and central New York.

⁂

The Americans did not know the destination of the British fleet that left Newport. Rebel forces remained beside Narragansett Bay until Washington decided where they should go. Stark and Angell enjoyed a few days of leisure while they waited for orders. By the second week in November, both officers led columns of ill-clad soldiers westward. General Heath watched these soldiers pass, "… barefooted over the hard frozen ground, and with an astonishing patience. Remember these things, ye Americans, in future times."[23]

Stark halted his troops at Danbury and housed them in whatever private dwellings remained after the British raid of 1777. Dr. James Thacher accompanied Stark's soldiers and noted, "Danbury was once a flourishing town, but the principal part of it has been destroyed by the enemy."[24] Private Joseph Plumb Martin had seen Danbury shortly after the raid. "The town had been laid in ashes," he wrote, "a number of the inhabitants murdered and cast into the burning houses, because they presumed to defend their persons and property. … I saw the inhabitants, after the fire was out, endeavouring to find the burnt bones of their relatives amongst the rubbish of their demolished houses."[25]

Colonel Angell continued his march until he reached the Hudson River across from West Point. The American forts on the heights impressed the Rhode Island soldier; it was an "American Gibralter," he thought.[26] Stark was equally impressed by West Point the first time he saw it. He worried that "The enemy, possessing it, would infallibly cut off all communications between the northern and southern states."[27] Controlling West Point might not win the war for America, but failing to control it could lose the war.

Stark and his men arrived at Pompton, New Jersey, on December 9 on their way to join Washington at Morristown. Two days of slogging through snow, then mud, then knee-deep water brought them to the heights outside Morristown. Here, the army would weather a harder winter than at Valley Forge. For a few bitterly cold weeks, officers who had fought together, but before now had little leisure to know one another, met and talked. The December chill aggravated Stark's rheumatism, so he found a billet at a nearby tavern, "The Half Moon."[28]

Regimental Surgeon, Doctor James Thacher met Stark at the Half Moon and wrote a portrait of him. "His manners were frank and unassuming," Thacher wrote, "but he manifested a peculiar sort of eccentricity and negligence which precluded all display of personal dignity and seemed to place him among those of ordinary rank in life."[29] Thacher admired genteel manners and proper address, the qualities exemplified by British officers. Stark, he concluded, did not measure up.

Patriot soldiers at Morristown set to work building their winter quarters, log huts "generally about twelve by fifteen or sixteen feet square," according to Private Martin. He described his new home as "fitted for the reception of gentlemen soldiers, with all their rich and gay furniture."[30]

The army suffered in deep snow and bitterly cold weather. A storm on January 2 and 3 piled up drifts four to six feet deep. Teamsters hauling provisions for the men could not reach the encampment. Of all his years soldiering, this was the time that Joseph Martin called "the hard winter." He wrote, "We were absolutely, literally starved;—I do solemnly declare that I did not put a single morsel of victuals into my mouth for four days and as many nights, except a little black birch bark which I gnawed off a stick of wood."[31]

General Stark had applied for leave to go home; his rheumatism pained him, and no campaigns were contemplated until spring. Before Stark left, Washington included in his general orders a short paragraph addressed to Stark's brigade: "It gives me pleasure to observe that your Brigade has fewer men improperly absent than any other. This circumstance does it great honor and the particular reports of the regiments exhibit fewer defects than most others."[32] With his commander's blessing, John Stark again rode home across snowy New England.

Washington passed a winter of constant distress over the pitiful condition of his soldiers. In December he had written to several governors that there was "every appearance that the army will infallibly disband in a fortnight."[33] Four months later the misery had still not abated: "The army is now on a most scanty allowance, and is seldom at the expiration of one day certain of a morsel of bread for the next."[34] Officers and enlisted men suffered alike; the Continental dollar was as useless to one as to the other. Resignations and threats of resignation came to the general.

The soldiers' bitterness at what they saw as their country's neglect seemed as galling to them as the cold and hunger. Private Martin expressed their despair: "The men were now exasperated beyond endurance; they could not stand it any longer; they saw no other alternative but to starve to death or break up the army, give all up and go home. … Here was the army starved and naked, and there their country sitting still and expecting the army to do notable things while fainting from sheer starvation."[35]

In May, Private Martin joined a mutiny at Morristown. Two regiments of the Connecticut line refused to leave an evening roll call. One man called out, "Who will parade with me?"[36] In a matter of moments, both regiments fell in with the angry soldier. Martin wrote, "We now concluded to go in a body to the other two regiments that belonged to our brigade and induce them to join us." Officers called upon two Pennsylvania regiments to surround the mutineers but, instead, the Pennsylvanians joined the revolt.[37]

Cool leadership by popular officers calmed the mutineers. Martin singled out Colonel Meigs of Connecticut ("an excellent man and brave officer") and Colonel Stewart of Pennsylvania ("much loved and respected by the troops") for their leadership. The enlisted men had vented their spleen, and that seemed to satisfy them.[38]

The mutiny brought no consequences except a temporary improvement in rations. The following year a full-blown mutiny of Pennsylvania soldiers would lead to summary executions of the ringleaders by firing squads.

Washington could be a rigid disciplinarian. Doctor Thacher wrote that he "possesses an inflexible firmness of purpose." One hundred lashes or more were laid on for relatively minor offenses. A deserter or a hardened criminal faced the hangman. The winter before the mutiny, seven men were condemned to hang at one public execution. They marched out in front of the assembled army. The chaplain spoke as they looked down at their coffins. Nooses were placed around their necks and blindfolds over their eyes; then an officer rode his horse to the scaffold and read a reprieve for six of the men. The seventh man was hanged.[39]

Some men accepted such arbitrary cruelty as an object lesson and thought their commander was magnanimous for pardoning the few. Others, like Private Martin, seethed inwardly. He once witnessed the execution of a deserter. The hangman, as usual, was a "ragamuffin fellow" who agreed to kill his fellow soldier for the dead man's clothing and boots. When the job was done, the hangman struggled to remove the boots from the swinging corpse. The soldiers watched for a while, and they grew disgusted. They began to stone the executioner and the officers in charge of the affair until these men retreated from the scene. Martin reported, "They were obliged to keep at a proper distance until the soldiers took their own time to disperse, when they returned and completed their honourable business."[40]

John Stark returned to the army in May, after the revolt of the Connecticut regiments but in time for the first battle of the year.[41] Early in June, disgruntled soldiers who only days before had defied their superiors again risked their lives for their ungrateful country.

All winter, Washington worried that an attack might come from the east, by way of Staten Island into New Jersey at Connecticut Farms and Springfield. A small detachment, including Private Joseph Plumb Martin, kept an uneasy watch on Newark Bay, across from Staten Island. It proved to be dangerous duty. Bands of Tories roamed the neighborhood. Patriot soldiers moved from house to house, trying to avoid raids. Martin's best friend in the army, a soldier named Twist, was caught by Loyalists and bayoneted to death—"massacred by his own countrymen," Martin wrote.[42]

The British failed to take advantage of the weakly guarded highway until June 7, when Hessian General Von Knyphausen led 5,000 soldiers across the water. They marched quickly toward Springfield, aiming to attack Morristown. British intelligence reported a mutinous, ill-prepared American army there, ripe for a surprise attack.[43]

"Old Knyp," as some soldiers called him, paused at the little village of Connecticut Farms long enough to set thirty homes afire together with the meetinghouse. Some of his men fired their muskets through a house window, killing young Hannah Caldwell, the wife of the minister, Reverend James Caldwell.[44]

The attackers moved west to a crossing of the Rahway River. There they met a stout unit of New Jersey militia under Colonel Sylvanus Seeley, who stopped them cold. The time the Hessians had spent burning the village of Connecticut Farms allowed the Americans to reinforce Seeley with a unit of

Lord Stirling's Continentals. Old Knyp wheeled his soldiers around and withdrew back to Newark Bay.[45]

On June 23 the British and Hessians returned to move against Morristown. Washington had briefly split his forces to defend against a feared attack at West Point, but he hurried his troops back toward northern New Jersey. The invaders attacked "Scotch Willie" Maxwell's regiment near Springfield and drove the Americans back. Stark and Angell arrived with their regiments and stiffened the defenses.[46]

Von Knyphausen's force now numbered more than 6,000, while Nathanael Greene commanded less than half that many. The Hessian commander hoped to encircle the rebels in a pincer attack and destroy them.[47]

Israel Angell stationed his men at a bridge over the Rahway River east of Springfield. His soldiers put up a fierce resistance for almost an hour until a flanking detachment of Jagers forced them to fall back. But, they had delayed attackers who outnumbered them five to one.[48]

Angell's troops ran out of paper wadding for their muskets. James Caldwell, the pastor whose young wife had just been murdered, learned of the need for paper. He rode to his parsonage and collected a stack of hymnals with pages filled with the songs of Isaac Watts. He distributed the volumes to the soldiers, yelling to them above the gunfire, "Give 'em Watts boys." Then he rode away.[49]

The northern arm of the British-Hessian attack came to a halt when General Stark's troops appeared on the heights above them. The British watched Stark's artillerists unlimber a cannon and swing it in their direction.

Despite a strong American defense of the town, von Knyphausen's soldiers occupied most of Springfield. Rebel soldiers on the hills watched while, one by one, houses caught fire. Tories torched a makeshift hospital in the Presbyterian Meetinghouse, roasting alive the American wounded. A German soldier remembered, "Their pleas for life were moving, but it did not help them." After the arson at Springfield, the German wrote, "not even a pig-sty was left standing."[50]

It took a while for the angry Americans to realize that their enemies were retreating. The British and Germans marched east, masked by the smoke and flames. General Greene ordered Stark to pursue them with two regiments, but the enemy had a head start and got away. Caleb Stark wrote that his grandfather "harassed" the enemy and "brought back several prisoners, and a quantity of baggage."[51]

Private Martin made a brief note of the battle of Springfield in his memoirs. He had just survived a winter and spring that tried his faith in Americans and in the army, but he kept his fighting spirit. "The enemy," he wrote, "soon recoiled into their shell again."[52] Martin and his comrades would still fight.

None of the combatants at Springfield could anticipate that the clash would be the last significant battle fought in the north during the Revolution. Most of them believed there would be future struggles for New York City and for West Point.

⊰❈⊱ ⊰❈⊱

The British failure to reach Morristown did nothing to ease Washington's burden. His army still lacked manpower, food, clothing, shoes and nearly everything else it needed to wage a military campaign.[53]

Bad news arrived from the south. General Benjamin Lincoln surrendered the garrison at Charleston, South Carolina, on May 12. The British imprisoned the entire force, including Lincoln himself.[54]

Then, on August 16, British General Cornwallis defeated a combined force of militia and Continentals commanded by Lincoln's replacement, Horatio Gates, near Camden, South Carolina. Gates had placed the militia at a critical place. The enemy charged, scattering the militia troops, leaving the Continentals to fight alone.[55] Gates himself "withdrew" alongside the retreating soldiers; he continued to withdraw until he had ridden 180 miles over a three-day period. Alexander Hamilton commented: "… was there ever an instance of a general running away, as Gates has done, from his whole army? … it disgraces the general and the soldier."[56]

⊰❈⊱ ⊰❈⊱

The week after Springfield, Washington again ordered Stark to return to New Hampshire to recruit "sound and healthy" Continental soldiers and a large force of militia. He instructed Stark to march them all to Claverack,

New York, by July 25. From Claverack they could travel south on the Hudson River.[57]

Stark had signed up his allotment by July 13. He wrote his commander, "The 500 men required are for the most part on their march; the 900 I hope will be able to march by the middle of next week."[58] Stark and his recruits joined Washington at Peekskill by August 1.[59]

Stark's brigade marched south toward Tappan on the Jersey border. His general orders of August 19 noted the poor appearance of his men: "All such men as have shoes must put them on for the time allotted for Exercise and Maneuvrings. It's notorious that many have come to the parade [without them] altho' possessed of them."[60]

Washington and his senior officers pondered their next moves. They knew that ships of the British and French fleets were at sea off the American coast, but they did not know the destinations or the schedules of the two navies.[61] Washington worried that a maritime attack might be made at West Point. On September 6 he called a council of war at Tappan. Six major generals and nine brigadiers attended the meeting, including John Stark.[62] Their commander asked them two questions: what should be their strategy; and should they send reinforcements south.[63]

General Stark answered, "… in the case the second [French Navy] should arrive, to push with all our force against New York." He did not think it advisable to split the army by sending a detachment south. The other general officers agreed—make no move until French ships arrived to challenge the British.[64]

The Americans took a brief rest. A group of Oneida Indians arrived to parley. They had been dependable allies, and Washington wanted to keep their loyalty. He ordered a grand review for them on September 13. Colonel Israel Angell wrote that the army was to "make as Great a Show as possible. … the Brigade of Genl. Starks was Reviewed about 9 in the Morning with Retinue of all the Genl. Officers of the Army and a Great part of the field Officers and all the savages of note, after which we attended at the Court."[65]

If being the centerpiece in the great show inflated General Stark's ego, an event the following week probably deflated it. Angell reported that the general and his aide, Major Caleb Stark, stopped to water their horses at a place called "the Stole." Their mounts became mired in mud. Caleb was able to spur his horse to dry land, but the general's horse, with the general in the saddle, remained stuck. "Genl. Stark was drawd out by the Soldiers," Angell wrote. He suffered no damage, "Except bedaubing himself with mud."[66]

Meanwhile, Washington rode to Hartford to meet with Rochambeau and other French officers. They agreed that, if the French fleet arrived, they would try to take New York. Otherwise a strong force would be sent south. Without the navy, they needed to make West Point impregnable; its loss would be a catastrophe. Washington left Hartford on September 23, intending to go directly to the fortress on the Hudson to examine it with its commander, Benedict Arnold.[67]

26

Arnold and André
Treason of the Blackest Dye

In 1779, Benedict Arnold was recovering from his leg wound in Philadelphia, where he wooed and won a vivacious young woman, Peggy Shippen. Peggy had declared no particular allegiance in the war, but she socialized with Loyalists and British officers like Major John André. The major took an interest in her new husband.[1]

André was handsome, cultivated and something of a dandy. In his spare time he produced amateur theatricals for Philadelphia society, including a magnificent pageant in honor of General Howe's retirement. André described his own costume for the gala, set off by, "A large pink scarf fastened on the right shoulder with a white bow crossed the breast and back, and hung in an ample loose knot with silver fringes, very low upon the left hip."[2]

His military service had not been all parties and pageants. Captured by Americans in Canada in 1775, he spent time as a prisoner in Pennsylvania until he was released on parole. Rather than return to England, André elected to remain in America and serve as a staff officer with Major General Charles Grey. Their regiment attacked a rebel force commanded by Anthony Wayne at Paoli and refused quarter to the Americans who surrendered.[3] Major André published an account of the butchery in a New York newspaper; his men, he wrote, put "to the bayonet all they came up with, and, overtaking the main herd of fugitives, stabbed great numbers."[4]

General Grey and Major André occupied the home of Benjamin Franklin in Philadelphia. Before he left, André looted the house, stealing a copy of Diderot's *Encyclopedie,* musical instruments and a portrait of Franklin himself painted by Benjamin Wilson, among other plunder. When Grey transferred to New York, he took his aide with him. Grey led a raid against Baylor's Virginia troops stationed in New Jersey near Tappan, New York. A Loyalist justice of the supreme court, Thomas Jones, in a manuscript published a century later, described Grey's methods:

> He surrounded the town, seized the sentinels, and with fixed bayonets entered the homes and barns where the rebels were sleeping, unsuspicious of danger, and before they could have recourse to their arms, the whole corps (a few who had concealed themselves excepted) were massacred in cold blood, and to the disgrace of Britons many of them were stabbed while upon their knees, humbly imploring and submissively begging for mercy.[5]

André noted the killings in his journal.

When General Grey went home to England, John André became aide to General Sir Henry Clinton, the new commander in chief of British forces in America. André later became adjutant general. By the spring of 1780, André was conducting a secret correspondence with a senior American general, Benedict Arnold.[6]

On May 23, Arnold wrote to André to tell him plainly what he expected: "… my property here secure and a revenue equivalent to the risk and service done." Then he acknowledged the warm feelings his wife harbored for the handsome major: "Madam Ar[nold] presents you her particular compliments."[7]

Washington had asked Arnold to command a wing of the army in 1779, but Arnold declined, citing his wound. He continued to complain of his disability in 1780, and he suggested that the command at West Point might be suitable for his condition. Washington reluctantly agreed and, by August 3, General Arnold commanded the American Gibraltar.[8] The month before, Arnold had advised André (now addressed by his code name, John Anderson) of his new post; he assured him, "The mass of the people are heartily tired of this war, and wish to be on their former footing." In the same letter Arnold revealed that the Americans planned to attack New York City once the French fleet arrived.[9]

Even before he took command at West Point, Arnold schemed to turn the fortress over to the British. On July 15 he wrote André to name the price for the deed: "twenty thousand pounds sterling I think will be a cheap purchase for an object of such importance."[10]

The deal was not yet done. The British hesitated to agree to the terms, though Arnold demanded "a full and explicit answer." He insisted on a face-to-face meeting with an officer who had Sir Henry Clinton's full confidence—a "man of his own mensuration"—John André.[11]

Clinton recognized the value of West Point. In addition to the multiple forts and batteries on the heights overlooking the river, a massive chain was stretched across the Hudson with artillery trained on it from both sides of the river. The east end of the chain was anchored at Constitution Island, where stone redoubts protected it. The links of the chain were a foot wide by eighteen inches long, forged of iron two inches thick, all kept afloat by a series of massive logs. So long as the chain barrier remained in place, no ships could pass.[12]

Sir Henry believed that Arnold commanded as many as 4,000 troops, and he knew the fortress bristled with cannon. The gunboats tied at the docks would be welcome additions to the British fleet. All this, Clinton thought, might be taken without hazard with the cooperation of the post commander. He considered Arnold's price a bargain. West Point, he wrote, "was to be pursued at every risk and at every expense."[13]

John André bore all the risk. On September 23, 1780, he boarded the British sloop of war *Vulture* and sailed upriver to a point on the west bank near the residence of a prominent Loyalist named Joshua Hett Smith.[14]

Men rowed Smith out to the *Vulture*, where he gave André a military pass signed by Arnold in the name of "John Anderson." Then, with André dressed in his regimental uniform, the two men went ashore to meet Arnold before all three men repaired to Smith's house. Arnold gave André detailed plans of West Point, written in his own, recognizable hand, together with minutes of the American council of war that had been held on September 6.[15]

When the meeting concluded, Arnold convinced André not to return to the sloop because, he said, there were "spyboats" on the river. A brief artillery duel had broken out between the *Vulture* and an American shore battery, so the British ship dropped downriver, out of range.[16]

Arnold advised André to change into civilian garb and to return to Manhattan by land with Joshua Hett Smith as a guide. The British major may not have known he was behind American lines where, if he were captured in uniform, he could expect to be treated as a prisoner of war. Any enemy officer wearing civilian clothing, however, would be considered a spy, subject to summary execution. André, unwisely, took Arnold's advice.[17]

The next day, Smith took the British officer across the Hudson and south as far as the Croton River, where he left André to travel through Westchester alone. Rebel militiamen stopped André near Tarrytown; they searched him and found Arnold's papers hidden under his stockings. Then they turned him over to Colonel John Jameson of the American dragoons. The colonel promptly sent off a letter to his commanding officer to report the capture of a suspicious character, one John Anderson. Colonel Jameson's commanding officer was General Benedict Arnold.[18]

Major Benjamin Tallmadge, Washington's chief of intelligence, arrived at Tarrytown and listened to Jameson's report. Tallmadge questioned the prisoner and observed him closely. "I became impressed," he wrote, "with the belief that he had been bred to arms." The suspicious American officer remained "constantly in the room with him." André, still pretending to be John Anderson, asked permission to write a letter to General Washington. When he finished writing, he handed the paper to Tallmadge to read. The letter, Tallmadge reported, "disclosed his true character to be 'Major John André, Adjutant-General to the British Army.'"[19]

Benedict Arnold received Colonel Jameson's letter from a horseman at the Beverly Robinson house, his headquarters on the east side of the Hudson. Arnold knew instantly that the plot had failed and he was in mortal danger. Washington was at that very moment on his way to meet Arnold. Alexander Hamilton had arrived at the Robinson house ahead of Washington. Arnold told Hamilton he had urgent business at West Point, bade a quick farewell to his wife Peggy, and fled down to a boat on the river. Unwitting soldiers rowed him downstream to safety on the *Vulture*.[20]

❦ ❧

George Washington knew nothing of these events as he rode south along the east bank of the river on the morning of September 25. He arrived at Arnold's headquarters at about 10:30 to find Arnold absent. After eating a quick break-fast, Washington and some of his retinue crossed to West Point, where they expected to encounter Arnold.[21]

From the boat landing up to Fort Putnam, they inquired for Arnold, but the scattered soldiers posted there had not seen their commander all day. "The impropriety of his conduct when he knew I was to be there," Washington said, "struck me very forcibly, and my mind misgave me; but I had not the least idea of the real cause."[22]

What he did see disturbed him even more—the redoubts were incom-plete, or they were constructed from wood that would burst into flames in a barrage. A skeletal crew manned the works; the forces Washington expected to be there were nowhere to be seen.[23] Doctor Thacher wrote that Arnold had sent some units away and had "disposed and arranged the remaining troops in such manner that little or no opposition could have been made, and an imme-diate surrender would have been inevitable."[24]

Back at the Robinson house, Colonel Alexander Hamilton handed Wash-ington the damning papers forwarded by Tallmadge together with André's let-ter that revealed everything. Washington sent Hamilton galloping downriver in a futile effort to stop Arnold. The traitor had escaped—the "spy" remained.[25]

❦ ❧

Major Tallmadge, with a "strong escort of cavalry," conducted André across the river to West Point and then south by barge to Tappan, the base of the American army.[26] There, André remained under vigilant guard at the tavern of Casparus Mabie, not far from Washington's headquarters at the Johannes DeWint house. In order to avoid prejudice, the American commander delib-erately avoided meeting the British officer.[27]

News of the plot by Arnold and André spread quickly through the army.

General Nathanael Greene's order of the day for September 26 opened with this statement: "Treason of the blackest dye was yesterday discovered." Greene identified Adjutant-General André as Arnold's coconspirator. André, Greene asserted, was a spy, a statement that might have raised eyebrows later when Greene presided over the council that tried André.[28]

The Americans expected that André faced summary execution by hanging if Washington ordered it; such was the universally accepted fate for spies. General Howe had hanged Nathan Hale without trial under just such circumstances.[29]

Instead, Washington commissioned a Board of General Officers, with Nathanael Greene as president, to hear André's case. Six major generals and eight brigadier generals made up the rest of the court. They were to sit at the Old Dutch Church at Tappan on Friday, September 29. Washington gave them specific instructions: "After a careful examination, you will be pleased as speedily as possible to report a precise state of his case, together with your opinion of the light in which he ought to be considered, and the punishment that ought to be inflicted."[30] Brigadier General John Stark was to sit as one of the judges.

André waited at Mabie's tavern, where Alexander Hamilton visited him several times. Like Benjamin Tallmadge, Hamilton became attached to the British officer. André told him frankly, "I foresee my fate, and though I pretend not to play the hero, or to be indifferent about life, yet I am reconciled to whatever may happen, conscious that misfortune, not guilt, has brought it upon me."[31]

The people of Tappan did not share Hamilton's sympathy. At night, patriots paraded before the tavern carrying makeshift coffins to remind André of the fate they hoped awaited him.[32]

The next day, Major André walked into the Dutch Church to confront the fourteen generals. In addition to Greene and Stark, the accused spy faced Stirling, St. Clair, Lafayette, Howe, von Steuben, Parsons, Clinton, Knox, Glover, Paterson, Hand and Huntington.[33] André seemed to be at ease before these grim-faced men in their blue and buff coats.[34]

English critics found much to complain of in Washington's choice of "jurymen." Greene was a blacksmith, Stark a lumberman and Glover a sailor; none of the panel of officers could boast of higher education, much less any knowledge of the law. The critics ignored the fact that, had a British general been in Washington's place, André would already have been swinging from the gibbet.[35]

No record was made of the trial except the notes kept by Advocate General John Lawrence, who conducted the inquiry. Lawrence first read Washington's order aloud, then introduced each general to the prisoner.[36]

Lawrence began the questioning by showing André his letter to Washington, written in the presence of Benjamin Tallmadge. André admitted he had written it, and he offered to change nothing in its text. Then, the British major identified the papers found in his stockings and acknowledged his earlier possession of them.[37]

Sir Henry Clinton had written to Washington after André's capture, demanding that his aide be released because he had come ashore under "a flag of truce" and had Arnold's "passport" to return to New York.[38] Advocate General Lawrence asked about the alleged flag of truce, and André answered that "it was impossible for him to suppose he came on shore under that sanction, and added, that if he came on shore under that sanction, he certainly might have returned under it."[39]

Thus, André admitted all the elements of the crime of espionage and rejected the excuse offered to him by Sir Henry Clinton. His only defense, as he stated in his first letter to Washington, was that Arnold had betrayed him "into the vile condition of an enemy in disguise within your posts." He was no spy, he believed, because he was "involuntarily an imposter."[40]

Advocate General Lawrence called no other witnesses; there was no need. "He put us to no proof," Baron von Steuben recalled, "but in open, manly manner confessed everything but a premeditated design to deceive."[41]

André had earlier requested that he not be questioned concerning any person other than himself, to be "excused from accusing any other." The council honored his wish; thus, he said nothing to implicate Joshua Hett Smith.[42] General Greene excused the prisoner, and André marched out under guard. Lawrence showed the generals letters from Benedict Arnold, Sir Henry Clinton and Beverly Robinson. All three letters proposed the nonexistent flag of truce as a complete defense.[43]

The Board of General Officers arrived at a speedy verdict: "… having maturely considered these facts," that Major André "…ought to be considered as a spy from the enemy, and that agreeably to the law and usage of nations it is their opinion he ought to suffer death."[44]

No record was made of the questions asked by the generals, or of their discussions on the evidence or the verdict. Their decision was unanimous, signed by each man and by Lawrence as judge advocate general.[45]

Caleb Stark, the general's grandson, later wrote that, "In regard to the execution of Major André, six members were in favor of his being shot, six others were of opinion that he ought to be hung as a spy. General Greene, the president, decided the question in favor of the latter." Actually, the board's verdict contained no recommendation as to the manner of André's execution. The customs of warfare demanded that spies be hanged; any other fate would be Washington's decision.[46]

The army waited. Washington delayed until the next day, September 30, before he issued his order of execution; Major André would die by hanging the following day, a Sunday, October 1, at 5:00 PM. While the Americans prepared for the event, a British messenger appeared bearing a white flag. Henry Clinton asked for a meeting between officers.[47]

The same courier brought a message for the commander in chief from Benedict Arnold, who threatened that if André were put to death, "I shall think myself bound by every tie of duty and honour to retaliate on such unhappy persons of your army as may fall within my power." Arnold concluded, "I call heaven and earth to witness that your Excellency will be justly answerable for the torrent of blood that may be spilt in consequence."[48]

Washington ignored Arnold's threat, but Clinton's request convinced him to postpone the execution. He sent Nathanael Greene to meet with Clinton's emissary, General James Robertson, who had only the "flag of truce" argument to offer. Washington wrote Clinton: "… it is evident Major André was employed in the execution of measures very foreign to the Objects of Flags of truce and such as they were never meant to authorise or countenance in the most distant degree." Besides, Washington pointed out, André had denied he had been under the protection of the flag.[49]

Colonel Israel Angell, officer-of-the-day for September 30, noted that Major André's servant arrived in the Tappan camp from New York. He brought with him André's regimental uniform, a sign the British knew their adjutant-general was doomed.[50]

༺ ༻

The trial was over, all appeals denied. The hanging would take place on Monday, October 2, at noon. André wrote a last request to the American commander, "… to adopt the mode of my death to the feelings of a man of honour." The spy wished to be informed that "I am not to die on a gibbet."[51]

General Washington did not reply. He had made up his mind—André would hang. Alexander Hamilton later explained his leader's thinking: "… this indulgence [death by firing squad], being incompatible with the laws of war, could not be granted, and it was therefore determined … to evade an answer, to spare him the sensations which a certain knowledge of the intended mode would inflict." If Washington had allowed André to be shot, doubt would remain whether the Americans truly believed André was a spy.[52]

On Monday morning André calmly ate a breakfast brought from Washington's table. Then he shaved and dressed in his regimentals. When he was satisfied with his appearance, he told his guards he was ready.[53]

A drummer tapped out an ominous cadence as the red-coated officer, accompanied by Tallmadge, walked to the place of his death. American soldiers lined the way. The Board of General Officers, mounted on horseback, watched. Colonel Alexander Scammel of New Hampshire, the officer in charge of the execution, waited by the gibbet.[54]

When André saw the horse-drawn wagon under the noose, Tallmadge said, he appeared to be startled "and inquired with some emotion whether he was not to be shot."[55] Upon being told he would hang, he quickly gathered himself. "It will be but a momentary pang," Hamilton remembered him saying.[56]

The executioner was a Tory named Strickland, recruited for the job by a promise of freedom. He had blackened his face to hide his identity.[57]

Colonel Scammel asked André if he had any last words. "Nothing but to request that you will witness to the world that I die like a brave man," André answered, and he climbed up on the tailgate of the wagon.[58]

Tallmadge shook hands with André and stepped away. The British officer tied a handkerchief over his own eyes and slipped the noose around his neck himself.[59] The hangman whipped the horse forward, and the body of John André swung. Doctor Thacher wrote, he "instantly expired."[60]

American witnesses—soldiers inured to violence and death—were strangely moved. The scene, Doctor Thacher thought, "was consecrated by the tears of thousands."[61]

Among the Americans, Benjamin Tallmadge probably knew André best. He remembered years later: "When I saw him swinging under the Gibbet, it seemed for a time as if I could not support it. … There did not appear to be one hardened or indifferent spectator in the multitude."[62]

Hamilton believed that, "in the midst of his enemies, he died universally esteemed and universally regretted."[63]

Not quite universally. Private Joseph Plumb Martin spoke for many:

He [André] was an interesting character. There has been a great deal said about him, but he was but a man, and no better, nor had he better qualifications than the brave Captain Hale, whom the British commander caused to be executed as a spy … without the shadow of a trial; denying him the use of a Bible or the assistance of a clergyman in his last moments, and destroying the letters he had written to his widowed mother and other relations. André had every indulgence allowed him that could be granted with propriety;—see the contrast—let all who pity André so much look at it and be silent.[64]

Thacher, Hamilton and Tallmadge admired André's courage but, above all, they admired his aristocratic manner. Thacher thought he had "proud and elevated sensibilities" with a "mien respectable and dignified."[65] Tallmadge called him "a most elegant and accomplished gentleman."[66] Hamilton found that André's elocution was handsome, his address easy, polite and insinuating."[67] Soldiers who had recently witnessed André's courage praised him instead for his vanity.

Major Caleb Stark and Lieutenant Archibald Stark witnessed the hanging, as did their father. Caleb, Jr., later wrote that, "a high minded soldier [André] who, in an evil hour, became the dupe of a traitor," met his death. It seems likely that the younger Starks shared the widespread admiration for André.[68]

John Stark left no comment on the affair other than his vote for a death sentence for the British officer. Had he known of André's history with the brutal General Grey, he might have thought, "Nothing in his life became him like the leaving of it."[69]

27

WEST POINT, ALBANY, AND WAR'S END

My Exile

On November 21, 1780, French Major General Francois-Jean de Beauvoir, the Marquis de Chastellux, with his retinue rode south from Fishkill along the east bank of the Hudson River into the Highlands. They rounded a bend, and the Marquis wrote, "my eyes were suddenly struck with the most magnificent picture I have ever beheld." Before him the river flowed through a deep chasm in the mountains; across the river stood "the fort of West Point and the formidable batteries which defend it." He dismounted and scanned the scene through a telescope until his aides urged him to push on. Major General William Heath, the new commander at West Point, awaited him.[1]

De Chastellux remounted and rode forward, and very soon, he wrote, "I perceived a corps of infantry of about two thousand five hundred men, ranged in battle formation on the bank of the river.[2]

General Heath and General Stark, both on horseback, greeted the Marquis. They had halted the march of Stark's corps for the French aristocrat to review the American soldiers.[3] Stark was leading six battalions, "a large foraging party," into Westchester County, all the way to the outskirts of New York City.[4]

The Marquis "passed before the ranks" with drums beating. He saw troops that were "ill clothed, but made a good appearance." He could find no fault with the officers. When his review was completed, the officers saluted one another. Stark arrayed his ranks for the march. Heath and the Marquis boarded a barge to cross to West Point.[5]

Bald, portly William Heath was a gentleman farmer from Massachusetts, wealthy enough to remain in the army "notwithstanding the want of pay," de Chastellux wrote, "which has compelled the less rich to quit it." The Frenchman sized up Heath quickly: "… if he has not been in the way of displaying his talents in action, it may at least be asserted that he is well adapted to what we call 'the business of the cabinet.'"[6]

Stark's foraging mission in desolate Westchester County was all ruse. The real mission was to draw the British out of Manhattan so that Lafayette could lead an attack on Staten Island.[7]

Henry Dearborn served on the Westchester expedition. He reported that they "marchd towards the Enemies lines as a covering party to several hundred teams that were collected & sent down as a forrageing party near the Enemies lines."[8]

In truth, the wagons were cover for the military tactics. Stark's soldiers marched through the territory of the "cowboys" and the "skinners," respectively Loyalist and patriot brigands who had laid waste to lower Westchester County, where civil war raged.[9] Stark wrote to Heath: "I hope the forage will turn out according to your wishes, but it does not equal my expectations. The country below White Plains is almost desolate on account of the ravages of both armies. Scarcely a farmer has more than one cow, and many who were once in affluent circumstances are now reduced to indiscriminate poverty."[10]

The soldiers marched and camped in the open in the chill November weather, often in heavy rain.[11] Forward units approached King's Bridge, at the northern tip of Manhattan. Stark kept out flanking columns, expecting a British attack at any time but, he complained, "the enemy either did not know of our approach, or did not choose to meet us."[12]

Heath, back at West Point, wrote to Stark expressing his eagerness to hear "an account of something interesting. … Heaven grant that it may be equal to our most sanguine expectations." Heath wanted a battle.[13]

The British, however, remained in New York, and Washington called off the attack on Staten Island. Dearborn wrote, "… after remaining out six nights without any covering but the heavens (three nights & three days exposed to heavy rains & hard marching) returnd to camp." Dearborn was disappointed. "We toock every meathod to provoke the Enemy to come out and attack us but to no purpose."[14]

The dampness and chill of the Westchester campaign aggravated Stark's ailments. He lived in constant pain. As soon as they reached camp at Peekskill Hollow, he wrote to Washington, "The impaired state of my health and the unsettled state of my accounts with the State of New Hampshire render my presence in that state the ensuing winter highly necessary."[15]

In another letter the general revealed a further problem. His absence, he told Sullivan, had left his farm "in a ruinous state for want of proper management and cultivation. … the decays of nature are irreparable." All the men in his family who could have corrected the decline of their farm served in the army.[16]

Stark needed to go home. He had reached his limit. But he left the door open to serving in the next campaign. Despite what he called his "shattered constitution," he hoped to "take the field for short periods." He was fifty-two years old. He had been at war for nearly a third of his adult life.[17]

Weeks went by without a response from Washington, who had moved to winter quarters at New Windsor, a short distance up the Hudson. The impatient Stark wrote to Congress for relief. On December 30, Washington approved his furlough in writing, adding, "The term of absence, if they choose to limit it, will depend on Congress." Congress had referred Stark's letter to Washington.[18]

He could go home, but how could he pay for the trip? Again, he importuned for "some cash advanced on account."[19] The commander responded, "there is not a single farthing in the military chest." Perhaps to demonstrate that he meant no slight to the brigadier, Washington added a postscript: "I have not been able to obtain any money for my own expenses or table for more than three months."[20]

John Stark, accompanied by his sons Caleb and Archibald, managed to get home to Derryfield in January of 1781. Perhaps they borrowed money for their expenses from fellow officers; they required lodging and meals at taverns, and feed for their saddle horses and pack animals (there being no pasture in January). Patriot soldiers had learned not to expect charity from their countrymen.

From January to May it was another winter of ferocious weather—a commonplace of the Revolutionary years. Matthew Patten recorded a series of "tedious and heavy" storms, with wind and drifting snow. Two inches of snow fell on May 8.[21]

That spring, Stark wrote to Sullivan, still complaining about his health. "The last," he wrote, "was one of the most severe winters we have had these ten year, and it is exceeding cold today."[22] But, he thought, the warmer weather to come might improve his health.

In late June orders arrived for him to travel to Saratoga to once again command the northern department. He would have only militia troops because, Washington explained, it was "necessary, for the operations of the campaign to recall the continental troops from the north."[23] The Americans were preparing the final effort against Cornwallis in Virginia.

Private Joseph Plumb Martin had been among those ordered south during the summer. His unit sailed down Chesapeake Bay to the mouth of the James River, where they saw the immense French fleet. Martin wrote, "they resembled a swamp of dry pine trees." He joined Lafayette's regiments at Williamsburg, and they moved on to Yorktown. "We now began preparations for laying close siege to the enemy," he wrote. "We had holed him and nothing remained but to dig him out."[24]

Washington left New York in August, bound for Virginia. His army would be too far away to offer support to the northern department in the event of trouble.[25] He instructed Stark to take advice from retired General Schuyler. Unspoken in the order was the hope that Stark would treat New York's Governor Clinton and the city fathers of Albany with some measure of respect.[26]

The independent folks of Vermont soon caused an alarm. The British made overtures to them, and patriots began to suspect that Vermonters might choose to remain loyal subjects of the King. Their militia made forays into territory claimed by New York and New Hampshire. Threats were exchanged.

John Stark had been a lifelong friend of Vermont; these maneuvers put him in a difficult position.[27]

He faced these perplexing problems with undependable militia, inadequate provisions and forage and, worst of all, hardly any rum. Scouts in the north woods, Stark wrote Washington, "ought to have a little grog in addition to their fresh beef and water."[28]

Complaining about the grog ration to his commander in chief demonstrated how removed Stark had become from the realities of the American Revolution. Posted in a backwater, beset by minor irritations, and frustrated by political problems for which he had no patience, Stark fumed. His strength was combat, and the nearest combat was hundreds of miles away in Virginia.

⁂

In October, Washington's army bagged the British army at Yorktown. With the American and French armies in front of him and the French Navy behind him, Cornwallis was trapped. For three weeks the two sides exchanged artillery fire while American sappers and miners dug works to move the Americans closer to the British lines.

Private Martin, one of the sappers, noted that one night a strange man, wearing a "surtout" (overcoat), appeared in the midst of his unit. They were dangerously close to the enemy lines, but the stranger moved about calmly and talked "familiarly with us." Later, Martin heard someone address the tall stranger as "Your Excellency," and the soldiers finally realized that their visitor was George Washington.[29]

One day, New Hampshire Colonel Alexander Scammel, a hero at Saratoga, led a reconnaissance near enemy lines. A musket shot wounded him, and he tried to surrender. A British soldier shot him in the back and killed him. News of the manner of his death reached the Americans.[30]

As the siege progressed, the cannonade on both sides grew fiercer. Dr. James Thacher described the weird beauty of a nighttime bombardment:

> The bombshells from the besiegers and the besieged are incessantly crossing each other's paths in the air. They are clearly visible in the

form of a black ball in the day, but in the night they appear like a fiery meteor with a blazing tail, most beautifully brilliant, ascending majestically from the mortar to a certain altitude and gradually descending to the spot where they are destined to execute their work of destruction.[31]

Two British redoubts situated in front of their main lines stalled the American advance. Colonel Alexander Hamilton led a bayonet attack on one of these positions, and Private Martin joined the fray. He heard a man shout, "the fort's our own" and "rush on boys."[32] The Americans captured several prisoners. An angry captain from New Hampshire threatened to kill a British major in revenge for Scammel's murder, "but Colonel Hamilton interposed, and not a man was killed after he ceased to resist."[33]

Cornwallis surrendered on October 19. The antagonists did not know it yet, but the American War for Independence was over. Strong British forces remained at Charleston and New York, but thereafter only peace negotiations passed between the enemies.

John Stark finally wrote a letter of congratulations to General Washington in December. Part of his message was graceful: "You have taught them [the British] the road to submission, and they have manifested to the world that they are vulnerable; and no doubt the warlike nations with whom they are at variance, stimulated by your noble example, will give them further proofs of their inability to trample on the laws of equity, justice and liberty with impunity."[34]

But Stark could not resist a hint of complaint: "My exile," he wrote, "has not been attended with any very interesting events." Washington had not included him in the final, glorious victory. The words "my exile" amounted to a bitter accusation.[35]

28

Old Soldiers
Live Free or Die

For almost two years the government of King George refused to acknowledge that the Americans had won the war. The British kept elements of their army and navy in America, and the Americans still regarded them as threats. Washington worried that victory at Yorktown would lead to a relaxation of rebel will, a weakness the enemy might exploit.[1]

Newburgh, New York, became the American headquarters and principal base in 1782. Located at the north end of the Hudson Highlands on the west bank of the Hudson, the site could resist attacks by land or water. It also offered the Americans a convenient route to Manhattan and other military objectives.

John Stark did not report for duty in 1782. His ailments kept him at home in Derryfield, where Molly had just given birth to their last child, a daughter, Sophia.[2] Washington heard nothing from Stark, received no "Intimations from him of his intentions."[3]

Finally, in September, Stark wrote to Washington to explain his absence. He complained of a "shattered constitution," and he elaborated: "During the course of the winter and the greater part of the spring and summer I was scarce able to ride five miles, but as the autumn began to advance I find my health gradually returning." Stark offered to serve "at any place in the army necessary for the good of my country."[4]

A month later Washington responded with a kind message. Citing the lack of action and Stark's precarious health, he wrote, "I do not wish or expect you should join the Army this Fall." However, the general made clear he would welcome Stark back and that he hoped "for a full Restoration of your Health and Usefulness."[5]

Stark's health was sufficiently restored that he travelled to Newburgh in the spring of 1783. The first indication of his presence with the army appeared in the general orders for April 18 when he was officer of the day.[6] He missed the drama of the previous month when disgruntled officers promoted what amounted to a military coup.

Arrears in pay and in reimbursement for expenses, and demands for pensions, caused many officers to turn against Congressional authority. Anonymous letters circulated suggesting that a separate military authority be established and urging the officers at Newburgh to assemble, without the sanction of higher authority, to consider their options.[7]

Washington was horrified. He ordered all officers to attend a meeting on March 15. He rose before the assemblage and tried to read from a prepared text: "This dreadful alternative of either deserting our Country in the extremest hour of her distress, or turning our Arms against it ... has something so shocking in it, that humanity revolts at the idea." His speech was strong, but its most effective words were not part of the text. He paused to take new spectacles from his coat, and the assembled officers waited while he put them on and adjusted them. "Gentlemen," he said, "you must pardon me. I have grown gray in your service and now find myself growing blind."[8]

This reminder of shared sacrifice turned the tide. The officers agreed to cease their threats, and they voted to renew their support for Congress.[9]

General Stark served as officer of the day, on average, once a week through the spring and early summer of 1783. The American army simply waited. Commissioners from both governments tried to reach agreement on the terms of a peace treaty that would officially end the Revolutionary War. Until then, military prudence dictated that the patriots remain at the ready.

The fate of the Loyalists remained a sticking point between the commissioners. The British wanted the rebels to return the lands and property they had seized, or they wanted the Loyalists to be indemnified for their losses. The

Americans flatly refused. Popular sentiment was so against the Tories that no national government could guarantee that the states would honor such a pro-Loyalist provision in a treaty.[10]

Benjamin Franklin, himself the father of a Loyalist, told the British diplomats bluntly that restitution and indemnification were impossible. "Your ministers require," he wrote, "that we should receive again into our bosom those who have been our bitterest enemies, and restore their property who have destroyed ours; and this while the wounds they have given us are still bleeding."[11]

Ultimately, Congress left it up to the states to deal with the confiscation of Loyalist estates on a voluntary basis, a result that satisfied no Loyalist.[12]

The peace treaty was signed in September; it had been so long expected that it came as an anticlimax. In December, Washington bade an emotional farewell to some of his officers at Fraunces Tavern in lower Manhattan. John Stark missed the occasion; he had returned to New Hampshire.[13]

Throughout the Revolution, Matthew Patten's diary of life in the Merrimack Valley only rarely recorded any hint of the violent political upheaval taking place in the land. He accounted for his daily chores, survey work, cases in his court and the price of rum. Any man who could record the birth of his child and the sale of a cow in the same sentence could not be expected to wax emotional about the fate of his country. Still, on December 11, 1783, Matthew wrote, all in capital letters: "WAS THANKSGIVEING THROUGHOUT THE UNITED STATES BY ORDER OF THE CONGRESS."[14]

General John Sullivan represented Patten in a lawsuit against Deacon Moor in the autumn of 1783 and won ten shillings damages with costs.[15] Sullivan had resigned from the army in 1779, expecting Congress to reject his resignation. Instead, the majority in Congress cheerfully put him out to pasture.[16]

John Stark had spent enough time at home during the winters of the war to know what conditions were like. He knew of the contrast between the comfortable lives of the civilians and the sacrifices of the soldiers. If his own farm was in ruinous condition, as he wrote, his neighbors prospered during the conflict.

The Marquis de Chastellux had visited New Hampshire in November of 1782. He found Portsmouth and the coastal region relatively hard up because the British Navy had halted commerce. By contrast, the farmers of the Merrimack Valley thrived. He wrote:

> [T]he losses of commerce have turned to the advantage of agriculture; the capital of the rich and the industry of the people having flowed back from the coasts towards the interior of the country, which has profited rapidly by this reflux. It is certain that the country has a very flourishing appearance, and that new houses are being built and new farms settled every day.[17]

The construction of new houses and barns boded well for the sawmill business. The war had silenced the Starks' mill; the equipment probably needed repair. Archibald, at twenty-two, and John, Jr., at twenty, were of an age to help, but Caleb went back to his grandfather's home in Dunbarton. He opened a store, began a successful career as a merchant, and built a handsome mansion.[18]

In addition to the older boys, John and Molly had seven minor children at home. The soldier needed to quickly transform himself back into the farmer and the lumberman. Unlike some of his military brethren, John Stark made the transition cheerfully.

After all their trials and suffering, many soldiers of the Revolution found it hard to leave their comrades—their brothers-in-arms. Those with the courage and grit to stay through the worst times regarded their comrades as family. When Private Joseph Plumb Martin came to the end of his service, he confessed to sadness at the parting: "… we were young men and had warm hearts. I question if there was a corps in the army that parted with more regret than ours did, the New Englanders in particular, Ah! It was a serious time."[19]

Many officers, too, wanted to continue their comradeship in some fashion. To that end Henry Knox proposed an association to be known as the Society of the Cincinnati. In May 1783 at Fishkill, New York, Alexander Hamilton chaired the first organizational meeting of the society, where its "institution" (bylaws) was adopted. The main purposes of the society were to provide a means of fellowship for brother officers of the Continental Army, to raise funds for needy officers, and to promote pensions for the surviving soldiers. George Washington took office as president of the society, and dozens of officers joined. John Stark refused to join.[20]

The name "Cincinnati" derived from the Roman farmer-soldier, Lucius Quintus Cincinatus, who led Rome through battles and hard times, and twice renounced all power and returned to his life as a farmer. The American society named for the Roman, however, carried as a core principle the survival of a military brotherhood. The permanence of the society was guaranteed by the right of the first-born son in each generation to inherit membership in the group—primogeniture. Some Americans, including Benjamin Franklin, thought this resembled the practices of British nobility.[21]

Washington tried to reform the institution by eliminating the right of hereditary membership. But the society, whose strength resided in thirteen separate state chapters, resisted the change. John Stark dismissed the society altogether. His grandson explained the general's view:

> Several officers at the time retained a partiality for orders of aristocracy. The establishment of the Cincinnati Society was the result. He [John Stark] made several objections to the formation of this order: one of which was that its principles had no affinity with the character and conduct of the illustrious Roman general whose name it had adopted.[22]

Support for, or opposition to, the Society of the Cincinnati foreshadowed a political divide that would soon cleave the United States. Thomas Jefferson saw something profoundly undemocratic about the organization. He wrote to James Madison in 1794 that the society was "carving out for itself hereditary distinctions, lowering over our Constitution eternally, meeting together in all parts of the Union, periodically, with closed doors, accumulating a capital in their separate treasury, corresponding secretly and regularly, and of which society the very persons denouncing the democrats are themselves the fathers, founders and high officers."[23] By the time Jefferson wrote those words, the partisan gulf between the Federalists and the Jeffersonian Republicans was a chasm. Americans were choosing sides in a new internal conflict.

When, at last, John and Molly Stark could live together in peacetime, he was fifty-five years old and she was forty-six. They were not elderly but, by eighteenth-century standards of longevity, they could not expect much time together. The death of family and friends disturbed their happiness all too often after the Revolution. Their son Archibald died in 1791 at age thirty. He had never married; he probably brought chronic ill health home from the war.[24]

Neighbor and friend Matthew Patten died in 1795. He was a worker to his last day, when he employed several men to mow a meadow near Bedford. At noontime he carried dinner to them in the field. Then, Matthew sat down in the shade of a tree, "where he was found dead in a short time." After his death, one of his sons took up the diary and recorded each day's events for two years, without ever noting that Matthew had died—the Patten custom of hard work simply continued.[25]

General John Sullivan also died in 1795 at fifty-five. He had become a hard drinker near the end of his life, and he became incompetent. His creditors hounded him. A contemporary described Sullivan's sad condition: "… he approached a state of idiocy, and was utterly incapable of holding a court or transacting any business. Early in the year 1794 he could neither feed, dress nor undress himself."[26]

A strange drama played out at Sullivan's funeral. Some of his creditors, to pressure his family into paying his debts, threatened to prevent his interment. General Joseph Cilley, pistols in hand, marched to the graveyard in front of the coffin and saw to it that Sullivan was properly buried.[27]

In London, Robert Rogers came to a similar end on May 18, 1795. Exiled from his American family, deeply in debt and broken by drink, Rogers was remembered in the British press for his "prodigious feats of valor" and "uncommon strength." But the same obituary observed that imprisonment for debt "had reduced him to the most miserable state of wretchedness."[28]

If John Stark knew of the passing of his old comrade, he never expressed his thoughts about it. Rogers had seemed such a giant of a man that his character flaws seemed to belong to another person altogether. Perhaps Stark grieved for his former friend, but a family tragedy soon eclipsed the loss of Rogers.

The Stark family kept a leather-bound account book, closed by brass hasps and marked by a shaky signature, "John Stark, His Book." It contained receipts for wages paid by "Capt Starks" in 1757. Someone in his family used the book for their own purposes years later, writing in it: "Charles Stark sailed from Boston in the Brig *Lipsburghe* Benjamin Wheelright Master Nov. __ 1796 & was heard of no more."[29]

Charles was twenty-two years old when he disappeared at sea in the ship owned by his older brother Caleb.[30]

⚜ ⚜

When General Stark returned to private life, he made a wholehearted commitment to privacy. Late in life he explained his pledge: "… since the close of the revolutionary war [I] have devoted my time entirely to domestic employments, and in the vale of obscurity and retirement, have tasted that tranquility which the hurry and bustle of a busy world can seldom afford."[31]

In 1782, Congress had promoted him to "Major General by Brevet," an honorary rank without increase in pay, and which remained uncertified until 1786.[32] Coming as late as it did, and placing him in the company of many officers of shorter service and lesser merit, the promotion probably meant little to him.

In October of 1789, President George Washington paid a triumphant visit to Portsmouth, New Hampshire, where he was welcomed by John Sullivan, as President of the State, and treated to a corps of light horse and an artillery salute. He spent three days of feasting, and he attended multiple church services with politicians and retired officers; he named them all in his diary. The one New Hampshire soldier notably absent from his list was John Stark.[33]

There is some evidence that Washington and Stark had a chilly relationship. The commander in chief struggled with the egos of his senior officers. Despite having a formidable ego himself, he usually exhibited great patience and understanding with them. In 1775 he quickly developed contempt for New England officers, but he came to tolerate the fiery independence of Arnold, Greene and Glover. Like Stark, these officers proved to be outstanding combat leaders. But when Washington socialized with General John Sullivan in Portsmouth after the Revolution, John Stark either wasn't invited to the festivities or he declined to attend.

Strangely, while the two men were poles apart socially, they had lived remarkably similar lives. Both began their careers in the wilderness—Washington as a surveyor, Stark as a trapper and hunter. Both survived the savage conflicts of the French and Indian War, learning their craft "in the hard school of danger," as Thucydides described it.[34] Both came to detest the protocols and orthodoxy of the King's army, and both witnessed the tragic slaughter occasioned by incompetent leaders.

Washington and Stark became able and disciplined veteran officers. They went into combat leading their men from the front. They made cool-headed decisions, and their calm examples stiffened the morale of their soldiers. Over time they developed a loyal following among their officers and enlisted men; when the American ranks threatened to evaporate after Trenton, they succeeded in holding together a fighting force.

Both officers dared to lead where others would not go; they did not hesitate to go against the grain of their subordinates' wishes. After Princeton, Washington directed humane treatment for his prisoners despite his troops' anger at the inhumanity of their enemies. After Bennington, Stark led by example in the generous treatment of his captives, even though these invaders had threatened the homes and families of his men. Both men rejected their foes' belief that "all stratagems are lawful in war." They took no polls; they demanded obedience, and they usually got it.

The consequences of their leadership reverberated, not only in their own times, but down through the years. Americans have not always lived up to the standards set by Washington, Stark and others of their generation but, when they haven't, their failures have been a continuing subject for debate. The traditions begun in the crucible of the Revolution remain the American standard.

Not every tradition was noble—one spawned ugly offspring. Stark and Washington conceived the expedition into Iroquois country in 1779. They were not alone. The attacks at Wyoming and Cherry Valley demanded action. But the Sullivan expedition served as a template for the abuse of Native Americans that went on for more than a century, usually without any provocation.

John Stark served several years as an officer in the Continental Army, but his greatest achievements came as a commander of militia at Bunker Hill and Bennington. When, to satisfy his sense of "honor," he resigned his Continental commission, he crossed a boundary that other officers, like Knox and Greene, had only threatened to cross.

Stark atoned later for leaving the army by serving faithfully under a succession of lesser commanders. But his "exile" may have resulted from Washington's sense that he was not sufficiently committed to the cause—that he might not be there when he was needed. His failing health, no doubt, contributed to that judgment.

Washington believed that the conflict with Britain could only be won by a standing force of soldiery wedded to the enterprise until the end. After the battle for Manhattan, when the militia "melted away," he concluded that the army must be organized with long enlistments and commanded with stern discipline. He wanted soldiers like Private Joseph Plumb Martin—men who complained, froze, starved and suffered, but who stayed, winter and summer, year after year.

Yet Private Martin, and hundreds like him, mutinied. In the eighteenth century, mutiny, or something like it, was almost an American tradition. The rangers under Robert Rogers revolted against constituted authority more than once. After Trenton, John Glover's Marblehead sailors, among the best of soldiers, went home when Washington needed them. A mutiny of General Wayne's Continental Line resulted in the execution of soldiers for treason in 1781. Only Washington's personal intercession convinced his officers to reaffirm their loyalty at Newburgh. Even Washington himself rejected his masters in the British Army establishment when he served under them.

Rebellion came naturally to American soldiers; they were an unruly lot. The corollary to their independence was that they thought for themselves in combat; they resisted responding like automatons. Like Stark, the best soldiers had the resourcefulness to act on their own and the self-confidence to take the initiative. Several of his fighters at Bennington remembered that "every man seemed to manage for himself" or fought "each on his own hook." With good leadership their independence, even their unruliness, became a virtue, not a fault.

John Stark was one of a small handful of outstanding combat officers in the war. Had he swallowed his pride in 1777 and stayed with the army, his legacy would be greater. But Stark was Stark—proud, obstinate and impulsive. He usually expressed his opinions no matter the cost, but whatever he thought of Washington, he kept to himself. His grandson Caleb wrote nothing disparaging about the commander in chief.

In January 1777, after Stark had served under Washington at Boston, Trenton and Princeton, Molly gave birth to their last-born son. They named the boy after the man who apparently was their favorite founding patriot— Benjamin Franklin.

Passage of the American Constitution presented the nation its first great issue in 1786 and 1787. Washington supported passage.[35] John Langdon and John Sullivan actively pushed for ratification in New Hampshire. John Stark's home ground, Hillsborough County, voted against ratification almost three to one, but there is no record that Stark actively opposed ratification.[36]

The old soldier expressed his political views in letters between 1804 and 1809. President Thomas Jefferson wrote to him in 1804, congratulating him on his long service.[37] Stark answered by alluding to the prior administrations of Washington and Adams: "I will confess to you, sir, that I once began to think that the labors of the revolution were in vain, and that I should live to see the system restored which I had assisted in destroying." Stark considered Jefferson's government, however, "correct and just."[38]

In July of 1809, he warned the Bennington memorial committee: "there is a dangerous British party in the country, lurking in their hiding places, more dangerous than all our foreign enemies."[39]

In December 1809, President Madison wrote to Stark expressing gratitude for his courageous service.[40] Stark responded with a cautionary observation: "But of all the dangers from which I apprehend the most serious evil to my country, and our republican institutions, none requires a more watchful eye than our internal British faction [the Federalists]."[41]

Stark's letter to Madison plainly stated his reasons for his distrust of the British and of their American admirers, whether Loyalists or Federalists: "If the enmity of the British is to be feared, their alliance is still more dangerous. I have fought by their side as well as against them, and have found them to be treacherous and ungenerous as friends, and dishonorable as enemies."[42] Lord Howe, killed at Ticonderoga, seems to have been the only British officer Stark ever admired.

As the general grew older, two clergymen took an interest in him. Reverend William Bentley, a Unitarian from Salem, Massachusetts, admired Stark from afar and decided to visit the soldier in Derryfield. They talked about religious matters. Stark apparently welcomed the visit and their subsequent letters.[43]

Elder James Randall also attempted to proselytize the general when they met in 1807. He encountered resistance: "if it were not for four things, which those called Christians hold," Stark told him, "namely anarchy, avarice, superstition and tradition I would be a Christian."[44]

Perhaps the clearest statement of his beliefs was reported by his son-in-law, Benjamin Stickney, in 1810: "a person asked Gen. Stark to subscribe money to send a missionary among the Indians to teach them religion. He told the gentleman that he would subscribe an equal sum to send for an Indian to teach us morality."[45]

John and Molly Stark needed all the spiritual support they could find as they passed into their dotage. They experienced a series of tragic losses:

Their daughter Sarah died in 1801, leaving four young children.

John's sister, Anna Gamble, burned to death in a fire in 1805.

Their son Benjamin Franklin Stark died in 1806, leaving a widow and two young children.

Their granddaughter Louisa Stickney, age three, burned to death in 1808.

Their daughter Elizabeth died in 1813, leaving several children.

Their granddaughter, Caleb's daughter Mary Ann, apparently committed suicide in the Merrimack River in 1815. Her brother Charles fell ill that same week and died several months later.[46]

In 1809 a committee of Vermonters, together with surviving veterans of the Battle of Bennington, planned a celebration in memory of the victory. They wrote to Stark and invited him to come, "that the young men may once have the pleasure of seeing the man who so gallantly fought to defend their sacred rights."[47]

General Stark, crippled by rheumatism, knew he was in no condition to make the journey. He regretfully declined the invitation, with a hint of humor: "You say you wish your young men to see me; but you who have seen me can tell them I never was worth much for show, and certainly can not be worth their seeing now."[48]

Instead of himself, Stark sent the Vermonters a toast in honor of courage and sacrifice: "Live free or die—death is not the worst of evils."[49]

Molly died from typhus on June 29, 1814, in her seventy-seventh year. The following month a few lines about Elizabeth (Molly) Stark appeared in the Concord *Patriot*: "She retained her strength of mind and bodily health with scarce a day's sickness from her youth." She had been ill five days before her death. Molly's funeral was held at the meetinghouse, where the widower spoke his farewell for all to hear: "Good bye, Molly, we sup no more together on earth."[50]

Caleb Stark applied for a veteran's pension to help support his father and, by 1818, the old soldier received $40 a month for his service. It took more than three decades for the United States to aid its old soldiers, a belated generosity to embittered men "who had spent their youthful, and consequently, their best days in the hard service of their country," enabling them "to eke out the fag end of their lives a little too high for the groveling hand of envy or the long arm of poverty to reach," as Private Martin wrote. His words fit John Stark, who had served America almost thirteen years of his "best days."[51]

General John Stark died on May 8, 1822. Before his final breath he was the last surviving American general of the Continental Army—the last to leave the field.[52]

Epilogue
John Stark Remembered

In September 1839, Henry David Thoreau and his brother John set out on a journey in a fifteen-foot "dory" they had built themselves, bound on a voyage Henry described in *A Week on the Concord and Merrimack Rivers*. Like most of Thoreau's travels, it was a metaphorical journey as well, evoking themes of which Henry was only partly aware.

After launching, they soon floated past "the first regular battleground of the Revolution," the vestigial abutments of North Bridge at Concord; then they passed down toward the Merrimack.[1] This watery world caused Henry to think of fish and fishing, and of men who formerly had "openly professed the trade of Fishermen" rather than "skulking through the meadows to a rainy afternoon sport"—real fishermen who caught "marvelous draughts of fishes," great hauls of shad, eels and alewives.[2]

Once on the wide Merrimack, Thoreau remembered the earliest inhabitants of the shores along the river: "It was in fact an old battle and hunting ground through which we were floating, the ancient dwelling-place of a race of hunters and warriors."[3]

They rowed upstream, past Londonderry, where Henry noted, "the Scotch-Irish settlers … were the first to introduce the potato into New England." Something about the scene there made him think of Homer's *Iliad*, "a book fit to be remembered in our finest hours."[4]

The Thoreau brothers pulled their oars against the Merrimack's "stately rolling flood," past the town where Captain Lovewell began his fatal enterprise, Lovewell's War.[5] They camped one night in Bedford "in a retired place," perhaps near Patten's seine.[6]

Thoreau's account of the trip gave him ample space to ruminate on nature, philosophy, religion and history, and of the great men who came before him.

He admired people of courage and conviction; his education led him to seek such heroes in antiquity. It chafed Henry that admirable folk were so rare in his own time, but he clung stubbornly to his belief that the heroic still existed; he felt a visceral connection between himself and the epic past. Years later he wrote: "I too am at least a remote descendant of that heroic race of men of whom there is tradition. I too sit here on the shore of my Ithaca, a fellow-wanderer and survivor of Ulysses." He continued the thought a few lines later: "And now where is the generation of heroes whose lives are to pass amid these our northern pines, whose exploits shall appear to posterity pictured amid these strong and shaggy forms?"[7]

One sunny day, Henry and John approached Amoskeag Falls, which they passed around by rowing through the canal and lock that had reduced the river's flow over the rapids. They pulled upstream for a mile or so when they looked up on the east bank and saw a granite obelisk, the monument to John Stark.[8]

The sight caused Henry to ponder Stark's life—a captain of rangers and leader at Bunker Hill and Bennington. "A hero of two wars," Thoreau called him. "His monument stands upon the second bank of the river … and commands a prospect several miles up and down the Merrimack." Then Henry repeated his lament: "It suggests how much more impressive in the landscape is the tomb of a hero than the dwellings of the inglorious living."[9]

Leaving the monument behind, they rowed toward the New Hampshire hills. The river became too shallow for the boat. The young men were still not satisfied. They cached the dory and proceeded on foot, following a track along the bank. Pine and spruce trees made a darker forest here in the foothills, and the river ran faster beside them. They followed "a dank forest path … more like an otter or marten's trail, or where a beaver had dragged his trap," up near the country where, a century before, Stark and his companions shook off the bonds of civilization.[10]

Finally, Henry Thoreau wrote, they wandered "on through notches which the streams had made, by the side of and over the brow of hoar hills and mountains." At the highest point of their expedition, they "at length crawled on prostrate trees over the Amonoosuck, and breathed the free air of Unappropriated Land."[11]

Live free.

APPENDIX

John Stark's Reply to the Invitation of the Bennington Committee

AT MY QUARTERS, Derryfield
    31st of July, 1809

My Friends and Fellow-Soldiers.

I received yours of the 22nd instant containing your fervent expressions of friendship, and your very polite invitation to meet with you, to celebrate the 16th of August in Bennington. As you say, I "can never forget, that" I commanded American troops on that day in Bennington. They were men who had not learned the art of submission, nor had they been trained to the arts of war. But our "astonishing success" taught the enemies of liberty, that undisciplined freemen are superior to veteran slaves.

Nothing could afford me greater pleasure than to meet your brave "sons of liberty" on the fortunate spot; but, as you justly anticipate, the infirmities of old age will not permit it, for I am now more than four score and one years old, and the lamp of life is almost spent. I have of late had many such invitations, but was not ready, for there was not oil in the lamp.

You say you wish your young men to see me; but you who have seen me can tell them, that I never was much for a show, and certainly can not be worth their seeing now.

In case of my not being able to attend, you wish my sentiments. These you shall have, as free as the air we breathe. As I was then, I am now, the friend of the equal rights of men, of representative democracy, of republicanism, and the declaration of independence—the great charter of our national rights—and of course the friend of the indissoluble union of these States. I am the enemy of all foreign influence, for all foreign influence is the influence of tyranny. This is the only chosen spot of liberty—this the only republic on earth.

You well know, gentlemen, that at the time of the event you celebrate, there was a powerful British faction in the country (called tories), a material part of the force we contended with. This force was rankling in our councils until it had laid a foundation for the subversion of our liberties; but, by having good sentinels at our outposts, we were apprised of our danger. The sons of freedom beat the alarm, and, as at Bennington, they came, they saw, they conquered.

These are my orders now, and will be my last orders to all my volunteers, to look to their sentries; for there is a dangerous British party in the country, lurking in their hiding places, more dangerous than all our foreign enemies; and whenever they shall appear, let them render the same account of them as was given at Bennington, let them assume what name they will.*

I shall remember, gentlemen, the respect you, and the inhabitants of Bennington and its neighborhood have shown me, until I go to the "country from whence no traveller returns." I must soon receive marching orders.

John Stark

P.S. I will give you my volunteer toast—Live free or die—Death is not the worst of evils.

*Some versions of Stark's letter to the Bennington committee omit his reference to the "dangerous British party in the country." This version is from Caleb Stark's *Memoir and Official Correspondence of Gen. John Stark*, 312–313.

NOTES

Prologue: August 15, 1777

1. Commager and Morris, *Spirit of 'Seventy-Six*, 568.
2. Ibid., 548.
3. Paine, *Common Sense*, 73.
4. Kenneth Roberts, *Northwest Passage*, 79.
5. Foster and Streeter, *Stark's Independent Command at Bennington*, 44.
6. Ibid.
7. Ibid.
8. Wasmus, *Eyewitness Account of the American Revolution*, 40–41.
9. Ibid.
10. Fischer, *Washington's Crossing*, 379.
11. Ibid. 376.
12. Paine, *Common Sense*, 74.
13. Burgoyne to Lord George Germaine, 20 August 1777, in Commager and Morris, *Spirit of 'Seventy-Six*, 577.

PART I: The French and Indian War

1. Origins: *A Hiding Place from the Wind*

1. Maney, *The Family of General John Stark*, 26.
2. Ibid., 30, 43.
3. Ibid., 27–29.
4. Brown, *Colonel John Goffe*, 22.
5. Leyburn, *The Scotch-Irish*, 104–105.
6. Ibid., 130.
7. Ibid., 159.
8. Maney, *The Family of General John Stark*, 26–27, 32.
9. Moore, *Life of General John Stark*, 26.
10. Ibid.
11. Ibid., 27–28.
12. Maney, *The Family of General John Stark*, 36–37.
13. Moore, *Life of General John Stark*, 28.
14. Brown, *Colonel John Goffe*, 29.
15. Ibid., 30.
16. Ibid., 30–31.
17. Ibid., 32–33.
18. Ibid., 35.
19. Ibid., 36.
20. Ibid., 40.
21. Ibid., 41–45.
22. Ibid., 45.
23. Moore, *Life of General John Stark*, 32.
24. Ibid., 31.
25. Ibid., 33–35.
26. Ibid., 33.
27. Patten, *Diary of Matthew Patten*. The story of the spring fishery at Amoskeag Falls is related annually in Patten's diary for thirty-four years.
28. Brown, *Colonel John Goffe*, 31.
29. Potter, *History of Manchester*, 635–690. Potter narrated the colorful history of the fishing at Amoskeag Falls from the Indians through the first white settlers.
30. Brown, *Colonel John Goffe*, 86.
31. Potter, *History of Manchester*, chapter 25.
32. Ibid.
33. Ross, *War on the Run*, 30–32.
34. Potter, *History of Manchester*, chapter 25.
35. Maney, *The Family of General John Stark*, 32.
36. Brown, *Colonel John Goffe*, 29.
37. Cuneo, *Robert Rogers*, 56.
38. Ibid., 6–7.
39. Roby, ed., *Reminiscences*, 2.
40. Leyburn, *The Scotch-Irish*, 258–259.
41. Roby, *Reminiscences*, 2.
42. Brown, *Colonel John Goffe*, 57.
43. Ibid., 60.
44. Cuneo, *Robert Rogers*, 8.
45. Ibid.
46. Brown, *Colonel John Goffe*, 62–63.
47. Ibid., 66.
48. Ibid., 67.
49. Hadley, *Where the Winds Blow Free: Dunbarton, New Hampshire*, 12.
50. Rogers, *Journals of Major Robert Rogers*, Todish, ed., 27. This edition of the Rogers *Journals* differs in some respects from the

version published by Luther Roby in 1831. Rogers published both the 1765 "London" version, later printed by Roby, and the 1769 "Dublin" version set forth in the book by Timothy Todish. See the introduction to the Todish book for a narrative of the history of the various editions of the *Journals*.

2. Captivity: *There'll Be War*

1. Patten, *Diary*, XV–XVI.
2. Hadley, *Dunbarton*, 12.
3. Cuneo, *Robert Rogers*, 9–10.
4. Hadley, *Dunbarton*, 17–18.
5. Ibid., 127.
6. Cuneo, *Robert Rogers*, 3, 13–15.
7. Moore, *Life of General John Stark*, 40.
8. Cuneo, *Robert Rogers*, 10–11.
9. Brown, *Colonel John Goffe*, 80.
10. Ibid.
11. Moore, *Life of General John Stark*, 514–528, for physical description of Stark; Scheer & Rankin, *Rebels and Redcoats*, 298, for Stark's face; Dearborn, *Revolutionary War Journals*, 377, for the intensity of Stark's gaze.
12. John Stark to State of New Hampshire, 30 July 1777, in Moore, *General John Stark*, 271–272, for Stark's speech patterns.
13. Ibid., 439.
14. Barney, *Rumney Then and Now; History*, 4.
15. Caleb Stark, *Memoir and Official Correspondence of Gen. John Stark*, 11.
16. Ibid., 12.
17. Brumwell, *White Devil*, 40.
18. Moore, *General John Stark*, 41.
19. Ibid.
20. Ibid., 43.
21. Ibid., 41.
22. Brumwell, *White Devil*, 31, 49.
23. Ibid., 44.
24. Williams, *The Redeemed Captive Returning to Zion*, 9–14.
25. Ibid., 26.
26. Ibid.
27. Caleb Stark, *Memoir and Official Correspondence*, 14.
28. Ibid.
29. Ibid., 15.
30. Moore, *General John Stark*, 42–44.
31. Caleb Stark, *Memoir and Official Correspondence*, 15.
32. Ibid., 107–108.
33. Ibid. 15.
34. Ibid.
35. Little, *The History of Weare, New Hampshire: 1735–1888*, 59. Little reported that Rogers, Stark and a man named Samuel Orr, while hunting in the woods, conferred with three Indians one rainy day in 1754. That evening Rogers left camp, murdered and scalped the three Indians and returned with their scalps. When Stark rebuked him, Little wrote, Rogers responded, "Oh, damn it! There'll be war before another year." We found no other source that corroborates this tale. Weare borders Dunbarton on the west. An inquiry with the Weare Historical Society in 2012 produced no other source for William Little's narrative.
36. Cuneo, *Robert Rogers*, 13. That one of the most famous men in American history, Robert Rogers, had a chance encounter in the New Hampshire woods with one of the most infamous men, Owen Sullivan, seems unlikely, but if their meeting was planned, no evidence of it survives.
37. Scott, *Counterfeiting in Colonial America*, 186–209.
38. Cuneo, *Robert Rogers*, 12–13.
39. Scott, *Counterfeiting in Colonial America*, 202.
40. Patten, *Diary*, 11–12.
41. Scott, *Counterfeiting in Colonial America*, 202.
42. Loescher, *The History of Rogers Rangers*, Vol. 1., "The Beginnings," 267.
43. Cuneo, *Robert Rogers*, 14.
44. Ibid., 18.
45. Scott, *Counterfeiting in Colonial America*, 207.

3. Stark and Rogers Go to War: *May God Be with Us*

1. Quoted in Parkman, *Montcalm and Wolfe*, 21.
2. Fowler, *Empires at War: The French and Indian War and the Struggle for North America*, 2–3.

3. Anderson, *Crucible of War*, 77.

4. Benjamin Franklin, *Autobiography and Other Writings*, 107.

5. Ibid., 108.

6. Freeman, *George Washington*, Harwell, ed., 36–46.

7. Ibid., 50–53.

8. Anderson, *Crucible*, 6.

9. Freeman, *George Washington*, 54.

10. Quoted in Flexner, *Washington: The Indispensable Man*, 14.

11. Ibid., 16.

12. Freeman, *George Washington*, 53–55.

13. Flexner, *Washington: The Indispensable Man*, 16.

14. Parkman, *Montcalm and Wolfe*, 74.

15. Quoted in Bellico, *Chronicles of Lake Champlain*, 52. Russell Bellico excerpted portions of Peter Kalm's *Travels in North America*, the first description of the wilderness that would become the northern front of the Seven Years War in America.

16. Ibid.

17. Ibid., 46, 55.

18. Ibid., 56.

19. Ibid., 61.

20. Ibid., 51, 61–62.

21. Ibid., 57.

22. Ibid., 65.

23. Ibid., 68–69.

24. Ibid., 26–27.

25. Ibid., 24–26.

26. Ibid., 23.

27. Ibid.

28. Ibid., 21–22.

29. Ibid.

30. Cuneo, *Robert Rogers*, 18.

31. Parkman, *Montcalm and Wolfe*, 149.

32. Moore, *General John Stark*, 54.

33. Brown, *Colonel John Goffe*, 186.

34. Quoted in Parkman, *Montcalm and Wolfe*, 101.

35. Ibid., 110–113.

36. Franklin, *Autobiography*, 152.

37. Cuneo, *Robert Rogers*, 20.

38. Ibid.

39. Ibid., 21.

4. Battle of Lake George:
The Bullets Flew Like Hailstones

1. Anderson, *Crucible of War*, 114–117.

2. O'Callaghan, *Documents Relating to the Colonial History of the State of New York*, Vol. X, Paris Documents, 1745–1774 (hereafter cited as *D.R.C.H.S.N.Y.*), 316.

3. Anderson, *Crucible of War*, 118.

4. Parkman, *Montcalm and Wolfe*, 153–155.

5. Thomas Williams to his wife, quoted in Bellico, *Chronicles of Lake George*, 35.

6. Anderson, *Crucible of War*, 121.

7. Parkman, *Montcalm and Wolfe*, 156.

8. Rogers, *Journals of Major Rogers*, 31.

9. O'Callaghan, *D.R.C.H.S.N.Y.*, Vol. X, 318.

10. Quoted in Parkman, *Montcalm and Wolfe*, 157.

11. O'Callaghan, *D.R.C.H.S.N.Y.*, Vol. X, 423.

12. Rogers, *Journals of Major Rogers*, 31.

13. Armand Francis Lucier, ed., *French and Indian War Notices Abstracted from Colonial Newspapers*, Vol. 2, 199 *et seq.*, contains an account of a ranger battle of January 21, 1757, known as the "First Battle on Snowshoes." Printed in a Boston newspaper on February 14, 1757, as an "Extract from Capt. Rogers Journal," it differs slightly from the later "London" version of Rogers's *Journals*, as reproduced in Roby, but it differs substantially from the "Dublin" version annotated by Timothy Todish. The difference is primarily that Rogers omitted to identify the participants and their contributions in the "Dublin" version.

14. Rogers, *Journals of Major Rogers*, 33–34.

15. Ibid., 35.

16. Ibid., 39.

17. O'Callaghan, *The Documentary History of the State of New York* (hereafter cited as *D.H.S.N.Y.*), Vol. 4, 269.

18. Rogers, *Journals of Major Rogers*, 40–41.

19. O'Callaghan, *D.H.S.N.Y.*, Vol. 4, 267.

20. Ibid.

21. Ibid., 220.

22. Ibid., 274–275.

23. Ibid., 276.

24. Ibid., 280–281.

25. Cuneo, *Robert Rogers*, 25.

26. Moore, *General John Stark*, 57.

27. Ibid.

28. Patten, *Diary of Matthew Patten*, 21.

29. Ibid., 22.

30. Ibid.

31. Rogers, *Journals of Major Rogers*, 41.

32. Baldwin, *The Revolutionary Journal of Col. Jeduthan Baldwin, 1775–1778*, 6. Notwithstanding the title, Baldwin's journal also recorded his service in the French and Indian War.

33. Ibid., 3–5.

34. Ibid.

35. Ibid., 8.

36. There were at least two officers named Putnam who occasionally accompanied Rogers—Ensign Timothy Putnam and Captain Israel Putnam. Their reports to General William Johnson are in *D.H.S.N.Y.*, Vol. 4, 264, 266.

37. Baldwin, *Revolutionary Journal*, 10.

38. Ibid.

39. Ibid., 11.

40. Ibid., 12.

41. Ibid., 12, 14.

42. Ibid., 16.

43. Ibid., 17.

44. Ibid., introduction, xviii.

5. Rogers Rangers:
An Independent Company of Rangers

1. Cuneo, *Robert Rogers*, 32.

2. Rogers, *Journals of Major Rogers*, 44.

3. Ibid.

4. Cuneo, *Robert Rogers*, 33.

5. Rogers, *Journals*, 44.

6. Ibid., 44–45.

7. Ibid.

8. Ibid.

9. Baldwin, *Revolutionary Journal*, 16.

10. The quoted material appears in Lucier, *French and Indian War Notices*, Vol. 2, pp. 13, 25, 30, 103–105.

11. Rogers, *Journals*, 45.

12. Ibid. 46.

13. Ibid.

14. Cuneo, *Robert Rogers*, 36.

15. Rogers, *Journals*, 46. See also Cuneo, *Robert Rogers*, note 1 on page 287, for a discussion of a possible route the rangers might have followed over the mountains from Lake George to Lake Champlain; see also Ross, *War on the Run*, 116.

16. Rogers, *Journals*, 47.

17. Ibid.

18. Ibid.

19. Ibid.

20. Ibid., 47, quotes Rogers's report from *D.H.S.N.Y.*, Vol. XI, 286.

21. Cuneo, *Robert Rogers*, 38.

22. Bougainville, *Adventures in the Wilderness: The American Journals of Louis Antoine de Bougainville, 1756–1760*, 46.

23. Ibid., 46–47.

24. Ibid.

25. Anderson, *Crucible of War*, 141.

26. Rogers, *Journals*, 47.

27. Ibid.

28. Hadley, *Dunbarton*, 18.

29. Flexner, *Washington: The Indispensable Man*, 27–29.

30. Freeman, *George Washington*, Harwell, ed., 97–99.

31. Parkman, *Montcalm and Wolfe*, 201.

32. Anderson, *Crucible of War*, 140.

33. Anderson, *Crucible of War*, 140, 145; Parkman, *Montcalm and Wolfe*, 192–193.

34. Anderson, *Crucible of War*, 146.

35. Chard Powers Smith, *The Housatonic*, 113–114.

36. Ibid., 136.

37. Rogers, *Journals of Major Rogers*, 49.

38. Ibid.

39. Ibid., 49, 53.

40. Bougainville, *Adventures in the Wilderness*, 44–47.

41. Anderson, *Crucible of War*, 153–155.

42. Parkman, *Montcalm and Wolfe*, 208.

43. Ibid., 196.

44. Cuneo, *Robert Rogers*, 44.

45. Rogers, *Journals*, 55–56.

46. Lord Loudon to Duke of Cumberland, quoted in Pargellis, ed., *Military Affairs in North America, 1748–1763*, 224.

47. Rogers, *Journals*, 54.

48. Ibid., 56.

6. First Battle on Snowshoes: *To Play at Bowls*

1. Maney, *The Family of General John Stark*, 35.
2. Patten, *Diary*, 32.
3. Rogers, *Journals of Major Rogers*, Gary Zaboly annotation, 82–83.
4. Lucier, *French and Indian War Notices*, Vol. 2, 199, Rogers's report published in a Boston newspaper on February 14, 1757.
5. Ibid., 200.
6. Rogers, *Journals*, 57.
7. Lucier, *French and Indian War Notices*, Vol. 2, p. 200.
8. Ibid.
9. O'Callaghan, *D.R.C.H.S.N.Y.*, Vol. X, Paris Documents, 569–570.
10. Rogers, *Journals*, 58–59.
11. Lucier, *French and Indian War Notices*, Vol. 2, p. 200.
12. Bougainville, *Adventures in the Wilderness*, 81.
13. Roby, *Reminiscences of the French War*, note 21, p. 135.
14. O'Callaghan, *D.R.C.H.S.N.Y.*, Vol. X, Paris Documents, 570.
15. Lucier, *French and Indian War Notices*, Vol. 2, p. 201.
16. Ibid., 201–202.
17. Roby, *Reminiscences of the French War*, note 21, p. 135.
18. Lucier, *French and Indian War Notices*, Vol. 2, pp. 201–202.
19. Ibid.
20. "A Narrative of Thomas Brown," in Bellico, *Chronicles of Lake George*, 49.
21. Ibid.
22. Ibid., 49–51.
23. Rogers, *Journals*, 59.
24. Ibid., 59–60.
25. O'Callaghan, *D.R.C.H.S.N.Y.*, Vol. X, Paris Documents, 570.
26. Parkman, *Montcalm and Wolfe*, 222.
27. Bougainville, *Adventures in the Wilderness*, 81.
28. See Rogers, *Journals*, 58, for a discussion by Timothy Todish of the options available to Robert Rogers and his rationale for making the choice he made.
29. Rogers, *Journals*, 62.
30. Ibid., 63.
31. Roby, *Reminiscences of the French War*, note 9, p. 231.

7. Fort William Henry: *Each Man for Himself*

1. Rogers, *Journals of Major Rogers*, 63.
2. Pargellis, *Lord Loudon in North America*, 302–303.
3. Rogers, *Journals*, 63–64.
4. Ibid., 64.
5. Anderson, *Crucible of War*, 181.
6. Rogers, *Journals*, 64.
7. Parkman, *Montcalm and Wolfe*, 223–224.
8. Ibid.
9. Ibid., 226.
10. Moore, *John Stark*, 79.
11. O'Callaghan, *D.R.C.H.S.N.Y.*, Vol. X, Paris Documents, 544.
12. Parkman, *Montcalm and Wolfe*, 225.
13. Anderson, *Crucible of War*, 179.
14. Rogers, *Journals*, 64–65.
15. Parkman, *Montcalm and Wolfe*, 234.
16. Moore, *John Stark*, 80–81.
17. Parkman, *Montcalm and Wolfe*, 247.
18. Ibid., 236.
19. Rogers, *Journals*, 68–69.
20. Louis Antoine Bougainville, quoted in Anderson, *Crucible of War*, 190.
21. Ibid.
22. Brown, *Colonel John Goffe*, 138.
23. Parkman, *Montcalm and Wolfe*, 241.
24. Ibid., 243.
25. Ibid., 247.
26. Ibid., 247–249.
27. Anonymous journal, quoted in Bellico, *Chronicles of Lake George*, 71.
28. Ibid.
29. Parkman, *Montcalm and Wolfe*, 250.
30. Ibid.
31. Anderson, *Crucible of War*, 195.
32. Anonymous journal, quoted in Bellico, *Chronicles of Lake George*, 72.
33. Brown, *Colonel John Goffe*, 141.
34. Parkman, *Montcalm and Wolfe*, 251.

35. Ibid., 252.

36. Anonymous journal, quoted in Bellico, *Chronicles of Lake George*, 73.

37. Quoted in Parkman, *Montcalm and Wolfe*, 252.

38. Colonel Samuel Angell, quoted in Bellico, *Chronicles of Lake George*, footnote page 74.

39. Brown, *Colonel John Goffe*, 146.

40. Moore, *John Stark*, 82.

41. Brown, *Colonel John Goffe*, 146–147.

42. Parkman, *Montcalm and Wolfe*, 255.

43. Anderson, *Crucible of War*, 230.

44. Ibid.

45. Brown, *Colonel John Goffe*, 148.

46. O'Callaghan, *D.R.C.H.S.N.Y.*, Vol. X, Paris Documents, 598.

47. Anonymous journal, quoted in Bellico, *Chronicles of Lake George*, 74.

48. Anderson, *Crucible of War*, 200–201.

49. Parkman, *Montcalm and Wolfe*, 234–235.

50. Rogers, *Journals*, 65, 70.

51. Franklin, *Autobiography*, 135.

8. The Misbehavior Scout: *A Set of Scoundrels*

1. Rogers, *Journals of Major Rogers*, 70.

2. Parkman, *Montcalm and Wolfe*, 302. Parkman quoted General James Wolfe, who called Howe, "the noblest Englishman that has appeared in my time, and the best soldier in the British army."

3. Ibid.

4. Roby, *Reminiscences of the French War*, 202.

5. Pargellis, *Lord Loudon in America*, 303.

6. Ibid., 303–304.

7. Cuneo, *Robert Rogers*, 62.

8. Loescher, *The History of Rogers Rangers*, Vol. 1, p. 192.

9. Ibid., 197.

10. Rogers, *Journals*, Gary Zaboly annotation, 82.

11. Cuneo, *Robert Rogers*, 62–62.

12. Ibid., 63–64.

13. Ibid., 64–65.

14. Rogers, *Journals*, 86.

15. Ibid., 87.

16. Moore, *John Stark*, 85.

17. Ibid.

18. Colonel Haviland, quoted in Cuneo, *Robert Rogers*, 71.

19. Ibid., 73–74.

20. Rogers, *Journals*, 89.

21. Ibid., 90.

22. Ibid., 91

23. Lucier, *French and Indian War Notices*, Vol. 3, p. 45. This passage appeared in a New York newspaper on March 27, 1757, citing a "Journal of a Scout of Capt. Robert Rogers, March 10, 1758."

24. O'Callaghan, *D.R.C.H.S.N.Y.*, Vol. X, Paris Documents, 838.

25. Rogers, *Journals*, 95–103. Gary S. Zaboly's annotation gives a thorough analysis of the "Rogers' Slide" story.

26. Ibid., 95, 104; see also Cuneo, *Robert Rogers*, 79. John Cuneo arrived at a slightly different, but equally appalling, number of casualties and survivors.

27. *Dictionary of Canadian Biography Online*, Vol. III, Marquis de Montcalm entry.

28. Bougainville, *Adventures in the Wilderness*, 201.

29. Ibid., 200.

9. Disaster at Ticonderoga: *They Fell Like Pigeons*

1. Parkman, *Montcalm and Wolfe*, 280.

2. Rogers, *Journals of Major Rogers*, 114–115.

3. Ibid., 117.

4. Cleaveland, *Journal of Rev. John Cleaveland*, in *Bulletin of the Fort Ticonderoga Museum* (*BFTM*), Vol. X, November 3, 1959, Number 3, p. 196.

5. Moneypenny, *Orderly Book*, in *BFTM*, Vol. XII, November 1969, Number 5, p. 356.

6. Ibid., 354.

7. Rogers, *Journals*, 118.

8. Bougainville, *Adventures in the Wilderness*, 221.

9. Cleaveland, *Journal*, in *BFTM*, Vol. X, November 3, 1959, Number 3, p. 196.

10. Bougainville, *Adventures in the Wilderness*, 222.

11. Ibid.

12. Ibid., 223.

13. Moneypenny, *Orderly Book*, in *BFTM*, Vol. XII, November 1969, Number 5, p. 438.

14. Cleaveland, *Journal*, in *BFTM*, Vol. X, November 3, 1959, Number 3, p. 197.

15. Parkman, *Montcalm and Wolfe*, 303.

16. Caleb Stark, *Memoir and Official Correspondence of Gen. John Stark*, 25.

17. Quoted in Wood, *Radicalism of the American Revolution*, 41–42.

18. Arnot, *Proceedings of the Army*, in *BFTM*, Vol. XVI, 1998, Number 1, p. 35.

19. Cleaveland, *Journal*, in *BFTM*, November 3, 1959, Number 3, p. 198.

20. Arnot, *Proceedings of the Army*, in *BFTM*, Vol. XVI, Number 1, p. 38.

21. Spicer, *Diary of Abel Spicer*, in Bellico, *Chronicles of Lake George*, 101.

22. Mante, *History of the Late War*, 147.

23. Bougainville, *Adventures in the Wilderness*, 229.

24. William Grant, *Copy of a Letter from North America*, in *BFTM*, Vol. XVI, 1998, Number 1, p. 56.

25. Rogers, *Journals*, 129.

26. Major General James Abercromby to Mr. James Abercromby, in *BFTM*, Vol. XVI, 1998, Number 1, pp. 74–75.

27. Caleb Stark, *Memoir and Official Correspondence*, 26.

28. Mante, *History of the Late War*, 147.

29. Spicer, *Diary of Abel Spicer*, in Bellico, *Chronicles of Lake George*, 101.

30. Major General James Abercromby to Mr. James Abercromby, in *BFTM*, Vol. XVI, 1998, Number 1, p. 74.

31. Ibid., 74–75.

32. Ibid.

33. Map of the terrain of Ticonderoga drawn by Captain Alexander Moneypenny in July 1758, in *BFTM*, Vol. XVI, 1998, Number 1, between pp. 54 & 55.

34. Bougainville, *Adventures in the Wilderness*, 229, 231–232.

35. Parkman, *Montcalm and Wolfe*, 310.

36. Bougainville, *Adventures in the Wilderness*, 232.

37. Rogers, *Journals*, 128.

38. Spicer, *Diary of Abel Spicer*, in Bellico, *Chronicles of Lake George*, 101.

39. Ibid., 102.

40. Arnot, *Proceedings of the Army*, in *BFTM*,

41. Captain James Murray to Mr. John Murray, in *BFTM*, Vol. XVI, 1998, Number 1, p. 48.

42. Letter in *The Scots Magazine*, footnote in Bellico, *Chronicles of Lake Champlain*, 93.

43. Louis Joseph de Montcalm, *Account of the Victory Won by the Royal Troops at Carillon on the 8th Day of July, 1758*, in Bellico, *Chronicles of Lake Champlain*, 93.

44. Bougainville, *Adventures in the Wilderness*, 232.

45. Montcalm, *Account of the Victory*, in Bellico, *Chronicles of Lake Champlain*, 93.

46. Bougainville, *Adventures in the Wilderness*, 235.

47. Ibid., 234.

48. Spicer, *Diary of Abel Spicer*, in Bellico, *Chronicles of Lake George*, 102–103.

49. Bellico, *Chronicles of Lake Champlain*, footnote, p. 94.

50. Parkman, *Montcalm and Wolfe*, Appendix G, p. 474.

51. Cleaveland, *Journal*, in *BFTM*, Vol. X, 1959, Number 3, 198–199.

52. Spicer, *Diary of Abel Spicer*, in Bellico, *Chronicles of Lake George*, 103.

53. Captain Hugh Arnot to Your Lordship [Loudon], in *BFTM*, Vol. XVI, 1998, Number 1, p. 28.

54. Major General James Abercromby to Mr. James Abercromby, in *BFTM*, Vol. XVI, 1998, Number 1, p. 76.

55. "Abercrombie the Engineer" letter forwarded to Lord Bute, in *BFTM*, Vol. XVI, 1998, Number 1, p. 69. "The Engineer" was the same Captain James Abercrombie who wrote the "play at bowls" letter to Robert Rogers in February 1757 and who disapproved of John Stark's performance on their one scout together.

56. Nicholas Westbrook annotations in *BFTM*, Vol. XVI, 1998, Number 1, pp. 63, 68, 91. Nicholas Westbrook was the executive director of Fort Ticonderoga from 1989 to 2009.

57. Cleaveland, *Journal*, in *BFTM*, Vol. X, 1959, Number 3, p. 200.

58. Spicer, *Diary of Abel Spicer*, in Bellico, *Chronicles of Lake George*, 103.

10. The Tide Turns:
I Rejoiced That I Was an Englishman

1. Maney, *The Family of General John Stark*, 32; and Hammond, ed., *Probate Records*, 276.

2. Hammond, ed., *Probate Records*, 276.

3. Moore, *John Stark*, 100.

4. Maney, *The Family of General John Stark*, 54–55.

5. Ibid.

6. Patten, *Diary of Matthew Patten*, 54–55.

7. Hammond, ed., *Probate Records*, 277.

8. Brown, *Colonel John Goffe*, 156–157. John Goffe's biographer, William Howard Brown, interpreted Patten's diary entry (which read, "writ a letter to Col. John Goffe by Capt. John Stark") to mean that John Stark carried Patten's letter to Col. Goffe. Given John Stark's recent marriage, his father's death, and the absence of his name from Rogers's *Journals* for the rest of 1758, Brown's interpretation seems in error. More likely, Patten had written a letter *on behalf* of John Stark.

9. Spicer, *Diary of Abel Spicer*, in Bellico, *Chronicles of Lake George*, 103–105.

10. Ibid.

11. Ibid.

12. Ibid., 109.

13. Parkman, *Montcalm and Wolfe*, 320–321.

14. Cleaveland, *Journal of Rev. John Cleaveland*, in *Bulletin of the Fort Ticonderoga Museum* (*BFTM*), Vol. X, 1959, Number 3, p. 210.

15. Bougainville, *Adventures in the Wilderness*, 262–263.

16. Adams, *Diary and Autobiography*, quoted in McCullough, *John Adams*, 43.

17. Cleaveland, *Journal*, in *BFTM*, Vol. X, 1959, Number 3, p. 229.

18. Spicer, *Diary of Abel Spicer*, in Bellico, *Chronicles of Lake George*, 111.

19. Ibid., 115, 117.

20. Rogers, *Journals of Major Rogers*, 150.

21. Ibid., 153, Colonel Haldiman's Orders to Rogers, March 3, 1759.

22. Freeman, *George Washington*, Richard Harwell, ed., 136–137.

23. Ibid.; Flexner, *Washington: The Indispensable Man*, 35.

24. O'Callaghan, *D.R.C.H.S.N.Y.*, Vol. VII, London Documents, 355.

25. Maney, *The Family of General John Stark*, 34–39, 63–65.

26. Patten, *Diary*, 58.

27. Ibid., 58, 61.

28. Ibid., 51, 61.

29. Rogers, *Journals*, 158.

30. Maney, *The Family of General John Stark*, 60.

31. Rogers, *Journals*, 155.

32. Ibid., 154–155.

33. Ibid.

34. Ibid., 156.

35. Ibid., 156–157.

36. Ibid., 158.

37. General Thomas Gage to Amherst and Haldiman, quoted in Cuneo, *Robert Rogers*, 92.

38. Ibid.

39. Ibid., 95–96.

40. Rogers, *Journals*, 159.

41. Ibid., 163, illustration and annotation by Gary Zaboly.

42. Bellico, *Chronicles of Lake George*, annotation 121–125.

43. Commissary Wilson's Orderly Book, quoted in Rogers, *Journals*, 164.

44. Lemuel Wood, *A Journal of the Canada Expedition*, in Bellico, *Chronicles of Lake George*, 130.

45. Ibid., 131.

46. Ibid., 132, 134.

47. Rogers, *Journals*, 164, 166; Cuneo, *Robert Rogers*, 97–98.

48. Lemuel Wood, *A Journal*, in Bellico, *Chronicles of Lake George*, 134–135.

49. Parkman, *Montcalm and Wolfe*, 314.

50. Amherst, *Journal of Jeffrey Amherst*, in Bellico, *Chronicles of Lake Champlain*, 119–120.

51. Rogers, *Journals*, 167.

52. Ibid., 168.

53. Ibid.

54. Amherst, *Journal*, in Bellico, *Chronicles of Lake Champlain*, 121–122.

55. Lemuel Wood, *A Journal*, in Bellico, *Chronicles of Lake George*, 136–137.

56. Quoted in Parkman, *Montcalm and Wolfe*, 344.

57. Ibid., 345.

58. Lemuel Wood, *A Journal*, in Bellico, *Chronicles of Lake George*, 137, 140.

59. Amherst, *Journal*, in Bellico, *Chronicles of Lake Champlain*, 123.

60. Lemuel Wood, *A Journal*, in Bellico, *Chronicles of Lake George*, 137, 140.

61. Parkman, *Montcalm and Wolfe*, 379; Amherst, *Journal*, in Bellico, *Chronicles of Lake Champlain*, 126, 131.

62. Rogers, *Journals*, 169–170.

63. Amherst, *Journal*, in Bellico, *Chronicles of Lake Champlain*, 131.

64. Webster, *Robert Webster's Journal*, in *BFTM*, Vol. II, July 1931, no. 4, p. 146.

65. Ibid., 146–147.

66. Ibid., 148.

67. Ibid.

68. Ibid.

69. Ibid., 141.

70. See Gary Zaboly annotation concerning "Suagothel" in Rogers, *Journals*, 184.

71. Ibid., 171.

72. Webster, *Robert Webster's Journal*, in *BFTM*, Vol. II, July 1931, no. 4, p. 145.

73. Anderson, *Crucible of War*, notes on 788–789.

74. Amherst, *Journal*, in Bellico, *Chronicles of Lake Champlain*, 138.

75. Patten, *Diary*, 72.

76. Caleb Stark, *Memoir and Official Correspondence of Gen. John Stark*, 27.

77. Original Receipts in the John Stark Papers at the New Hampshire Historical Society, Concord, New Hampshire.

78. Patten, *Diary*, 202.

11. Domestic Interlude: *Capt. Starks Mill*

1. Maney, *The Family of General John Stark*, 73–74.

2. McCullough, *John Adams*, 53.

3. Hadley, *Dunbarton*, 121.

4. Gipson, *Coming of the Revolution*, 121.

5. Diary of Judge Samuel Sewall, quoted in Pike, *Tall Trees, Tough Men*, 40.

6. Ibid., 40, 44–45.

7. Maney, *The Family of General John Stark*, 45.

8. Caleb Stark, *Memoir and Official Correspondence of Gen. John Stark*, 345. Caleb Stark, Jr., wrote of his father's childhood: "The good Captain Page entertaining a strong affection for the child who had been born under his roof, and had received his Christian name, was desirous of retaining and adopting him. To this proposition his father made no objection, and he remained under the indulgent care of his maternal grandfather until the 16th of June, 1775."

9. Moore, *John Stark*, 119.

10. Patten, *Diary of Matthew Patten*, 94.

11. Russell, *Long Deep Furrow*, 94.

12. Ibid., 89.

13. Patten, *Diary*, 102, 127.

14. Ibid., 95–96.

15. Ibid., 121, 129.

16. Gipson, *Coming of the Revolution*, 13–14.

17. Ibid., 15–17.

18. Ibid., 22–24.

19. Hulton, *Letters of a Loyalist Lady*, VIII.

20. Gipson, *Coming of the Revolution*, 55, 59.

21. Moore, *John Stark*, 118.

22. Patten, *Diary*, xiv, 139.

23. Pike, *Tall Trees, Tough Men*, 175–176. There are numerous videos online showing sawmills in operation that were patterned after eighteenth-century mills, including the sound effects.

24. Patten, *Diary*, 141.

25. Ibid., 152, 182.

26. Ibid., 161.

12. Rebellion Begins: *That Nest of Locusts*

1. Shy, *Toward Lexington*, 111–112, 125.

2. Gipson, *Coming of the Revolution*, 70.

3. Ibid., 72–73.

4. McCullough, *John Adams*, 59.

5. Gipson, *Coming of the Revolution*, 82.

6. Quoted in McCullough, *John Adams*, 60.

7. Ibid., 61–62.

8. Washington, *Writings*, 116–117.

9. Franklin, *Autobiography*, 256.

10. Gipson, *Coming of the Revolution*, 90–91.

11. Ibid., 92.

12. Potter, *History of Manchester*, 385.

13. Maier, *From Resistance to Revolution*, 60, 68.

14. Gipson, *Coming of the Revolution*, 100.

15. Dickinson, *Letters from a Farmer*, 38.

16. Maney, *The Family of General John Stark*, 61.

17. Ibid., 27.

18. Moore, *John Stark*, 121.

19. Gipson, *Coming of the Revolution*, 173–175, 180.

20. Ibid., 181.

21. Ibid., 190–192.

22. Washington, *Writings*, 130.

23. Gipson, *Coming of the Revolution*, 193.

24. McCullough, *John Adams*, 65–66.

25. Gipson, *Coming of the Revolution*, 203.

26. Maney, *The Family of General John Stark*, 61.

27. Patten, *Diary of Matthew Patten*, 204, 208, 221.

28. Maney, *The Family of General John Stark*, 45.

29. Patten, *Diary*, 227, 250, 296.

30. Ibid., 247.

31. McCullough, *John Adams*, 67–68.

32. Hulton, *Letters of a Loyalist Lady*, 23–24.

33. Brown, *Colonel John Goffe*, 238–239.

34. Ibid., 240.

35. Patten, *Diary*, 281.

36. Major General Haldiman to Earl of Dartmouth, quoted in Gipson, *Coming of the Revolution*, 218, note 10.

37. Ibid., 220.

38. Commager and Morris, *Spirit of 'Seventy-Six*, 1.

39. "A Retrospect of the Boston Tea Party," quoted in Commager and Morris, *Spirit of 'Seventy-Six*, 5.

40. Ibid., 4, 6.

41. Hulton, *Letters of a Loyalist Lady*, 69–71.

42. Adams, *Diary and Autobiography*, Vol. II, 86.

43. Gipson, *Coming of the Revolution*, 224.

44. "Debates in Parliament," in Commager and Morris, *Spirit of 'Seventy-Six*, 11–12.

45. Ibid., 15.

46. Ibid., 10.

47. George Washington to George William Fairfax, in Washington, *Writings*, 150.

48. Lamb, *A British Soldier's Story*, 15.

49. Patten, *Diary*, 297, 320, 322.

50. Brown, *Colonel John Goffe*, 243–245.

51. Patten, *Diary*, 325.

52. Brown, *Colonel John Goffe*, 246.

53. Patten, *Diary*, 325.

54. Whittemore, *A General of the Revolution*, 13.

55. "Diary of a British Officer," in Commager and Morris, *Spirit of 'Seventy-Six*, 36.

56. Whittemore, *A General of the Revolution*, 16.

57. Commager and Morris, *Spirit of 'Seventy-Six*, 53–58.

58. Ibid., 59.

59. Ibid., 60.

60. Ketchum, ed., *American Heritage Book of the Revolution*, 99.

61. Ibid., 99–100.

PART II: The American Revolution

13. First Actions:
Raw, Undisciplined, Cowardly Men

1. Ketchum, *Decisive Day*, 14–15, 18.

2. Force, *American Archives*, 4th series, Vol. I, 1682–1683.

3. Major Pitcairn to Earl of Sandwich, March 4, 1775, in Commager and Morris, *Spirit of 'Seventy-Six*, 62.

4. Ketchum, ed., *American Heritage Book of the Revolution*, 100–101.

5. Hugh, Earl Percy to Governor Gage, April 20, 1775, in Commager and Morris, *Spirit of 'Seventy-Six*, 88.

6. Hulton, *Letters of a Loyalist Lady*, 77.

7. Diary of Lieutenant Frederick MacKenzie, entry for April 19, 1775, in Commager and Morris, *Spirit of 'Seventy-Six*, 87.

8. "Official Patriot Account, April 26, 1775," in Brown, *Major Problems*. Dr. Samuel A. Forman's biography, *Dr. Joseph Warren*, 271–271, reported that Benjamin Church, Eldridge Gerry and Thomas Cushing prepared the "official" account of the battle, and Dr. Warren signed it before sending it to Great Britain.

9. Committee of Safety to Massachusetts

Towns, April 28, 1775, in Commager and Morris, *Spirit of 'Seventy-Six*, 92.

10. Ibid., diary of Dr. Ezra Stiles, entry for April 19, 1775, 10 o'clock at night.

11. Storrs, *Diary of Experience Storrs*, 84.

12. Commager and Morris, *Spirit of 'Seventy-Six*, 69.

13. Ibid., 76, John Adams to William Barrell, April 19, 1775.

14. Patten, *Diary of Matthew Patten*, 342.

15. Benjamin Stickney, quoted in Moore, *John Stark*, 130.

16. Maney, *The Family of General John Stark*, 61.

17. Moore, *John Stark*, 130–131.

18. Patten, *Diary*, 342.

19. Gage to Earl of Dartmouth, April 22, 1775, in Rhodehamel, ed., *Writings from the War*, 20.

20. Patten, *Diary*, 343.

21. Hulton, *Letters of a Loyalist Lady*, 78–79.

22. Gage to Lord North, in Ketchum, *Decisive Day*, 25.

23. Ibid., 1–7.

24. Moore, *John Stark*, 134.

25. Caleb Stark, *Memoir and Official Correspondence of Gen. John Stark*, 109–110.

26. Potter, *Military History of New Hampshire*, 264.

27. Ibid.

28. Bosson, *The Battle of Chelsea*, 24, 36.

29. Ibid., 25, 36.

30. Ibid., 25, 34.

31. Ibid., 20.

32. Ibid., 26–27, 45.

33. Ibid., 28. See also Philbrick, *Bunker Hill*, 186.

34. Caleb Stark, *Memoir and Official Correspondence*, 110–111.

35. Moore, *John Stark*, 141.

36. Potter, *Military History of New Hampshire*, 264.

37. Moore, *John Stark*, 142.

38. Potter, *Military History of New Hampshire*, 264.

39. Ibid., 265–266.

40. Ketchum, *Decisive Day*, 56, 66.

41. Ibid., 54, 75, 78, 98.

42. Flexner, *Washington: The Indispensable Man*, 58–59, 61.

14. Bunker Hill: *Good God How the Balls Flew*

1. Lord George Germaine to Lord Suffolk, June 16 or 17, 1775, in Commager and Morris, *Spirit of 'Seventy-Six*, 119.

2. Ibid., 119–120.

3. Ibid., 96–97, General Gage's Proclamation.

4. Ketchum, *Decisive Day*, 72.

5. Commager and Morris, *Spirit of 'Seventy-Six*, 116, 121.

6. Ibid., 135, letter from a British Officer, July 5, 1775.

7. Ketchum, *Decisive Day*, 75–79.

8. Ibid., 81–82.

9. Peter Brown to his mother, June 28, 1775, in Commager and Morris, *Spirit of 'Seventy-Six*, 123.

10. Ibid., 122–123, diary of Amos Farnsworth, entry for June 16, 1775.

11. Ibid., 130, Lord Rawdon to his uncle, June 20, 1775.

12. Ibid., 123, Peter Brown to his mother, June 28, 1775.

13. Ibid.

14. John Stark to New Hampshire Provincial Congress, June 19, 1775, in Caleb Stark, *Memoir and Official Correspondence of Gen. John Stark*, 112.

15. Brown, *Colonel John Goffe*, 249–251.

16. Caleb Stark, *Memoir and Official Correspondence*, 345–346. This tale of the runaway boy joining his soldier father on the eve of the first great battle of the Revolution is probably romanticized. Stark biographer Howard Parker Moore pointed out that both Caleb and his younger brother Archibald had been on the payroll of Captain John Moore's militia company since April of 1775. Caleb did fight at Bunker Hill and went on to serve honorably for eight more years.

17. Ibid.

18. Moore, *John Stark*, 154.

19. Ketchum, *Decisive Day*, 138.

20. Ibid., 118.

21. Ibid., 142.

22. Fisk, *The American Revolution*, 138–139.

23. "An Account of the Battle of Bunker Hill by Major General Henry Dearborn," published in Heath, *Memoirs of Major-General Heath*, 376–377.

24. Ibid.

25. Ibid.

26. Ketchum, *Decisive Day*, 136.

27. Moore, *John Stark*, 156.

28. Samuel Webb to his brother, in Rhodehamel, ed., *The American Revolution*, 37.

29. Ibid.

30. "An Account of the Battle of Bunker Hill by Major General Henry Dearborn," published in Heath, *Memoirs of Major-General Heath*, 377.

31. Ibid., 377–378.

32. Ibid.

33. Ibid.

34. Lockhart, *Whites of Their Eyes*, 271–272.

35. Potter, *Military History of New Hampshire*, 271.

36. Ketchum, *Decisive Day*, 154–155.

37. Ibid., 151–152.

38. Diary of Amos Farnsworth, entry for June, 17, 1775, in Commager and Morris, *Spirit of 'Seventy-Six*, 122.

39. Ibid., 128, part of a letter from Boston, June 23, 1775.

40. "An Account of the Battle of Bunker Hill by Major General Henry Dearborn," published in Heath, *Memoirs of Major-General Heath*, 379, 382.

41. Ketchum, *Decisive Day*, 158–159.

42. Ibid., 133–134, Burgoyne to Lord Stanley, June 25, 1775.

43. "An Account of the Battle of Bunker Hill by Major General Henry Dearborn," published in Heath, *Memoirs of Major-General Heath*, 379, 382.

44. Ibid., 130, Lord Rawdon to his uncle, June 20, 1775.

45. Ketchum, *Decisive Day*, 124.

46. McCullough, *John Adams*, 22.

47. Ketchum, *Decisive Day*, 161–162.

48. Ibid., 164–165.

49. Ibid., 172–173.

50. Ibid., 177.

51. Samuel Webb to his brother, in Rhodehamel, ed., *The American Revolution*, 38.

52. Moore, *John Stark*, 172.

53. Burgoyne quoted in Ketchum, *Decisive Day*, 181.

54. Ibid., 183, 193.

55. "An Account of the Battle of Bunker Hill by Major General Henry Dearborn," published in Heath, *Memoirs of Major-General Heath*, 386.

56. Affidavits of Reverend David Chapman and Reverend John Bullard in Heath, *Memoirs of Major-General Heath*, 395. William Heath went to some pains in his *Memoirs* to gather narratives that would discredit General Israel Putnam's performance at the Battle of Bunker Hill, which suggests that Heath had some motive beyond historical accuracy.

57. Lord Rawdon to his uncle, June 20, 1775, in Commager and Morris, *Spirit of 'Seventy-Six*, 130–131.

58. Ibid., 134, Burgoyne to Lord Stanley, June 25, 1775.

59. Ibid., Gage to Lord Barrington, Secretary of State for War, June 26, 1775.

60. Ibid., 131–132, William Howe, letter to an anonymous recipient, June 22 and 24, 1775.

61. Ibid., 135–136, anonymous letter from a British Officer, July 5, 1775.

62. Freeman, *George Washington*, Richard Harwell, ed., 225.

15. Boston Falls: *New Lords New Laws*

1. Freeman, *George Washington*, Richard Harwell, ed., 228–229.

2. Quoted in McCullough, *1776*, 42–43.

3. Washington to Lund Washington, August 20, 1775, in Rhodehamel, ed., *George Washington: Writings*, 184.

4. Ibid., 175–176.

5. John Adams to Abigail Adams in Rhodehamel, ed., *The American Revolution*, 32–33.

6. John Stark to New Hampshire Provincial Congress, June 19, 1775, in Force, ed., *American Archives*, 4th Series, Vol. 2, p. 1029.

7. Ibid., 1063, 1069.

8. Ibid.

9. Whittemore, *A General of the Revolution*, 19–20.

10. McCullough, *1776*, 30–31.

11. Reverend William Emerson to his wife, July 17, 1775, in Commager and Morris, *Spirit of 'Seventy-Six*, 153.

12. Ibid., 162, Washington to President of Congress, September, 21, 1775.

13. Ibid., 184, Congress to General Schuyler, June 27, 1775.

14. Ketchum, ed., *American Heritage Book of the Revolution*, 122–123.

15. Commager and Morris, *Spirit of 'Seventy-Six*, 192.

16. Ibid., 200, journal of Dr. Isaac Senter, entry for November 1, 1775.

17. Ibid., 165.

18. Ibid., 166–167, letter from an English officer, August 18, 1775.

19. Burrows, *Forgotten Patriots*, 37.

20. Washington to Gage, August 11, 1775, Rhodehamel, ed., *George Washington: Writings*, 181.

21. Ibid., 182–183.

22. Burrows, *Forgotten Patriots*, 38–41.

23. Commager and Morris, *Spirit of 'Seventy-Six*, 170.

24. Ibid., 171.

25. Ibid., 172, H. Mowat, Captain, to the People of Falmouth, October 16, 1775.

26. Ibid., 172–173, Report of the Selectmen of Falmouth.

27. Ibid., 173, Washington to President of Congress.

28. Adams, *Diary and Autobiography*, Vol. II, 177.

29. Ibid., 178.

30. Cuneo, *Robert Rogers*, 257–258.

31. Ibid., 258–259.

32. Sullivan to Washington, December 17, 1775, Force, ed., *American Archives*, 4th Series, Vol. 4, p. 300.

33. Caleb Stark, quoted in Moore, *John Stark*, 215.

34. Ibid., 216–217.

35. Ibid.

36. Isaacson, *Benjamin Franklin*, 280–281.

37. Moore, *John Stark*, 219.

38. Ketchum, ed., *American Heritage Book of the Revolution*, 125.

39. Ibid.

40. Annotation in Commager and Morris, *Spirit of 'Seventy-Six*, 272.

41. Paine, *Common Sense*, 13.

42. Ibid., 18.

43. Ibid., 46.

44. McCullough, *John Adams*, 373–374.

45. Maney, *The Family of General John Stark*, 61.

46. Commager and Morris, *Spirit of 'Seventy-Six*, 157–158.

47. Ibid., 175–176.

48. Fischer, *Washington's Crossing*, 25.

49. Israel Trask, quoted in Fischer, *Washington's Crossing*, 25.

50. Colonel Charles Stuart to Lord Bute, April 28, 1776, in Commager and Morris, *Spirit of 'Seventy-Six*, 181–182.

51. Pension Application of Samuel Larrabee, in Dann, ed., *The Revolution Remembered*, 10.

52. Colonel Charles Stuart to Lord Bute, April 28, 1776, in Commager and Morris, *Spirit of 'Seventy-Six*, 182.

53. Ibid., 183, Journal of Timothy Newell, a Selectmen of Boston, March 17, 1776.

54. Pension Application of Samuel Larrabee, in Dann, ed., *The Revolution Remembered*, 10.

55. McCullough, *John Adams*, 104.

56. Wilkinson, *Memoirs of My Times*, 32.

57. Ibid., 33.

16. Retreat from Canada: *Not an Army, but a Mob*

1. Caleb Stark, *Memoir and Official Correspondence of Gen. John Stark*, 114.

2. Freeman, *George Washington*, Richard Harwell, ed., 254, 262.

3. Caleb Stark, *Memoir and Official Correspondence*, 114.

4. Hancock to Canadians, January 24, 1776, in Force, ed., *American Archives*, 4th Series, Vol. 4, p. 1653.

5. Hancock to Washington, in Freeman, *George Washington*, Richard Harwell, ed., 267.

6. Ketchum, ed., *American Heritage Book of the Revolution*, 142.

7. Benjamin Franklin, quoted in Isaacson, *Benjamin Franklin*, 306.

8. Ketchum, ed., *American Heritage Book of the Revolution*, 142.

9. Freeman, *George Washington*, Richard Harwell, ed., 268.

10. Patten, *Diary of Matthew Patten*, 360.

11. Caleb Stark, *Memoir and Official Correspondence*, 34.

12. Whittemore, *A General of the Revolution*, 26.

13. Fenn, *Pox Americana*, 69–70.

14. Beebe, *Journal of a Physician*, 325–326.

15. Ibid., 327.

16. Wasmus, *Eyewitness Account of the American Revolution*, 18.

17. Sullivan to Hancock, June 1, 1776, in Commager and Morris, *Spirit of 'Seventy-Six*, 214–215.

18. Caleb Stark, *Memoir and Official Correspondence*, 34.

19. Commager and Morris, *Spirit of 'Seventy-Six*, 216–217.

20. Ibid., 210, Benedict Arnold to Hannah Arnold, January 6, 1776.

21. Jones, *Conquest of Canada*, 81–82.

22. Charles Cushing to his brother, July 8, 1776, in Force, ed., *American Archives*, 5th Series, Vol. 1, p. 130.

23. Stark to Congress, September 23, 1776, in Moore, *John Stark*, 237.

24. Jones, *Conquest of Canada*, 88.

25. Ibid., 89.

26. Ibid., 88.

27. Charles Cushing to his brother, July 8, 1776, in Force, ed., *American Archives*, 5th Series, Vol. 1, p. 128.

28. Moore, *John Stark*, 232.

29. Beebe, *Journal*, 336.

30. Fenn, *Pox Americana*, 18.

31. Jones, *Conquest of Canada*, 93.

32. Patten, *Diary*, 361.

33. Caleb Stark, *Memoir and Official Correspondence*, 35.

34. Beebe, *Journal*, 338.

35. Baldwin, *Revolutionary Journal*, 58.

36. Beebe, *Journal*, 338–339.

37. Ibid.

38. Baldwin, *Revolutionary Journal*, 60.

39. John Trumbull to his father, July 12, 1776, in Commager and Morris, *Spirit of 'Seventy-Six*, 221.

40. Whittemore, *A General of the Revolution*, 30–31.

41. Sullivan to Schuyler, July 6, 1776, in Force, ed., *American Archives*, 5th Series, Vol. 1, p. 235.

42. Ibid., Schuyler to Sullivan, July 7, 1776.

43. Moore, *John Stark*, 234.

44. Beebe, *Journal*, 340.

45. Trumbull, *John Trumbull at Ticonderoga*, in *Bulletin of the Fort Ticonderoga Museum* (*BFTM*), Vol. III, January 1933, Number 1, p. 5.

46. Ibid.

47. Generals' resolution of July 6, 1776, in Force, ed., *American Archives*, 5th series, Vol. 1, p. 233. Engineer Jeduthan Baldwin noted in his *Journal* that he was ordered to examine Mt. Independence the next day, July 7, 1776; he reported no prior familiarity with the site.

48. In *Journal of a Physician*, 341, Dr. Beebe reported that the generals made their decision with "no consultation."

49. "Remonstrance" in Force, ed., *American Archives*, 5th Series, Vol. 1, p. 233.

50. Wells, *Journal of Bayze Wells*, in Bellico, *Chronicles of Lake Champlain*, note p. 206.

51. Schuyler to his officers, July 9, 1776, in Force, ed., *American Archives*, 5th series, Vol. 1, p. 234.

52. Ibid., 232, Schuyler to Washington, July 12, 1776.

53. Ibid., 176, Hastings to Gates, July 10, 1776.

54. Ibid., 444, Washington to Congress, July 19, 1776.

55. Ibid.

17. Independence: *Now We Are a People*

1. Baldwin, *Revolutionary Journal*, 58–60.

2. Trumbull, *John Trumbull at Ticonderoga*, in *Bulletin of the Fort Ticonderoga Museum* (*BFTM*), Vol. III, January 1933, Number 1, pp. 5–6.

3. Moore, *John Stark*, 220.

4. Caleb Stark, *Memoir and Official Correspondence of Gen. John Stark*, 349.

5. Beebe, *Journal of a Physician*, 344.

6. Colonel Anthony Wayne to a fellow officer, quoted in Bellico, *Chronicles of Lake Champlain*, 207.

7. Trumbull, *John Trumbull at Ticonderoga*, in *BFTM*, Vol. III, January 1933, Number 1, p. 6.

8. Roby, *Reminiscences of the French War*, Appendix, 184.

9. Force, ed., *American Archives*, 5th Series, Vol. 1, p. 630.

10. Beebe, *Journal*, 344.

11. Moore, *John Stark*, 236.

12. Ibid., 238.

13. Wayne's Orderly Book, in *BFTM*, Vol. XI, September 1963, Number 2, pp. 99, 101.

14. Ibid., 143.

15. Ibid., 104.

16. Patten, *Diary of Matthew Patten*, 362.

17. Lamb, *A British Soldier's Story*, 28.

18. Ibid.

19. Nelson, *Benedict Arnold's Navy*, 23, 227.

20. Baldwin, *Revolutionary Journal*, 72.

21. Ibid., 62–63.

22. Ibid., 64–65.

23. Ibid., 73.

24. Quoted in Schecter, *Battle for New York*, 99.

25. Ketchum, ed., *American Heritage Book of the Revolution*, 179.

26. Ibid., 173.

27. Scheer & Rankin, eds., *Rebels & Redcoats*, 182–185.

28. Ibid., 186.

29. Commager and Morris, *Spirit of 'Seventy-Six*, 444.

30. Force, ed., *American Archives*, 5th Series, Vol. 1, pp. 1259–1260.

31. Ibid.

32. Tallmadge, *Memoir of Colonel Benjamin Tallmadge*, quoted in Commager and Morris, *Spirit of 'Seventy-Six*, 445.

33. Martin, *Narrative of a Revolutionary Soldier*, 26.

34. Scheer & Rankin, *Rebels & Redcoats*, 191.

35. Tallmadge, *Memoir*, quoted in Commager and Morris, *Spirit of 'Seventy-Six*, 446.

36. Scheer & Rankin, *Rebels & Redcoats*, 194.

37. Baldwin, *Revolutionary Journal*, 70–71, 78–79.

38. Trumbull, *John Trumbull at Ticonderoga*, in *BFTM*, Vol. III, January 1933, Number 1, pp. 7–8.

39. Ibid.

40. Ibid., 9.

41. Gates's Order of August 7, 1776, Force, ed., *American Archives*, 5th Series, Vol. 1, p. 826.

42. Ibid., 1002, Arnold to Gates.

43. Nelson, *Benedict Arnold's Navy*, 260.

44. Ibid.

45. Ibid., 261.

46. Wells, *Journal of Bayze Wells*, in Bellico, *Chronicles of Lake Champlain*, 209.

47. Nelson, *Benedict Arnold's Navy*, 257.

48. Ibid., 282.

49. Ibid.

50. Ibid., 296, 298.

51. Wells, *Journal*, in Bellico, *Chronicles of Lake Champlain*, 229.

52. Journal of Lt. James Hadden of the Royal Artillery, in Commager and Morris, *Spirit of 'Seventy-Six*, 224.

53. Marine Joseph Cushing, quoted in Bellico, *Chronicles of Lake Champlain*, note, p. 231.

54. Ibid., Wells, *Journal*.

55. Baldwin, *Revolutionary Journal*, 81.

56. Ibid., 82.

57. Beebe, *Journal*, 356.

58. Trumbull, *John Trumbull at Ticonderoga*, in *BFTM*, Vol. III, January 1933, Number 1, p. 12.

59. Benjamin Stickney, "Biographical Sketch of General John Stark," in *New Hampshire Patriot*, Number II, April 1810.

60. Captain John Lacey memoir, in Commager and Morris, *Spirit of 'Seventy-Six*, 225.

61. Beebe, *Journal*, 357.

62. Gates's General Orders, thanking troops, October 29, 1776, in Commager and Morris, *Spirit of 'Seventy-Six*, 225.

63. Beebe, *Journal*, 357.

64. Lamb, *A British Soldier's Story*, 29–30.

18. Retreats and Defeats:
   Times That Try Men's Souls

1. Beebe, *Journal of a Physician*, 357.

2. Ibid., 359.

3. Patten, *Diary of Matthew Patten*, 366.

4. Maney, *The Family of General John Stark*, 61.

5. Patten, *Diary*, 366.

6. Ketchum, ed., *American Heritage Book of the Revolution*, 199–200.

7. Excerpt from *The American Crisis*, in Commager & Morris, *Spirit of 'Seventy-Six*, 505.

8. Ibid., 449, Franklin to Lord Howe.

9. Ibid., 274, Benjamin Rush quoting John Adams.

10. Ibid., 451.

11. Ibid., 448, Journal of Sir George Collier, Commander of the *Rainbow*.

12. Ibid., 457, Greene to Washington, September, 5, 1776.

13. Schecter, *Battle for New York*, 204–205.

14. Ibid., 207–208.

15. Ibid., 210–214.

16. Hutson, *Nathan Hale Revisited*.

17. Ibid.

18. Cuneo, *Robert Rogers*, 267.

19. Hutson, *Nathan Hale Revisited*.

20. Ibid.

21. Schecter, *Battle for New York*, 213.

22. Ibid., 214.

23. Dwyer, *The Day Is Ours*, 132.

24. Ibid., 132, 138–139.

25. Ibid., 132, 138.

26. Wilkinson, quoted in Dwyer, *The Day Is Ours*, 139–140.

27. Fischer, *Washington's Crossing*, 129, 131.

28. Solomon Clift, quoted in Scheer & Rankin, *Rebels & Redcoats*, 231–233.

29. Ibid., 233, Washington to Captain Enoch Anderson.

30. Fischer, *Washington's Crossing*, 132.

31. Collins, ed., *Ravages at Princeton*, 4, 14–15.

32. Fischer, *Washington's Crossing*, 178–179.

33. General Howe's order, in Scheer & Rankin, *Rebels & Redcoats*, 236.

34. Charles Wilson Peale, quoted in Fischer, *Washington's Crossing*, 132–133.

35. Washington to Lund Washington, December 17, 1776, in Commager and Morris, *Spirit of 'Seventy-Six*, 504.

36. Ketchum, ed., *American Heritage Book of the Revolution*, 189.

37. Scheer & Rankin, *Rebels & Redcoats*, 236–237.

38. Ketchum, *Winter Soldiers*, 222.

39. Washington to Lund Washington, December 10, 1776, in *George Washington: Writings*, 260–261.

40. General Lee to Horatio Gates, December 13, 1776, in Commager & Morris, *Spirit of 'Seventy-Six*, 500.

41. Fischer, *Washington's Crossing*, 211.

19. Crossing the Delaware: *The Dauntless Stark*

1. Scheer & Rankin, *Rebels & Redcoats*, 238.

2. Ibid., 240.

3. Washington to Joseph Reed, December 23, 1776, in Commager and Morris, *Spirit of 'Seventy-Six*, 511.

4. Scheer & Rankin, *Rebels & Redcoats*, 240.

5. Fischer, *Washington's Crossing*, 203.

6. Benjamin Stickney, "Biographical Sketch of General John Stark," in *New Hampshire Patriot*, No. II, April 1810. Benjamin Franklin Stickney married John Stark's daughter Mary. The Maney genealogy of the Stark family, p. 89, reported that Stickney collected "many interesting particulars in the life of Gen. John Stark, which have since been used in the biographies published of him." This "particular" might be the figment of an old man's memory, but Stark could be astonishingly tactless, and the story might be true.

7. Ibid.

8. Dwyer, *The Day Is Ours*, 219.

9. Ibid., 220.

10. Fischer, *Washington's Crossing*, 204–205.

11. Anonymous aide to Washington, quoted in Scheer & Rankin, *Rebels & Redcoats*, 240.

12. James Wilkinson, quoted in Dwyer, *The Day Is Ours*, 231.

13. Ketchum, *Winter Soldiers*, 248.

14. Fischer, *Washington's Crossing*, 206.

15. Wilkinson, *Memoirs of My Own Times*, Vol. 1, 128.

16. Ibid.

17. Ibid.

18. Ketchum, *Winter Soldiers*, 253.

19. Memoirs of Elisha Bostwick, in Commager and Morris, *Spirit of 'Seventy-Six*, 512.

20. Anonymous aide to Washington, quoted in Scheer & Rankin, *Rebels & Redcoats*, 241.

21. Fischer, *Washington's Crossing*, 208–209.

22. Ibid., 234.

23. Dwyer, *The Day Is Ours*, 247.

24. Wilkinson, *Memoirs*, 129.

25. Dwyer, *The Day Is Ours*, 251.

26. Fischer, *Washington's Crossing*, 239.

27. Anonymous aide to Washington, in Scheer & Rankin, *Rebels & Redcoats*, 242.

28. Dwyer, *The Day Is Ours*, 253–255.

29. Fischer, *Washington's Crossing*, 223.

30. Wilkinson, *Memoirs*, 130.

31. Fischer, *Washington's Crossing*, 247.

32. Henry Knox to his wife, December 28, 1776, in Commager and Morris, *Spirit of 'Seventy-Six*, 512–513.

33. Wilkinson, *Memoirs*, 129–130.

34. Fischer, *Washington's Crossing*, 248.

35. Johannes Reuber, quoted in Dwyer, *The Day Is Ours*, 267.

36. Ibid., 260–261.

37. Wilkinson, *Memoirs*, 131.

38. Anonymous aide to Washington, in Scheer & Rankin, *Rebels & Redcoats*, 243.

39. Johannes Reuber, quoted in Dwyer, *The Day Is Ours*, 269.

40. Washington to John Hancock, *George Washington: Writings*, 263.

41. Fischer, *Washington's Crossing*, 256.

42. Ibid., 265.

43. Ibid., 265–266.

44. Ibid., 270.

45. Sergeant "R," in Commager and Morris, *Spirit of 'Seventy-Six*, 519–520.

46. Fischer, *Washington's Crossing*, 273–274.

47. Ibid., 272.

48. Dwyer, *The Day Is Ours*, 291.

49. Ibid.

50. Fischer, *Washington's Crossing*, 288–289.

51. Ibid., 293.

52. Washington to Robert Morris, January 1, 1777, in *George Washington: Writings*, 265.

53. Fischer, *Washington's Crossing*, 298–301.

54. Dwyer, *The Day Is Ours*, 323.

55. Fischer, *Washington's Crossing*, 302–303.

56. Ibid., 312.

57. Ibid., 313–315.

58. Washington to President of Congress, January 5, 1777, in Scheer & Rankin, *Rebels & Redcoats*, 247.

59. General Mercer, quoted in Dwyer, *The Day Is Ours*, 308.

60. "The American Liberty Song," in Royster, *A Revolutionary People at War*, 111.

61. Dwyer, *The Day Is Ours*, 330–331.

62. Ibid., 331–332.

63. Scheer & Rankin, *Rebels & Redcoats*, 248–249.

64. Dwyer, *The Day Is Ours*, 342, 344.

65. Ibid., 354.

66. Collins, ed., *Ravages at Princeton*, 37.

67. Dwyer, *The Day Is Ours*, 362.

68. Ibid., 365.

69. Washington's order, quoted in Fischer, *Washington's Crossing*, 379.

70. Ibid., 376–377.

20. The Road to Bennington:
Our Friend John Stark

1. Martha Bland to Fanny Randolph, in Scheer & Rankin, *Rebels & Redcoats*, 255.

2. Dwyer, *The Day Is Ours*, 292.

3. Martin, *Narrative of a Revolutionary Soldier*, 54–55.

4. James Martin, *Benedict Arnold*, 304–305.

5. Ibid., 306.

6. Washington to Arnold, in *George Washington: Writings*, 270.

7. Moore, *John Stark*, 252.

8. Twohig, ed., *Papers of George Washington 8*, pp. 503–504.

9. Bouton, ed., *Documents and Records, State of New Hampshire*, Vol. VIII, 518.

10. Caleb Stark, *Memoir and Official Correspondence of Gen. John Stark*, 42.

11. Potter, *Military History of New Hampshire*, note p. 336.

12. Freeman, *George Washington*, Richard Harwell, ed., 339.

13. Sullivan to John Hancock, quoted in Whittemore, *A General of the Revolution*, 53.

14. Freeman, *George Washington*, Richard Harwell, ed., 346.

15. Ibid., 345.

16. Scheer & Rankin, *Rebels & Redcoats*, 285.

17. Ibid.

18. Ibid., 286.

19. Wasmus, *Eyewitness Account of the American Revolution*, 50.

20. Ibid., 53, 57, 58.

21. Ibid., 58–59.

22. Ibid., 52, 55, 58.

23. Lamb, *A British Soldier's Story*, 35.

24. Scheer & Rankin, *Rebels & Redcoats*, 289.

25. Petersen, *Seth Warner*, 90–91.

26. Ibid., 14–18.

27. Ibid., 33, 45.

28. Ibid., 66–67.

29. Ibid., 69.

30. Ibid., 92.

31. Journal of Lt. William Digby of the Shropshire Regiment, entry for July 4, 1777, in Commager and Morris, *Spirit of 'Seventy-Six*, 553.

32. Lamb, *A British Soldier's Story*, 35.

33. Wasmus, *Eyewitness Account*, 59.

34. Journal of Lt. William Digby of the Shropshire Regiment, entry for July 5, 1777, in Commager and Morris, *Spirit of 'Seventy-Six*, 554.

35. Thacher, *An Army Surgeon*, 83–84.

36. Petersen, *Seth Warner*, 100–105.

37. Ibid.

38. Patrick Cogan to John Stark, July 17, 1777, in Moore, *John Stark*, 260–261.

39. Thacher, *An Army Surgeon*, 85–86.

40. Tuckerman, *General Philip Schuyler*, 187, 193.

41. Hall, *History of Vermont*, 256–258.

42. Foster and Streeter, *Stark's Independent Command*, 24.

43. John Langdon, quoted in Moore, *John Stark*, 262.

44. Ibid., 263.

45. Foster and Streeter, *Stark's Independent Command*, 26.

46. Ibid., 20–27.

47. Caleb Stark, *Memoir and Official Correspondence*, 47.

48. President Weare, quoted in Moore, *John Stark*, 265.

49. Foster and Streeter, *Stark's Independent Command*, 29.

50. Ibid., 29–31.

51. Moore, *John Stark*, 271–272.

52. Foster and Streeter, *Stark's Independent Command*, 32–33.

53. Moore, *John Stark*, 277.

54. Ibid., 278–279, Stark to New Hampshire Committee of Safety, August 7, 1777.

55. Ibid., 279, Benjamin Lincoln to Schuyler, August 7, 1777.

56. Ibid., 277, Captain Peter Clark to his wife.

57. Lamb, *A British Soldier's Story*, 41.

58. Scheer & Rankin, *Rebels & Redcoats*, 296.

59. Riedesel, *Letters and Journals*, 92–93.

60. Wasmus, *Eyewitness Account*, 63.

61. Ibid., 66.

62. Ketchum, *Saratoga*, 272–274.

63. Nickerson, *Turning Point of the Revolution*, 235–238.

64. Foster and Streeter, *Stark's Independent Command*, 28; see also, Randall, *Benedict Arnold: Patriot and Traitor*, 87.

65. Riedesel, *Letters and Journals*, 96.

66. Nickerson, *Turning Point of the Revolution*, 238.

67. Ketchum, *Saratoga*, 295.

68. Nickerson, *Turning Point of the Revolution*, 239–240; Gabriel, *Battle of Bennington*, 18.

69. Ketchum, *Saratoga*, 296.

70. Wasmus, *Eyewitness Account*, 68.

71. Washington to Schuyler, July 22, 1777, excerpted in Foster and Streeter, *Stark's Independent Command*, 35.

72. Washington to Schuyler, July 22, 1777, excerpted in Allen, ed., *George Washington: A Collection*, 89.

21. The Battle of Bennington: *A Continual Clap of Thunder*

1. Frederic Kidder, quoted in Commager and Morris, *Spirit of 'Seventy-Six*, 568.

2. Ibid., 569.

3. Smith, *The Housatonic*, 173–174.

4. Ketchum, *Saratoga*, 298.

5 Coburn, *Centennial History*, 30, 35–36.

6. Schuyler to Washington, in Foster and Streeter, *Stark's Independent Command*, note p. 63.

7. Ibid., 42.

8. Gabriel, "Incident at the Bennington Meeting House, August 17, 1777," *The Hessians: The Journal of the Johannes Schwalm Historical Association*, Volume 14, p. 89.

9. Reminiscences of Levi Beardsley, in Gabriel, *Battle of Bennington*, 84.

10. Ibid., 87, Pension Application of Joseph Rudd.

11. Wasmus, *Eyewitness Account of the American Revolution*, 69.

12. Ibid.

13. Baum to Burgoyne, August 14, 1777, in Lord, *War over Walloomscoick*, 7.

14. Lord, *War over Walloomscoick*, 7.

15. Ibid., 6.

16. Stark to Gates, August 26, 1777, in Caleb Stark, *Memoir and Official Correspondence of Gen. John Stark*, 130.

17. Ibid. The stony soil made it impossible to dig entrenchments, according to Asa Fitch, quoted in Gabriel, *Battle of Bennington*, 45.

18. Wasmus, *Eyewitness Account*, 70.

19. Ibid. Wasmus spelled his name MacKay.

20. Nickerson, *Turning Point of the Revolution*, 240.

21. Coburn, *Centennial History*, 40.

22. Lord, *War over Walloomscoick*, 7–9.

23. Ketchum, *Saratoga*, 301.

24. Wasmus, *Eyewitness Account*, 71.

25. Ibid.

26. Caleb Stark, *Memoir and Official Correspondence of Gen. John Stark*, 58.

27. Ibid.

28. Ibid.

29. Lord, *War over Walloomscoick*, 10–11.

30. Ibid.

31. Moore, *John Stark*, 310.

32. Ibid.

33. Nickerson, *Turning Point*, 252.

34. Pension Application of David Holbrook, in Dann, *The Revolution Remembered*, 89.

35. Stark to Gates, August 26, 1777, in Caleb Stark, *Memoir and Official Correspondence*, 130.

36. Wasmus, *Eyewitness Account*, 71.

37. Ibid.

38. Ibid.

39. Ibid., 72.

40. Pension Application of David Holbrook, in Dann, *The Revolution Remembered*, 89.

41. Thomas Mellen, quoted in Lord, *War over Walloomscoick*, 60.

42. Silas Walbridge and Jessee Field, quoted in Moore, *John Stark*, 313.

43. Ibid.

44. Wasmus, *Eyewitness Account*, 72.

45. Nickerson, *Turning Point*, 252–253.

46. Ibid.

47. Lord, *War over Walloomscoick*, 54–55.

48. Ibid.

49. Ibid., 57.

50. Ibid., 81.

51. Ibid., 82.

52. Ketchum, *Saratoga*, 311–312.

53. Potter, *Military History of New Hampshire*, 320.

54. Thomas Mellen, quoted in Moore, *John Stark*, 315.

55. Austin Wells, quoted in Lord, *War over Walloomscoick*, 160.

56. Ibid., 58.

57. Nickerson, *Turning Point*, 254.

58. Levi Beardsley, quoted in Gabriel, *Battle of Bennington*, 84.

59. Wasmus, *Eyewitness Account*, 72.

60. Ibid., 73.

61. Nickerson, *Turning Point*, 255.

62. Skene to Earl of Dartmouth, quoted in Moore, *John Stark*, 319.

63. Pension Application of David Holbrook, in Dann, *The Revolution Remembered*, 89–90.

64. Letterbook of Asa Fitch, quoted in Gabriel, *Battle of Bennington*, 65.

65. Nickerson, *Turning Point*, 257.

66. Pension Application of David Holbrook, in Dann, *The Revolution Remembered*, 90–91.

67. Ibid., 91.

68. Stark to Gates, August 26, 1777, in Caleb Stark, *Memoir and Official Correspondence*, 131.

69. Thomas Mellen, quoted in Moore, *John Stark*, 323.

70. Gabriel, *Battle of Bennington*, 94.

71. Stark to Gates, August 26, 1777, in Caleb Stark, *Memoir and Official Correspondence*, 131.

72. Thomas Mellen, quoted in Moore, *John Stark*, 324.

73. Ibid.; see also Petersen, *Seth Warner*, 136, and Stark's report to Gates in Caleb Stark, *Memoir and Official Correspondence*, 131.

74. Moore, *John Stark*, 324.

75. Ibid.

76. Gabriel, *Battle of Bennington*, 28.

22. A Storm Gathers at Saratoga:
The Fate of America May Be Determined

1. Gabriel, *Battle of Bennington*, 27–28.

2. Nickerson, *Turning Point of the Revolution*, 263.

3. Wasmus, *Eyewitness Account of the American Revolution*, 72.

4. Ibid., 73.

5. Ibid.

6. Ibid., 74.

7. Gabriel, "Incident at the Bennington Meeting House, August 17, 1777," *The Hessians: The Journal of the Johannes Schwalm Historical Association*, Volume 14, p. 88.

8. Wasmus, *Eyewitness Account*, 74.

9. Ibid.

10. Ibid.

11. Ibid.

12. Ibid., 74–75.

13. Ibid., 75.

14. Lamb, *A British Soldier's Story*, 55–56.

15. General Riedesel, *The American Campaign*, excerpted in Frederika Riedesel's *Letters and Journals*, 97.

16. James Martin, *Benedict Arnold*, 361–364.

17. General Riedesel, *The American Campaign*, excerpted in Frederika Riedesel's *Letters and Journals*, 98.

18. Dearborn, *Revolutionary War Journals*, 101–107.

19. James Martin, *Benedict Arnold*, 350.

20. Scheer & Rankin, *Rebels & Redcoats*, 311–312.

21. Ketchum, *Saratoga*, 337.

22. Caleb Stark, *Memoir and Official Correspondence of Gen. John Stark*, 350.

23. Ibid., note p. 351.

24. Ibid.

25. Stark to Gates, quoted in Moore, *John Stark*, 365, 369.

26. Baldwin, *Revolutionary Journal*, 119.

27. Commager and Morris, *Spirit of 'Seventy-Six*, 576.

28. Moore, *John Stark*, 379.

29. Ibid., 379–380, Wilkinson to General St. Clair, October 7, 1777.

30. Ibid., 374, Stark to "the Commanding Officer of the Militia destined for the Northern Army from the State of New Hampshire, September 17, 1777."

23. Stark's Knob:
They Go There To Serve under Genl Stark

1. Potter, *Military History of New Hampshire*, 336–340; Dearborn, *Revolutionary War Journals*, 104.

2. Scheer & Rankin, *Rebels & Redcoats*, 128.

3. Wilkinson, *Memoirs of My Own Times*, quoted in Scheer & Rankin, *Rebels & Redcoats*, 315.

4. Morrison, *Oxford History of the American People*, Vol. 1, p. 327.

5. Dearborn, *Revolutionary War Journals*, 107.

6. Wilkinson, *Memoirs*, quoted in Scheer & Rankin, *Rebels & Redcoats*, 321.

7. Recollections of Captain E. Wakefield, in Commager and Morris, *Spirit of 'Seventy-Six*, 581.

8. Ibid.

9. Caleb Stark, *Memoir and Official Correspondence of Gen. John Stark*, 351.

10. Ketchum, *Saratoga*, 397.

11. Lamb, *A British Soldier's Story*, 52–53.

12. New Hampshire Committee of Safety to John Stark, September 10, 1777, in Moore, *John Stark*, 374–375.

13. Ibid., 381.

14. Ketchum, *Saratoga*, 417.

15. General Riedesel, *The American Campaign*, excerpted in Frederika Riedesel, *Letters and Journals*, 101.

16. Ketchum, *Saratoga*, 427.

17. Journal of Lt. William Digby of the Shropshire Regiment, in Commager and Morris, *Spirit of 'Seventy-Six*, 605.

18. Frederika Riedesel, *Letters and Journals*, 134–135.

19. Caleb Stark, *Memoir and Official Correspondence*, note p. 351.

20. Lamb, *A British Soldier's Story*, 54.

21. Ibid., 55–59.

22. Wasmus, *Eyewitness Account of the American Revolution*, 78, 83.

23. Schuyler to General Lincoln, quoted in Moore, *John Stark*, 364.

24. Carrington, *Battles of the Revolution*, 353.

24. Albany: *They Do Very Well in the Hanging Way*

1. Washington to Congress, quoted in Commager and Morris, *Spirit of 'Seventy-Six*, 625,

2. Ibid., 655–656, Benjamin Rush to Patrick Henry, January 12, 1778.

3. Ibid., 652, Washington to Richard Henry Lee, October 17, 1777.

4. Freeman, *George Washington*, Richard Harwell, ed., 367.

5. Washington to General Thomas Conway, November 9, 1777, quoting Conway's own statement in a letter to Horatio Gates, Commager and Morris, *Spirit of 'Seventy-Six*, 653.

6. Ibid., 655, Washington to Gates, January 4, 1778.

7. Moore, *John Stark*, 387.

8. Stark's appointment as brigadier general, in Caleb Stark, *Memoir and Official Correspondence of Gen. John Stark*, 138–139.

9. Patten, *Diary of Matthew Patten*, 375.

10. Freeman, *George Washington*, Richard Harwell, ed., 382, 387–388.

11. Resolution of Congress, December 3, 1777, quoted in Caleb Stark, *Memoir and Official Correspondence*, 77.

12. Ibid., 79, James Duane to Stark, December 16, 1777.

13. Ibid., 142, Gates to Stark, January 24, 1778.

14. Stark to Lafayette, February 7, 1778, quoted in Moore, *John Stark*, 409–410.

15. Freeman, *George Washington*, Richard Harwell, ed., 379.

16. Ibid.

17. Lafayette to Washington, quoted in Moore, *John Stark*, 411–412.

18. Berleth, *Bloody Mohawk*, 252.

19. Ibid., 247–253; also, Graymont, *The Iroquois*, 164–165.

20. Freeman, *George Washington*, Richard Harwell, ed., 390.

21. Moore, *John Stark*, 404.

22. Wood, *Radicalism of the American Revolution*, 223–224.

23. Forman, *Dr. Joseph Warren*, 111.

24. Ibid.

25. Franklin, *Autobiography*, 317.

26. McCullough, *John Adams*, 204.

27. Caleb Stark, *Memoir and Official Correspondence*, 80.

28. Graymont, *The Iroquois*, 2 *et seq.*

29. Ibid., 105.

30. Ibid., Chapter 5.

31. Ketchum, ed., *American Heritage Book of the Revolution*, 319.

32. Taylor, *The Divided Ground*, 18.

33. Ketchum, ed., *American Heritage Book of the Revolution*, 319.

34. Stark to the Brigadier of Hampshire County, Mass., June 24, 1778, Caleb Stark, *Memoir and Official Correspondence*, 168.

35. Ibid., 147, Stark to Gates, May 21, 1778.

36. Graymont, *The Iroquois*, 165–166.

37. Stark to Ten Broeck, June 1, 1778, Caleb Stark, *Memoir and Official Correspondence*, 157.

38. Ibid., 156, Stark to Gates, May 31, 1778.

39. Washington to Stark, May 20, 1778, Washington, *Writings of George Washington*, Fitzpatrick, ed., Vol. 11, p. 427.

40. Stark to Washington, June 8, 1778, Caleb Stark, *Memoir and Official Correspondence*, 160.

41. Ibid.

42. Washington to Stark, May 26, 1778, Washington, *Writings of George Washington*, Fitzpatrick, ed., Vol. 11, p. 461.

43. Stark to Committee of Safety of Tryon County, June 16, 1778, Caleb Stark, *Memoir and Official Correspondence*, 163.

44. Ibid., 146, John Barclay, Mayor of Albany, to Stark, May 20, 1778.

45. Ibid., 147, Stark to Gates, May 21, 1778.

46. Ibid., 159, Stark to Gates, June 4, 1778.

47. Ibid., 164–165, Ethan Allen to Stark, June 18, 1778.

48. Ibid., 165, Stark to Ethan Allen, June 20, 1778.

49. Ibid., 172–173, Stark to the President of the New Hampshire Congress, June 28, 1778.

50. Ibid., 184–185, note p. 185, Stark to Colonel Ichabod Alden, August 15, 1778.

51. Ibid., 178, Stark to Vermont Governor Chittenden, July 5, 1778.

52. Ibid., 177, Stark to Gates, July 15, 1778.

53. Governor Clinton to Washington, July 20, 1778, Moore, *John Stark*, 427.

54. Ibid., 428, Governor Clinton to John Jay.

55. Commager and Morris, *Spirit of 'Seventy-Six*, 1005.

56. Washington to Stark, July 18, 1778, Caleb Stark, *Memoir and Official Correspondence*, 178.

57. Ibid., 182, Stark to Washington, July 24, 1778.

58. Berleth, *Bloody Mohawk*, 265, 267.

59. Stark to Gates, June 20, 1778, Caleb Stark, *Memoir and Official Correspondence*, 166.

60. Ibid., 181, Gates to Stark, July 14, 1778.

61. Berleth, *Bloody Mohawk*, 266–267.

62. Washington to Stark, August 5, 1778, Washington, *Writings of George Washington*, Fitzpatrick, ed., Vol. 12, p. 283–284.

63. Stark to Washington, August 10, 1778, Caleb Stark, *Memoir and Official Correspondence*, 184.

64. Graymont, *The Iroquois*, 181.

65. Stark to Washington, October 28, 1778, Caleb Stark, *Memoir and Official Correspondence*, 194.

66. Graymont, *The Iroquois*, 185–186.

67. Ibid., 186–191.

68. Frank Moore, *Diary of the American Revolution*, 330–332.

69. Washington to Governor Clinton, September 25, 1778, Washington, *Writings of George Washington*, Fitzpatrick, ed., Vol. 12, note 46, p. 496.

70. Moore, *John Stark*, 279.

71. Washington to Stark, October 19, 1778, Washington, *Writings of George Washington*, Fitzpatrick, ed., Vol. 13, p. 112.

25. The Last Significant Battle in the North: *Give 'em Watts Boys*

1. Freeman, *George Washington*, Richard Harwell, ed., 405.

2. Angell, *Diary of Israel Angell*, 4.

3. Ibid., 31.

4. Ibid., 33, 35–36.

5. Patten, *Diary of Matthew Patten*, 394.

6. Stark to Gates, May 21, 1779, quoted in Moore, *John Stark*, 434.

7. Angell, *Diary*, 88–90.

8. Ibid., 84–85.

9. Ibid., 85–86.

10. Caleb Stark, *Memoir and Official Correspondence of Gen. John Stark*, 81.

11. Angell, *Diary*, 87.

12. Commager and Morris, *Spirit of 'Seventy-Six*, 1011.

13. Dearborn, *Revolutionary War Journals*, 155.

14. Graymont, *The Iroquois*, 196.

15. Dearborn, *Journals*, 157.

16. Ibid., 159; Washington had ordered "that the [Iroquois] country may not be merely overrun, but destroyed."

17. Ibid., 172, 179.

18. Barton, "Journal of Lieutenant William Barton," quoted in Commager and Morris, *Spirit of 'Seventy-Six*, 1014.

19. Dearborn, *Journals*, 188.

20. Barton, "Journal," quoted in Commager and Morris, *Spirit of 'Seventy-Six*, 1015.

21. Dearborn, *Journals*, 193.

22. Archibald Stark logbook, quoted in Caleb Stark, *Memoir and Official Correspondence*, 195.

23. *Memoirs of General Heath*, quoted in Moore, *John Stark*, 436.

24. Thacher, *Army Surgeon*, 180.

25. Joseph Plumb Martin, *Narrative of a Revolutionary Soldier*, 55.

26. Angell, *Diary*, 96–97.

27. Stark to Mesech Weare, December 14, 1779, Caleb Stark, *Memoir and Official Correspondence*, 197.

28. Moore, *John Stark*, 438.

29. Thacher, *Eyewitness to the American Revolution*, quoted in Moore, *John Stark*, 439.

30. Joseph Plumb Martin, *Narrative*, 145.

31. Ibid., 145–146.

32. General Orders, January 16, 1780, Washington, *Writings of George Washington*, Fitzpatrick, ed., Vol. 17, p. 428.

33. Fleming, *Forgotten Victory*, 60.

34. Freeman, *George Washington*, Richard Harwell, ed., 431.

35. Joseph Plumb Martin, *Narrative*, 157.

36. Freeman, *George Washington*, Richard Harwell, ed., 434.

37. Joseph Plumb Martin, *Narrative*, 158.

38. Ibid., 158–161.

39. Thacher, *Eyewitness*, 186, 196.

40. Joseph Plumb Martin, *Narrative*, 143.

41. Caleb Stark, *Memoir and Official Correspondence*, 81–82.

42. Joseph Plumb Martin, *Narrative*, 150–155.

43. Fleming, *Forgotten Victory*, 18–19.

44. Commager and Morris, *Spirit of 'Seventy-Six*, 728.

45. Ibid., 728, Diary of Colonel Sylvanus Seeley of the New Jersey Militia, June 7 & 8, 1780.

46. Thacher, *Eyewitness*, 201.

47. Fleming, *Forgotten Victory*, 230–231.

48. Ibid., 261–262.

49. Ibid., 262–263.

50. Ibid., 280–281.

51. Caleb Stark, *Memoir and Official Correspondence*, 82.

52. Joseph Plumb Martin, *Narrative*, 163.

53. Ibid., 164.

54. Freeman, *George Washington*, Richard Harwell, ed., 436.

55. Commager and Morris, *Spirit of 'Seventy-Six*, 1124.

56. Ibid., 1135, Alexander Hamilton to James Duane, September 6, 1780.

57. Washington to Stark (2 letters), June 30, 1780, Washington, *Writings of George Washington*, Fitzpatrick, ed., Vol. 19, pp. 102–103; July 28, 1780, p. 276.

58. Stark to Washington, July 13, 1780, quoted in Moore, *John Stark*, 445.

59. General Orders, August 1, 1780, Washington, *Writings of George Washington*, Fitzpatrick, ed., Vol. 19, p. 299.

60. Stark's Orderly Book for August 9, 1780, in "Stark Papers," New Hampshire Historical Society.

61. Freeman, *George Washington*, Richard Harwell, ed., 442.

62. Caleb Stark, *Memoir and Official Correspondence*, 202.

63. Washington, *Writings of George Washington*, Fitzpatrick, ed., Vol. 20, p. 5.

64. Caleb Stark, *Memoir and Official Correspondence*, 202.

65. Angell, *Diary*, 116.

66. Ibid., 121.

67. Freeman, *George Washington*, Richard Harwell, ed., 442.

26. Arnold and André:
Treason of the Blackest Dye

1. Ketchum, ed., *American Heritage Book of the Revolution*, 267.

2. Flexner, *The Traitor and the Spy*, 202.

3. Ibid., 143, 146, 150–151.

4. Journal of Major John André, in Commager and Morris, *Spirit of 'Seventy-Six*, 622.

5. Van Doren, *Secret History*, 91, for the looting of Franklin's home; see also Thomas Jones, *History of New York During the Revolutionary War*, Vol. 1, p. 286, for the raid at Tappan.

6. Flexner, *The Traitor and the Spy*, 263.

7. Arnold to André, May 23, 1779, Commager and Morris, *Spirit of 'Seventy-Six*, 748.

8. Freeman, *George Washington*, Richard Harwell, ed., 403, 437.

9. Arnold to John Anderson (André), July 12, 1780, Commager and Morris, *Spirit of 'Seventy-Six*, 748.

10. Ibid., 749, Arnold to André, July 15, 1780.

11. Ibid., 749–750, Sir Henry Clinton to Lord George Germaine, October 11, 1780.

12. Thacher, *Eyewitness to the American Revolution*, 216.

13. Sir Henry Clinton to Lord George Germaine, October 11, 1780, Commager and Morris, *Spirit of 'Seventy-Six*, 750.

14. Ibid., 751, Intelligence Report of Andrew Elliot, October 4 & 5, 1780.

15. Ibid., 759–760, Hamilton to John Laurens, October 1780.

16. Flexner, *The Traitor and the Spy*, 349–350.

17. Intelligence Report of Andrew Elliot, October 4 & 5, 1780, Commager and Morris, *Spirit of 'Seventy-Six*, 751.

18. Ketchum, ed., *American Heritage Book of the Revolution*, 268.

19. Tallmadge, *Memoir of Colonel Benjamin Tallmadge*, 36.

20. Diary of Tobias Lear, private secretary to Washington, entry of October 23, 1786, Commager and Morris, *Spirit of 'Seventy-Six*, 756–758.

21. Ibid.

22. Ibid.

23. Freeman, *George Washington*, Richard Harwell, ed., 442.

24. Thacher, *Eyewitness*, 232.

25. Diary of Tobias Lear, private secretary to Washington, entry for October 23, 1786, Commager and Morris, *Spirit of 'Seventy-Six*, 758.

26. Tallmadge, *Memoir*, 37.

27. Hatch, *Major John André*, 251, 258.

28. Nathanael Greene's Order of the Day, September 26, 1780, Commager and Morris, *Spirit of 'Seventy-Six*, 755–756.

29. Hatch, *Major John André*, 259.

30. Thacher, *Eyewitness*, 221–222.

31. Hamilton to John Laurens, October 1780, Commager and Morris, *Spirit of 'Seventy-Six*, 763–765.

32. Hatch, *Major John André*, 255.

33. Thacher, *Eyewitness*, 224.

34. Hatch, *Major John André*, 260.

35. Walsh, *Execution of Major André*, 3.

36. Van Doren, *Secret War*, 356.

37. Ibid., 357.

38. Sir Henry Clinton to Washington, September 26, 1780, Commager and Morris, *Spirit of 'Seventy-Six*, 761.

39. Van Doren, *Secret War*, 357.

40. André to Washington, September 24, 1780, Commager and Morris, *Spirit of 'Seventy-Six*, 760–761.

41. Von Steuben, quoted in Hatch, *Major John André*, 262.

42. Ibid., 261.

43. Ibid.

44. Thacher, *Eyewitness*, 224.

45. Ibid.

46. Caleb Stark, *Memoir and Official Correspondence of Gen. John Stark*, 83.

47. Tallmadge, *Memoir*, 37.

48. Arnold to Washington, October 1, 1780, Commager and Morris, *Spirit of 'Seventy-Six*, 762.

49. Washington to Sir Henry Clinton, September 30, 1780, Washington, *Writings of George Washington*, Fitzpatrick, ed., Vol. 20, pp. 103–104.

50. Angell, *Diary of Israel Angell*, 126.

51. André to Washington, October 1, 1780, Commager and Morris, *Spirit of 'Seventy-Six*, 762–763.

52. Ibid., 763–765, Hamilton to John Laurens, October 1780.

53. Ibid., 765–766, Dr. Thacher.

54. Hatch, *Major John André*, 273.

55. Tallmadge, *Memoir*, 38.

56. Hamilton to John Laurens, October 1780, Commager and Morris, *Spirit of 'Seventy-Six*, 763–765.

57. Hatch, *Major John André*, 273.

58. Hamilton to John Laurens, October 1780, Commager and Morris, *Spirit of 'Seventy-Six*, 763–765.

59. Tallmadge, *Memoir*, 38.

60. Dr. Thacher, in Commager and Morris, *Spirit of 'Seventy-Six*, 766.

61. Ibid.

62. Tallmadge, *Memoir*, 38.

63. Hamilton to John Laurens, October 1780, Commager and Morris, *Spirit of 'Seventy-Six*, 765.

64. Joseph Plumb Martin, *Narrative of a Revolutionary Soldier*, 178.

65. Dr. Thacher, in Commager and Morris, *Spirit of 'Seventy-Six*, 766–767.

66. Tallmadge, *Memoir*, 37–38.

67. Hamilton to John Laurens, October 1780, Commager and Morris, *Spirit of 'Seventy-Six*, 765.

68. Caleb Stark, *Memoir and Official Correspondence*, 83–84.

69. Shakespeare, *Macbeth*, Act I, Scene IV.

27. West Point, Albany, and War's End: *My Exile*

1. de Chastellux, *Travels in North America*, Vol. 1, p. 89.
2. Ibid.
3. Ibid., 90.
4. Dearborn, *Revolutionary War Journals*, 207.
5. de Chastellux, *Travels*, Vol. 1, p. 90.
6. Ibid., 92–93.
7. Caleb Stark, *Memoir and Official Correspondence of Gen. John Stark*, 84.
8. Dearborn, *Journals*, 209.
9. Flexner, *The Traitor and the Spy*, 356.
10. Stark to General William Heath, November 28, 1780, Caleb Stark, *Memoir and Official Correspondence*, 203–204.
11. Dearborn, *Journals*, 209.
12. Stark to General William Heath, November 28, 1780, Caleb Stark, *Memoir and Official Correspondence*, 204.
13. Ibid., 204–205, General William Heath to Stark, November 23, 1780.
14. Dearborn, *Journals*, 209.
15. Stark to Washington, November 30, 1780, Caleb Stark, *Memoir and Official Correspondence*, 206.
16. Stark to General Sullivan, November 28, 1780, quoted in Moore, *John Stark*, 455–456.
17. Ibid.
18. Ibid., 454, Washington to Stark, December 30, 1780.
19. Stark to Washington, January 1, 1781, Caleb Stark, *Memoir and Official Correspondence*, 207–208.
20. Ibid., 210, Washington to Stark.
21. Patten, *Diary of Matthew Patten*, 426, 428–430.
22. Stark to General Sullivan, spring 1781, quoted in Moore, *John Stark*, 459.
23. Washington to Stark, June 25, 1781, Caleb Stark, *Memoir and Official Correspondence*, 211.
24. Joseph Plumb Martin, *Narrative of a Revolutionary Soldier*, 196, 198.
25. Freeman, *George Washington*, Richard Harwell, ed., 473.
26. Washington to Stark, June 28, 1781, Caleb Stark, *Memoir and Official Correspondence*, 213.
27. Ibid., 275–276, Samuel Robinson to Stark, October 16, 1781.
28. Ibid., 216, Stark to Washington, August 9, 1781.
29. Joseph Plumb Martin, *Narrative*, 198–199.
30. Commager and Morris, *Spirit of 'Seventy-Six*, note p. 1228.
31. Ibid., 1232–1233, Dr. Thacher.
32. Joseph Plumb Martin, *Narrative*, 202.
33. Dr. Thacher, quoted in Commager and Morris, *Spirit of 'Seventy-Six*, 1233.
34. Stark to Washington, December 21, 1781, Caleb Stark, *Memoir and Official Correspondence*, 303.
35. Ibid.

28. Old Soldiers: *Live Free or Die*

1. Freeman, *George Washington*, Richard Harwell, ed., 493.
2. Maney, *The Family of General John Stark*, 61.
3. Washington to Lt. Col. George Reid, *Writings of George Washington*, Fitzpatrick, ed., Vol. 25, p.477.
4. Stark to Washington, September 23, 1782, quoted in Moore, *John Stark*, 479.
5. Washington to Stark, October 23, 1782, *Writings of George Washington*, Fitzpatrick, ed., Vol. 25, p. 286.
6. Ibid., Vol. 26, p. 334.
7. Commager and Morris, *Spirit of 'Seventy-Six*, 1282–1283.
8. Freeman, *George Washington*, Richard Harwell, ed., 501.
9. Ibid.
10. Commager and Morris, *Spirit of 'Seventy-Six*, 1268.
11. Ibid., 1270.
12. Ibid., 1268.
13. Moore, *John Stark*, 483.
14. Patten, *Diary of Matthew Patten*, 475.
15. Ibid., 471–472.
16. Whittemore, *A General of the Revolution*, 150–151.
17. de Chastellux, *Travels in North America*, Vol. 2, p. 488.
18. Maney, *The Family of General John Stark*,

61, 66, 75.

19. Joseph Plumb Martin, *Narrative of a Revolutionary Soldier*, 241.

20. The story of the Society of the Cincinnati is told in detail on the society's Web site: http://www.society of the Cincinnati.org/about/history/founding.

21. Freeman, *George Washington*, Richard Harwell, ed., 520.

22. Caleb Stark, *Memoir and Official Correspondence of Gen. John Stark*, 87.

23. Jefferson to James Madison, December 28, 1794, Jefferson, *Selected Writings*, 529.

24. Maney, *The Family of General John Stark*, 61.

25. Patten, *Diary*, 543, 549.

26. Whittemore, *A General of the Revolution*, 224–226.

27. Ibid.

28. Cuneo, *Robert Rogers*, 278.

29. Account Book in "Stark Papers," New Hampshire Historical Society, Concord, New Hampshire.

30. Maney, *The Family of General John Stark*, 61. The name of the vessel is spelled "Shipsburg" in the Maney work.

31. Stark to Jefferson, October 1806, Caleb Stark, *Memoir and Official Correspondence*, 309.

32. Moore, *John Stark*, 488.

33. Washington, *Diary of George Washington, 1789–1791*, Vol. 4, Benson J. Lossing, ed., 42–43.

34. Thucydides, *The Peloponnesian War*, 23.

35. Freeman, *George Washington*, Richard Harwell, ed., 550.

36. Whittemore, *A General of the Revolution*, 216–219.

37. Caleb Stark, *Memoir and Official Correspondence*, 308–309.

38. Ibid., 309–310, Stark to Jefferson, October 1805.

39. Ibid., 313, Stark to Committee at Bennington, July 31, 1804.

40. Ibid., 316, Madison to Stark, December 26, 1809.

41. Ibid., 316–317, Stark to Madison, January 21, 1810.

42. Ibid.

43. Ibid., 320–325. Caleb Stark published several letters sent from the Reverend William Bentley to John Stark over a period of several years.

44. Quoted in Moore, *John Stark*, 498.

45. Ibid., 499.

46. Maney, *The Family of General John Stark*, 35, 61, 86–88, 92–93.

47. Caleb Stark, *Memoir and Official Correspondence*, 311.

48. Ibid., 312, Stark to Bennington Committee, July 31, 1809.

49. Ibid., 313.

50. Moore, *John Stark*, 507.

51. Joseph Plumb Martin, *Narrative*, 251.

52. General Thomas Sumter of South Carolina, a militia officer, and the Marquis de Lafayette, a Frenchman, outlived John Stark.

Epilogue: John Stark Remembered

1. Thoreau, *A Week*, 14.

2. Ibid., 32–33.

3. Ibid., 84.

4. Ibid., 93–98.

5. Ibid., 123.

6. Ibid., 248.

7. Thoreau's journal entry for July 7, 1845, in *Selected Journals of Henry David Thoreau*, Carl Bode, ed., 80.

8. Thoreau, *A Week*, 268–269.

9. Ibid.

10. Ibid., 333.

11. Ibid., 334.

Bibliography

Adams, John. *The Adams Papers: Diary & Autobiography of John Adams: Diary 1771–1781*. New York: Atheneum Press, 1964.

Allen, Thomas, B. *Tories: Fighting for the King in America's First Civil War*. New York: Harper Collins, 2010.

Allen, W.B., ed. *George Washington: A Collection*. Indianapolis: Liberty Fund, 1988.

Amherst, Lord Jeffrey. *The Journal of Jeffrey Amherst 1759*. In Bellico, *Chronicles of Lake Champlain: Journeys in War and Peace*. Fleischmanns, N.Y.: Purple Mountain Press, 1999.

Anderson, Fred. *Crucible of War: The Seven Years' War and the Fate of Empire in British North America, 1754–1766*. New York: Random House–Vintage Books, 2001.

———. *A People's Army: Massachusetts Soldiers and Society in the Seven Years War*. Chapel Hill, N.C.: University of North Carolina Press, 1984.

Angell, Israel. *Diary of Colonel Israel Angell commanding the Second Rhode Island Continental Regiment during the American Revolution*. Providence: Preston and Rounds, 1899.

Arnot, Hugh. *A Journal or Proceedings of the Army Under the Command of Majr. Genl. Abercromby*. In "'Like Roaring Lions Breaking from their Chains': The Highland Regiment at Ticonderoga," *Bulletin of the Fort Ticonderoga Museum (BFTM)*, Nicholas Westbrook, ed., Vol. XVI, 1998, Number 1, pp. 61–91.

Baldwin, Jeduthan. *The Revolutionary Journal of Col. Jeduthan Baldwin, 1775–1778*. Bangor, Me.: The DeBurians, 1906.

Barney, Jesse A. *Rumney Then and Now: History*. Salem, Mass.: Higginson Book Co., 1967.

Beebe, Louis. *Journals of a Physician on the Expedition against Canada, 1776*. The *Pennsylvania Magazine of History and Biography*, Volume LIX, No. 4, October 1935.

Belknap, Jeremy. *The History of New Hampshire, Vol. 1*. 1784. Reprint, Dover, N.H.: C.C. Stevens, 1831.

Bellico, Russell P. *Chronicles of Lake Champlain: Journeys in War and Peace*. Fleischmanns, N.Y.: Purple Mountain Press, 1999.

———. *Chronicles of Lake George: Journeys in War and Peace*. Fleischmanns, N.Y.: Purple Mountain Press, 1995.

———. *Empires in the Mountains: French and Indian War Campaigns and Forts in the Lake Champlain, Lake George and Hudson River Corridor*. Fleischmanns, N.Y.: Purple Mountain Press, 2010.

Berleth, Richard. *Bloody Mohawk: The French and Indian War & American Revolution on New York's Frontier*. Delmar, N.Y.: Black Dome Press, 2009.

Bosson, Albert D. *The Battle of Chelsea: Historical Address and Notes*. Boston: Register of Old Suffolk Chapter, Sons of the American Revolution, 1900.

Bougainville, Louis Antoine de. *Adventure in the Wilderness: The American Journals of Louis Antoine de Bougainville, 1776–1783*. Edward P. Hamilton, ed. Norman, Okla.: University of Oklahoma Press, 1964.

Bouton, Nathaniel, ed. *Documents and Records Relating to the State of New Hampshire during the Period of the American Revolution from 1776–1783*. Vol. VII. Concord, N.H.: 1874.

Brookhiser, Richard. *Alexander Hamilton: American*. N.Y.: Simon & Schuster, 1999.

Brown, Richard, ed. *Major Problems in the Era of the American Revolution, 1760–1791: Documents and Essays*. Lexington, Mass.: D.C. Heath and Company, 1992.

Brown, William Howard. *Colonel John Goffe: Eighteenth Century New Hampshire*. Manchester, N.H.: Lew A. Cummings Co., 1950.

Brumwell, Stephen. *White Devil: A True Story of War, Savagery, and Vengeance in Colonial America*. Cambridge, Mass.: Da Capo Press, 2004.

Bulletin of the Fort Ticonderoga Museum (BFTM). Articles cited by author's name as published in the *Bulletin*, abbreviated *BFTM*.

Burrows, Edwin G. *Forgotten Patriots: The Untold Story of American Prisoners during the Revolutionary War*. New York: Basic Books–Perseus Books Group, 2008.

Calloway, Colin G. *New Worlds for All: Indians, Europeans and the Remaking of Early America*. Baltimore: Johns Hopkins University Press, 1997.

Carrington, Henry B. *Battles of the American Revolution 1775–1781: Historical and Military Criticism*. New York: A.S. Barnes & Company, 1881.

Chastellux, Marquis de. *Travels in North America in the Years 1781 and 1782*. Two volumes. Chapel Hill, N.C.: University of North Carolina Press, 1963.

Chidsey, Donald Barr. *The Loyalists: The Story of Those Americans Who Fought against Independence*. New York: Crown Publishers, 1973.

Cleaveland, Rev. John. *Journal of Rev. John Cleaveland: June 14, 1758–October 25, 1758*. In *Bulletin of the Fort Ticonderoga Museum (BFTM)*, Vol. X, Nov. 3, 1959, No. 3, 192–233.

Coburn, Frank Warren. *The Centennial History of the Battle of Bennington: 1777–1877*. Boston: George E. Littlefield, 1877.

Collins, Varnum Lansing. *A Brief Narrative of the Ravages of the British and Hessians at Princeton in 1776–1777: A Contemporary Account of the Battles of Trenton and Princeton*. Princeton, N.J.: The University Library, 1906.

Commager, Henry Steele, and Richard B. Morris. *The Spirit of 'Seventy-Six; The Story of the American Revolution as Told by the Participants*. One-volume edition. New York: Harper & Row, 1958.

Crannell, Karl. *John Stark: Live Free or Die*. Stockton, N.J.: OTTN Publishing, 2007.

Cuneo, John R. *Robert Rogers of the Rangers*. Ticonderoga, N.Y.: Fort Ticonderoga Museum, 1988.

Dann, John C. ed. *The Revolution Remembered: Eyewitness Accounts of the War for Independence*. Chicago: University of Chicago Press, 1999.

Dearborn, Henry. *Revolutionary War Journals of Henry Dearborn, 1775–1783*. Chicago: The Caxton Club, 1939.

Dickinson, John. *Letters from a farmer in Pennsylvania: to the inhabitants of the British colonies*. Philadelphia: David Hall and William Sellers (Sabin Americana reprint), 1768.

Dwyer, William M. *The Day Is Ours: An Inside View of the Battles of Trenton and Princeton, November 1776–January 1777*. New Brunswick, N.J.: Rutgers University Press, 1998.

Fenn, Elizabeth A. *Pox Americana: The Great Smallpox Epidemic of 1775–82*. New York: Farrar, Straus and Giroux, 2001.

Fischer, David Hackett. *Paul Revere's Ride*. New York and Oxford: Oxford University Press, 1994.

———. *Washington's Crossing*. New York and Oxford: Oxford University Press, 2004.

Fiske, John. *The American Revolution: Volume 1*. Boston and New York: Houghton Mifflin Company, 1891.

Fleming, Thomas. *The Forgotten Victory: The Battle for New Jersey–1780*. New York: Reader's Digest Press, 1973.

———. *Washington's Secret War: The Hidden History of Valley Forge*. New York: Harper Collins, Smithsonian Books, 2005.

Flexner, James Thomas. *The Traitor and the Spy: Benedict Arnold and John André*. Boston: Little, Brown and Company, 1975.

———. *Washington: The Indispensable Man*. New York: A Mentor Book, New American Library, 1969.

Force, Peter. *American Archives: Consisting of a Collection of Authentick Records, State Papers, Debates, and Letters and Other Notices of Public Affairs*. 4th Series. 9 vols. Washington, D.C.: M. St. Clair and Peter Force, 1837–1853.

Forman, Samuel A. *Dr. Joseph Warren: The Boston Tea Party, Bunker Hill and the Birth of American Liberty*. Gretna, La.: Pelican Publishing Company, 2012.

Foster, Herbert D., and Thomas W. Streeter. "Stark's Independent Command at Bennington." Paper published in *Proceedings of the New York State Historical Association*, 1905.

Fowler, William M., Jr. *Empires at War: The French and Indian War and the Struggle for North America, 1754–1763*. New York: Walker & Company, 2005.

Franklin, Benjamin. *The Autobiography and Other Writings*. New York: The Penguin Group, 1961.

Freeman, Douglas Southall. *George Washington: Volume IV: Leader of the Revolution*. New York: Scribner, 1951.

———. *George Washington*. An abridgement in one volume. Richard Harwell, ed. New York: Simon & Schuster, 1968.

Gabriel, Michael P. *The Battle of Bennington: Soldiers and Civilians*. Charleston: The History Press, 2012.

———. "Incident at the Bennington Meeting House, August 17, 1777." *The Hessians: The Journal of the Johannes Schwalm Historical Association*. Volume 14. 2011.

Gerloch, Don R. *Proud Patriot: Philip Schuyler and the War of Independence: 1775–1783*. Syracuse, N.Y.: Syracuse University Press, 1987.

Gipson, Lawrence Henry. *The Coming of the Revolution, 1763–1775*. New York: Harper & Row, 1962.

Graymont, Barbara. *The Iroquois in the American Revolution*. Syracuse, N.Y.: Syracuse University Press, 1972.

Hadley, Alice M. *Dunbarton, New Hampshire: Where the Winds Blow Free*. Canaan, N.H.: Dunbarton History Committee, Phoenix Publishing, 1976.

Hall, Hiland. *The History of Vermont from its Discovery to its Admission into the Union in 1791*. Albany, N.Y.: Joel Munsell, 1868.

Hammond, Otis G., ed. *Probate Records of the Province of New Hampshire, Vol. 6, 1757–1760*. State Papers Series. Volume 36. State of New Hampshire, 1938.

Hatch, Robert McConnell. *Major John André: A Gallant in Spy's Clothing*. Boston: Houghton Mifflin, 1986.

Heath, William. *Memoirs of Major-General William Heath by Himself*. William Abbatt, ed. New York: William Abbatt, 1961.

Hulton, Anne. *Letters of a Loyalist Lady*. Cambridge, Mass.: Harvard University Press, 1927.

Hurd, D. Hamilton. *History of Hillsborough County, New Hampshire*. Philadelphia: J. W. Lewis & Co., 1885.

Hutson, James. *Nathan Hale Revisited: a Tory's Account of the Arrest of the First American Spy*. Library of Congress Information Bulletin, retrieved May 1, 2012. www.Loc.Gov./Loc/lcib/0307-8/hale.html.

Isaacson, Walter. *Benjamin Franklin: An American Life*. New York: Simon & Schuster, 2003.

Jefferson, Thomas. *The Life and Selected Writings of Thomas Jefferson*. New York: The Modern Library, 1944.

Jellison, Charles A. *Ethan Allen: Frontier Rebel*. Syracuse, N.Y.: Syracuse University Press, 1969.

Jones, Charles Henry. *History of the Campaign for the Conquest of Canada: From the Death of Montgomery to the Retreat of the British Army under Sir Guy Carleton*. Philadelphia: Porter & Coates, 1882.

Jones, Thomas. *History of New York during the Revolutionary War and of the Leading Events in the Other Colonies at that Period*. Vol. 1. New York: New-York Historical Society, 1879.

Kalm, Peter. *Travels in North America*. Excerpted in Bellico, *Chronicles of Lake Champlain: Journeys in War and Peace*, 45–71.

Ketchum, Richard M., ed. *The American Heritage Book of the Revolution*. New York: American Heritage Publishing Company, 1958.

———. *Decisive Day: The Battle for Bunker Hill*. Garden City, N.Y.: Doubleday & Company, 1962.

———. *Saratoga: Turning Point of America's Revolutionary War*. New York: Henry Holt & Company, 1997.

———. *The Winter Soldiers: The Battles for Trenton and Princeton*. New York: Henry Holt & Company, 1973.

Lamb, Roger. *A British Soldier's Story: Roger Lamb's Narrative of the American Revolution*. Don D. Hagist, ed. Baraboo, Wis.: Ballindalloch Press, 2004.

Leach, Douglas Edward. *Roots of Conflict: British Armed Forces and Colonial Americans, 1677–1763*. Chapel Hill, N.C.: University of North Carolina Press, 1986.

Leyburn, James G. *The Scotch-Irish: A Social History*. Chapel Hill, N.C.: University of North Carolina Press, 1962.

Little, William. *The History of Weare, New Hampshire: 1735–1888*. Lowell, Mass.: Town of Weare, 1888.

Lockhart, Paul. *The Drillmaster of Valley Forge: The Baron De Steuben and the Making of the American Army*. New York: Smithsonian Books, Harper Collins, 2008.

———. *The Whites of Their Eyes: Bunker Hill, the First American Army, and the Emergence of George Washington*. New York: Harper Collins, 2011.

Loescher, Burt Garfield. *The History of Rogers Rangers. Vol. I: The Beginnings, Jan. 1755–April 6, 1758*. San Francisco: self-published, 1946.

———. *Genesis: Rogers Rangers: Vol. II. The First Green Berets: The Corps and the Revivals: April 6, 1758–December 24, 1783*. San Mateo, Calif.: self-published, 1969.

———. *The History of Rogers Rangers, Vol. III: Officers and Non-Commissioned Officers.* Burlingame, Calif.: self-published, 1957.

———. *The History of Rogers Rangers: Vol. 4. The St. Francis Raid.* Heritage Book Reprint, 2002.

Lord, Philip, Jr. *War over Walloomscoick: Land Use and Settlement Pattern on the Bennington Battlefield–1777.* Albany, N.Y.: New York State Museum, 1989.

Lucier, Armand Francis. *French and Indian War Notices Abstracted from Colonial Newspapers.* Bowie, Md.: Heritage Books, 1999.

Luzader, John F. *Saratoga: A Military History of the Decisive Campaign of the American Revolution.* New York: Savas Beatie, 2008.

Maier, Pauline. *From Resistance to Revolution: Colonial Radicals and the Development of American Opposition to Britain, 1765–1776.* New York and Boston: W.W. Norton & Company, 1972.

Maney, Jane Elizabeth Stark. *The Family of General John Stark, 1728–1822, of New Hampshire.* Northborough, Mass.: Higginson Book Company Reprint, 2002.

Mante, Thomas. *The History of the Late War in North America and the Islands of the West Indies, Including the Campaigns of MDCCLXIII and MDCCLXIV against His Majesty's Indian Enemies.* New York: Research Reprints, 1970.

Martin, James Kirby. *Benedict Arnold: Revolutionary Hero: An American Warrior Reconsidered.* New York: New York University Press, 1997.

Martin, Joseph Plumb. *A Narrative of a Revolutionary Soldier: Some of the Adventures, Dangers and Sufferings of Joseph Plumb Martin.* New York: Signet Classic, 2001.

McCullough, David. *John Adams.* New York: Simon & Schuster, 2001.

———. *1776.* New York: Simon & Schuster, 2005.

Moneypenny, Alexander. *Orderly Book: March 23–June 29, 1758.* Published in the *Bulletin of the Fort Ticonderoga Museum* (*BFTM*). Vol. XII, Dec. 1969, No. 5.

Moore, Frank. *The Diary of the American Revolution.* Abridged and edited by John Anthony Scott. New York: Washington Square Press, 1967.

Moore, Howard Parker. *A Life of General John Stark of New Hampshire.* New York: self-published, 1949.

Morrison, Samuel Eliot. *The Oxford History of the American People. Vol. I. Prehistory to 1789.* New York: New American Library, 1971.

Nelson, James L. *Benedict Arnold's Navy.* Camden, Me.: McGraw Hill, 2006.

New Hampshire, State of. *State Papers, Documents and Records Relating to the State of New Hampshire during the Period of the American Revolution, from 1776 to 1783.* Concord, N.H.: 1874.

Nickerson, Hoffman. *The Turning Point of the Revolution: or Burgoyne in America.* Port Washington, N.Y.: Kennikat Press, 1967.

O'Callaghan, Edmund Bailey, ed. *The Documentary History of the State of New York.* Albany: Weed, Parsons and Co., 1849.

———. *Documents Relating to the Colonial History of the State of New York, Vol. VII, London Documents, 1745–1774.* Albany: Weed, Parsons & Co.

———. *Documents Relating to the Colonial History of the State of New York, Vol. X, Paris Documents, 1745–1774.* Albany: Weed, Parsons & Co., 1856.

Paine, Thomas. *Common Sense.* New York: Penguin Books, 2005.

Pargellis, Stanley McCrory. *Lord Loudon in North America.* New Haven, Ct.: Yale University Press, 1933.

———, ed. *Military Affairs in North America, 1748–1765: Selected Documents from the Cumberland Papers in Windsor Castle.* New York and London: D. Appleton–Century Company, 1937.

Parkman, Francis. *Montcalm and Wolfe.* New York: The Modern Library, 1999.

Patten, Matthew. *The Diary of Matthew Patten of Bedford, New Hampshire from 1754 to 1788.* Camden, Me.: Picton Press, 1993.

Petersen, James E. *Seth Warner.* Middlebury, Vt.: Dunmore House, 2001.

Philbrick, Nathaniel. *Bunker Hill: A City, a Siege, a Revolution.* New York: Viking Penguin Group, 2013.

Pike, Robert E. *Tall Trees, Tough Men: An Anecdotal History of Logging and Log-Driving in New England.* New York: W.W. Norton & Company, 1984.

Potter, Chandler E. *The History of Manchester Formerly Derryfield in New Hampshire; Including that of Ancient Amoskeag, or the Middle Merrimack Valley.* Manchester, N.H.: C.E. Potter, 1856.

———. *Military History of the State of New Hampshire*. Concord, N.H.: C.E. Potter, 1869.

Randall, Willard Sterne. *Benedict Arnold: Patriot and Traitor*. New York: William Morrow and Company, 1990.

Rhodehamel, John H. *The American Revolution: Writings from the War of Independence*. New York: Library of America, 2001.

Richardson, Robert D., Jr. *Henry Thoreau: A Life of the Mind*. Berkeley, Calif.: University of California Press, 1986.

Riedesel, Mrs. General (Frederika). *Letters and Journals Relating to the War of the American Revolution and the Capture of the German Troops at Saratoga*. William L. Stone, trans. Albany, N.Y. Joel Munsell, 1867.

Roberts, Kenneth. *Northwest Passage*. New York: Fawcett Books, 1964.

Roby, Luther. *Reminiscences of the French War and Robert Rogers' Journal and a Memoir of General Stark*. Freedom, N.H.: Reprint, Freedom Historical Society, 1988.

Rogers, Robert. *The Annotated and Illustrated Journals of Major Robert Rogers*. Timothy Todish, ed., Gary Zaboly, illus. Fleischmanns, N.Y.: Purple Mountain Press, 2002.

Rose, Ben Z. *John Stark: Maverick General*. Waverly, Mass.: TreeLine Press, 2007.

Ross, John F. *War on the Run: The Epic Story of Robert Rogers and the Conquest of America's First Frontier*. New York: Bantam Books, 2009.

Royster, Charles. *A Revolutionary People at War: The Continental Army & American Character, 1775–1783*. Chapel Hill, N.C.: University of North Carolina Press, 1979.

Russell, Howard S. *A Long, Deep Furrow: Three Centuries of Farming in New England*. Hanover, N.H.: University Press of New England, 1982.

Schecter, Barnet. *The Battle for New York: The City at the Heart of the American Revolution*. New York: Walker & Company, 2002.

Scheer, George F., and Hugh F. Rankin, eds. *Rebels and Redcoats: The American Revolution through the Eyes of Those Who Fought and Lived It*. New York: New American Library, 1957.

Scott, Kenneth. *Counterfeiting in Colonial America*. New York: Oxford University Press, 1957.

Shy, John. *Toward Lexington: The Role of the British Army in the Coming of the American Revolution*. Princeton, N.J.: Princeton University Press, 1965.

Smith, Chard Powers. *The Housatonic: Puritan River*. New York: Rinehart & Company, 1946.

Spicer, Abel. *Diary of Abel Spicer: 1758*. In Bellico, *Chronicles of Lake George: Journeys in War and Peace*. Fleischmanns, N.Y.: Purple Mountain Press, 1995.

Stark, Caleb. *Memoir and Official Correspondence of Gen. John Stark*. Boston: Gregg Press, 1972.

Steele, Ian. *Betrayals: Fort William Henry and the "Massacre."* New York, Oxford: Oxford University Press, 1990.

Stephenson, Michael. *Patriot Battles: How the War of Independence Was Fought*. New York: Harper Collins, 2007.

Stickney, Benjamin. "Biographical Sketch of General John Stark." *New Hampshire Patriot*. No. 2, April 1810.

Storrs, Experience. *The Diary of Colonel Experience Storrs*. Wladimir Hagelin and Ralph A. Brown, eds. *The New England Quarterly*. Vol. 28, No. 1, March 1955.

Tallmadge, Benjamin. *Memoir of Colonel Benjamin Tallmadge. Eyewitness Accounts of the American Revolution*. New York: New York Times and Arno Press, 1968.

Taylor, Alan. *The Divided Ground: Indians, Settlers, and the Northern Borderland of the American Revolution*. New York: Alfred A. Knopf, 2006.

Thacher, James. *Eyewitness to the American Revolution: The Battles and Generals as Seen by an Army Surgeon*. Longmeadow Press, 1994.

Thoreau, Henry David. *The Natural History Essays*. Salt Lake City: Peregrine Smith Books, 1980.

———. *Selected Journals of Henry David Thoreau*. Carl Bode, ed. New York: New America Library, 1967.

———. *A Week on the Concord and Merrimack Rivers*. Boston: Houghton Mifflin, 1961.

Trevelyan, Sir George Otto. *The American Revolution Part II, Volume II*. New York and London: Longmans Green & Co., 1903.

Trumbull, John. *John Trumbull at Ticonderoga: From His Autobiography*. In *Bulletin of the Fort Ticonderoga Museum*. Vol. III, No. 1, January 1933.

Tuchman, Barbara W. *The First Salute*. New York: Alfred A. Knopf, 1988.

Tuckerman, Bayard. *Life of General Philip Schuyler, 1733–1804*. New York: Dodd, Meade and Company, 1903. Reprint, BiblioBazaar Reproduction.

Twohig, Dorothy, ed. *George Washington's Diaries: An Abridgement*. Charlottesville: University Press of Virginia, 1999.

———, ed. *The Papers of George Washington. Revolutionary War Series 8, January–March 1777*. Charlottesville: University Press of Virginia.

Upton, Richard Francis. *Revolutionary New Hampshire: An Account of the Social and Political Forces Underlying the Transition from Royal Province to American Commonwealth*. Hanover, N.H.: Dartmouth College Publications, 1936.

Van Doren, Carl. *Secret History of the American Revolution*. New York: The Viking Press, 1941.

Walsh, John Evangelist. *The Execution of Major André*. New York: Palgrave for St. Martin's Press, 2001.

Washington, George. *Writings*. New York: Library of America, 1997.

———. *The Writings of George Washington*. Volumes 11–22. John C. Fitzpatrick, ed. Washington, D.C.: Government Printing Office, 1940.

Wasmus, Julius F. *An Eyewitness Account of the American Revolution and New England Life; The Journal of J.F. Wasmus, German Company Surgeon, 1776–1783*. Helga Doblin, trans. Mary C. Lynn, ed. New York: Greenwood Press, 1990.

Webster, Robert. *Robert Webster's Journal: Fourth Connecticut Regiment, Amherst Campaign, April 5ᵗʰ to November 23ʳᵈ, 1759*. In *Bulletin of the Fort Ticonderoga Museum*. Vol. II, July 1931, No. 4.

Wells, Bayze. *Journal of Bayze Wells*. In Bellico, *Chronicles of Lake Champlain: Journeys in War and Peace*. Fleischmanns, N.Y.: Purple Mountain Press, 1999.

Whittemore, Charles P. *A General of the Revolution: John Sullivan of New Hampshire*. New York: Columbia University Press, 1961.

Wilkinson, James. *Memoirs of My Own Times*. Volume I. Philadelphia: Abraham Small, 1816.

Williams, John. *The Redeemed Captive Returning to Zion*. 1704. Ann Arbor, Mich.: University Microfilms.

Wood, Gordon S. *The American Revolution: A History*. New York: Modern Library, 2003.

———. *The Creation of the American Republic: 1776–1787*. New York: W.W. Norton & Company, 1969.

———. *The Radicalism of the American Revolution*. New York: Random House–Vintage Books, 1991.

INDEX

De Woedtke, Gen. Friedrich William, Baron, 197
Diamond Island (Lake George), 100
Diana (British schooner), 158
Dickey, John, 7
Dickinson, John, 118
Dickinson, Gen. Philemon, 227
Digby, Lt. William, 245, 279
Dinwiddie, Gov. Robert, 24–25, 49
Donop, Col. Carl von, 232–233, 300
Doolittle, Capt., 37
Dorchester Heights, 162, 187
Dover, New York (the "Oblong"), 21
Drowned Lands, 26
Duane, James, 284
Dunbarton, New Hampshire, 121, 331
Durbin, Col. 302
Durham boats, 225
Dutch Church, Old (Tappan, New York), 316–317

E

East India Company, 123–124
Eastman, Amos, 14–18
Eastman, Capt. Ebenezer, 10
Eastman, Stilson, 61
East River, 205–206
Edgerton, Eleazar, 256
Emerson, Rev. William, 177, 233
Erskine, Sir Harry, 91
Estaing, Adm. Charles Hector, Count d', 298
Ewing, Gen. James, 227
Exeter, New Hampshire, 128, 157–158, 183, 239, 248
Eyre, Lt. Col. William, 63

F

Falmouth (Portland), Maine, 181
Farnsworth, Amos, 163
Fay, John, 270
Fay, Stephen, 243, 270
Federalists, 333, 338
Field, Jesse, 261
First Narrows (Lake George), 27, 37, 54, 76, 83
Fishkill, New York, 322
Folsom, Nathaniel: in command of New Hampshire troops (1775), 157, 175–176; as delegate to Congress, 127–128
Fonda, Lt. Jelles, 37
Forbush, Chaplain, 81
Fort at Number Four, 4, 44, 104–106, 249
Fort Chambly (Quebec), 193
Fort Dummer, 30
Fort Duquesne, 29
Fort Edward: in French and Indian War, 32, 44–45, 52–54, 67–70, 74–77, 80–81, 96–98; in Revolution, 251, 278
Fort George, 100–101, 201, 205, 214
Fort Lee, 215
Fort Niagara, 287, 301
Fort Oswego, 52, 68
Fort Putnam (West Point), 315
Fort Stanwix (Fort Schuyler), 255, 272, 293, 294, 300
Fort St. Frederic, 9, 26, 29. *See also* Crown Point
Fort Ticonderoga: Americans, as base for, 197–199, 201–208, 211–212, 214, 217; Amherst, captured by, 103; Arnold and Allen, captured by, 161; Burgoyne, captured by, 242–246, 248. *See*

also Carillon
Fort William and Mary (New Hampshire), 128
Fort William Henry, 28, 38, 40–41, 44–45, 47, 52–54, 59–60: siege of, 62–63, 65–71; in ruins, 80
Francis, Col. Turbott, 245
Franklin, Benjamin, 26, 284, 330, 332: at Albany Conference, 23; *Autobiography*, 31, 71–72; Canadian mission of, 189–190; as freemason, 186; home looted, 311; Howe brothers, and conference with, 216; Parliament, testimony in 117
Franklin, Temple, 183
Franklin, William, 183
Fraser, Gen. Simon, 245, 251, 277
Fraunces Tavern (New York City), 330
Freeman, Douglas Southall, 96
Freeman's Farm (Saratoga), 268, 274, 276–277
Freemasonry, 286–287
French fleet: Americans waiting for (1780), 309–310, 312; at Rhode Island, 298–299; at Yorktown, 325
French Lines (Carillon), 210–202, 242

G

Gage, Brig. Gen Thomas: Amherst, replacement for, 116, 119, 129; at Fort Edward, 99–100; Massachusetts, as military governor of, 152, 154–157, 161–162, 173, 180
Gamble, William, 54
Gansevoort, Col. Peter, 293
Gates, Gen. Horatio, 246, 267, 308: in 1775 campaign, 189, 196, 199: in 1776 campaign, 208–210, 212, 219–221; in 1777 campaign, 272–274, 276, 278–279, 282, 284–286: in 1778 campaign, 288, 292–293, 295; in 1779 campaign, 299
General Arnold (privateer), 299
General Stark (privateer), 299
George III, King, 113, 126, 185, 195, 241, 266, 328
Germaine, Lord George, 161
German Flats (New York), 285
Germantown (Pennsylvania), 282
Gist, Christopher, 24
Glover, Col. John, 186, 335–336: André, and trial of, 317; at Long Island, 208; at Saratoga, 276, 280; at Trenton, 223–224
Goffe, "Hunter John," Jr., 29, 93, 123, 126, 155, 164: at Derryfield, 13, 14; as Indian fighter, 4, 5, 8, 9, 10; at Fort William Henry, 66, 68; Provincial Assembly, member of, 126
Goffe, Squire John, Sr., 2,4
Greene, Gen. Nathanael: 203, 240, 273, 335–336: André, and trial of, 316, 318–319; at Long Island, 207; at New York, 216; at Rhode Island, 298–299; at Springfield, 307; at Trenton, 223–224
Greenwood, John (fifer), 227
Gregg, Col. William, 256
Grey, Maj. Gen. Charles, 311–312, 321

H

Hadden, Lt. James, 211
Haldiman, Lt. Col. Frederick, 96, 99, 123
Hale, Capt. Nathan, 217–218, 316, 320
Half Moon Tavern (Morristown, New Jersey), 303
Halifax, Nova Scotia, 71, 187

ABOUT THE AUTHORS

The Polhemus brothers grew up in a small town where their family and teachers encouraged their interest in history. Their first book, *Up on Preston Mountain: The Story of an American Ghost Town* (Purple Mountain Press, 2005) celebrated their native hills.

John Polhemus obtained a degree in aeronautics and astronautics at MIT and spent his working life in that field. He closed his career with seventeen years of global travel, marketing aircraft engines and providing customer service in Asia and Europe. He retired in 1997, giving him time for history, genealogy, golf and family.

Richard Polhemus majored in American history in college. He worked in construction for several years, then attended law school at night and practiced law for thirty years. He retired to pursue his love for hiking, history and grandchildren.